learn

Word 97, Second Edition

Robert L. Ferrett
John Preston
Sally Preston

Learn Word 97, Second Edition

Copyright© 1999 by Que® Education and Training

All rights reserved. Printed in the United States of America. No part of this book may be used or reproduced in any form or by any means, or stored in a database or retrieval system, without prior written permission of the publisher, except in the case of brief quotations embodied in critical articles and reviews. Making copies of any part of this book for any purpose other than your own personal use is a violation of United States copyright laws. For information, address Que Education and Training, Macmillan Computer Publishing, 201 W. 103rd Street, Indianapolis, IN 46290.

Library of Congress Catalog No: 98-89900

ISBN:1-58076-326-x

This book is sold as is, without warranty of any kind, either express or implied, respecting the contents of this book, including but not limited to implied warranties for the book's quality, performance, merchantability, or fitness for any particular purpose. Neither Que Education and Training nor its dealers or distributors shall be liable to the purchaser or any other person or entity with respect to any liability, loss, or damage caused or alleged to be caused directly or indirectly by this book.

01 00 99 98   4 3 2 1

Screens reproduced in this book were created using Collage Plus from Inner Media, Inc., Hollis, NH.

This book was produced digitally by Macmillan Computer Publishing and manufactured using computer-to-plate technology (a film-less process) by GAC/Shepard Poorman, Indianapolis, Indiana.

Credits

Publisher
Robert Linsky

Executive Editor
Jon Phillips

Technical Editors
Linda Bartella
Asit Patel

Series Editors
Robert L. Ferrett
John Preston
Sally Preston

Development Editor
Susan E. Gilbert

Director of Product Marketing
Susan L. Kindel

Operations Manager
Christine Moos

Software Coordinator
Angela Denny

Team Coordinator
Melody Layne

Designer
Louisa Klucznik

Senior Editor
Karen A. Walsh

Copy Editor
Leah D. Williams

Layout
Michael J. Poor

Indexer
Sandy Henselmeier

About the Authors

Robert L. Ferrett is the Director of the Center for Instructional Computing at Eastern Michigan University. His center provides computer training and support to the faculty at the university. He has authored or coauthored nearly 20 books on Access, PowerPoint, Excel, and Word, and he was the editor of the 1994 ACM SIGUCCS Conference Proceedings. He has been designing, developing, and delivering computer workshops for more than a decade. He has a B.A. in Psychology, an M.S. in Geography, and an M.S. in Interdisciplinary Technology from Eastern Michigan University. He is ABD in the Ph.D. program in Instructional Technology at Wayne State University.

John Preston is an Associate Professor at Eastern Michigan University in the College of Technology, where he teaches microcomputer application courses at the undergraduate and graduate levels. He has been teaching, writing, and designing computer-training courses since the advent of the personal computer. He has authored and coauthored nearly 20 books on Microsoft Word, Excel, Access, and PowerPoint. He has received grants from the Detroit Edison Institute and the Department of Energy to develop Web sites for energy education and alternative fuels, respectively. He has also developed one of the first Internet-based microcomputer applications courses at an accredited university. He received a B.S. from the University of Michigan in Physics, Mathematics, and Education and an M.S. from Eastern Michigan University in Physics Education. He is ABD in the Ph.D. program in Instructional Technology at Wayne State University.

Sally Preston is President of Preston & Associates, a computer software training firm. She combines her extensive business experience as a bank vice-president in charge of branch operations with her skills in training people on new computer systems. She provides corporate training through Preston & Associates and through the Institute for Workforce Development at Washtenaw Community College, where she teaches computer courses part-time. She has coauthored more than a dozen books on Access, Excel, and PowerPoint. She has an M.B.A. from Eastern Michigan University.

Trademark Acknowledgments

All terms mentioned in this book that are known to be trademarks or service marks have been appropriately capitalized. Que Education and Training cannot attest to the accuracy of this information. Use of a term in this book should not be regarded as affecting the validity of any trademark or service mark.

Preface

Que Education and Training is the educational publishing imprint of Macmillan Computer Publishing, the world's leading computer book publisher. Macmillan Computer Publishing books have taught more than 20 million people how to be productive with their computers.

This expertise in producing high-quality computer tutorial and reference books is evident in every Que Education and Training title we publish. The same tried-and-true writing and product-development process that makes Macmillan Computer Publishing books bestsellers is used to ensure that educational materials from Que Education and Training provide the most accurate and up-to-date information. Experienced and respected computer application experts write and review every manuscript to provide class-tested pedagogy. Quality assurance editors check every keystroke and command in Que Education and Training books to ensure that instructions are clear, accurate, and precise.

Above all, Macmillan Computer Publishing and, in turn, Que Education and Training, have years of experience in meeting the learning demands of students across all disciplines.

Philosophy of the Learn Series

The Learn Series has been designed for students who need to master the basics of a particular software program quickly. The books are visual in nature to help students master the basics easily. Most steps are accompanied by figures that show the results of the steps. Visual cues are given in the form of highlights and callouts to help direct students to the location in the window that is being used in a particular step. Explanatory text is minimized in the actual steps but is included when appropriate in additional pedagogical elements. Every lesson includes reinforcement exercises to give students a chance to practice their skills immediately.

Structure of a Learn Series Book

Each of the books in the Learn series is structured in the same way for the sake of consistency. The following elements are included in each book.

Introduction

Each book has an introduction designed to provide students with an overview of what they will be learning. This consists of an introduction to the series (how to use this book), a brief introduction to the Windows 95 operating system, and an introduction to the software.

Lesson Introduction

The introduction to each lesson includes a lesson number, title, and a brief introduction to the topics covered in the lesson.

Task Introduction

All tasks included in the lesson are listed on the opening page of each lesson to give students a road map. Each task is explained in a section at the beginning of the task.

Completed Project

A screen capture or printout of the results of the lesson is included at the beginning of the lesson to provide an example of what is accomplished in the lesson.

"Why would I do this?"

At the beginning of each task is a "Why would I do this?" section, which is a short explanation of the relevance of the task. This section illustrates why a particular element of the software is important and how it can be used effectively.

Figures

Steps have accompanying figures, which are placed to the right or left of the steps. The figures show what the result of the steps will be. The figures provide the reader with visual reinforcement of the task at hand, and also highlight buttons, menu choices, and other screen elements used in the task.

Pedagogical Elements

Three recurring elements are found in the Preston Ferrett Learn series:

In Depth: Detailed look at a topic or procedure or another way of doing something.

Quick Tip: Faster or more efficient way of doing something.

Pothole: Area where trouble may be encountered, along with instructions on how to recover from and/or avoid these mistakes.

Glossary

New words or concepts are printed in italic the first time they are presented. Definitions of these words or phrases are included in the glossary at the back of the book.

End-of-Lesson Material

The end-of-lesson material includes Student and Application Exercises. The Student Exercises consist of the following:

True/False questions. Ten True/False questions enable students to test their understanding of the new material in the lesson.

Visual Identification. A captured screen or screens offer students the opportunity to test their familiarity with various screen elements introduced in the lesson.

Matching. Ten Matching questions are included to give students a chance to assess their familiarity with concepts and procedures introduced in the lesson.

Application Exercises, included at the end of each lesson, consist of three to five exercises that provide practice in the skills introduced in the tasks. These exercises generally follow the sequence of the tasks in the lesson. Each exercise usually builds on the previous exercise, so it is a good idea to do them in the order in which they are presented.

Student Data Files

To access the student data files that accompany this book, click on the CD-ROM drive in Windows Explorer or My Computer. The files are arranged by lesson number within the **Student** folder. To open **Less0401**, for example, follow these steps:

1 Double-click the CD-ROM drive from Windows Explorer.

2 Double-click the **Lesson04** folder.

3 Double-click on **Less0401**. Word will launch and display **Less0401**.

Annotated Instructor's Edition

If you have adopted this text for use in a college classroom, you will receive, upon request, an Annotated Instructor's Edition (AIE) at no additional charge. The Annotated Instructor's Edition is a comprehensive teaching tool that contains the student text with margin notes and tips for instructors and students. The AIE also contains suggested curriculum guides for courses of varying lengths, answers to the end-of-chapter material, test questions and answers, and PowerPoint slides. Data files and solutions for each tutorial and exercise, along with a PowerPoint presentation, are included on disc with the AIE. Please contact your local representative or write to us on school or business letterhead at Macmillan Computer Publishing, 201 West 103rd Street, Indianapolis, IN 46290-1097, Attention: Que Education and Training Sales Support.

Managing Files with Windows Explorer

Throughout most of this book, you work in the Microsoft Word program. At times, however, you are asked to find, retrieve, and rename files on your data disc or a hard disk. This review helps you manage files. It shows how to do so using the Windows Explorer, although all these procedures can also be accomplished using My Computer. Use whichever method is most comfortable for you.

Launch the Windows Explorer

You can usually perform any operation in Windows 95 or in Microsoft applications in two or three ways. Many people place a Windows Explorer (not to be confused with the Internet Explorer!) icon on the Windows desktop. If this icon is available, double-click it. Windows Explorer is launched.

If the icon does not exist, move to the taskbar at the bottom of the screen. The taskbar contains the Start button, any open applications, and the time. The taskbar may appear at the bottom of the screen, or it may be hidden. If it is hidden, move the pointer to the bottom of the screen and it should pop up.

Click the **Start** button and move the pointer to the **Programs** option. A list of available programs is displayed. Your list of programs will be different from the one shown. Windows Explorer is at or near the end of the list. Launch **Windows Explorer** by moving the pointer over it and clicking the left mouse button.

Navigate the Drives and Folders

Windows Explorer is divided into two windows. The window on the left side, labeled All Folders, displays icons for each disk drive that is accessible from your computer. Folders may be within folders to make up several layers of files. If additional folders (subfolders) are available, a plus sign (+) is placed to the left of the icon.

The All Folders section gives you an overview of the relationship between these layers, whereas the Contents window on the right displays the details of the selected drive or folder. You can choose to show details of the files and folders or show the files and folders as icons by clicking buttons on the toolbar. Your Windows Explorer screen will look much different from the one shown, but it will contain the same elements.

To move to another disk drive, click once on the disk drive icon, such as 3 1/2 Floppy (A:). To open a file folder, double-click the Folder icon. Doing so opens the folder and displays the contents in the right-hand window.

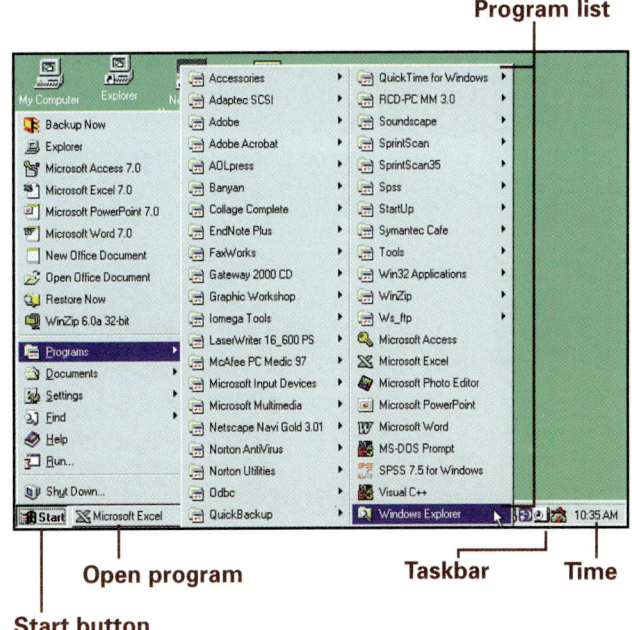

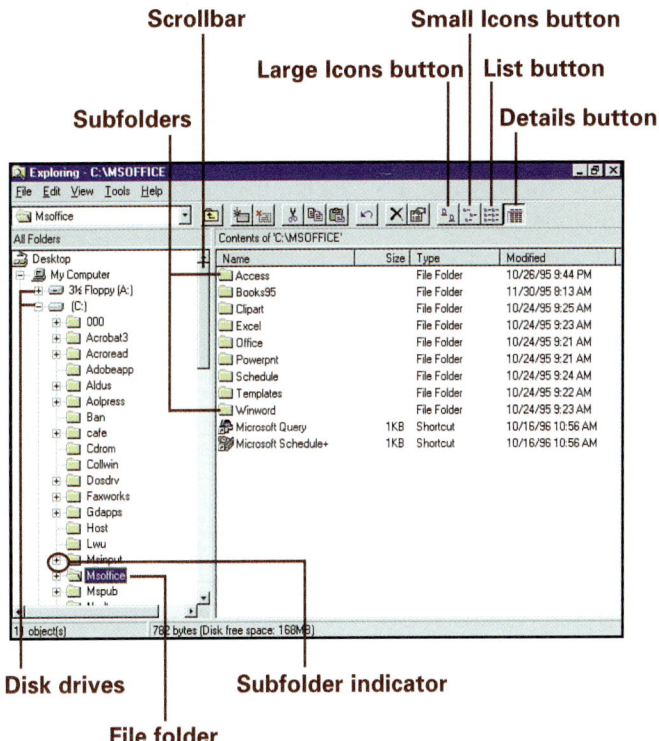

Preface vii

Find Files

Disk drives are capable of storing thousands of files. If you do not know which drive and folder a particular file is stored in, it could take a long time to open each one and read the list of its contents. Windows Explorer finds a file for you if you know at least part of its name.

The project files for this book all begin with the letters **Less**. In the example shown, the student files have been moved from the data disc to the hard drive for the purposes of illustration.

To find all the files that contain the letters **Less**, click on the disk drive you want to search. Select **Tools**, **Find**, **Files or Folders** from the menu. In the **Find** window, type **Less** in the **Named** box and then click **Find Now**. All the files and file folders with those letters are listed in the bottom of the **Find** window.

After you have found a list of files, click the file you want. The location of the file is shown to the right of the filename in the **In Folder** column.

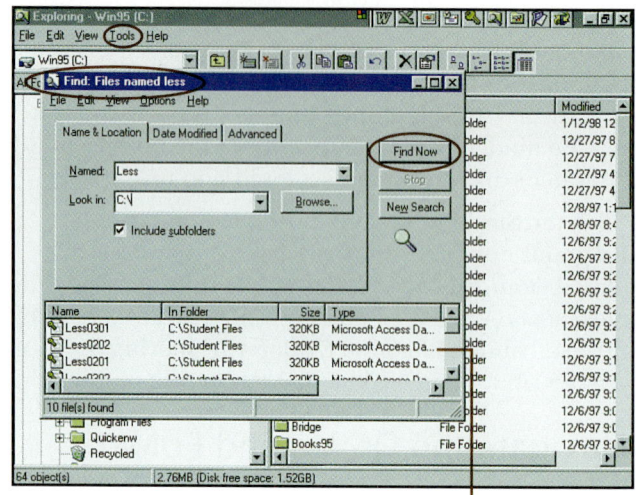

List of files found

Make Copies of Existing Files

After you have found the location of the file you need, go to the folder containing the file. Click once on the file to highlight it. Choose **Edit**, **Copy** from the menu, and then choose **Edit**, **Paste**. This puts a copy of the file in the same location as the original. If you want to copy the file to another folder or disk drive, move to the new location before you perform the Paste command.

Rename Files

When you have made a copy of a file and pasted it into the desired location, you will often want to rename it. To rename a file, click it and then choose **File**, **Rename**. The filename is highlighted. At this point, you can simply type a new name, or you can put the cursor in the filename and edit it as you would edit text in a word processor.

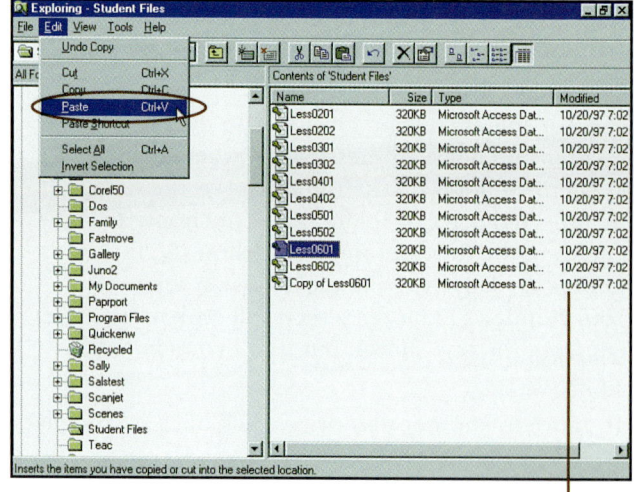

Copy of file

Open Documents and Launch Associated Applications Automatically

You can open a file in two ways. The first is to run the application (such as PowerPoint) and then use the **File**, **Open** commands from the menu. The second is to locate the file in Windows Explorer or My Computer and double-click on the filename.

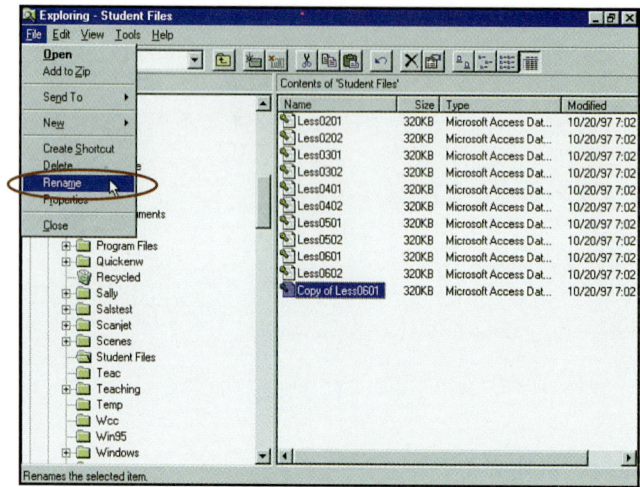

Introduction to Word

Microsoft Word is a word processing application program. A word processing program allows you to enter text and then change it by editing existing text, moving blocks of text, or changing the appearance of the letters. The document is stored electronically, so it can be duplicated, printed, copied, and shared with others more conveniently than paper documents.

How Word Processors Work

The computer screen is used to represent a page of paper. In Word, you can choose to work in a simulated page, called Page Layout view, that shows the page with its edges, margins and any headers, footers, or automatic page numbers. This view uses an inch or so at each side to display the margins, so the available space for viewing each line is reduced. For this reason, most people work in the Normal view, which utilizes the full width of the screen for displaying text.

When you type on the keyboard, your text appears on the screen. A vertical, flashing line indicates the insertion point so that you can tell where your text will go when you start to type. A short, horizontal line marks the end of the existing text. When you are typing and reach the end of a line, just continue to type. The program decides whether the last word will fit. If it will not, it moves down to the next line. You press the **Enter** key when you get to the end of a paragraph or when you want to create empty lines to add extra space between paragraphs.

If you want to add words anywhere in an existing paragraph, move the insertion point to the desired location and start typing. The text that comes after your new text moves down the page automatically. The program determines where each new line of the paragraph will end and makes all the necessary adjustments to the paragraph. You can move the insertion point by using the four arrow keys on the keyboard or by moving the mouse pointer to the desired location and clicking the left mouse button one time.

To replace, move, delete, or enhance text, you need to select it first. After it is selected, you can press **Del** on the keyboard to delete it, or you can choose any of several buttons on the toolbar to change the size, color, alignment, font style, or any number of other text characteristics.

Word has many additional features that you can use for special purposes. It is not necessary for you to learn them all. After you have mastered the basics, you can add the skills that are most useful in your pursuits.

How to Identify Parts of the Word Window

You can use two methods to quickly identify parts of the Word screen. They are ScreenTips and What's This?. A ScreenTip appears if you place the pointer on a toolbar button and leave it there for a moment. The ScreenTip displays the name of the button. (If this feature does not work on your computer, you can turn it on by selecting **Tools**, **Customize** from the menu. Then click the **Options** tab and click the **Show ScreenTips on toolbars** check box.)

If you would like a more detailed description, you may choose **Help**, **What's This?** from the menu. After you select this help option, the pointer has a question mark attached to it until you click on part of the screen, at which time a more detailed paragraph describing the function of the object you clicked appears.

Parts of the Word Window

The Word window has several components that you will learn how to use in this book. For a brief overview of the layout of the window and its parts, see the accompanying figure.

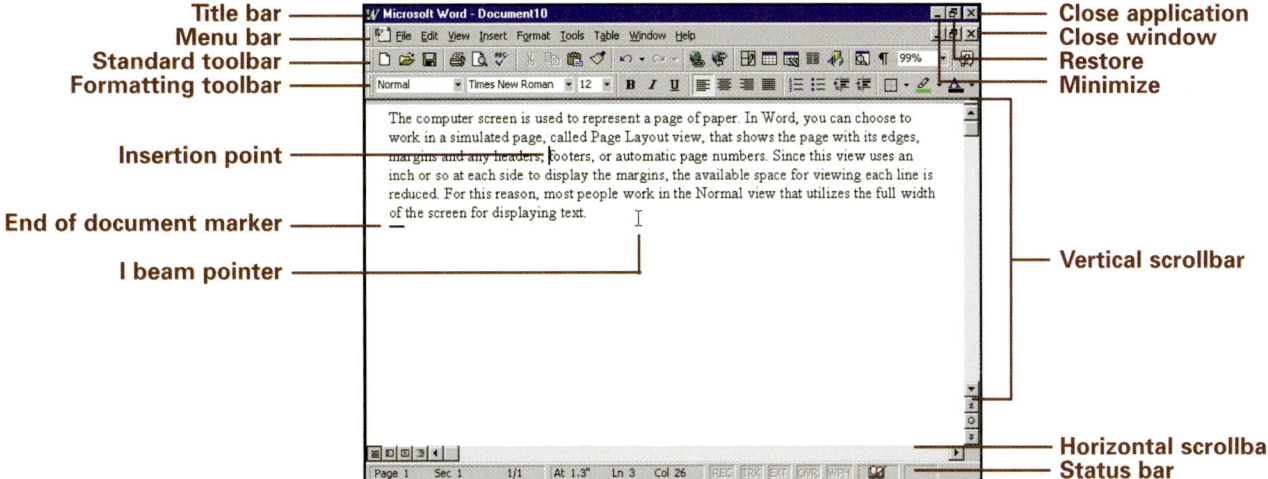

Preface ix

How to Launch Word

The Word program may be initiated (launched) in several ways. When the Word program was installed on your computer, its name was added to the list of programs that may be found when you click the **Start** button on the Windows taskbar and then click **Programs**. The Word program may be listed by itself, or you may have to open a folder, such as Microsoft Office, to find the icon that represents the program. When you find it, click on it and the program launches. There may be other shortcut methods of launching Word on your computer, but this method is the one that will work on most machines.

You can launch Word in several faster ways. It is possible to add the Word program icon to the list of commonly used programs that appears immediately when you click **Start**. The Word icon could be placed on the desktop, or it could be part of a small toolbar at the top of the screen. In general, if you see the Word icon, you can click or double-click on it to launch Word.

If you are using the Windows Explorer or My Computer program to search for files, you may notice that the Word files have a small Word icon displayed next to their names. When this is the case, you can double-click on the filename. Word launches automatically and then opens the file as well.

Exit Word

When you are done with the Word program, you should close it before you turn off the computer. To do this, you can click the **Close** button on the title bar. If you have not saved your most recent changes, you are asked if you want to do so before the program closes. You may also close Word by using the **File** and **Close** options from the menu.

The Concept of This Book

This book is designed for students who are new to Word and would like to know how to use it in real-life applications. The authors have combined their many years of business experience and classroom teaching to provide a basic step-by-step approach that leads to the development of skills advanced enough to be useful in the workplace. We have designed the book so that you will be successful immediately and will create a useful document in the first lesson. In the lessons that follow, you will learn how to edit the document, add tables, check spelling and grammar, add clip art, and integrate Word with other programs. (Do not close your document at the end of each task. Do close your document and Word after each lesson.) Finally, we recognize that few people can remember everything that they learn in class, so we conclude the book by showing you how to get help from the online manuals, from the Internet, and from additional textbooks.

Welcome to the Learn On-Demand Series

Congratulations on choosing the most innovative interactive learning product available for today's software applications: the Learn On-Demand Series by Que Education and Training.

Learn On-Demand is unique in that it allows you to learn while you work. Learn On-Demand users gain a well-rounded knowledge of software functionality—complete with conceptual understanding and hands-on experience—by learning how to use a program in both a simulated environment and with "live" data. The down-time often associated with off-site or classroom learning can be virtually eliminated because of Learn On-Demand's capability to allow students to learn while they work.

System Requirements

Learn On-Demand uses advanced multimedia technology to deliver training in a network or standalone environment efficiently. The minimum system requirements for Learn On-Demand are as follows:

- An IBM-compatible PC with a minimum of 486SX CPU
- 8MB RAM (16MB recommended)
- Microsoft Windows 95
- Microsoft Office 97
- VGA display adapter and monitor (640×480 or better)
- Two-button mouse
- Audio sound card (optional, but recommended)
- 4x speed or faster CD-ROM

 **Pothole:** A CD-ROM is not required to access Learn On-Demand from a network server, but it is required to complete the installation process.

Hard disk space requirements for Learn On-Demand vary according to your system configuration and the Learn On-Demand titles you are going to install. You can use the following table to determine how much disk space Learn On-Demand requires in your environment.

FILE TYPES	ESTIMATED HARD DISK SPACE REQUIREMENTS
Learn On-Demand program files	2MB
Application support files	1MB per application
Content files (for example, graphics and lesson files)	3.5MB per Lesson
Sound files	20–25MB (optional)

If you want to access Learn On-Demand's audio content on a standalone computer, you can run sound files directly from the CD-ROM. For network distribution, the sound files must be installed on a server. Sound files average 20–25MB per module.

Working with the Files from the CD-ROM

If you are working on a computer in a lab, verify that you can save the files to the hard drive. Some schools and universities do not allow you to save files to the computers in the computer labs. If the files have been installed on a network or by a lab assistant, your instructor will inform you where the files are located.

After inserting the CD-ROM, an installation screen will appear. The screen has three options:

- Install—This option gives you the option to install the student data files that accompany the text and the Learn On-Demand software.

- Browse—This option opens Windows Explorer and displays the contents of the CD-ROM. This is one option you can use to access the student data files directly from the CD-ROM.

- Exit—This option closes the installation window and returns you to the Windows desktop.

Installing the Files to Your Hard Drive

If you have been instructed to install the files on a lab computer or if you are installing them on your home computer, follow these steps:

1 From the installation screen, click the **Install** button.

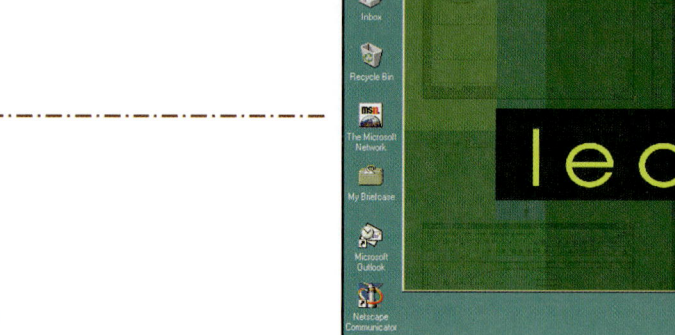

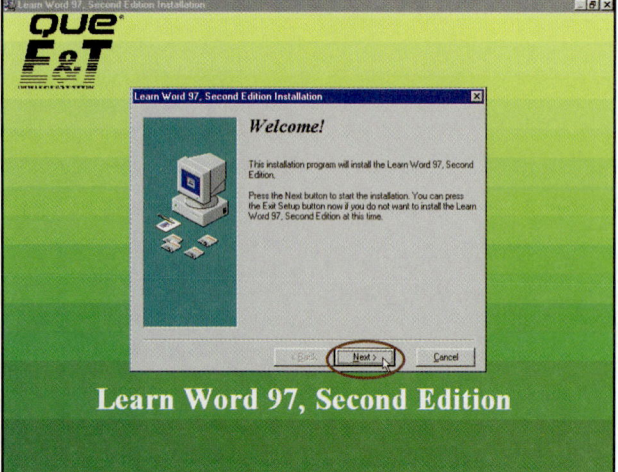

2 The **Welcome** dialog box is displayed. Click the **Next** button.

xii **Learn Word 97, Second Edition**

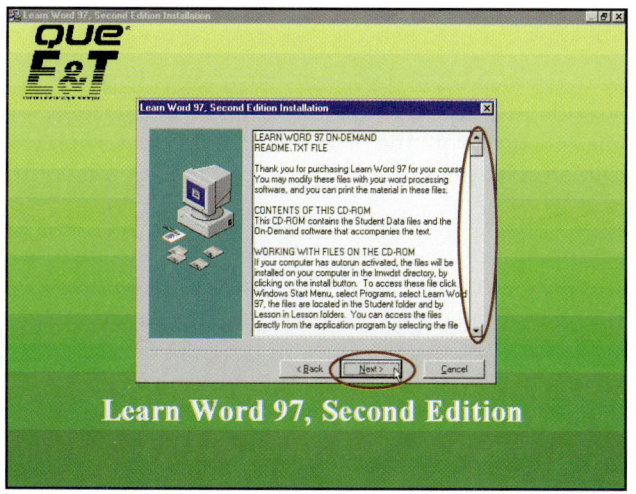

3 The Readme.txt appears. The Readme.txt gives you important information regarding the installation. Make sure you use the scrollbar to view the entire Readme.txt file. When you are finished reading the Readme.txt, click the **Next** button.

4 The Select Destination Directory is displayed. This option applies only to the student data files. If you install Learn On-Demand, you will see a similar screen during that installation. Unless instructed otherwise by your instructor, the default location is recommended. Click **Next**.

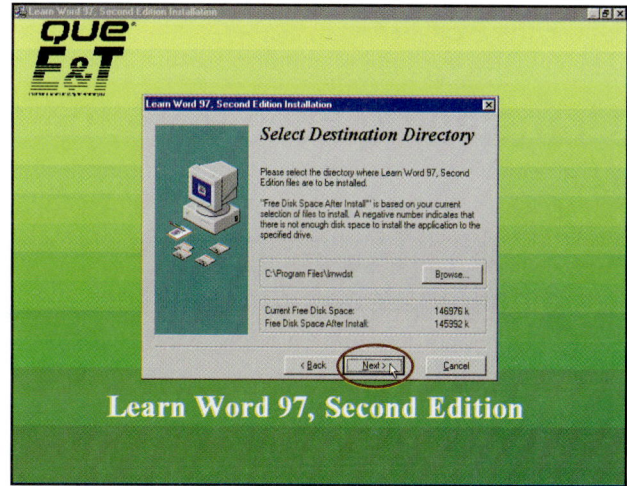

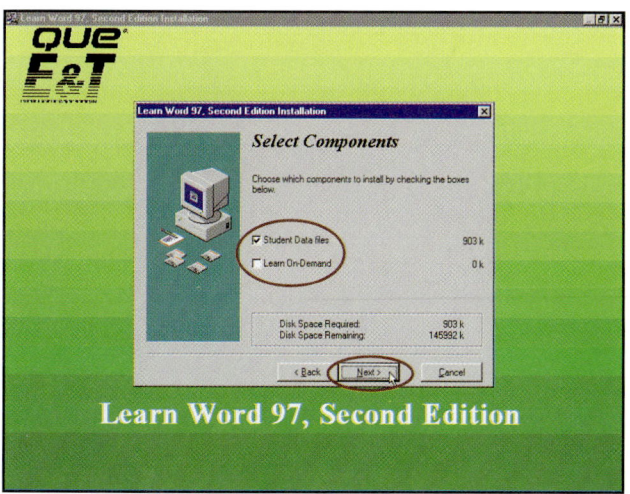

5 The Select Components screen opens. The default for this screen is to install only the student data files. To override the default, click on the check box beside each option. You can choose to install either one or both of the components listed. Select the components you want to install and click the **Next** button.

6 The Ready to Install screen appears. Click **Next** to begin the installation.

7 The components you selected will be installed.

- If you choose to install the student data files, a directory will be created on your hard drive where the student files will be installed. The installation of the student data files allows you to access the data files from the **Start** menu programs. To access the student data files from the **Start** menu, click **Start**, click **Programs**, and then click **Learn Word 97, Second Edition**. The student data files are located in the Student folder and arranged by lesson.

- If you choose to install the On-Demand software, a second installation program runs within the current installation. Follow the directions as they appear on your screen. You have three installation options: Minimal Install, Standard Install, and Full Install. Minimal Install copies the basic program files to your computer, but requires the CD for graphics and sound. Standard Install copies all program files to your computer, but requires the CD for sound. Full Install copies all program and sound files to your computer. If you accept the default directory\folder to install Learn On-Demand, all Learn On-Demand files are placed in \Learn\Ondemand. If you choose another location to install Learn On-Demand, all the files are copied to the directory\folder you specify. Files are not copied to any other location during the install. Learn On-Demand appears automatically in the Start menu programs after installation. The Learn On-Demand shortcut appears in the item's submenu.

8 A dialog box appears confirming that the installation is complete.

Uninstalling Files from the CD

When you have completed the course, you may decide you don't need Learn On-Demand or the student data files anymore. If that's the case, you have the capability to uninstall them. This section covers the uninstall process for both Learn On-Demand and the student data files.

Uninstalling Learn On-Demand

Learn On-Demand includes an uninstall program. You can use this program to remove specific titles from Learn On-Demand. If all titles are removed from Learn On-Demand, most program files will also be removed from your computer, as well as the shortcuts from the Programs submenu; however, the \Learn\Ondemand directory structure where Learn On-Demand was originally installed will still exist.

Use the following procedure to uninstall a title from Learn On-Demand:

1 Click **Start**.

2 Click **Find**.

3 Click **Files or Folders**.

4 In the **Named** text box, type **Uninst.exe**.

5 In the **Look in** box, type the drive where Learn On-Demand is installed.

6 Click the **Find Now** button.

7 When the file is displayed in the results list, double-click **Uninst.exe** that is located in the Learn\On-Demand folder.

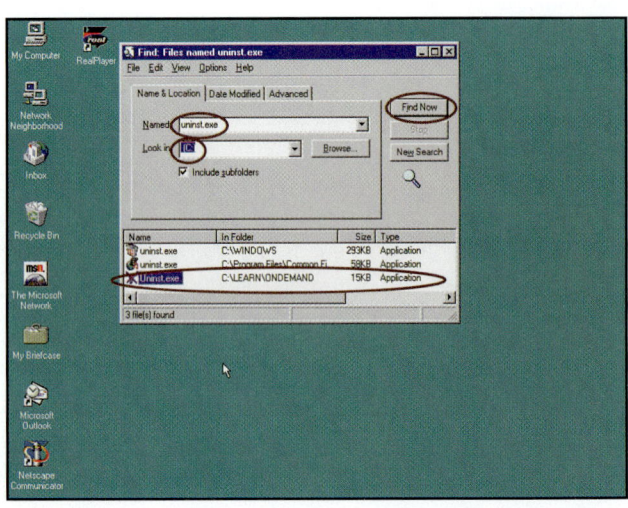

8 From the **On-Demand Uninstallation** dialog box, select the title you want to uninstall and click the **Uninstall** button.

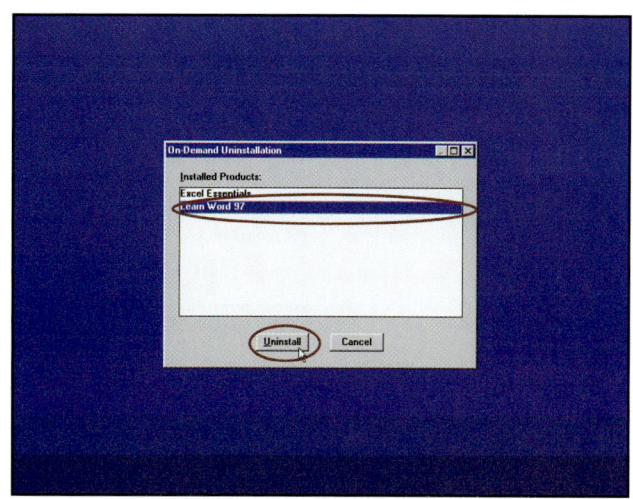

Uninstalling the Student Data Files

There is also a program to uninstall the student data files. The following steps walk you through the process:

1 Click on the **Start** menu and then click **Programs**.

2 Click **Learn Word 97, Second Edition**.

3 Click **Uninstall Learn Word 97, Second Edition**.

4 Click one of the Uninstall methods listed:

- Automatic—This method deletes all files in the directory and all shortcuts created.
- Custom—This method allows you to select the files you want to delete.

5 Click **Next**.

6 The **Perform Uninstall** dialog box appears. Click **Finish**. The Student data files and directories will be deleted.

Starting Learn On-Demand

To start Learn On-Demand, do the following:

1 From the Taskbar, click the **Start** menu. The **Start** menu appears.

2 Click **Programs**. The **Programs** menu appears.

3 Click the **Learn On-Demand** program group. The **Learn On-Demand** sub-menu appears.

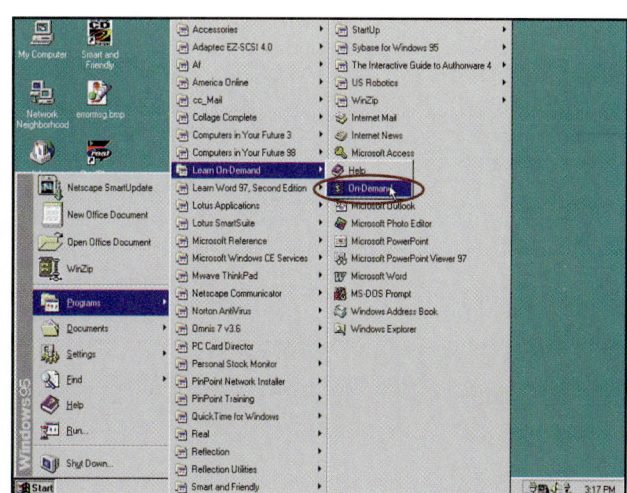

Learn On-Demand toolbar

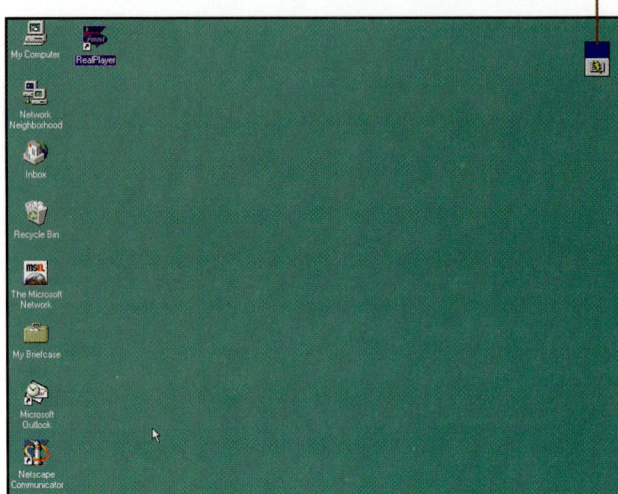

4 Click **On-Demand**. The Learn On-Demand toolbar floats on the Windows desktop.

Learn On-Demand toolbar — Teacher button

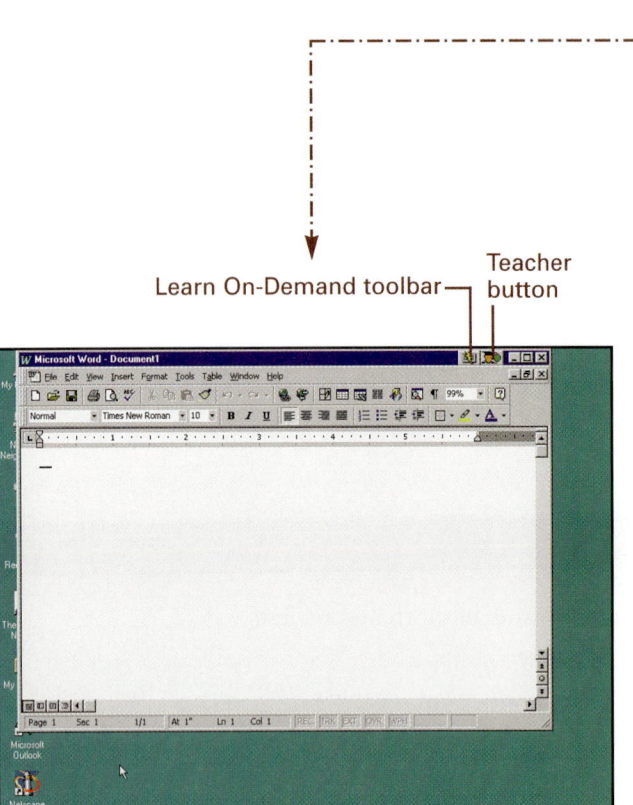

5 The Teacher button appears when you are in an application for which you have a Learn On-Demand title installed. At this point, you need to open Word.

6 The Learn On-Demand toolbar appears on the application title bar.

Using Learn On-Demand

Through interactive training, Learn On-Demand teaches students how to use a software program's features to complete tasks. This process makes students more productive because they can get the training they need when they need it. Specific tasks are covered in *topics*. You can learn about a topic using any of the four Learn On-Demand playback modes: Concept, Concurrent, Teacher, or Demo. These modes are individually covered later in this tutorial.

The **Interactive Training—Lesson Selection** dialog box is the central location from which you can find and view available training modules, lessons, and topics. From this location, you can launch a desired topic in any of Learn On-Demand's training modes. The dialog box contains three tabbed pages: **Contents**, **Search**, and **Topics for**. The purpose of each page is to help you view and locate training relevant to your specific needs, which are reviewed later in this tutorial.

 Click the **Teacher** button on the application title bar to open the **Interactive Training—Lesson Selection** dialog box. You are now ready to select the desired topic and training mode.

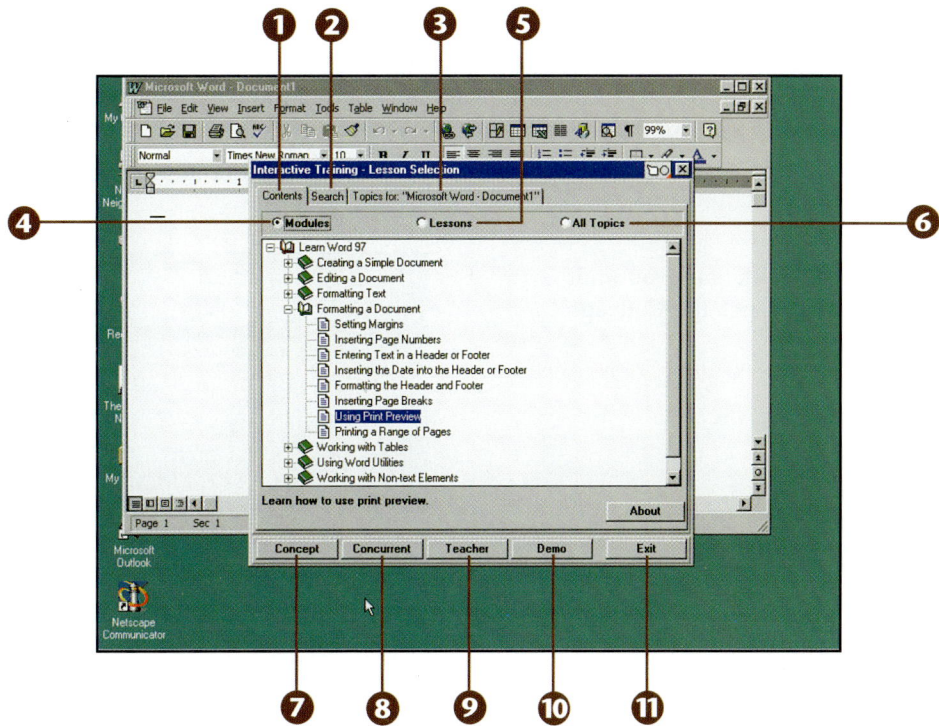

① Displays all the modules, lessons, or topics available. Click the plus (+) box to expand the listings and click the minus (-) box to contract the listings. A description of each selected topic appears below the list box.

② Enables you to quickly locate topics of interest. You can enter a *keyword* to find all related topics.

③ Displays only those topics that relate to your working application. A description of each selected topic appears below the list box.

④ When selected, displays the Learn On-Demand titles (modules) that are applicable to the working application. Expanding modules displays the lessons within them. The lessons can then be further expanded to display the individual topics.

⑤ When selected, groups the topics by lesson that are applicable to the working application. Expanding lessons displays the topics within them.

⑥ When selected, displays all topics that are applicable to the working application.

⑦ Provides a description of the key concept of the current topic.

⑧ Enables you to learn while you work.

⑨ Prompts you to enter mouse clicks or keystrokes as you complete tasks in a simulated environment.

⑩ Displays an animated demonstration of the task being completed in a simulated environment.

⑪ Closes the **Interactive Training—Lesson Selection** dialog box and returns you to your application. This button does not close Learn On-Demand. The Learn On-Demand icon still appears on your application title bar.

Using Concept Mode

Although it is important to learn how to perform a task, it is also important to learn when and why a task is performed. Learn On-Demand's *Concept mode* displays the key concept of a topic to help students gain a better understanding of how the topic relates to everyday uses of the application.

Use the following procedure to learn how to use Learn On-Demand's Concept mode:

1 Select a topic describing the task you want to learn how to complete. Click the **Concept** button.

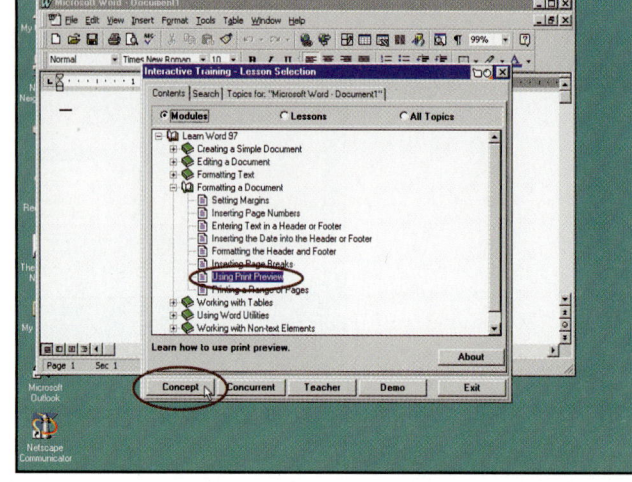

Key concept

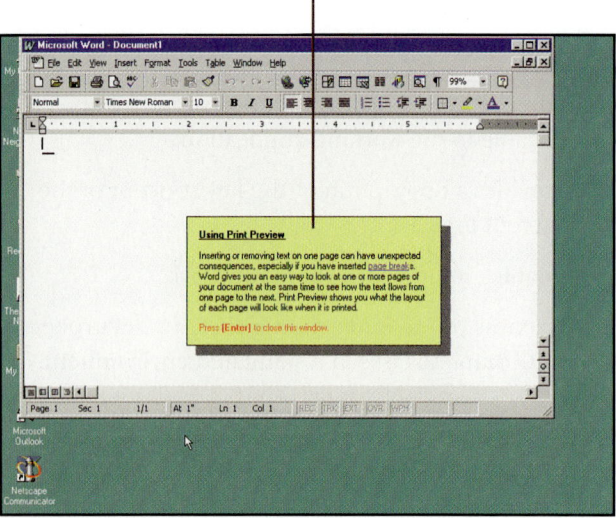

2 Learn On-Demand displays the key concept for the topic. When you have finished viewing the topic, click anywhere or press any key. The concept information disappears from your screen and returns you to the **Interactive Training— Lesson Selection** dialog box.

Using Concurrent Mode

With Learn On-Demand's *Concurrent mode*, students can learn interactively while working with the "live" application and data. This unique mode makes it possible for students to accomplish real tasks with actual data.

When Concurrent mode is selected, the **Topic** dialog box opens within the application. This dialog box includes a series of steps that need to be followed in sequence to complete the selected task. A red check mark appears when a step has been completed. Note: You must follow these steps *exactly* as directed.

1 Concurrent mode prompts the student with a *hotspot* around the area of the screen needing action.

2 The hotspot is outlined with a red marquee.

3 The red line drawn from the hotspot to the current step provides easy and clear onscreen directions.

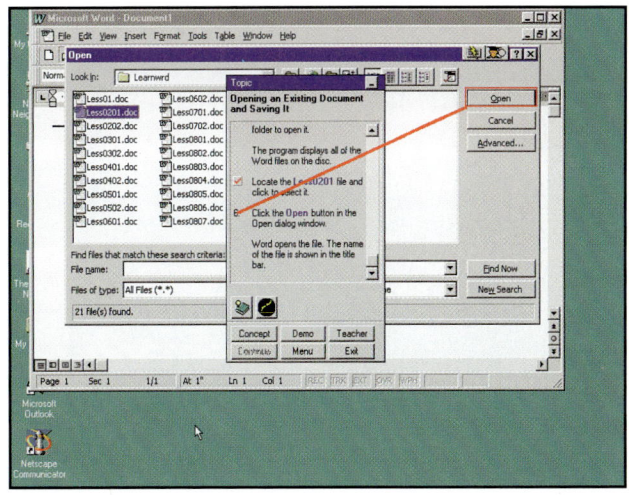

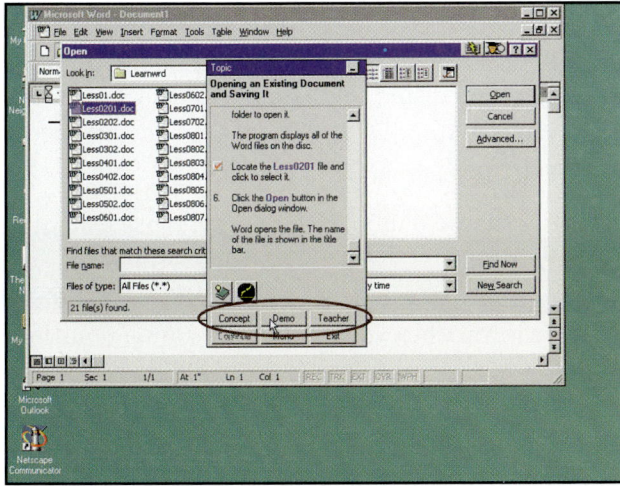

If you need further assistance during your concurrent training session, you can switch to another training mode by clicking the **Concept**, **Demo**, or **Teacher** mode buttons.

Using Teacher Mode

Teacher mode prompts students to enter the necessary mouse clicks or keystrokes to complete tasks in a simulated environment. When you are working in Teacher mode, Learn On-Demand places a hotspot over the location where you need to complete an action. The hotspot is outlined with a red marquee. If you make a mistake, Learn On-Demand prompts you to try again. Notice that Teacher mode provides a simulated environment, so active data and system settings in your application are protected. You can control Teacher mode using the buttons that appear at the bottom of the Teacher mode screen. Use the following procedure to learn how to complete a task in Learn On-Demand's Teacher mode:

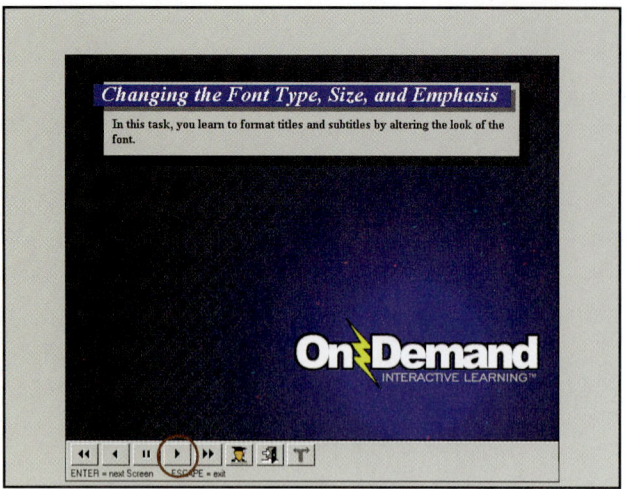

1. Click the **Teacher** button to open the **Interactive Training—Lesson Selection** dialog box, if necessary.

2. Select a topic describing the task you want to learn how to complete. With the topic selected, click the **Teacher** button.

3. Learn On-Demand displays an opening screen with the objective of the topic in Teacher mode.

Click the Forward button to begin training. The training for the selected topic appears in Teacher mode.

Buttons appear at the bottom of the Topic dialog box. You can use the buttons, which are described in the following figure, to perform additional Learn On-Demand functions.

❶ Enables you to move to the beginning screen within a topic. (Applicable for multiple-step topics only.)

❷ Enables you to move backward one step at a time.

❸ Pauses Teacher mode.

❹ Enables you to move forward one step at a time.

❺ Enables you to move to the last screen within a topic.

❻ Returns you to the **Interactive Training—Lesson Selection** dialog box. From this dialog box, you can select another topic.

❼ Exits Teacher mode.

❽ Alternative button. If this button is black, it will show an alternative way to complete a task.

❾ Displays the key concept for the selected topic. Tells you when you would use a software function and why.

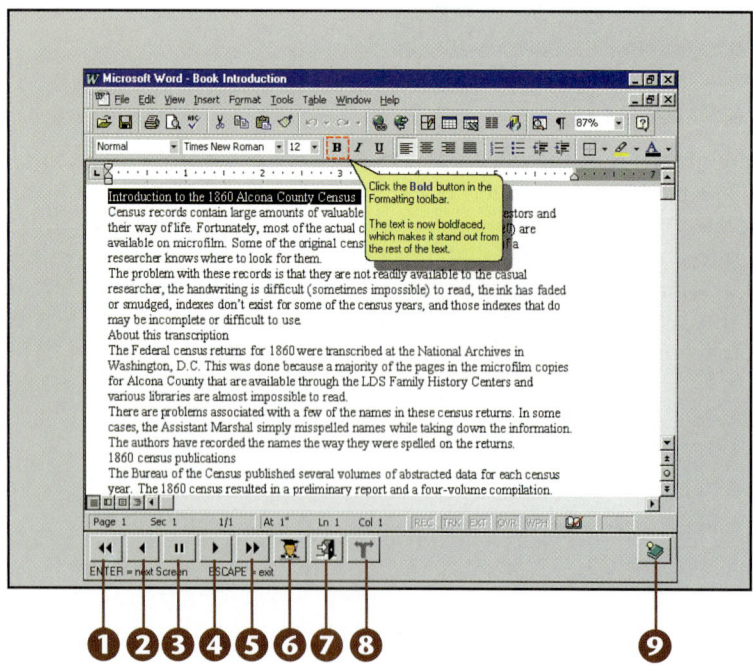

In addition to the buttons, pressing the ↵Enter key advances Teacher mode one frame at a time. Pressing the Esc key exits Teacher mode.

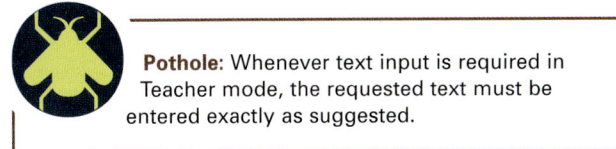

Pothole: Whenever text input is required in Teacher mode, the requested text must be entered exactly as suggested.

Using Demo Mode

Demo mode enables students to learn by watching an animated demonstration of operations being performed. All required activities, such as moving the mouse and selecting menu items, are completed automatically.

When students are working in Demo mode, they can stop the demonstration at any time by pressing the Esc key. They can also pause the animation by holding the ⇧Shift key. Releasing the ⇧Shift key resumes the demonstration.

Use the following procedure to learn how to complete a task in Learn On-Demand's Demo mode:

1 Click the **Teacher** button to open the **Interactive Training—Lesson**. The **Interactive Training—Lesson Selection** dialog box opens.

2 Select the topic describing the task you want to learn how to complete. Click the **Demo** button. Learn On-Demand displays an animation that demonstrates how to complete the task.

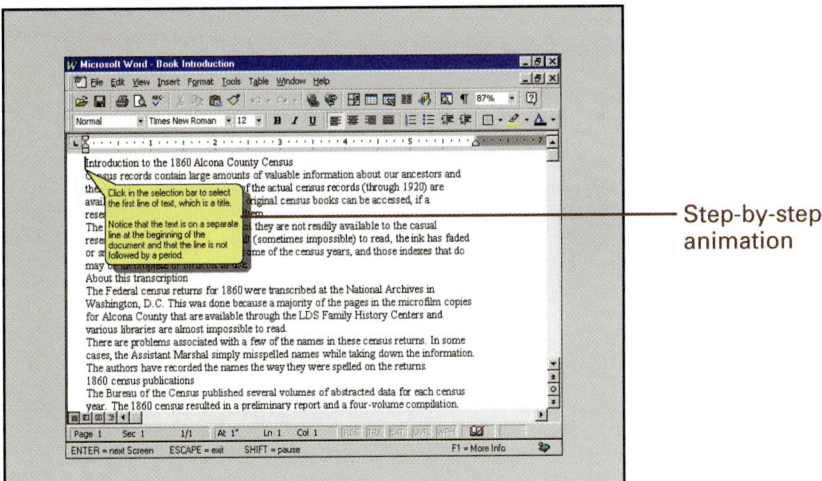

Step-by-step animation

3 You can obtain more information about a topic at any time while using Demo mode by pressing the F1 key to display the **Concept** button. Clicking this button once displays conceptual information about the task, and clicking it again removes the information from your screen. Pressing the Esc key removes the button. Depending on the topic being viewed, other buttons may also appear, including the **In Depth**, **Quick Tip**, or **Pothole** buttons.

Searching by Topic

After you have started Learn On-Demand and are in the application (with your file open) for which you want training, you can select a topic. Simply choose a selection from the list of available modules, lessons, or topics from the **Search** tab in the **Interactive Training—Lesson Selection** dialog box.

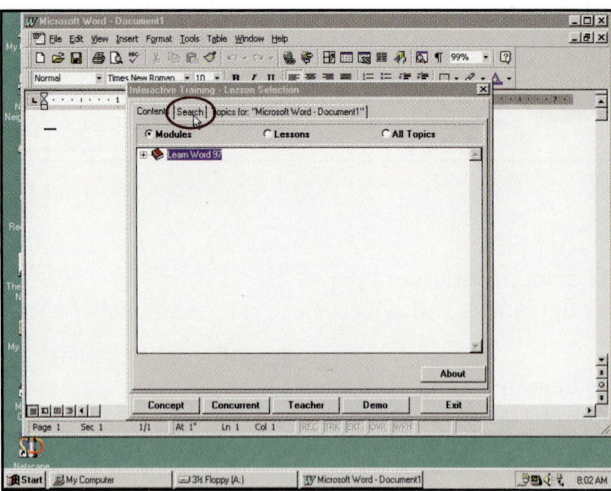

1 Click the **Search** tab. The **Search** page appears.

2 Type the keyword **format**.

3 Related keywords of **format** appear in the **Select a keyword from the list** box. Select **Format** from the list.

4 Related topics appear in the **Pick the topic** list box.

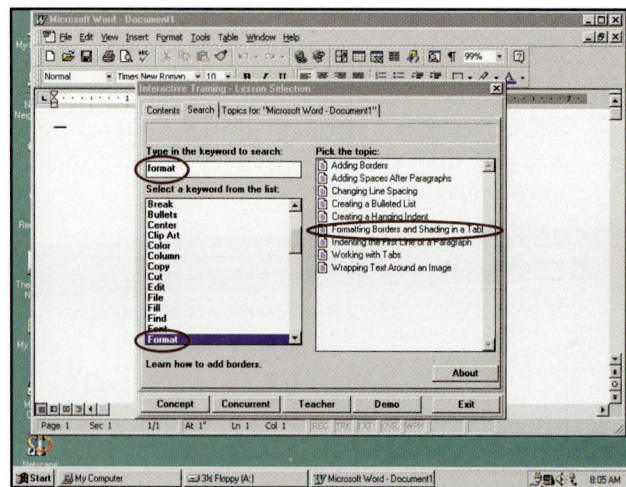

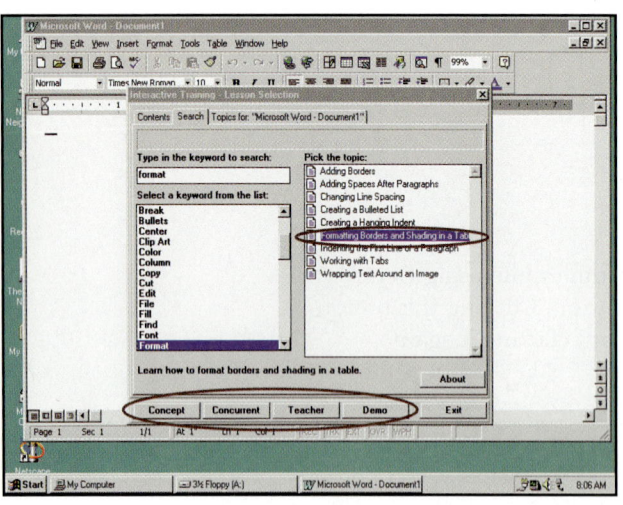

5 Select a topic from the **Pick the topic** frame.

6 Select your desired mode: **Concept**, **Concurrent**, **Teacher**, or **Demo**. Follow the steps as outlined on your screen.

Exiting Learn On-Demand

Use the following procedure to exit Learn On-Demand:

1. Click the **Learn On-Demand** button on the application title bar. The **Learn On-Demand** menu appears.

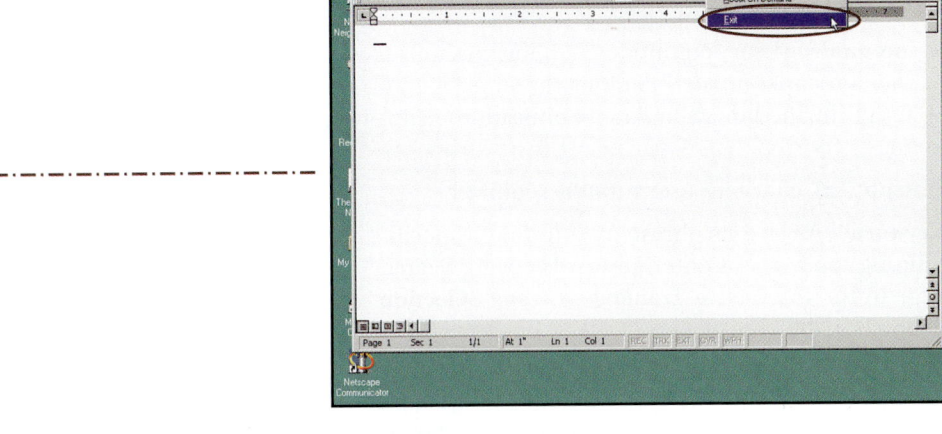

2. Click the **Exit** command. The **On-Demand—Exit** dialog box opens.

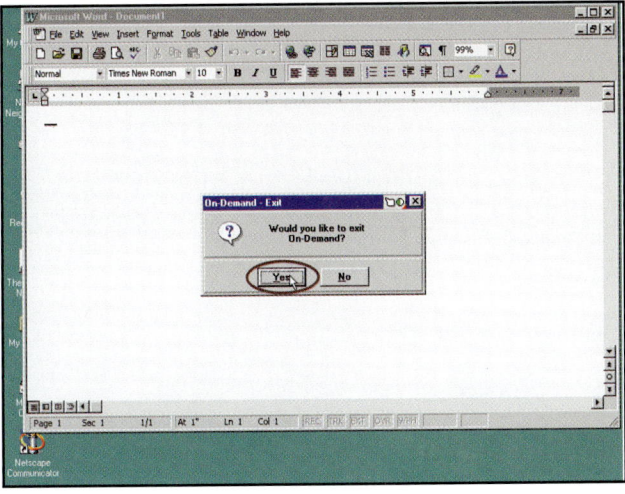

3. Click **Yes**. Learn On-Demand closes.

Technical Support

Should you need assistance installing or operating Learn On-Demand, email Macmillan Technical Support at **support@mcp.com**.

Glossary of Terms

Concept mode   Learning mode displaying the key concept of a topic. Explains when, where, and why you would use a program's features, as well as any other important conceptual information about a topic.

Concurrent mode   Learning mode enabling you to learn interactively while you work without leaving your "live" application.

Content files   Graphics and lesson files associated with Learn On-Demand.

Demo mode   Learning mode enabling you to learn by watching an animated demonstration of operations being performed in a simulated application environment.

Hotspot   Area where user input is required.

Keyword   A word or phrase used to find a specific training topic. Users enter keywords on the **Search** page in the **Interactive Training—Lesson Selection** dialog box.

Teacher mode   Learning mode enabling you to learn interactively by prompting you to enter mouse clicks or keystrokes as you complete tasks in a simulated application environment.

Topic   The most specific level of organization within PTS courseware titles. Each topic provides all the information required to complete a specific task within an application.

Table of Contents at a Glance

Lesson 1: Creating a Simple Document	**2**
Lesson 2: Editing a Document	**22**
Lesson 3: Formatting Text	**42**
Lesson 4: Formatting a Document	**74**
Lesson 5: Working with Tables	**100**
Lesson 6: Using Word Utilities	**124**
Lesson 7: Working with Non-text Elements	**148**
Lesson 8: References to Other Documents and Getting Help	**168**
Glossary	**196**
Index	**198**

Table of Contents

Lesson 1: Creating a Simple Document — 2

Task 1	Opening a New Document and Entering Text	3
Task 2	Moving Around in a Document	6
Task 3	Correcting Errors Using the Backspace and Delete Keys	8
Task 4	Correcting Spelling and Grammar Errors	10
Task 5	Saving a Document	13
Task 6	Printing and Closing a Document	14
	Student Exercises	16
	True-False	16
	Identifying Parts of the Word Screen	16
	Matching Questions	17
	Application Exercises	17

Lesson 2: Editing a Document — 22

Task 1	Opening an Existing Document and Saving It with a Different Name	23
Task 2	Inserting Text	26
Task 3	Selecting and Deleting Text	28
Task 4	Selecting and Replacing Text	30
Task 5	Moving Text Using Cut and Paste	32
Task 6	Using Undo and Redo	34
Task 7	Moving Text Using Drag and Drop	36
Task 8	Printing a Document Using the Menu	38
	Student Exercises	39
	True-False	39
	Identifying Parts of the Word Screen	39
	Matching Questions	40
	Application Exercises	40

Lesson 3: Formatting Text — 42

Task 1	Changing the Font Type, Size, and Emphasis	43
Task 2	Aligning Text in a Paragraph	46
Task 3	Changing Line Spacing	48

Task 4	Creating a Bulleted List	50
Task 5	Indenting the First Line of a Paragraph	54
Task 6	Using the Format Painter	56
Task 7	Creating a Hanging Indent	58
Task 8	Adding Spaces After Paragraphs	60
Task 9	Working with Tabs	62
Task 10	Printing Selected Text	66
	Student Exercises	68
	True-False	68
	Identifying Parts of the Word Screen	68
	Matching Questions	69
	Application Exercises	70

Lesson 4: Formatting a Document — 74

Task 1	Setting Margins	75
Task 2	Inserting Page Numbers	78
Task 3	Entering Text in a Header or Footer	80
Task 4	Inserting the Date into the Header or Footer	82
Task 5	Formatting the Header and Footer	84
Task 6	Inserting Page Breaks	86
Task 7	Using Print Preview	88
Task 8	Printing a Range of Pages	92
	Student Exercises	95
	True-False	95
	Identifying Parts of the Word Screen	95
	Matching Questions	96
	Application Exercises	97

Lesson 5: Working with Tables — 100

Task 1	Inserting a Table	101
Task 2	Entering Information into a Table	102
Task 3	Adding Rows to a Table	104
Task 4	Formatting Text in a Table	106
Task 5	Aligning Text in a Table	109
Task 6	Formatting Borders and Shading in a Table	110

Task 7	Using the AutoFormat and AutoFit Tools	114
Task 8	Centering a Table	116
	Student Exercises	119
	True-False	119
	Identifying Parts of the Word Screen	119
	Matching Questions	120
	Application Exercises	120

Lesson 6: Using Word Utilities — 124

Task 1	Using the Shortcut Menu to Check Spelling and Grammar	125
Task 2	Using the Spelling and Grammar Checker	127
Task 3	Tracking Changes	130
Task 4	Using AutoCorrect	134
Task 5	Using AutoText	137
Task 6	Finding Text	140
Task 7	Finding and Replacing Text	142
	Student Exercises	145
	True-False	145
	Identifying Parts of the Word Screen	145
	Matching Questions	146
	Application Exercises	147

Lesson 7: Working with Non-text Elements — 148

Task 1	Adding Borders	149
Task 2	Adding Clip Art	152
Task 3	Resizing and Moving Clip Art	154
Task 4	Adding a Picture	156
Task 5	Wrapping Text Around an Image	158
Task 6	Using WordArt	161
	Student Exercises	164
	True-False	164
	Identifying Parts of the Word Screen	164
	Matching Questions	165
	Application Exercises	165

Lesson 8: References to Other Documents and Getting Help — 168

Task 1	Moving Information Between Documents	169
Task 2	Adding Bookmarks	172
Task 3	Linking Word Documents Together	176
Task 4	Linking to Pages on the Internet	180
Task 5	Using the Office Assistant	182
Task 6	Using the Help Menu	184
Task 7	Getting Help on the Internet	186
Task 8	Finding Reference Books and Self-help Textbooks	190
	Student Exercises	192
	True-False	192
	Identifying Parts of the Word Screen	192
	Matching Exercises	193
	Application Exercises	193

Glossary — 196

Index — 198

Lesson 1
Creating a Simple Document

Task 1: Opening a New Document and Entering Text

Task 2: Moving Around in a Document

Task 3: Correcting Errors Using the Backspace and Delete Keys

Task 4: Correcting Spelling and Grammar Errors

Task 5: Saving a Document

Task 6: Printing and Closing a Document

Introduction

Microsoft Word is a program that can be used by individuals at varying levels of expertise. It can be used to do basic word processing tasks, such as writing a memo, an essay, or a letter. It is also a very robust program that can do the most complex word processing tasks. After you have mastered the fundamental skills necessary to produce a basic document, you can build up your repertoire by adding advanced skills one at a time.

In this lesson, you learn how to create a new document and enter and edit text. You also learn how to save, print, and close a document.

Visual Summary

By the time you have completed this lesson, you will have created a document that looks like this:

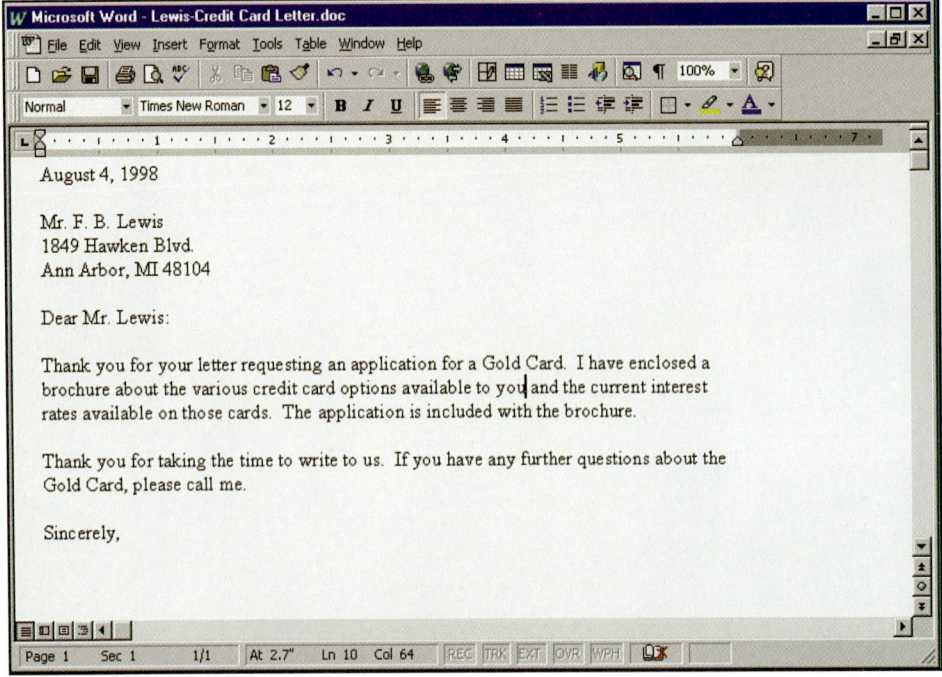

Task 1

Opening a New Document and Entering Text

Why would I do this?

Word processing programs are used to create written documents—letters, memos, research papers, and so forth. Launching Word automatically creates a blank document where you can begin entering text. It is just like taking a blank piece of paper and writing with a pen or pencil except that you write using a computer keyboard.

In this task, you learn to create a new document.

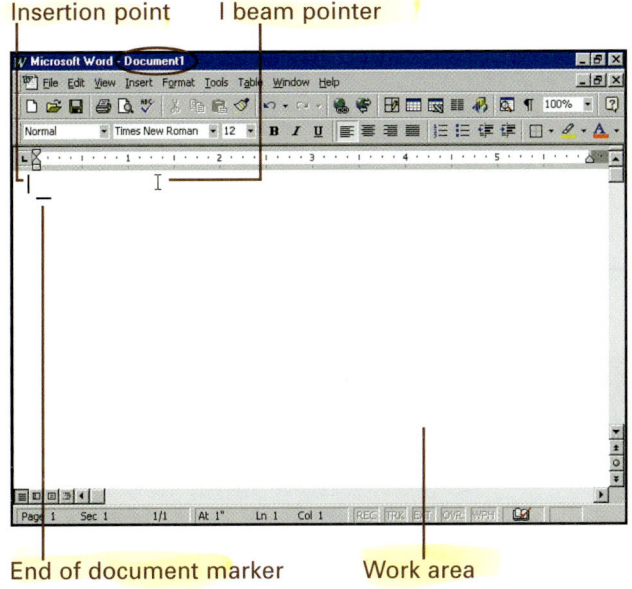

Insertion point · I beam pointer · End of document marker · Work area

1 Launch Microsoft Word. A new document called **Document1** is displayed. The *insertion point*, or cursor, where you begin typing appears in the upper-left corner of the work area, and the end of document marker appears below the insertion point. The *I beam pointer* showing the location of the mouse indicator also appears somewhere on the screen. If you need help launching Word, refer to the Preface of this book.

> **Pothole:** When you first use Word, you may have a little trouble distinguishing between the pointer—which shows the movement or location of the mouse—and the blinking insertion point—which is the point at which you begin to type. Whatever you type always appears at the insertion point location, never at the pointer location. The mouse pointer appears as an I beam on the document and as a white arrow when on the toolbars or at the left edge of a document.

2 If your screen does not look like the one shown in step 1, click the **Normal View** button.

> **In Depth:** The view buttons located on the status bar are used to change the way the document appears on your screen. The Normal view used in this book shows document formatting with a simplified page layout for quick and easy typing. The Page Layout view is used so that you can see how the text appears on the page and can edit margins, breaks between pages, and other page layout features.

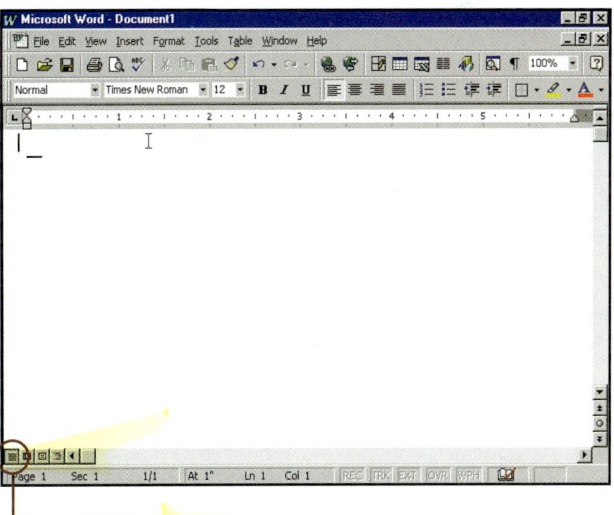

Normal View button

3 Type the following date: **August 4, 1998**.

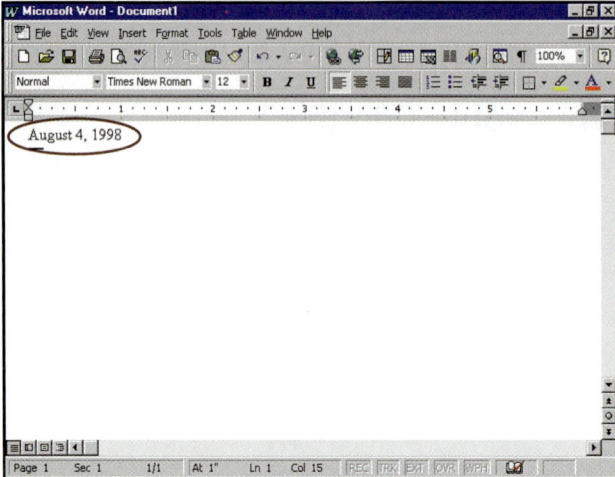

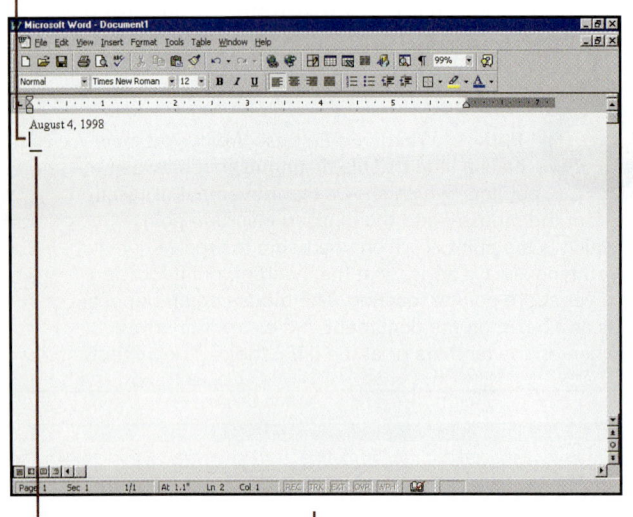

4 Press `Enter`. The insertion point and the end of document marker move down a line.

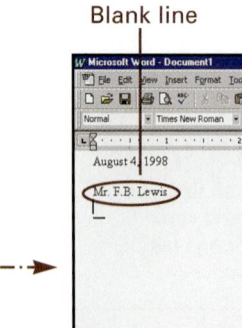

5 Press `Enter` again to create a blank line, type in **Mr. F. B. Lewis**, and then press `Enter`. The new line of text is displayed.

4 Learn Word 97, Second Edition

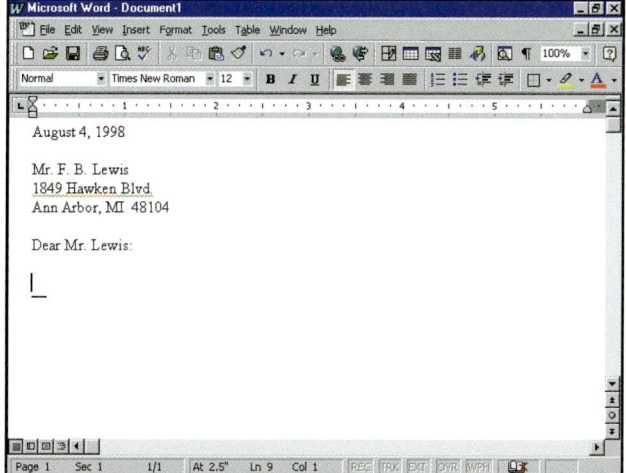

6 Finish the address with the following text:
1849 Hawken Blvd.
Press ⏎Enter
Ann Arbor, MI 48104
Press ⏎Enter twice
Dear Mr. Lewis:
Press ⏎Enter
Press ⏎Enter again to create a blank line after the salutation.

> **In Depth:** The Office Assistant may open on your screen at this point and ask if you need assistance writing a letter. Click the **Cancel** button to close the Office Assistant.

> **In Depth:** Jagged lines may appear below some of the text you have entered. A red broken line means that the word is not in the dictionary, and a green broken line means that the program thinks there may be a grammatical mistake. To verify that these options are turned on, click **Tools, Options** on the menu bar. Click the **Spelling & Grammar** tab and make sure a check mark is in the box next to **Check spelling as you type** and in the box next to **Check grammar as you type**. Then click **OK** to close the **Options** dialog box.

7 Type in the following text. Do not press ⏎Enter at the end of each line. Only press it after the last word of the paragraph. (Note: Misspell **application** in the last sentence, as shown in the following passage.)

Thank you for your letter requesting an application for a Gold Card. I have enclosed a brochure about the various credit card options available to you, and the current interest rates we charge on those cards. The appliction is included with the brochure.

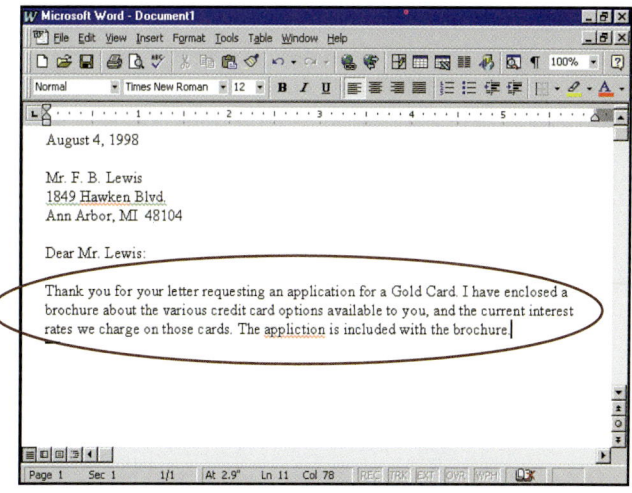

> **In Depth:** The insertion point for the text moves from one line to the next because of a feature called *word wrap*. With word wrap, the first word to reach the right margin automatically moves to the next line. You do not press ⏎Enter until you get to the end of a paragraph. The words on your screen may not wrap in the same way they do in the figure. This may be due to a difference in font size setting. The font size used in this figure is 12 point Times New Roman. The *default* font setting for Word is 10 point Times New Roman. (You'll learn more about fonts and sizes in Lesson 3, "Formatting Text.") Do not be concerned if the words wrap at a different place in the paragraph.

Lesson 1: Creating a Simple Document

8 Press ⏎Enter twice to create a blank line between the paragraphs. Then finish the letter by typing in the following:

Thank you for taking the time to write to us. If you have any further questions about the Gold Card, please call me.

Press ⏎Enter twice. Then type:

Sincerely,

Press ⏎Enter four times. Then type:

\<your name\>
Vice President, Credit Administration

Make sure you type in your name in the second-to-last line. Keep the document open and proceed to task 2.

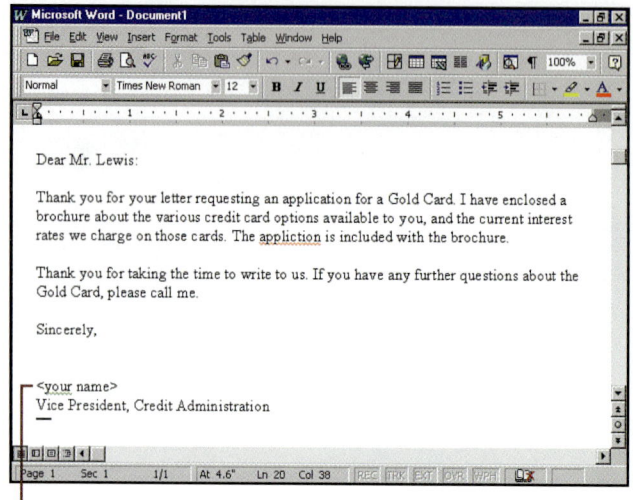

Type your name in here.

Pothole: If the letter is longer than can be seen on the screen, the top of the letter scrolls up out of sight when you type in your name and title. Don't be concerned. In the next lesson, you will learn how to move around in your document.

Task 2

Moving Around in a Document

Why would I do this?

When you typed the letter in the first task, the insertion point moved automatically as you typed or when you pressed the ⏎Enter key. When you reached the end of the letter, the screen automatically scrolled the text up and out of view so that you could see the new lines you were typing. In this task, you learn how to move around in the document so that you can select text, enter new text, edit existing text, or see different parts of your document. You can move around in a document in many different ways. You can use the pointer to move the insertion point to a new location. You can use arrow keys to move up, down, left, or right in the text. You can also use the scrollbars or use combinations of keys that move you up or down a screen at a time. Knowing how to move around in your document enables you to enter and edit text much faster.

Keyboard Key	Description
PgUp	Takes you up one page from where the cursor is placed
PgDn	Takes you down one page from where the cursor is placed
Home	Takes you to the beginning of the line where the cursor is placed
Ctrl + Home	Takes you to the beginning of the document
End	Takes you to the end of the line where the cursor is placed
Ctrl + End	Takes you to the end of the document

In this task, you learn how to use the *scrollbar*. You also learn how to move left and right a character at a time, up and down a line at a time, and up and down a page at a time.

1 Click the arrow at the top of the vertical scrollbar several times to scroll to the top of your letter. Notice that the screen scrolls up one line at a time. If you click the arrow and hold down the left mouse button, your screen scrolls rapidly.

> **In Depth:** The vertical scrollbar located at the right edge of the window and the horizontal scrollbar located at the bottom of the window can be used to move the portion of the document that shows on your screen. The vertical scrollbar moves the document up and down on your screen. The horizontal scrollbar moves the document left and right on your screen.

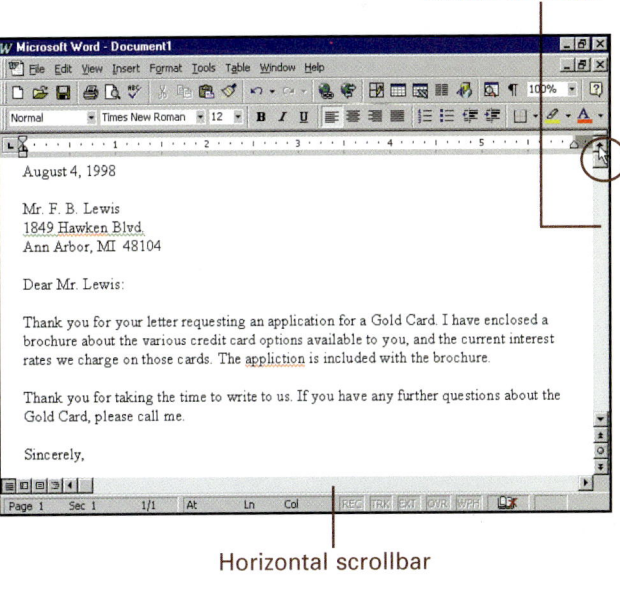

Vertical scrollbar

Horizontal scrollbar

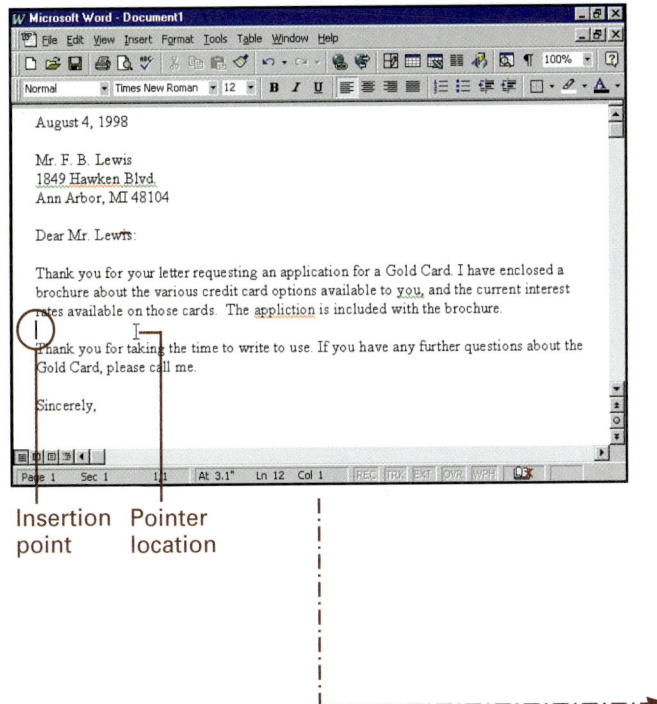

Insertion point   Pointer location

2 Position the pointer on the blank line between the two paragraphs and click once with the left mouse button. The insertion point is moved to the beginning of the blank line. If you begin typing, the words appear at the insertion point location, not at the pointer location.

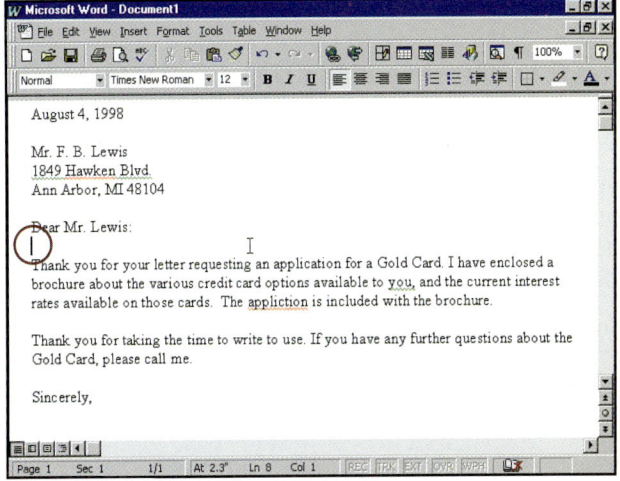

3 Press ↑ on your keyboard four times. Notice that the insertion point is now just below the salutation. Try using the other arrow keys found on your keyboard to move around in the text. Using the arrow keys changes the location of the insertion point in your document. If needed, the text showing on your screen will scroll up or down so that you can continue to see the insertion point.

Lesson 1: Creating a Simple Document

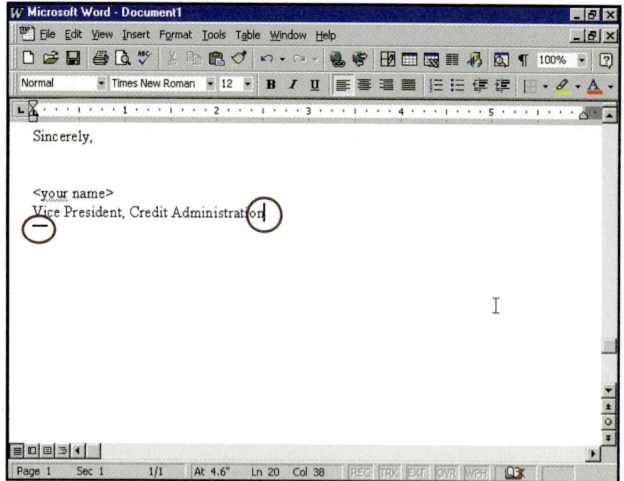

4 Press the `PgDn` key to move down one screen. Notice that the insertion point moves and only the bottom of the letter is now displayed. You can also see the end of document marker.

5 Press the `PgUp` key to return to the place in the document where you were before you pressed `PgDn`. Notice that the top of the letter is displayed and that the insertion point has moved to the top of the letter. This feature is very helpful for longer documents.

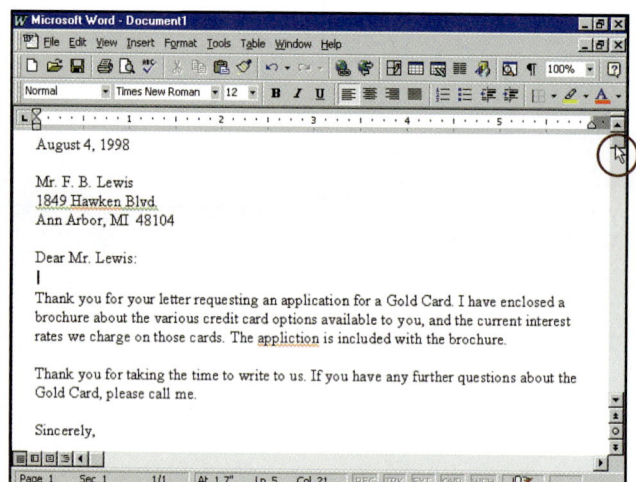

> **In Depth:** Notice the box in the vertical scrollbar. This box lets you know your location in the document—it is at the top of the scrollbar when you are at the top of the document and at the bottom of the scrollbar when you are at the end of the document. You can point to the box, click and hold the left mouse button, and then drag the box up or down the scrollbar to move quickly to a new location in your document. This action moves the text showing on your screen, but it does not change the location of the insertion point. You need to click at the point where you want to begin to type to move the insertion point to that location.

Task 3

Correcting Errors Using the Backspace and Delete Keys

Why would I do this?

When you are composing a document, you will often make typographical errors that you want to correct immediately. You will also find changes that you want to make when you proofread what you've written. You can correct errors in several ways. The two most common methods are to use the `Backspace` and `Del` keys. The `Backspace` key deletes text to the left of the insertion point, and the `Del` key deletes text to the right of the insertion point.

In this task, you learn to edit text using the `Backspace` and `Del` keys.

1 Use the pointer to place the insertion point immediately to the left of the word **charge** in the first full paragraph.

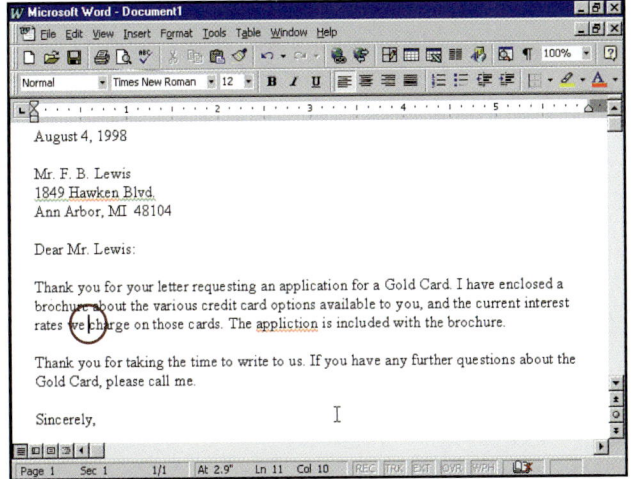

2 Press `Backspace` once. Notice that the insertion point moves to the left and removes the space between the words **we** and **charge**.

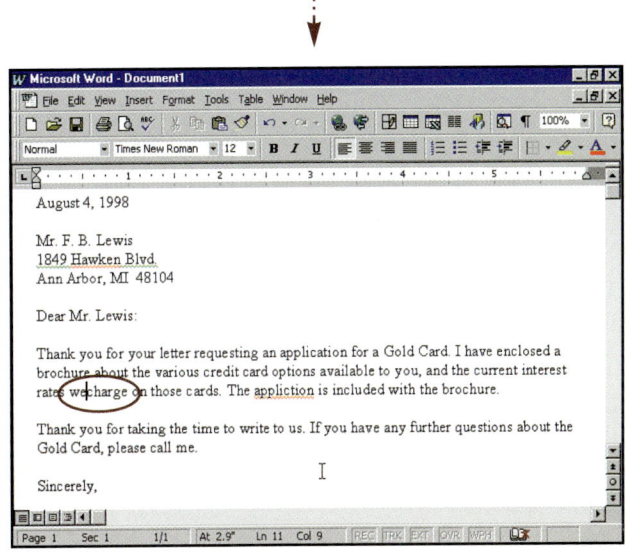

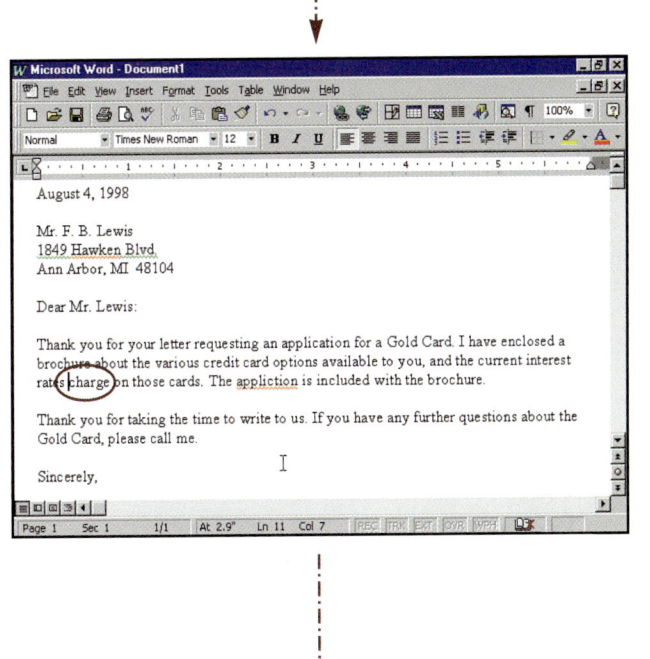

3 Press `Backspace` twice more. Notice that the word **we** has now been deleted.

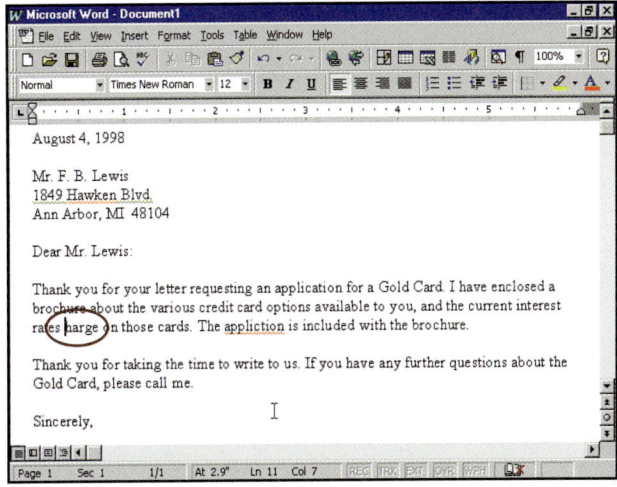

4 Press `Del` once. Notice that the first letter of the word **charge** to the right of the insertion point is removed, even though the insertion point didn't move.

Lesson 1: Creating a Simple Document   9

5 Press Del five more times. The word **charge** is now removed. Do not remove the space to the right of the word.

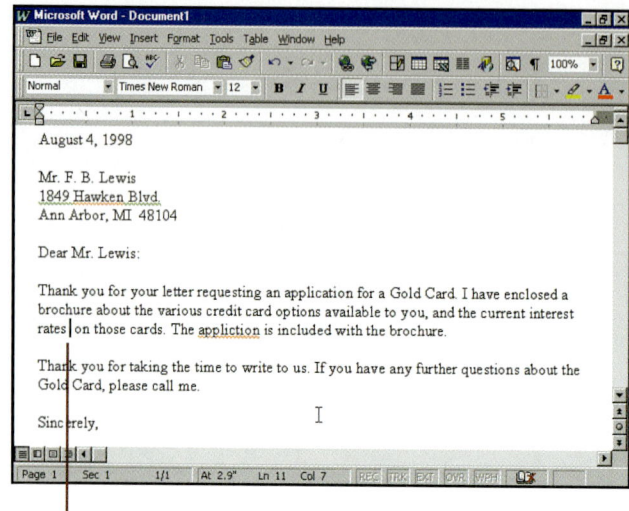

Two spaces with the insertion point in the middle

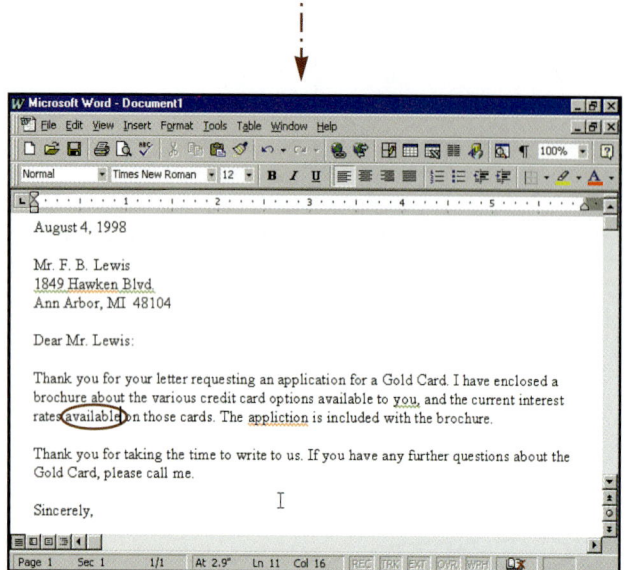

6 Type in the word **available** at the insertion point. The word is inserted and the existing text is moved to the right.

Task 4

Correcting Spelling and Grammar Errors

Why would I do this?

Spelling and grammar errors in a document reduce the credibility and effectiveness of the message. Microsoft Word has two ways to check spelling and grammar. The first is a program that gives you a great deal of flexibility in checking and correcting the errors. The second is a shortcut that can save a considerable amount of time in a long document.

In this task, you learn how to use a shortcut menu to correct spelling and grammar errors.

1 Position the pointer on the misspelled word **appliction** and click with the right mouse button. A shortcut menu opens that suggests the correct spelling. The top section of the shortcut menu contains suggestions for replacing the misspelled word.

> **In Depth:** The spelling program uses a dictionary that has thousands of words in it. When you type a word that is not in its dictionary, the word is shown with a red, jagged line. Just because the word is not in the program's dictionary does not mean that it is misspelled—it could be a proper noun, a technical term, or an unusual word.

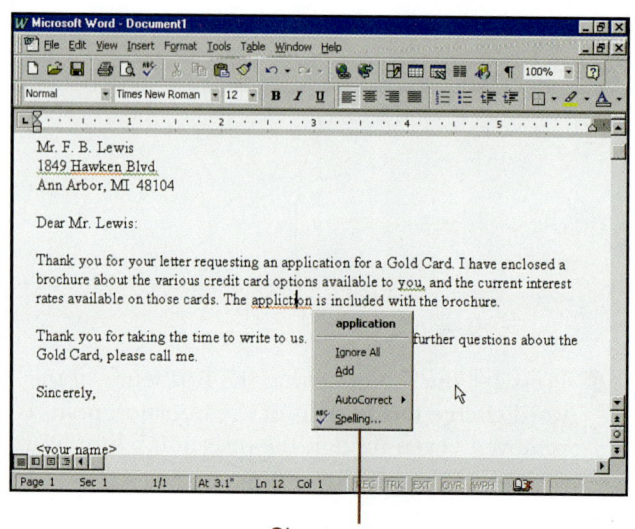

Shortcut menu

Learn Word 97, Second Edition

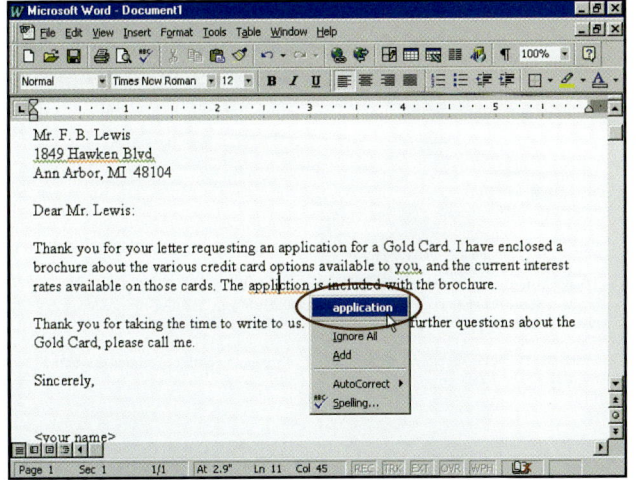

2 The suggestion is correct. Move the pointer to the word in the shortcut menu to select it.

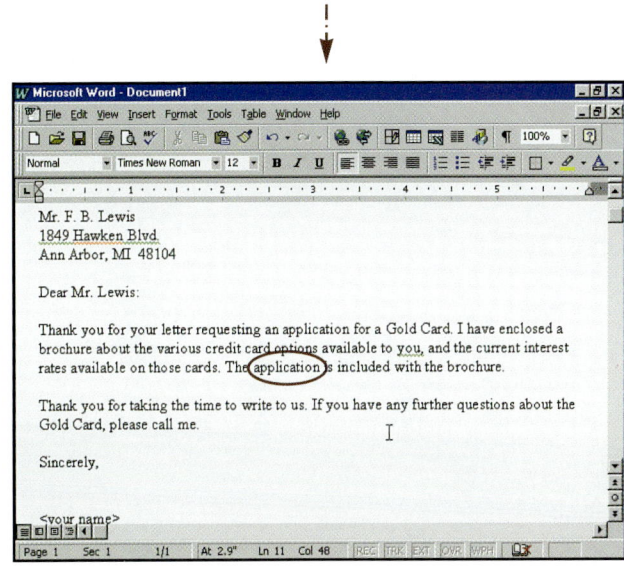

3 Click on the selected word with the left mouse button. The misspelled word is replaced with the correctly spelled word, and the shortcut menu closes.

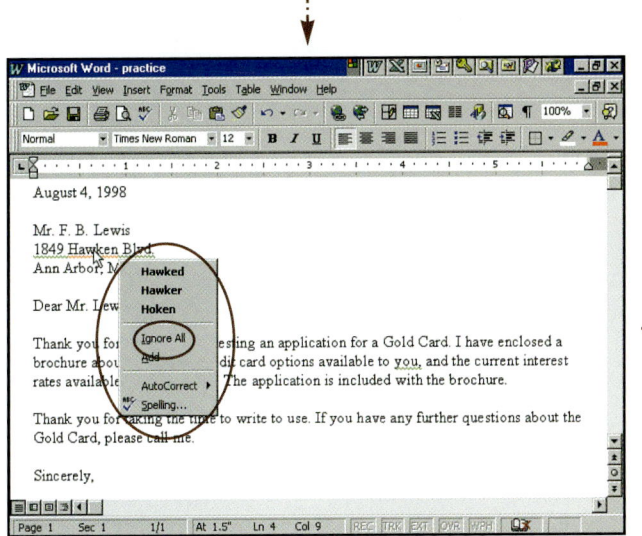

4 Right-click the word **Hawken** in the address line. The shortcut menu opens with suggestions, but none of the suggestions are correct.

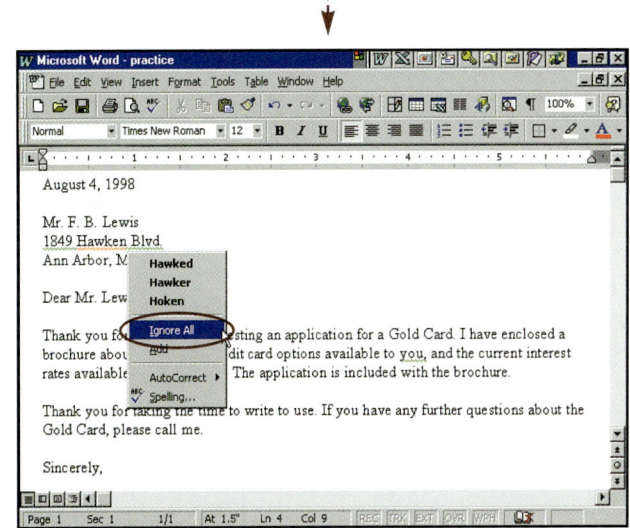

5 Click the **Ignore All** button to ignore all further occurrences of the word in this document.

Pothole: When the program identifies a word that is not in the dictionary, you have the option of adding it. Be very careful! If you add a misspelled word to the dictionary, it accepts the word in the future without warning. In general, do not add words to the dictionary if you are using someone else's computer or are working in a computer laboratory.

Lesson 1: Creating a Simple Document

6 The green lines indicate grammar errors. The same technique can be used to correct the grammar errors. Right-click on the address line. The shortcut menu opens. Because of the period at the end of **Blvd.**, the grammar checker thinks this line is a sentence fragment.

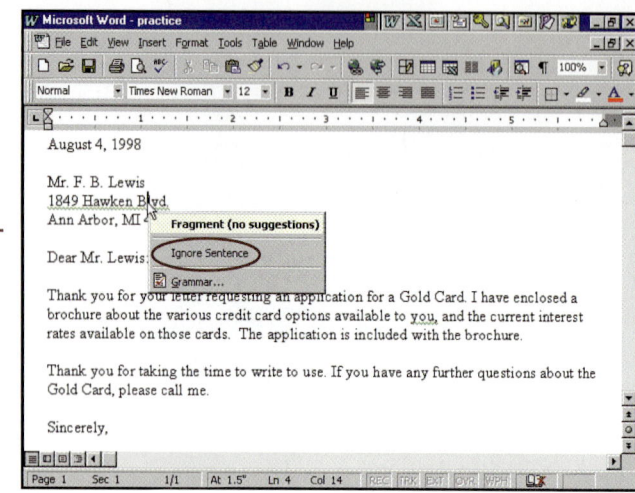

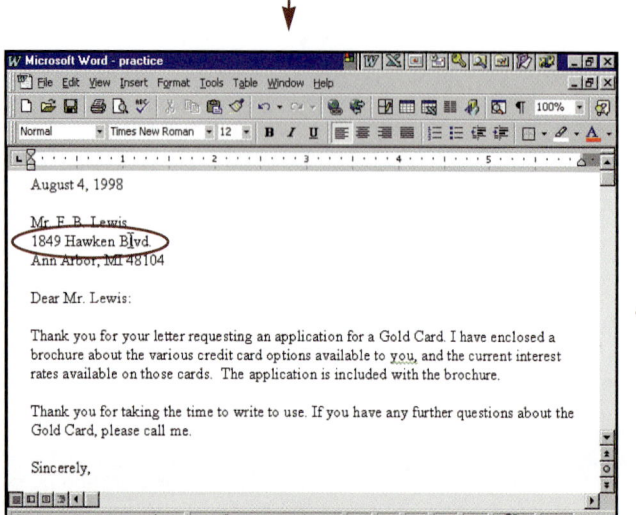

7 Click **Ignore Sentence** to ignore the address line. The green line disappears.

8 Right-click the word **you** that is followed by a comma and is underlined with a jagged green line. The shortcut menu appears and suggests that the comma is not necessary.

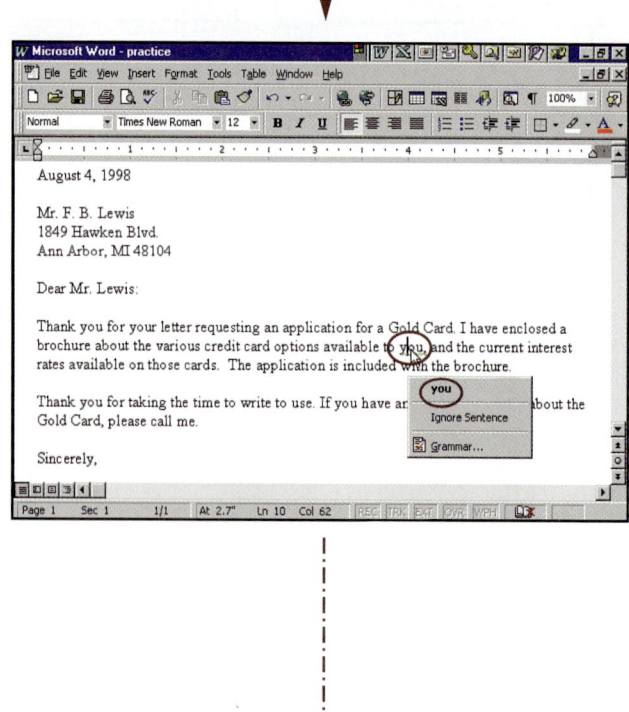

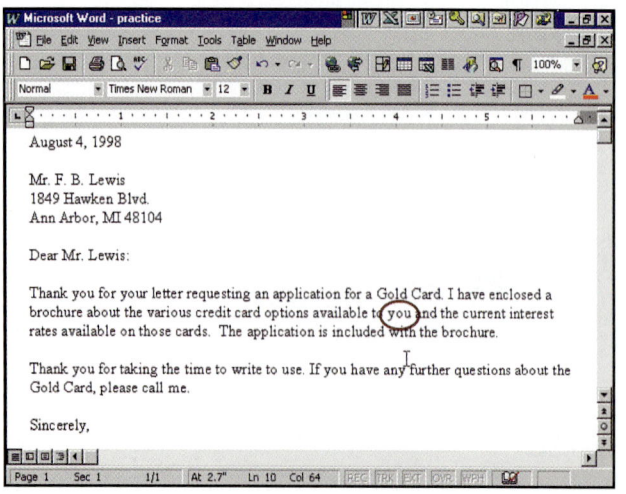

9 Click **you** in the shortcut menu to select it. This action replaces **you,** in the sentence, and the green line disappears.

Learn Word 97, Second Edition

Task 5
Saving a Document

Why would I do this?

When you write a letter, memo, or other type of document, you generally want to save a permanent record of it. As you are writing, the program works with Random Access Memory (RAM), which is temporary memory in your computer. If you turn off your computer without saving your document, you will have no record of your work. To create a permanent record, you need to save your work on some permanent storage media, such as a hard disk or a floppy disk. When you are working on a long document, save your work every ten minutes or so. The first time you save a document, you are asked to give the document a name, as well as the location where you want it saved.

In this task, you learn to save a new document.

1 Click the **Save** button on the Standard toolbar. The **Save As** dialog box is displayed.

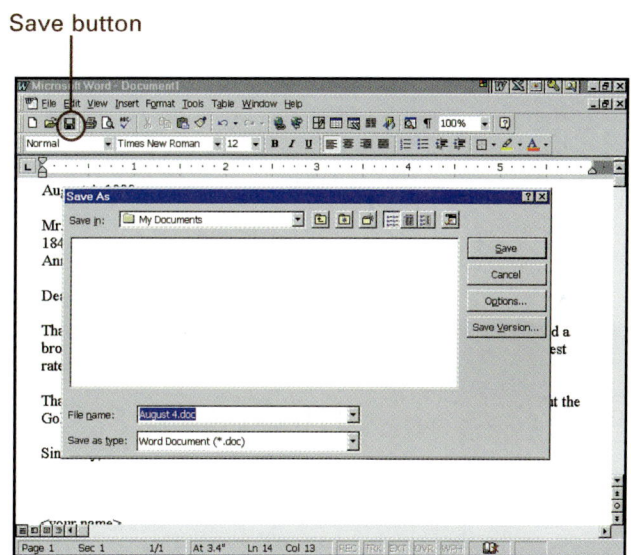

2 The text in the **file name** text box is highlighted. Type **Lewis-Credit Card Letter**.

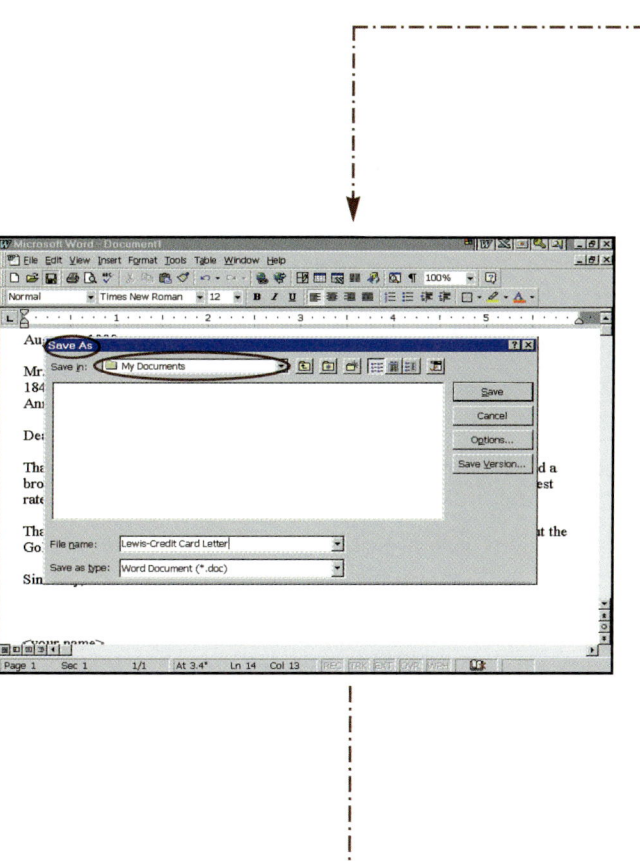

3 Because we will be saving to a floppy disk, please insert a disk now. To specify where you want to save the file, click the down arrow to the right of the **Save in** box. A drop-down list opens.

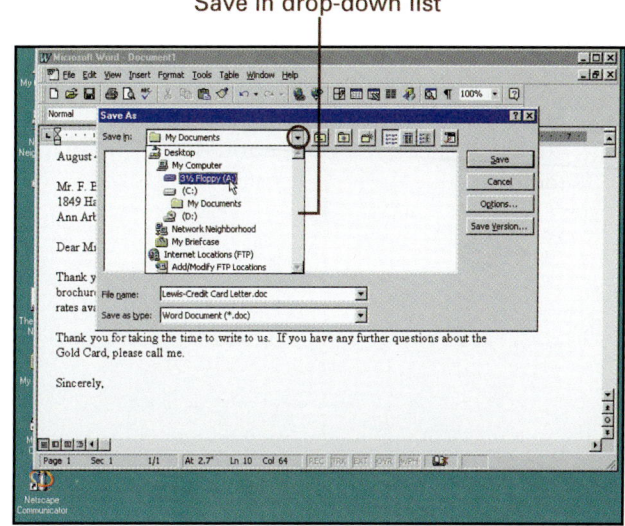

Lesson 1: Creating a Simple Document   13

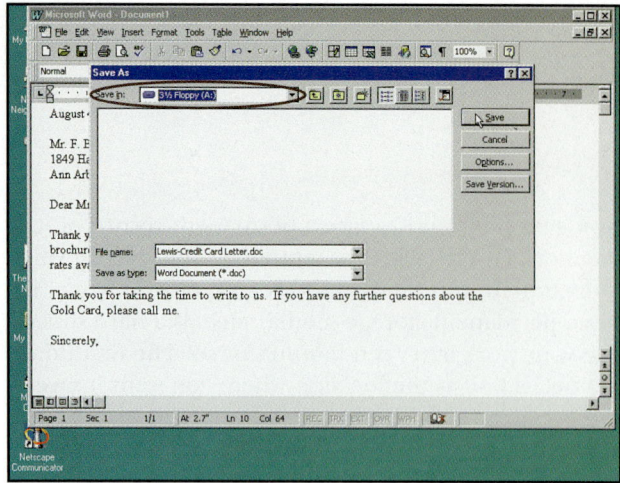

4 Choose the A: drive to store your document.

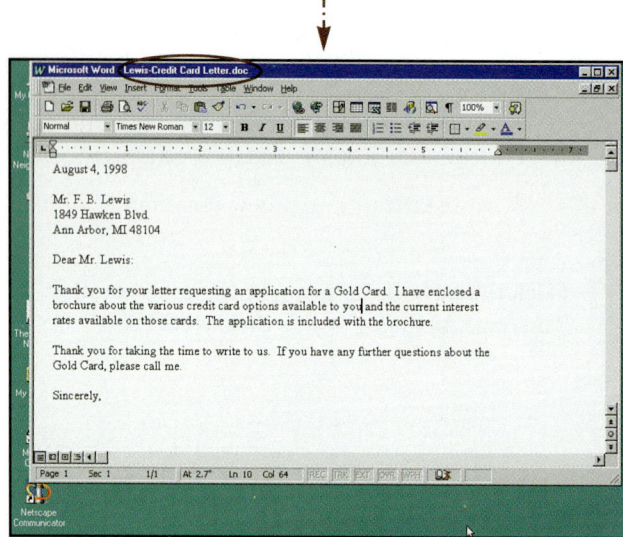

5 Click the **Save** button in the dialog box. Notice that the name of the document in the Word title bar has changed to **Lewis-Credit Card Letter**.

Task 6

Printing and Closing a Document

Why would I do this?

Letters and other documents are written to communicate with others. In most cases, you need a printed copy of your document to send to others. The easiest and quickest way to print is to click the **Print** button on the toolbar. When you do so, the entire document is sent to the printer automatically using the default settings.

In the Preface to this book, you learned how to close Microsoft Word. Sometimes, however, you will want to close the document but leave Word open to create a new, unrelated document.

In this task, you learn how to use the Print button to print a document and also how to close the document.

Print button

1 Make sure your printer is turned on and selected. Then click the **Print** button on the Standard toolbar.

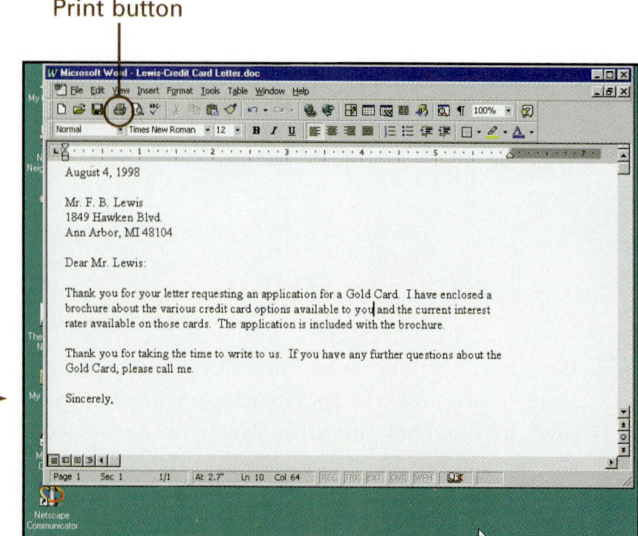

Save button · Close Window button · Close Application button

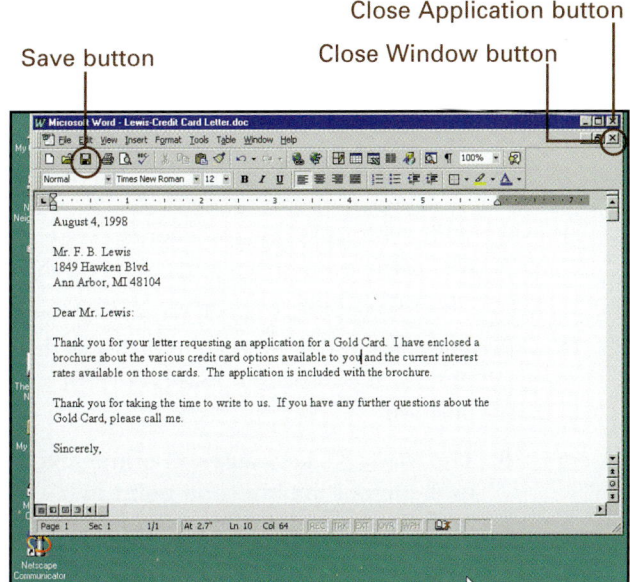

2 Click the **Save** button in the Standard toolbar to save your work if you have made any changes.

3 Click the document **Close Window** button at the right end of the menu bar. Make sure you don't click the application Close button in the title bar, which closes Word.

> **In Depth:** If you have not saved your changes when you click on either Close button, the program asks you whether you want to save them.

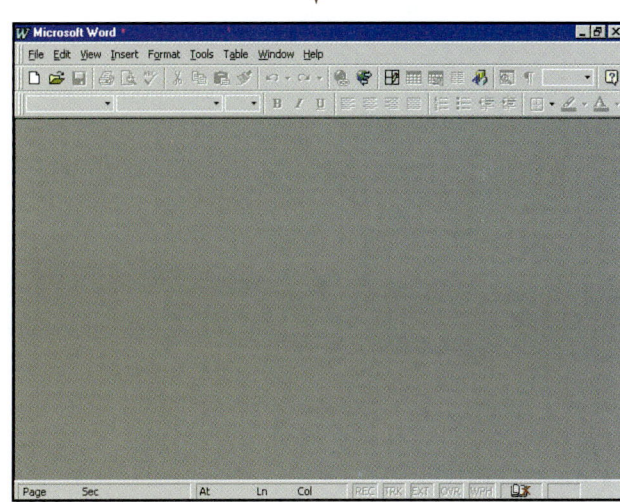

Lesson 1: Creating a Simple Document **15**

Student Exercises

True-False

Circle either T or F.

T F 1. When you launch Word, it automatically opens a blank document named Document1.

T F 2. To create a blank line between lines of text, you press the Insert Blank Line button.

T F 3. To move the insertion point in your document, you can use the arrow keys on your keyboard.

T F 4. If you are typing a paragraph that will not fit on a single line, you press ↵Enter at the end of each line of text.

T F 5. The spell check program identifies all of the incorrectly spelled words in the document, even if they are proper names or technical terms.

T F 6. When you type, the new characters go where the pointer happens to be when you start typing.

T F 7. The Del key deletes the character to the right of the insertion point's current position.

T F 8. The ←Backspace key causes all of the text to the left of the insertion point to be moved to the left by one space each time the ←Backspace key is pressed.

T F 9. Spelling errors are indicated by a red jagged underline, and grammar errors are indicated by a green jagged underline.

T F 10. The first time you try to save a new document by pressing the Save button, the Save As dialog box opens to give you the opportunity to change the name and location of the file.

Identifying Parts of the Word Screen

Refer to the figure and identify the numbered parts of the screen. Write the letter of the correct label in the space next to the number.

1. _____
2. _____
3. _____
4. _____
5. _____
6. _____
7. _____
8. _____

A. Save button
B. Vertical scrollbar
C. Close Window button
D. Horizontal scrollbar
E. Pointer
F. Print button
G. End of document marker
H. Insertion point

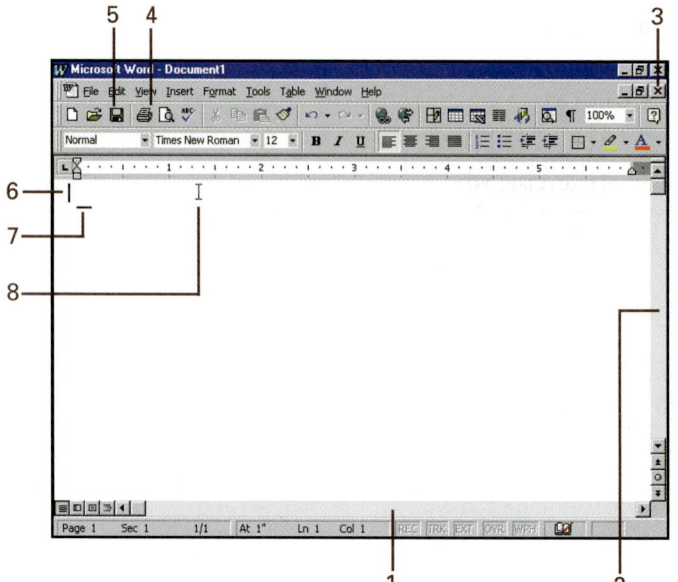

16 Learn Word 97, Second Edition

Matching Questions

Match the following statements to the word or phrase from the list on the right. Write the letter of the matching word or phrase in the space provided next to the number.

1. ____ Deletes the character to the left of the insertion point
2. ____ Used to move the insertion point around in the document one space at a time
3. ____ Indicates that the sentence or phrase does not match the rules for structure that the program uses
4. ____ Deletes the character to the right of the insertion point
5. ____ Indicates the end of the document
6. ____ Sends the document to the printer using the default settings
7. ____ Stores the document on disk
8. ____ Closes the document window but not the Word program
9. ____ Indicates that the word is not in its dictionary
10. ____ Moves the view of the document down one screen

A. End of document marker
B. Save
C. Spell check
D. Grammar check
E. [Del] key
F. [Backspace] key
G. Arrow keys
H. Print button
I. Close Window button on the menu bar
J. Page down

Application Exercises

The following exercises produce and use a single document. They should be performed in sequence.

Exercise 1—Launch Word and Enter a Date, Name, and Salutation

In this exercise, you launch Word and type a business letter from a bank executive to a customer. Refer to the figures to see how the text in the paragraphs wraps. Two intentional spelling mistakes and two intentional grammar errors are in this text. These mistakes (as well as any additional typing errors that you make) are fixed in a later exercise. The figures shown assume that the font size is 12 point and the font is Times New Roman. Click on the arrow next to the **Font Size** box on the Formatting toolbar. Choose **12** points from the **Font Size** drop-down list. For help, see Lesson 3, Task 1 as reference.

1. Launch MS Word.
2. Type today's date—for example, September 10, 1998.

3. Press ⏎Enter to end the first line and move to the next line. Press ⏎Enter again to create a blank line between the date and the name and address lines.

4. Type the following name and address. Press ⏎Enter at the end of each line.

   Bill Williams

   1835 Long Lake Road

   Ann Arbor, MI 48104

5. Press ⏎Enter twice after the postal code and type the salutation:

   Dear Mr. Williams:

6. Press ⏎Enter twice and type the first paragraph of the letter:

   Thank you for your letter concerning the rate on the Gold Card you hold with our bank.

7. Press ⏎Enter twice and then type in the next paragraph:

   The account you have is a variable rate account. The rate are tied to the prime rate, as quoted in the Wall Street Journal. It is going down to 11.8%, effective today, based on the reccent decline in the prime rate. If you pay your credit card account in full each month, you can take advantage of the 25-day grace period before interest is assessed. The benefit is that accounts that are paid in full each month do not acummulate interest charges. These feature is not available on all variable rate accounts.

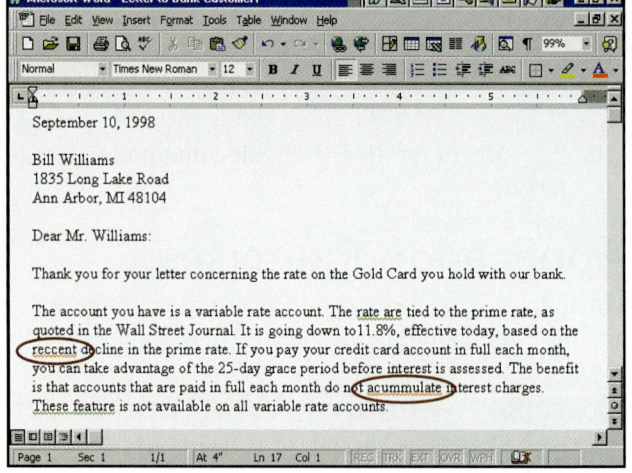

8. Press ⏎Enter twice and then type in the next paragraph:

   Thank you for taking the time to write to us to share your thoughts. If you have further questions please call me at (313) 555-1234.

9. Press ⏎Enter twice and then type the following:

   Sincerely,

10. Press ⏎Enter three times to make room for the signature and then type the following: (Press ⏎Enter at the end of each line.)

    Sara A. Johnson

    Vice President

    Branch Adminitration

Learn Word 97, Second Edition

11. Press ⏎Enter twice and then type the following:

    cc: Revolving Credit

12. Leave the document open for use in the next exercise.

Exercise 2—Move the View and the Insertion Point and Correct Spelling and Grammar Errors

1. Use the vertical scrollbar, up arrow, or PgUp to move the view to display the top half of the letter.

2. Right-click the words **rate are** and choose **rate is** from the shortcut menu.

3. Right-click the word **reccent** and select **recent**.

4. Right-click the misspelled word, **acummulate**. Replace it with **accumulate**.

5. Right-click the phrase **These feature** and replace it with the first choice, **This feature**.

6. Use the vertical scrollbar, down arrow, or PgDn to move the view to display the bottom half of the letter.

7. Right-click on the word **Adminitration** and choose **Administration**.

8. Use this method to find and fix any other spelling or grammar errors that you may have made while typing the document. All red and green jagged lines should be removed.

9. Leave the document open for use in the next exercise.

Exercise 3—Edit the Document

1. Move the insertion point to Sara Johnson's name at the end of the document. Use Del or ⌫Backspace to delete her name and type in your name.

2. Leave the document open for use in the next exercise.

Exercise 4—Save the Document

1. Click the **Save** button on the toolbar.

2. In the Save As dialog box, type **Letter to a Bank Customer** in the **File name** box.

3. In the **Save in** box, select the folder where you want to save the document. (You probably want to save it to a floppy disk in drive A: if you are working in a computer lab.)

4. Click the **Save** button.

Exercise 5—Print the Document and Close It

1. Make sure the printer that is hooked up to your computer is turned on.

2. Click the **Print** button on the toolbar.

3. Click the **Close Window** button at the upper-right corner of the document window to close the document.

4. Click the **Close Application** button at the upper-right corner of the Word document window to close Word.

Lesson 2
Editing a Document

Task 1: Opening an Existing Document and Saving It with a Different Name

Task 2: Inserting Text

Task 3: Selecting and Deleting Text

Task 4: Selecting and Replacing Text

Task 5: Moving Text Using Cut and Paste

Task 6: Using Undo and Redo

Task 7: Moving Text Using Drag and Drop

Task 8: Printing a Document Using the Menu

Introduction

You will probably need to alter nearly every document you create. These alterations will be necessary because you will make typographical errors or will want to delete, change, or add to your text. Word gives you many ways to edit a document. The most basic of these methods is the insertion, selection, deletion, and replacement of text. Word also provides ways to copy and paste, or move, text.

In this lesson, you learn how to use several techniques to edit text in a document.

Visual Summary

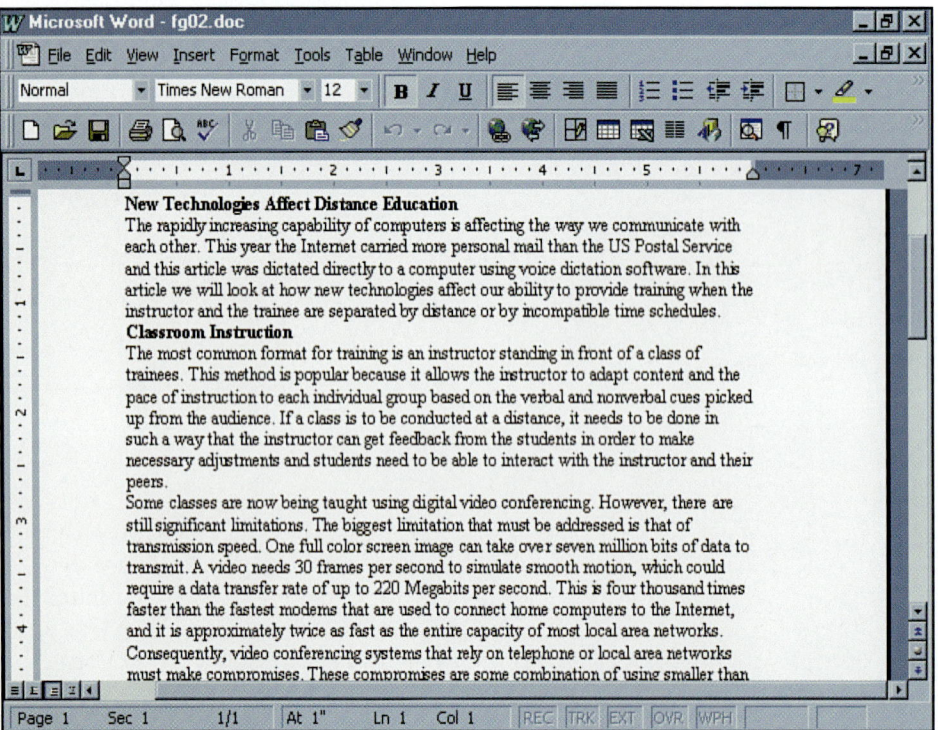

By the time you have completed this lesson, you will have created a worksheet that looks like this:

Task 1

Opening an Existing Document and Saving It with a Different Name

Why would I do this?

Creating a document involves both writing and editing. While writing is the first step, proofing and editing is the second (and sometimes third) step in the process. Often, you will create a draft of a document, save it and close it, and then edit it at a later time. In some instances, you will want to open an existing document and use it as the basis for a new document. You can open an existing document, make changes to it, and then save it with a new name. This retains the original document without any changes and creates a second document with a different name.

In this task, you learn to open a document that was created earlier and stored on a disk. You will save the document with a new name on a *floppy disk* in drive A:. Place a formatted disk in drive A: before you start this task.

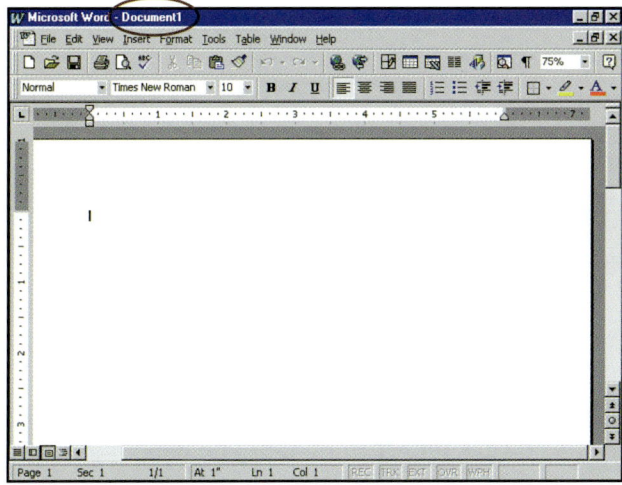

1 Launch Word. Word opens and an empty document called **Document1** is displayed.

2 Place the CD-ROM that is included with the book in your computer and click the **Open** button. The **Open** dialog box is displayed.

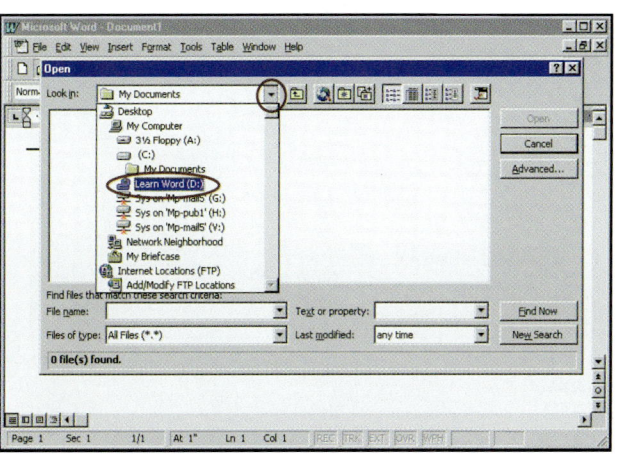

3 Click on the arrow to the right of the **Look in** list. Then, click the drive where you see **Learn Word**, the title of the CD-ROM. (Notice the CD icon to the left of the title.) The drive letter in this example is D:, although the drive letters associated with the CD-ROM drive will vary depending on how the computer is set up.

4 Double-click the **Student** folder from the list of files included on the CD. This will display the contents of the **Student** folder.

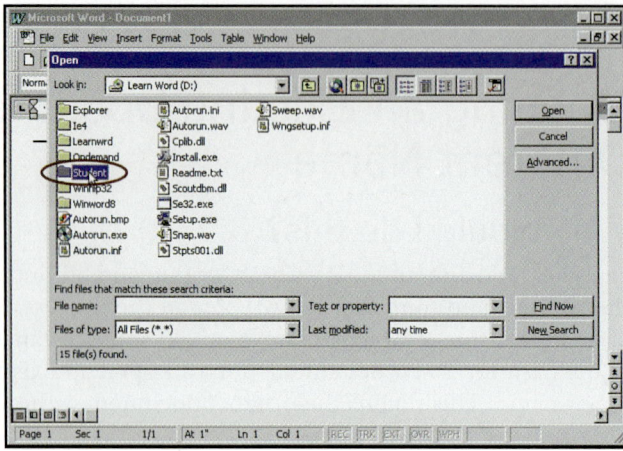

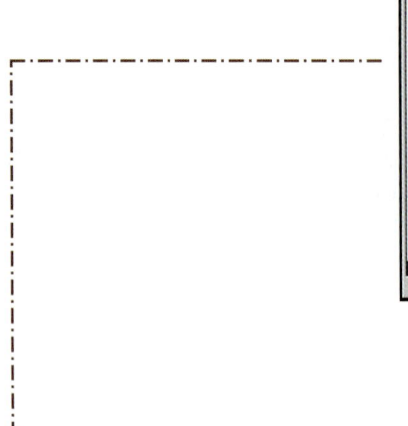

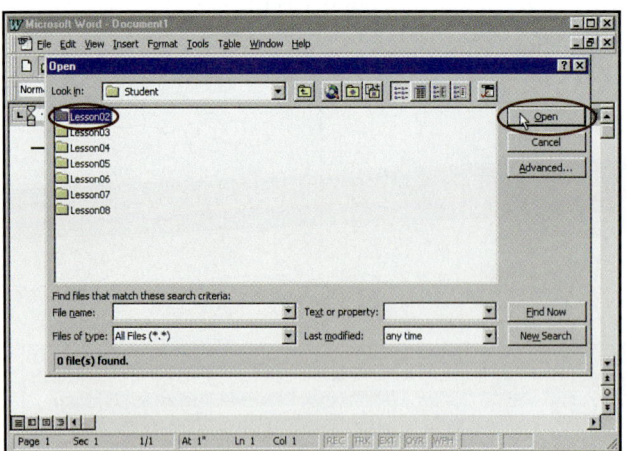

5 Click on the **Lesson02** folder to select it, and then click the **Open** button. The folder is opened and the Word files for **Lesson02** are displayed.

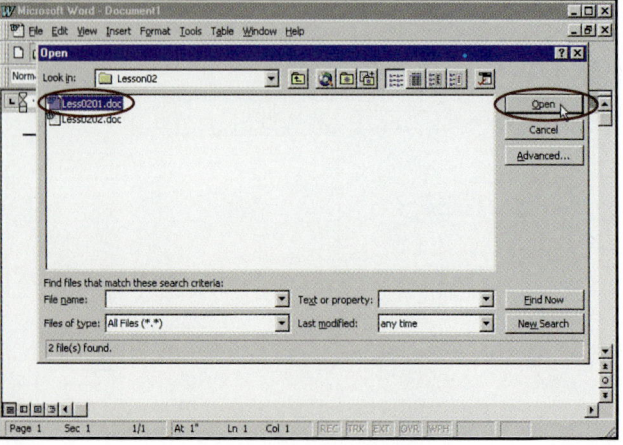

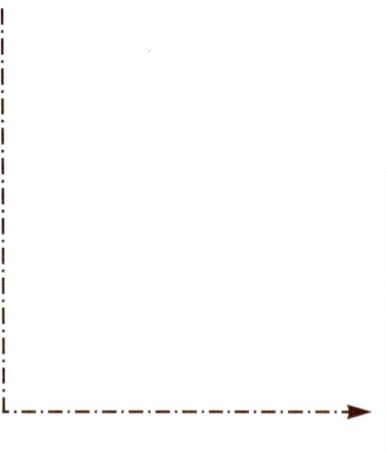

6 Locate the **Less0201** file and click to select it. Click the **Open** button in the **Open** dialog box.

24 Learn Word 97, Second Edition

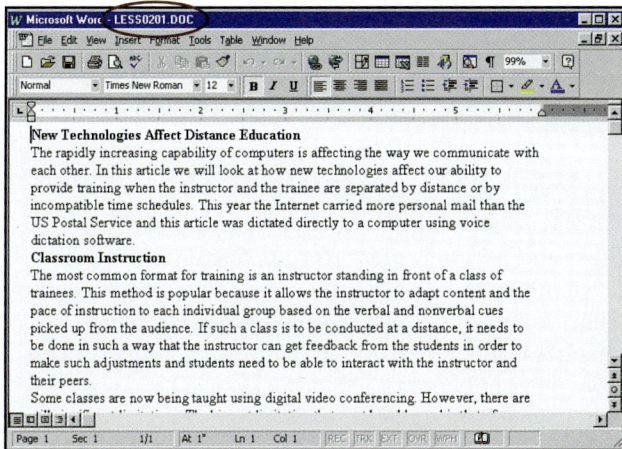

7 Word opens the document. Notice that the filename is shown in the title bar.

8 Click on **File** and **Save As** from the menu bar. The **Save As** dialog box is displayed.

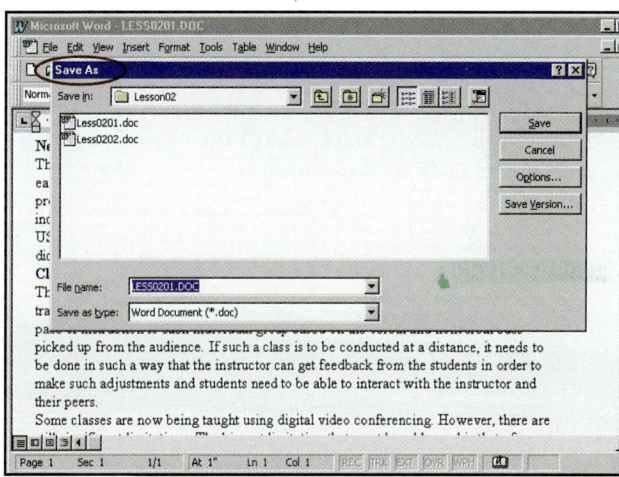

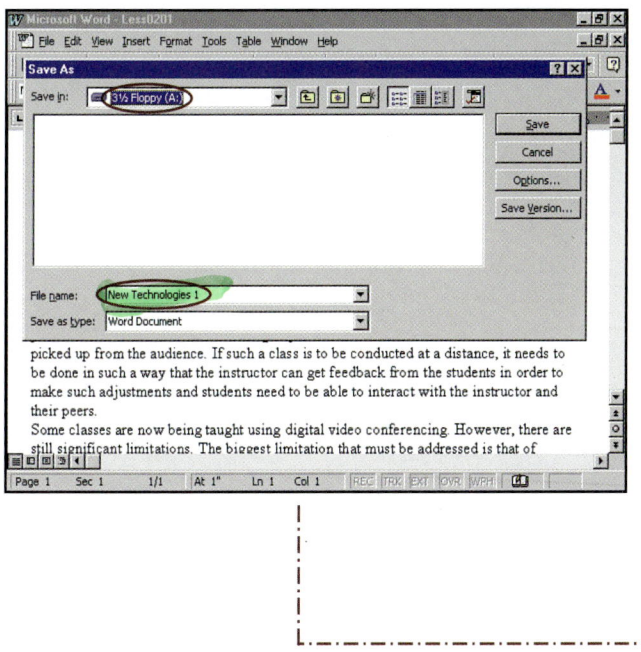

9 The text in the **File name** box should be highlighted. If it isn't, select the text by clicking on the left mouse button and moving it across the text. Type **New Technologies 1**. Select the floppy disk (drive A:) from the **Save in** drop-down list.

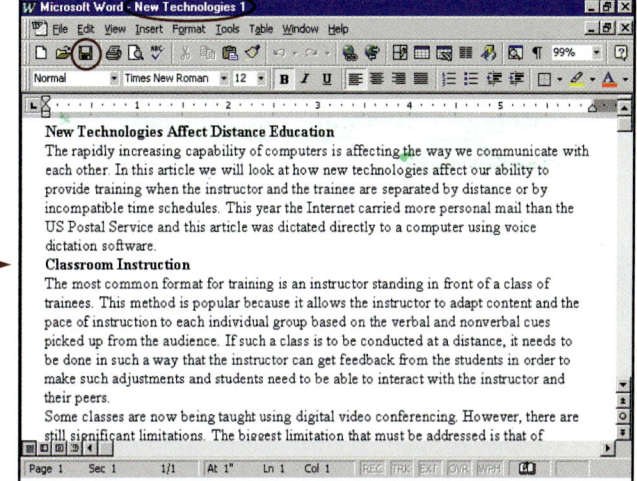

10 Click on the **Save** button. The document is saved on the floppy disk, and the new name is displayed on the title bar.

Lesson 2: Editing a Document

Task 2
Inserting Text

Why would I do this?

In most cases, the first draft of a document is written quickly to record your initial thoughts. During the proofing and editing process, you may want to expand on the existing text and add new ideas to your document. If you allowed the computer to wrap the text at the end of each line when you created the document, the program automatically adjusts the existing text to make room for whatever text you insert. This freedom to express your thoughts quickly and to then make extensive additions and changes is a major advantage of using a word processor over a typewriter.

In this task, you learn how to insert text into an existing document.

1 Click the down arrow on the vertical scrollbar to scroll down in the **New Technologies 1** file. Stop when the last paragraph and the end of document marker are displayed.

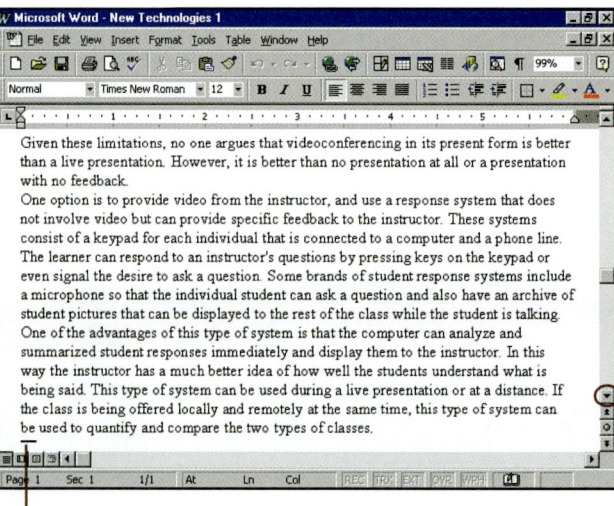

End of document marker

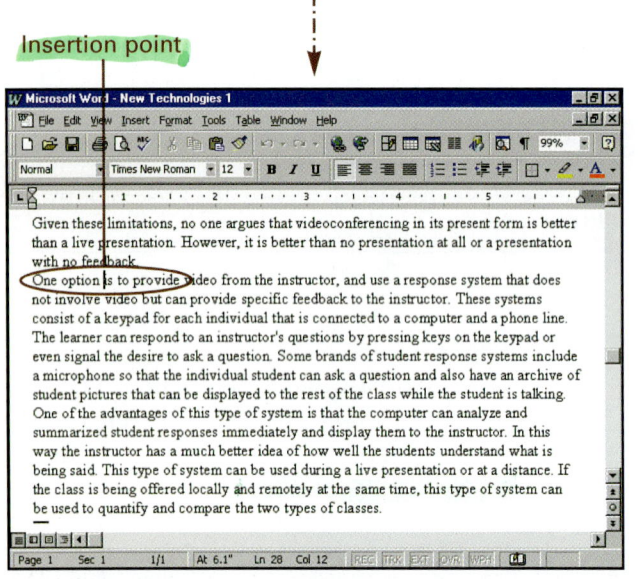

2 Place the insertion point just before the word **is** in the first line of the last paragraph.

3 Type in the words **for distance courses** at the insertion point. Make sure you add a space at the end of the inserted text.

> **In Depth:** When you are first learning to use the mouse, you may sometimes place the insertion point in the wrong location. You can use the right and left arrows on the keyboard to move the insertion point one character at a time to the right or left. You can also insert spaces by pressing Spacebar when needed.

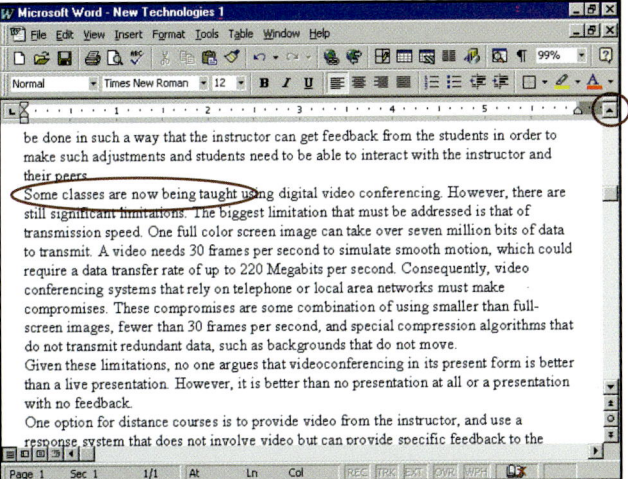

4 Use the up arrow on the vertical scrollbar to display the paragraph that begins, **Some classes are now being taught**.

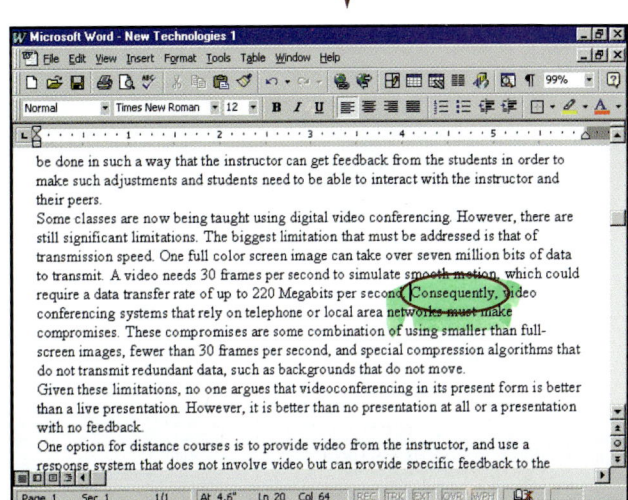

5 Place the insertion point just before the word **Consequently** in the fifth line of this paragraph.

6 Type in the following sentence to help expand on the previous sentence:
This is four thousand times faster than the fastest modems that are used to connect home computers to the Internet, and it is approximately twice as fast as the entire capacity of most local area networks.

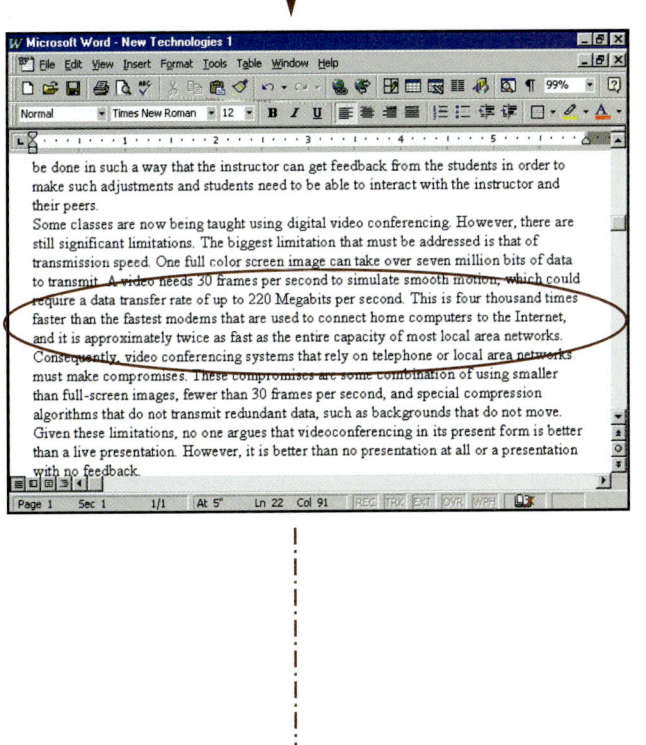

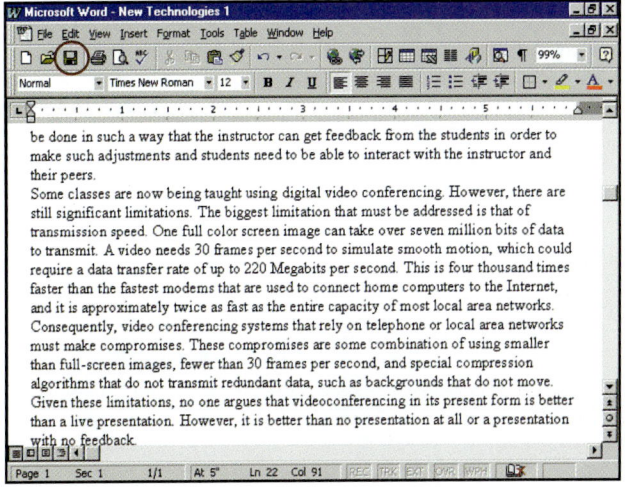

7 Click the **Save** button on the Standard toolbar to save your changes.

Lesson 2: Editing a Document   27

Task 3

Selecting and Deleting Text

Why would I do this?

In Lesson 1, you learned how to use the [Backspace] and [Del] keys to delete one character at a time. If you want to remove words, phrases, sentences, or even whole paragraphs, using these two procedures can be tedious. You can select and delete multiple characters in a way that will save you a great deal of time during the editing process.

In this task, you learn to select text and delete it.

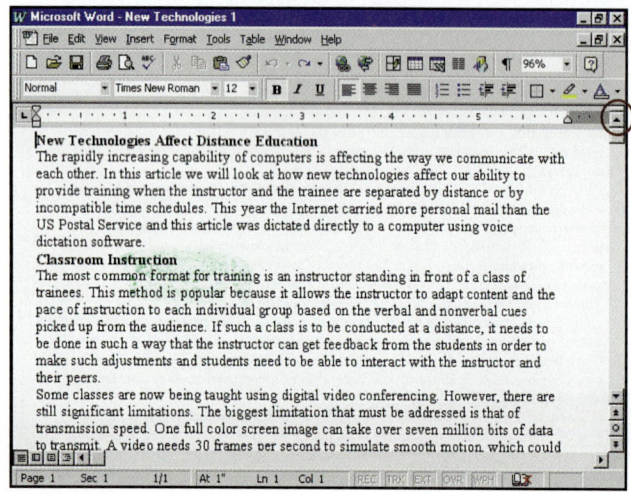

1 Use the up arrow on the vertical scrollbar to move back to the top of the **New Technologies 1** document.

2 Double-click on the word **such** in the fourth line of the second paragraph. The word, along with the following space, is selected.

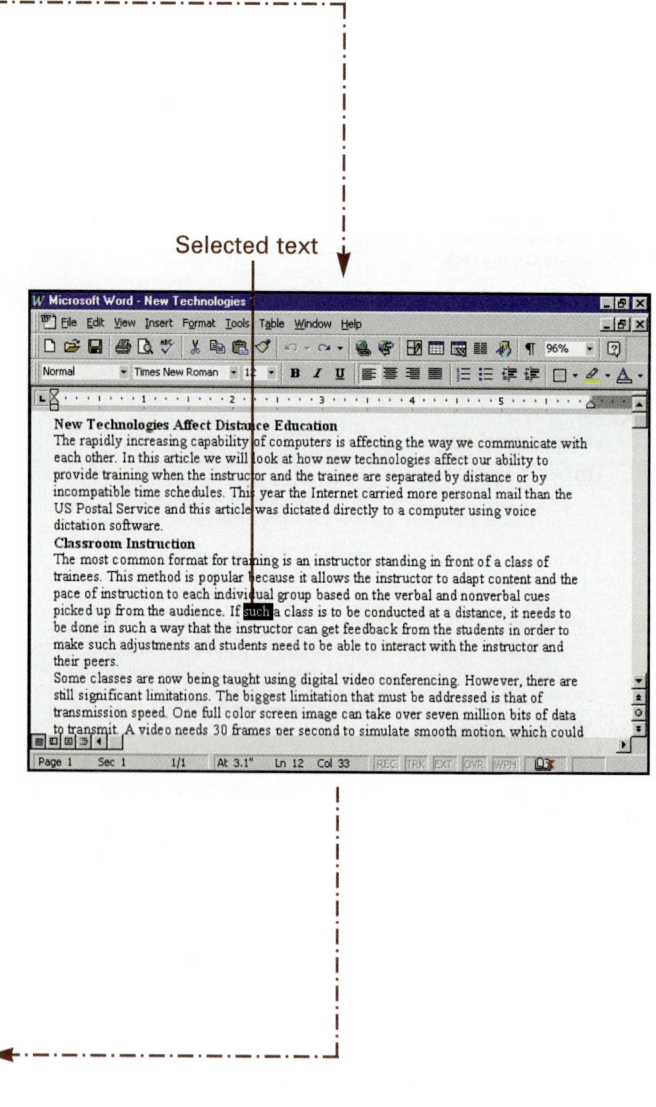

Selected text

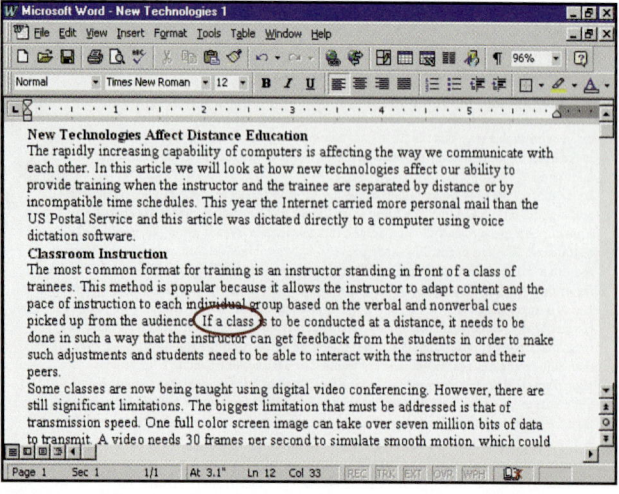

3 Press [Del] on your keyboard to delete the selected word. The word is removed from the text.

28 Learn Word 97, Second Edition

4 Use the down arrow on the vertical scrollbar to move to the bottom of the document. The end of document marker should be near the bottom of the screen.

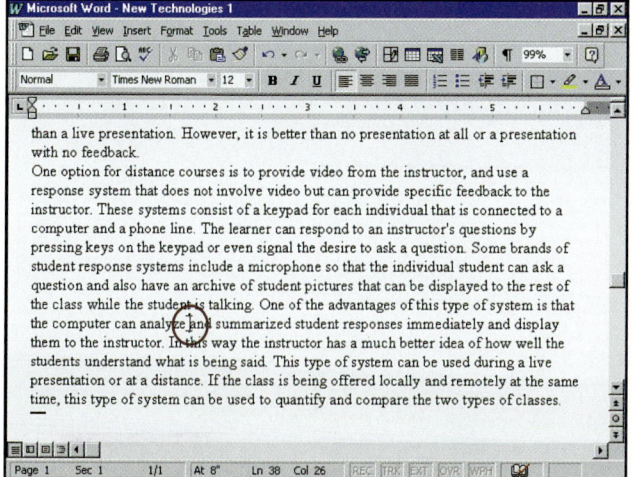

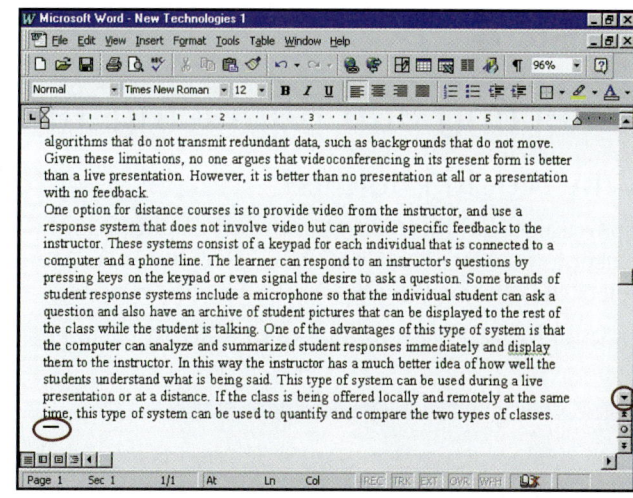

5 Click and hold down the left mouse button just to the left of the phrase **and summarized** in the bottom paragraph, as shown in the figure.

6 Drag to the right until you have selected the words **and summarized**, and then release the left mouse button.

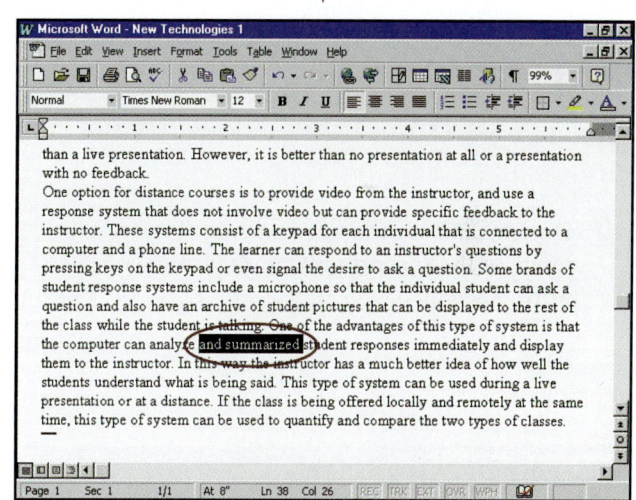

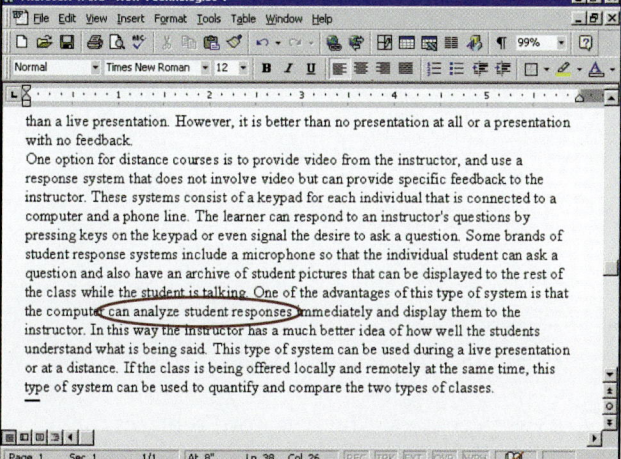

Pothole: If the words you want to select are located on two lines, you need to click in the same location with the left mouse button and then drag down and to the left until the two words are selected. You may have to try this procedure several times until you feel comfortable selecting text.

7 Press Del to delete the selected words.

Lesson 2: Editing a Document **29**

Task 4

Selecting and Replacing Text

Why would I do this?

Sometimes you think of a better word or phrase and want to make a replacement. You could select and delete the existing word or phrase and then insert its replacement, but it is faster to combine these two steps and simply select the old word or phrase and type in a new one.

In this task, you learn to select and replace existing text in a document.

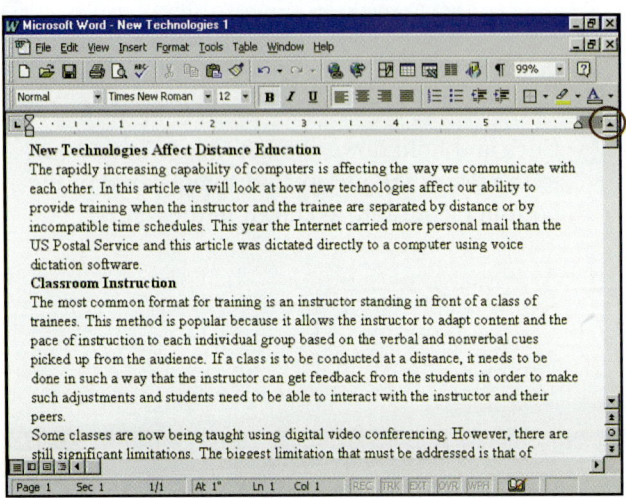

1 Use the up arrow on the vertical scrollbar to move back to the top of the **New Technologies 1** document.

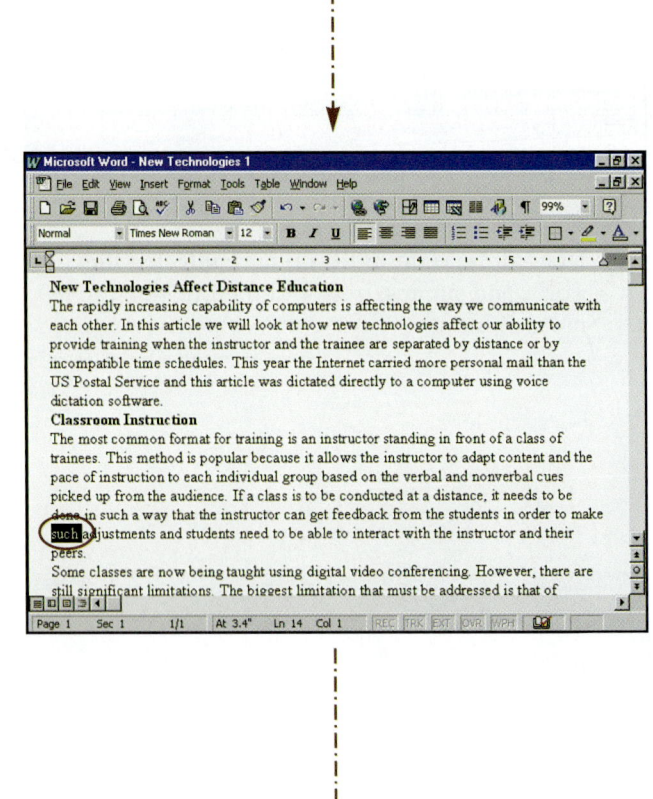

2 Double-click on the word **such** in the last sentence of the second paragraph, as shown. The word is selected.

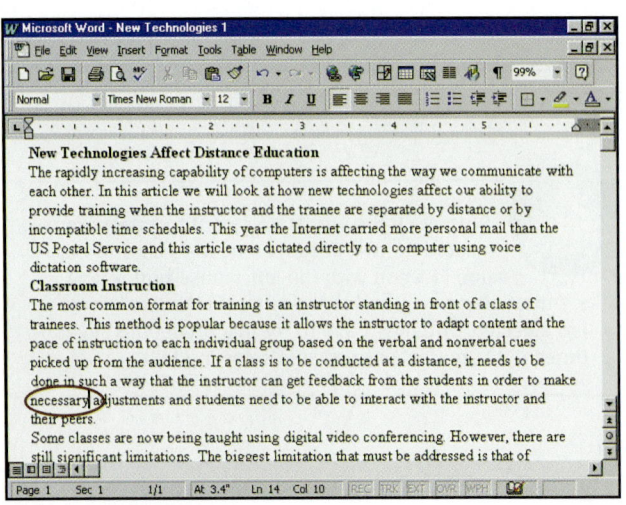

3 Type **necessary**. The new word replaces the selected word.

30 Learn Word 97, Second Edition

4 Scroll down to the bottom of the document. The end of document marker should be near the bottom of the screen.

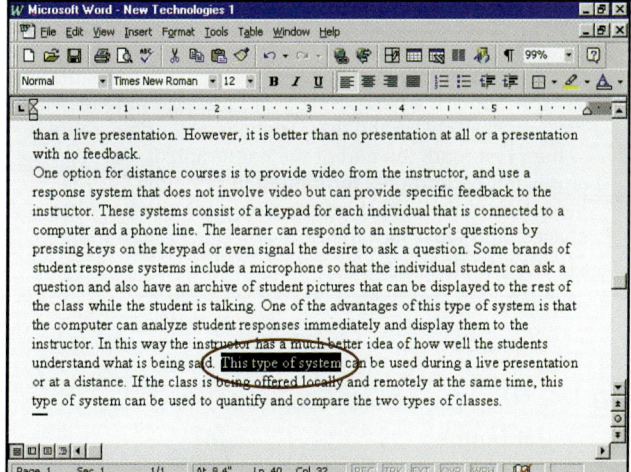

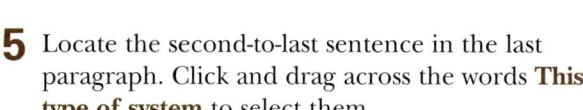

5 Locate the second-to-last sentence in the last paragraph. Click and drag across the words **This type of system** to select them.

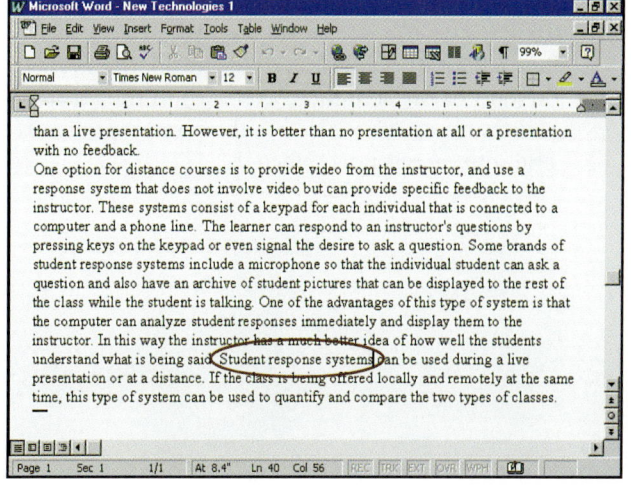

6 Type **Student response systems** to replace the words you selected.

Lesson 2: Editing a Document   31

Task 5

Moving Text Using Cut and Paste

Why would I do this?

If you want to relocate text in a document, you could use the skills you learned earlier in this lesson—that is, you could delete the text in its original location, move the insertion point to the new location, and retype the text. Moving the text using the *cut-and-paste* method is a quicker, easier way to relocate text without having to do any additional typing. This method removes the selected text from one location, stores it temporarily in a location known as the *Clipboard*, and then pastes the text to a new location when the Paste button is used.

In this task, you learn how to move text by cutting text from one location and pasting it in a new location.

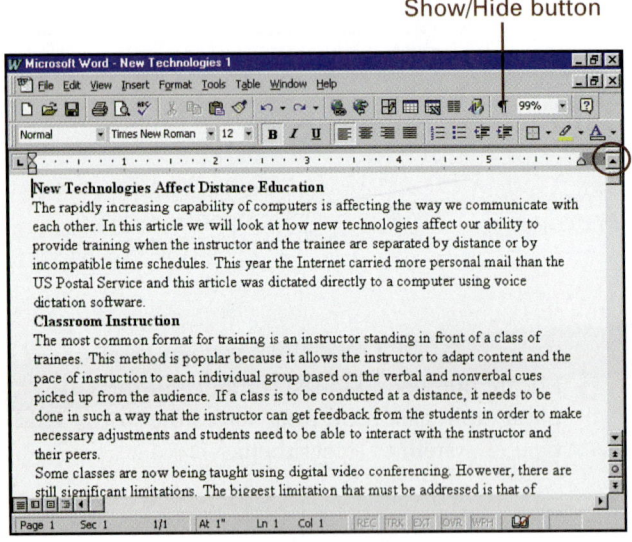

1 Use the up arrow on the vertical scrollbar to move back to the top of the **New Technologies 1** document. Click the **Show/Hide** button to reveal the hidden paragraph marks.

In Depth: When you press ↵Enter to mark the end of a paragraph, Word places a hidden character in the text. That character does more than just mark the end of the paragraph; it also stores the paragraph's formatting information. To see hidden characters, such as the paragraph mark, spaces, and tabs, click the Show/Hide button on the Standard toolbar.

2 Click just to the left of the last sentence in the first paragraph and drag down to the period at the end of the sentence, as shown in the figure. Make sure you don't delete the paragraph mark. The sentence is now selected.

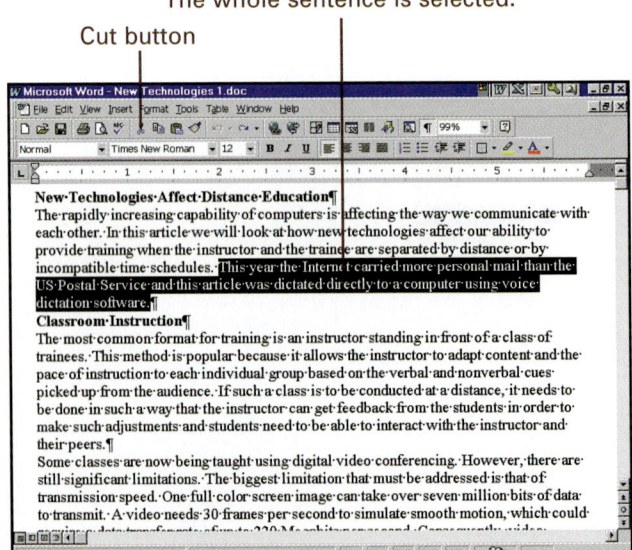

Cut button   Copy button

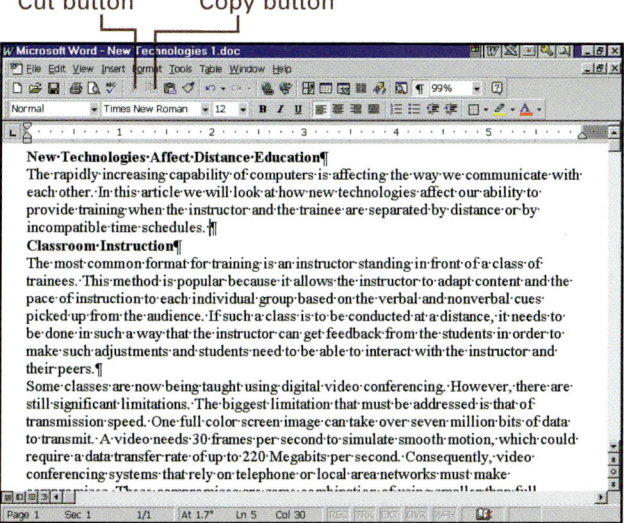

3 Click the **Cut** button on the Standard toolbar. The sentence disappears. It has been placed in the Clipboard. Notice that the Cut and Copy buttons are now grayed out.

Quick Tip: Another option for cutting and pasting is to right-click the selected text and use the **Cut** and **Paste** options in the shortcut menu.

In Depth: The Copy button, found just to the right of the Cut button on the Standard toolbar, also places the selected text in the Clipboard, but it leaves the text in its original location. *Copy* is used to duplicate text. That text then can be pasted into another location in the same or in a new document without any of the original text being moved. Notice that the Copy and Cut buttons are currently dimmed and are not available for use. Text must first be selected for these buttons to be used.

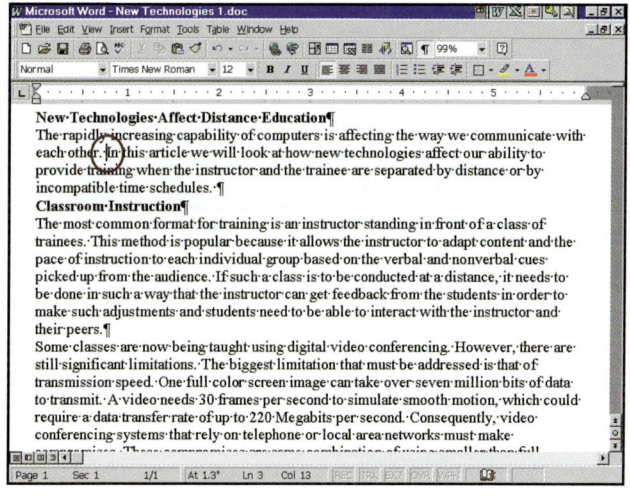

4 Place the insertion point to the right of the period at the end of the first sentence in the first paragraph, as shown in the figure.

Paste button

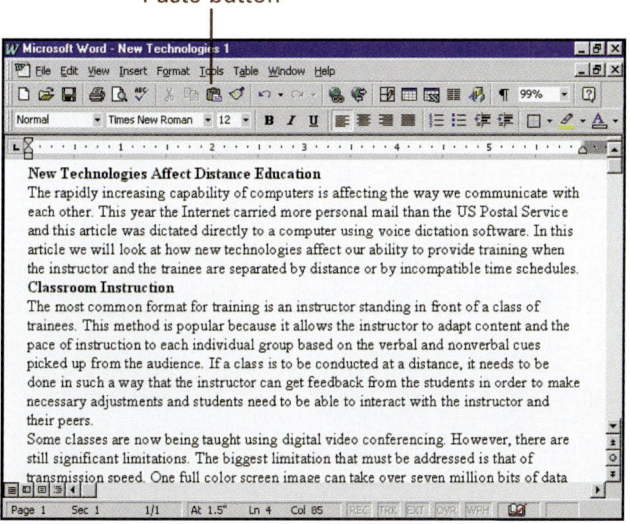

5 Click the **Paste** button on the Standard toolbar. The sentence you cut is now pasted at the insertion point. Click the Show/Hide button to hide the paragraph marks. Do not save or close your document at this time.

Lesson 2: Editing a Document

Task 6

Using Undo and Redo

Why would I do this?

Sometimes you may accidentally delete text or paste something in the wrong location. You also, on occasion, may make several changes in a document and then decide that you would rather not use the changes you have made. Word gives you the option of undoing and redoing changes you have made. This capability saves you from having to retype text. It also prevents you from leaving out a step you made previously when you change back to the original version.

In this task, you learn to undo and redo changes that you have made.

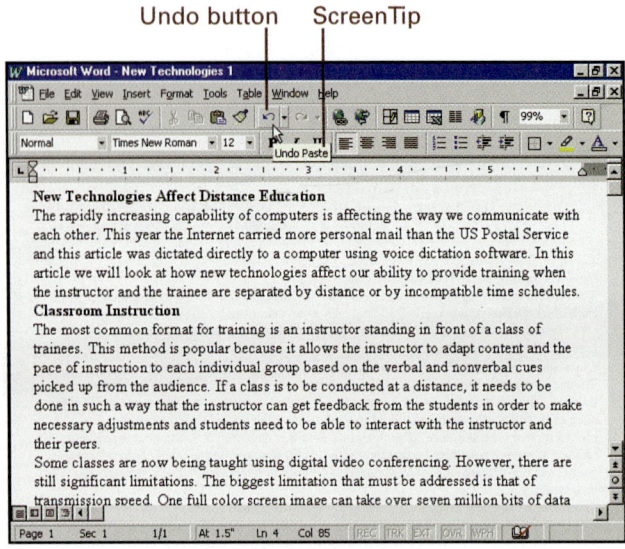

1 With the top of the **New Technologies 1** document on the screen, move the pointer to the **Undo** button on the Standard toolbar. A ScreenTip that says **Undo Paste** is displayed. The Paste function was the last one you used.

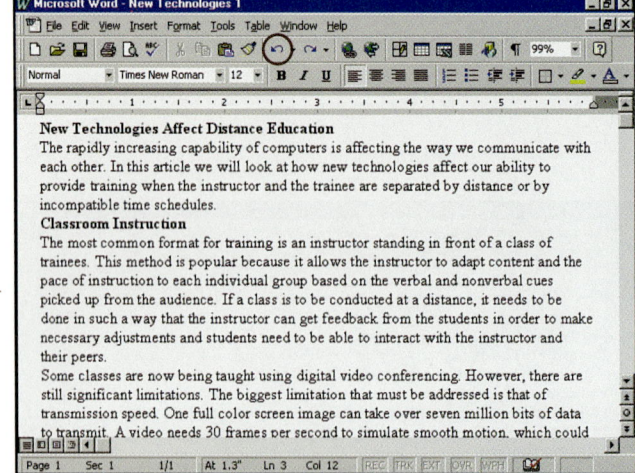

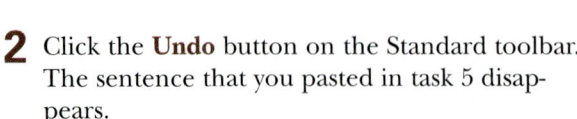

2 Click the **Undo** button on the Standard toolbar. The sentence that you pasted in task 5 disappears.

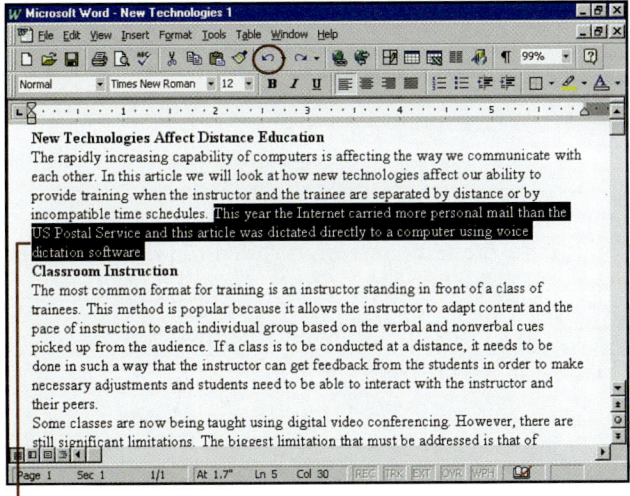

This sentence is returned to its original location.

3. Click the **Undo** button again. The sentence you cut is now returned to its original location. You have undone the last two edits you made to the document.

**In Depth:** An arrow is to the right of both the Undo and the Redo buttons. Each of these arrows gives you a drop-down list of prior changes. You can use this feature to undo or redo multiple steps with a single action. You can undo an entire sequence of steps to a previous condition by clicking the Undo arrow and dragging across all the actions you want to undo. You cannot undo a single task from the list unless it is the first item in the list.

Redo button

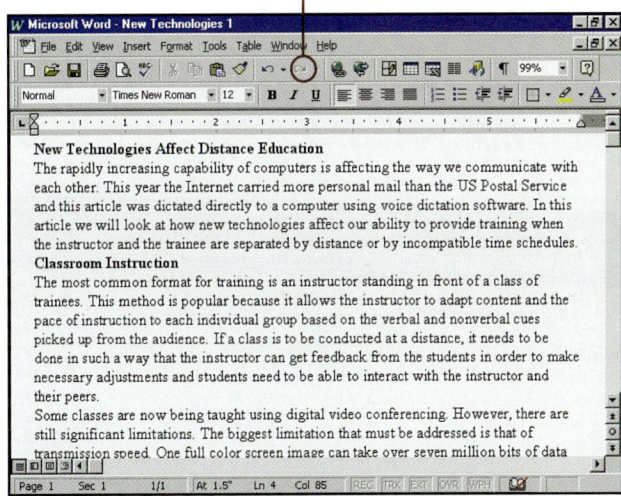

4. Click the **Redo** button twice to redo the last two steps. Notice that the Redo button becames grayed out. Press the [Spacebar] to add a space between sentences. Leave the file open for the next task.

Lesson 2: Editing a Document 35

Task 7

Moving Text Using Drag and Drop

Why would I do this?

The cut-and-paste method of moving text is faster than deleting and retyping. An even quicker way to move text around, particularly if the text to be moved and the destination are on the same screen, is called the *drag-and-drop* method. With this method, you move text from one location to another by dragging it from the original to the desired location on your screen—hence the name drag-and-drop.

In this task, you learn how to move text by using drag and drop.

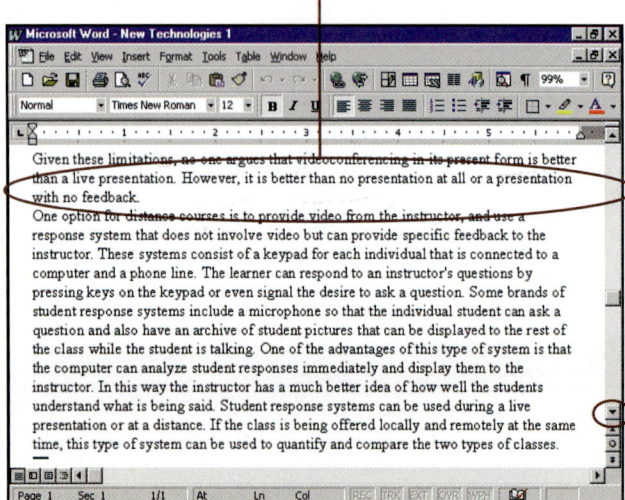

1 Use the down arrow on the vertical scrollbar to move near the bottom of the **New Technologies 1** document. The sentence ending with the word **feedback** should be visible. This sentence will be rearranged.

Pothole: If the drag-and-drop technique covered in this task does not work, choose **Tools**, **Options** from the menu and select the **Edit** tab. Click the **Drag-and-drop text editing** option box to turn this feature on.

2 Select the words **a presentation with no feedback**, but do not select the period.

Learn Word 97, Second Edition

3 Move the pointer on top of the selected text. The pointer changes to an arrow.

Arrow pointer

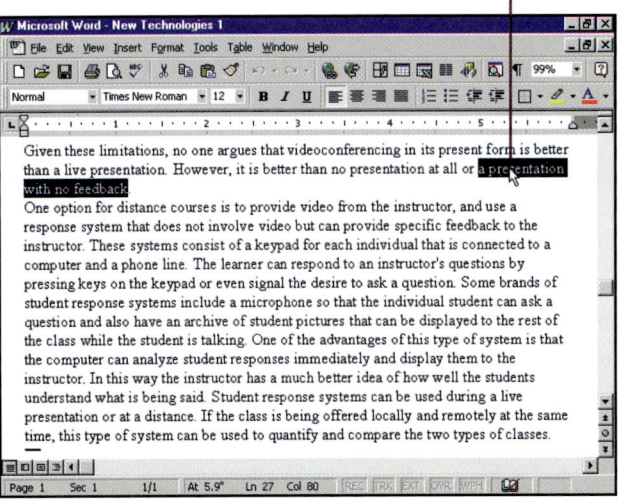

Insertion point

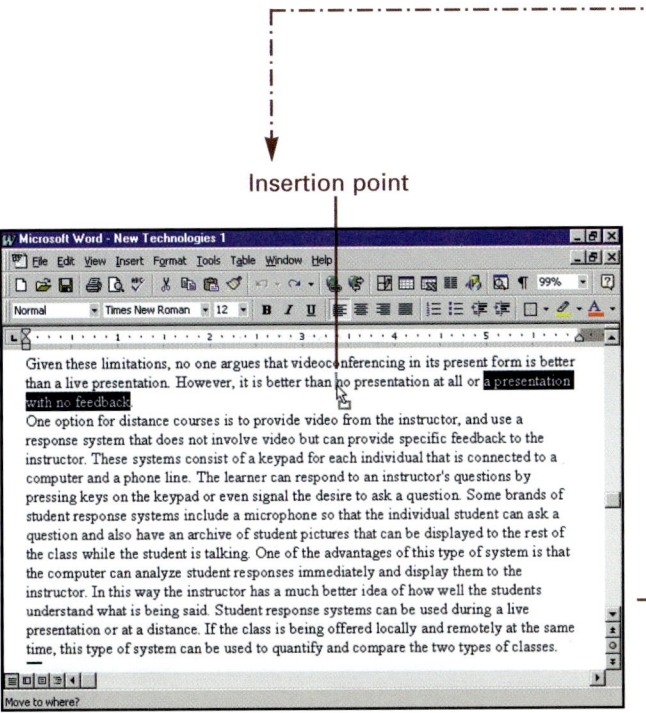

4 Click on the selected text and hold down the left mouse button while moving the pointer to the left of the phrase **no presentation at all** in the same sentence. The pointer is shaped like an arrow with a small box attached to the bottom.

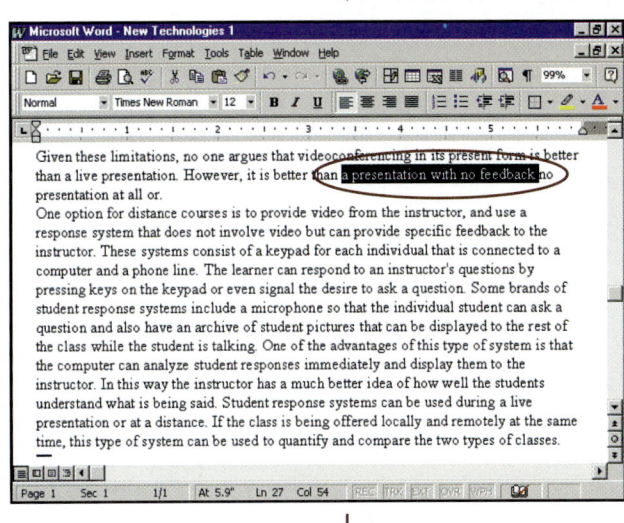

5 Release the mouse button. The highlighted text is dropped at the new location.

Pothole: If you accidentally drop the text too soon or miss the drop location, click the **Undo** button and try again.

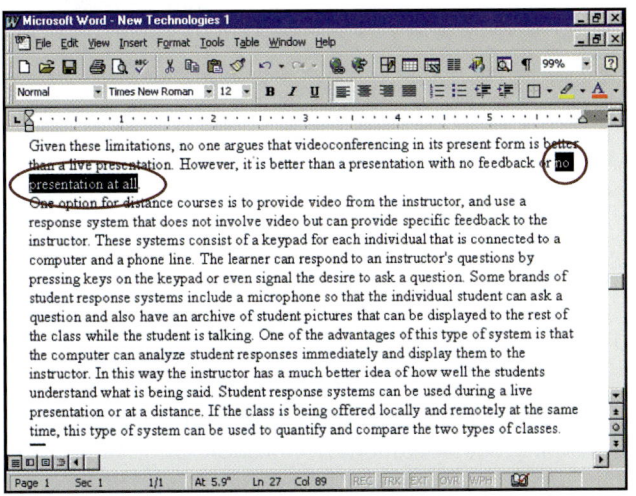

6 Select the phrase **no presentation at all** and drag and drop it to the right of the word **or** in the same sentence. Leave the file open for the next task.

Lesson 2: Editing a Document   37

Task 8
Printing a Document Using the Menu

Why would I do this?

The easiest way to print a document is to click the **Print** button on the Standard toolbar, as you did in Lesson 1. Sometimes you need more control than the **Print** toolbar button gives you, however. In that case, use the menu option, which displays a dialog box offering many printing choices.

In this task, you learn to print a document using the menu.

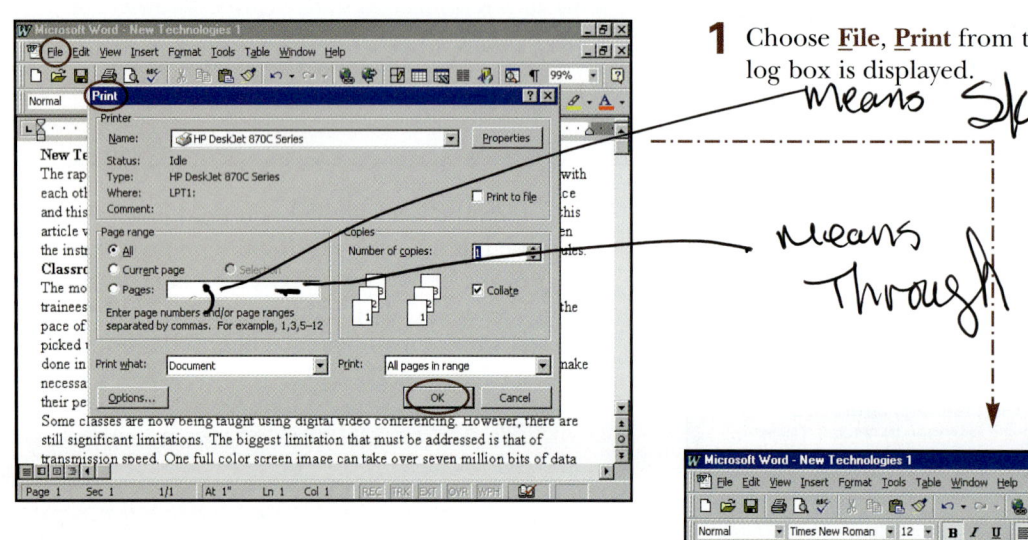

1 Choose **File**, **Print** from the menu. The **Print** dialog box is displayed.

, means skip

– means Through

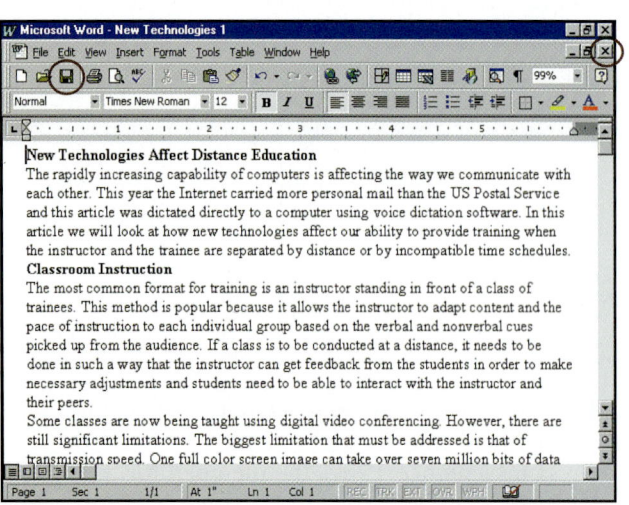

2 Make sure your printer is turned on and click **OK** to send your document to the printer.

3 Click the **Save** button to save your document. Click the document Application **Close** button to close the document and close Word.

Learn Word 97, Second Edition

Student Exercises

True-False
Circle either T or F.

T F **1.** To open a document that is stored on floppy disk, you click on the button on the Standard toolbar that looks like a small floppy disk.

T F **2.** The insertion point is indicated by the tip of the pointer arrow. New text goes wherever the pointer is when you start to type.

T F **3.** If text is selected, you can delete it by pressing Del.

T F **4.** When you make a mistake, you can reverse your error by clicking the Undo button.

T F **5.** If you want to undo a mistake, you must do so before you type anything else. The program can only undo one previous action.

T F **6.** The Redo button is the opposite of the Undo button. It allows you to change your mind and restore the actions that you chose to undo.

T F **7.** If you have made ten changes to the text and notice that the change you made six steps ago is wrong, you may click on the list arrow next to the Undo button, pick that one action from the list, and undo it. The other actions are not affected.

T F **8.** Drag and drop refers to a method of erasing blocks of text in which you drag the selected text to the Recycle Bin.

T F **9.** Using the Print option on the File menu gives you more options for printing than simply clicking on the Print button on the toolbar.

T F **10.** When you cut selected text, that text is stored in a memory area called the Clipboard.

Identifying Parts of the Word Screen

Refer to the figure and identify the numbered parts of the screen. Write the letter of the correct label in the space next to the number.

1. ____
2. ____
3. ____
4. ____
5. ____
6. ____
7. ____
8. ____
9. ____
10. ____

A. Insertion point
B. Copy selected item
C. Drag-and-drop pointer
D. Selected text
E. Undo previous step
F. Cut selected item
G. List of actions to undo
H. Redo previous undo
I. Paste contents of Clipboard at insertion point
J. List of actions to redo

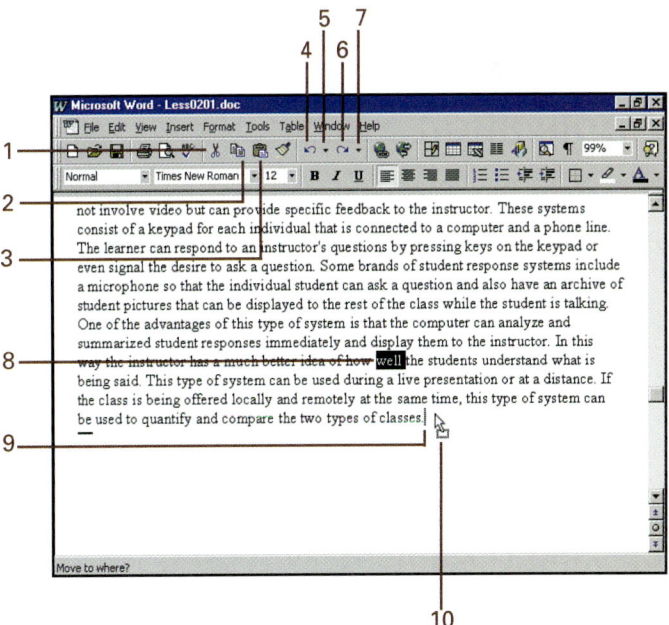

Matching Questions

Match the following statements to the word or phrase from the list on the right. Write the letter of the matching word or phrase in the space provided next to the number.

1. ____ Moves the selected text to a new location by using the mouse to click and drag the text
2. ____ An area that is used for temporary storage of information that has been cut or copied
3. ____ Reverses the Undo action and returns the text to its condition prior to the use of the Undo
4. ____ Compact disc–read-only memory, a storage medium used to store programs, files, and other computer reference materials that cannot be changed
5. ____ Removes text from the document and stores it in the Clipboard
6. ____ Places the selected text in the Clipboard, while at the same time leaving it in the document
7. ____ Places the contents of the Clipboard at the insertion point
8. ____ Reverses the previous action
9. ____ A file storage medium that can be easily removed from the computer; it consists of a flexible (floppy) plastic disk enclosed in hard plastic
10. ____ A vertical line that indicates where text goes if it is typed or dropped

A. CD-ROM
B. Copy
C. Drag and drop
D. Clipboard
E. Paste
F. Cut
G. Moving text
H. Undo
I. Floppy disk
J. Redo
K. Insertion point

Application Exercises

Exercise 1—Open an Existing File and Save It Under a Different Name

1. Launch Word. Open **Less0202** from the student files.
2. Use the **File**, **Save** **As** menu options to save the file on a floppy disk in drive A: with the name **New Technologies 2**.

Exercise 2—Insert Text into an Existing Document

1. Scroll to the beginning of the document.
2. Place the insertion point in front of the first word of the first paragraph.

3. Type **Edited by:** , followed by your name.

4. Press ↵Enter.

5. Click the **Save** button to save your changes.

Exercise 3—Selecting and Deleting Text

1. Select the second full paragraph in the section on self study. (This paragraph starts with the phrase **There are several**.)

2. Press Del to delete the paragraph.

3. Click the **Save** button to save your work.

Exercise 4—Selecting and Replacing Text

1. Scroll down to the section **Future Technologies**.

2. Select the title, **Future Technologies**, and replace it by typing **Anticipated Increases in Transmission Speed**.

3. Click the **Save** button to save your work.

Exercise 5—Move Text Using Cut and Paste and Drag and Drop— Then Print the Page

1. Locate the sentence in the first paragraph that begins with **Many people try**.

2. Move this sentence to the beginning of the paragraph using the cut-and-paste method.

3. Click **Undo** twice.

4. Select the same sentence and move it to the beginning of the paragraph using the drag-and-drop method.

5. Check the spacing between the sentence you just moved and the following sentence. Insert a space if necessary to provide at least one space between them.

6. Compare your document to the example in the figure.

7. Select **File**, **Print**, and **OK** to print the page.

8. Click **Save** to save your changes.

9. Close the document and exit Word.

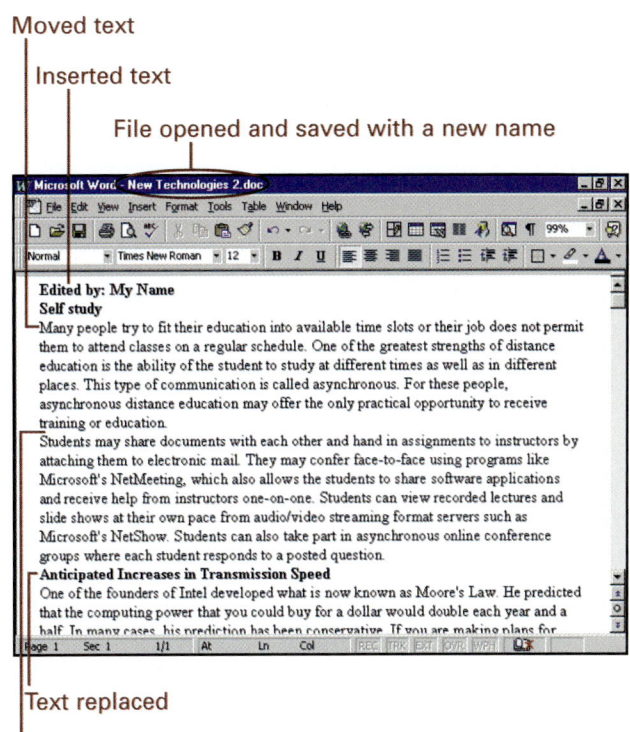

Moved text

Inserted text

File opened and saved with a new name

Text replaced

Paragraph deleted

Lesson 2: Editing a Document

Lesson 3
Formatting Text

- **Task 1:** Changing the Font Type, Size, and Emphasis
- **Task 2:** Aligning Text in a Paragraph
- **Task 3:** Changing Line Spacing
- **Task 4:** Creating a Bulleted List
- **Task 5:** Indenting the First Line of a Paragraph
- **Task 6:** Using the Format Painter
- **Task 7:** Creating a Hanging Indent
- **Task 8:** Adding Spaces After Paragraphs
- **Task 9:** Working with Tabs
- **Task 10:** Printing Selected Text

Introduction

When you create documents, you will want to have the ability to emphasize words, phrases, titles, subtitles, and so forth. In addition, you will need to have the ability to give the text a professional look that conveys information quickly and is aesthetically pleasing.

Microsoft Word gives you many tools to help you format text effectively. You can emphasize text to make it stand out from the surrounding text. Formatting tools allow you to indent paragraphs in two distinct ways, change line spacing, and align text. You can also align columns of text and format attractive, effective lists of information.

In this lesson, you learn how to use the most important Word formatting tools.

Visual Summary

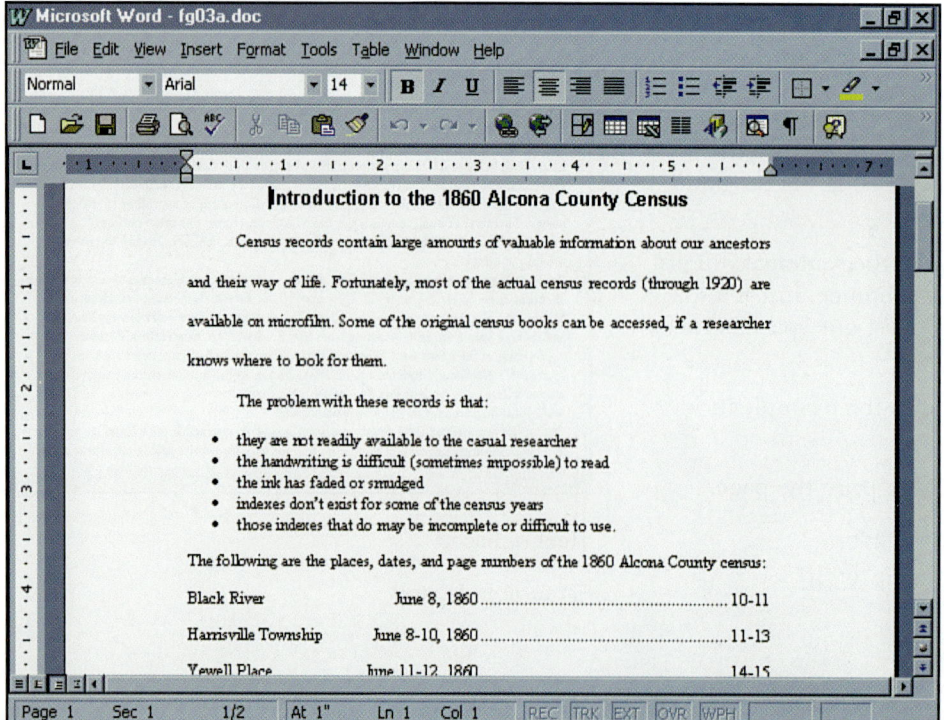

When you have completed this lesson, you will have created a document that looks like this:

Task 1

Changing the Font Type, Size, and Emphasis

Why would I do this?

Text formatting is used to emphasize important elements of a document. It helps you create effective, readable documents. When you open the document used in this chapter, you will notice that it is difficult to read. At first glance, all of the text looks similar, even though it contains titles and subtitles. Changing font size and style and adding emphasis by applying bold, italic, or underline characteristics to text help lead the reader through a document and aid in its overall organization.

In this task, you learn to format titles and subtitles by altering the look of the font.

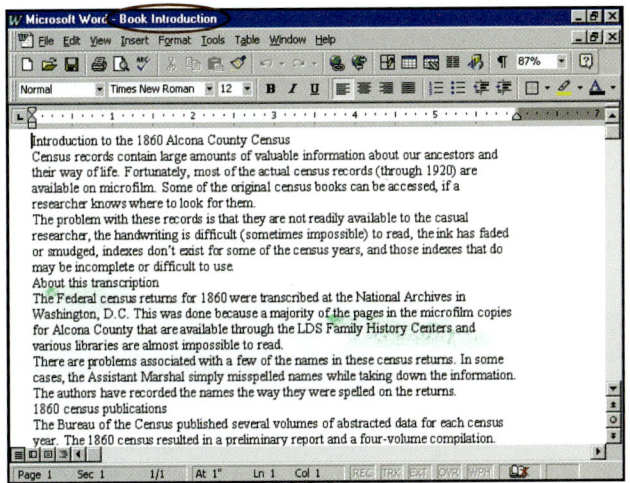

1 Launch Microsoft Word. Open **Less0301** from the student files. Save the file as **Book Introduction**.

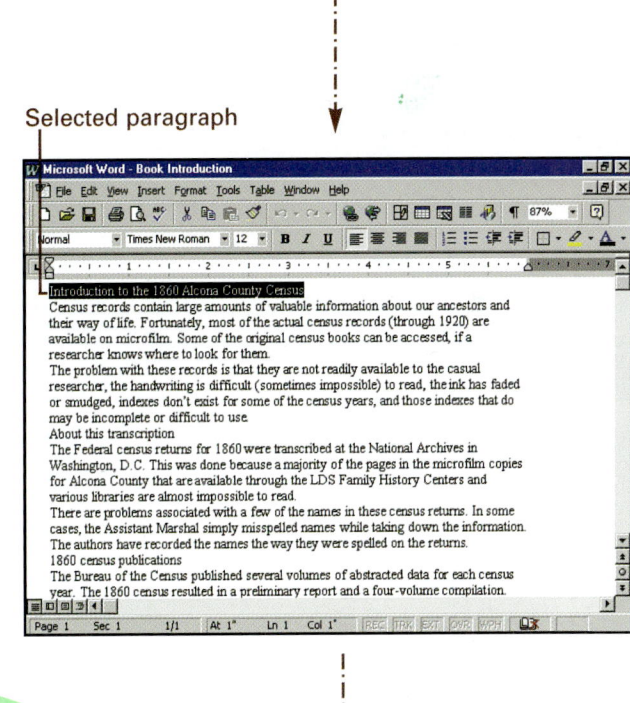

2 Select the first line of text, which is a title. Notice that the text is on a separate line at the beginning of the document and that the line is not followed by a period.

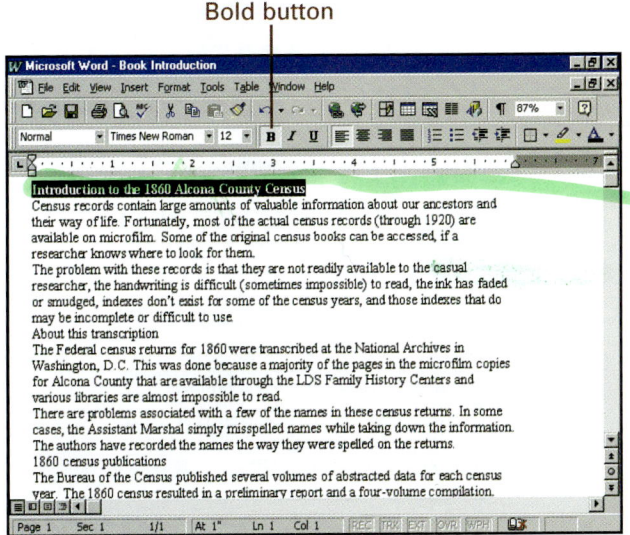

3 Click the **Bold** button in the Formatting toolbar. The first line of text is now boldfaced, which makes it stand out from the rest of the text.

4 With the first line still selected, click on the arrow to the right of the **Font** button. Choose **Arial** from the Font drop-down list. The style of the text is changed.

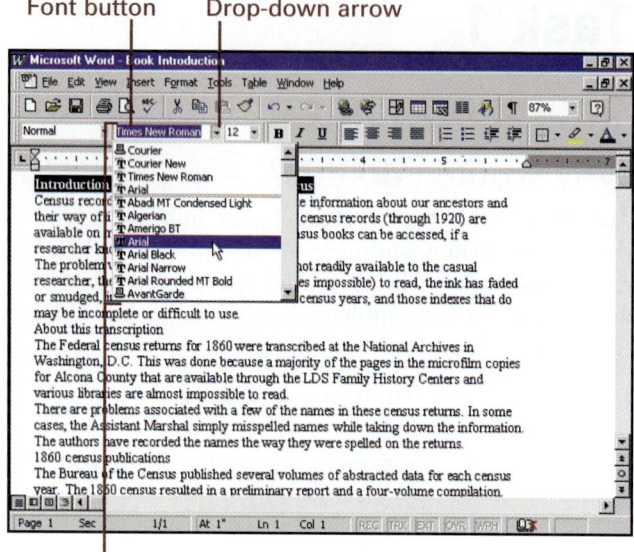

Font button   Drop-down arrow

Font drop-down list box

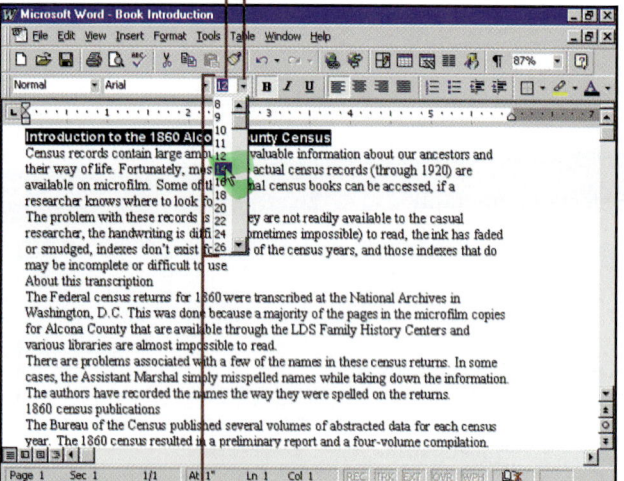

Font Size button   Drop-down arrow

Font Size drop-down list box

5 Click on the arrow to the right of the **Font Size** button. Choose **14** point from the Font Size drop-down list. The size of the text is increased.

In Depth: The larger the font size, the larger the text looks when you print the document. Font size is measured in points. There are 72 points per inch.

6 Highlight the first subtitle, **About this transcription**, and click the **Bold** button to boldface the text. Deselect the text by clicking anywhere else in the document. Notice that this one step enables you to find the subtitle quickly.

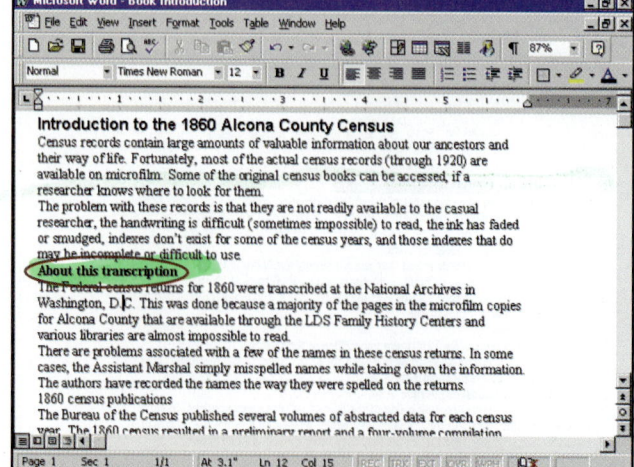

Learn Word 97, Second Edition

7 Highlight the second subtitle, **1860 census publications**, and click the **Bold** button to boldface the text. Deselect the text by clicking anywhere else in the document.

> **In Depth:** You can also add emphasis to selected text by using italics or underline. On the Formatting toolbar click the *I* button to add italics or the U to add an underline to selected text. You can also change formatting through keyboard shortcuts. Press Ctrl + **B** to add bold, Ctrl + **I** for italic, and Ctrl + **U** for underline.

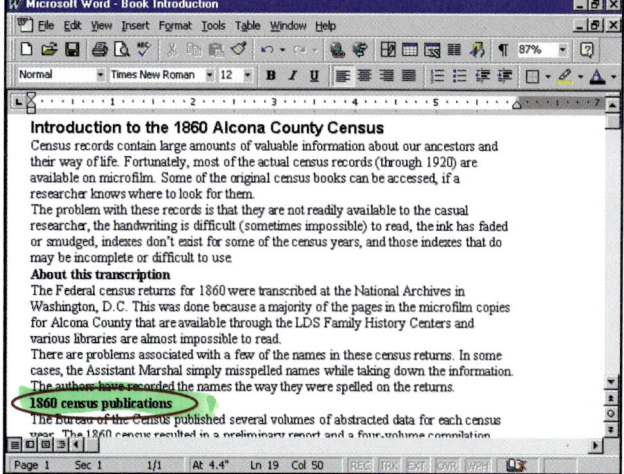

Task 2

Aligning Text in a Paragraph

Why would I do this?

Most text is arranged on the page so that a uniform margin is between the left edge of the paper and the beginning of each line. Because the words in each line are of different lengths, the right edge of the paragraph is usually uneven, or ragged. This type of alignment is called *Left Justified*.

The computer calculates the length of a line and the available space between margins. If you want to center a line of text, the computer uses this information to position the line in the center of the available space. *Centering* is a type of alignment used to make titles distinct from other parts of the document and to draw the reader's attention.

If you are doing a newsletter or prefer to have the text line up on both sides, you can specify an alignment that is called *Justified*. To accomplish this, the computer adjusts the size of the spaces between the words in each line. When you are trying to align text, it is important to remember that the computer does not consider a space to be a consistent size.

In this task, you learn how to center titles and to justify text.

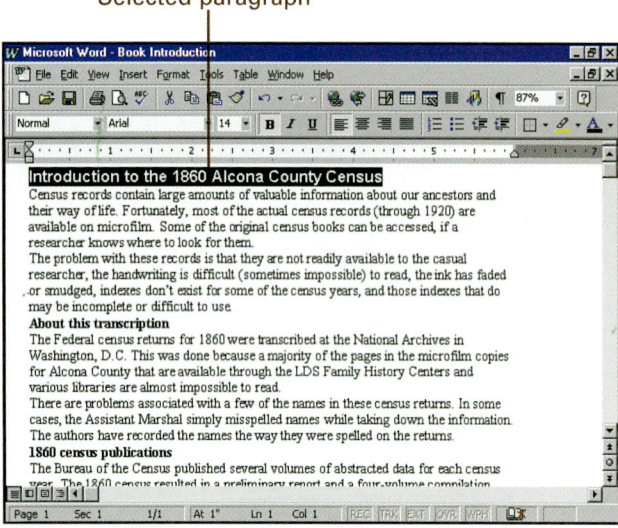

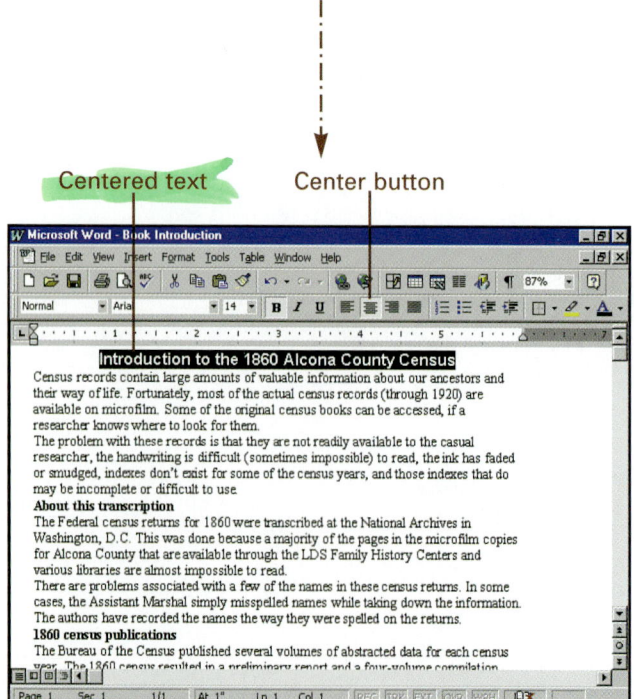

1 With your **Book Introduction** file still active, select the first line, which is the title of the document.

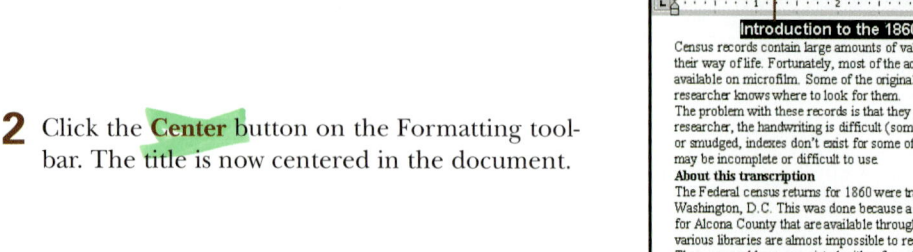

2 Click the **Center** button on the Formatting toolbar. The title is now centered in the document.

Selected text

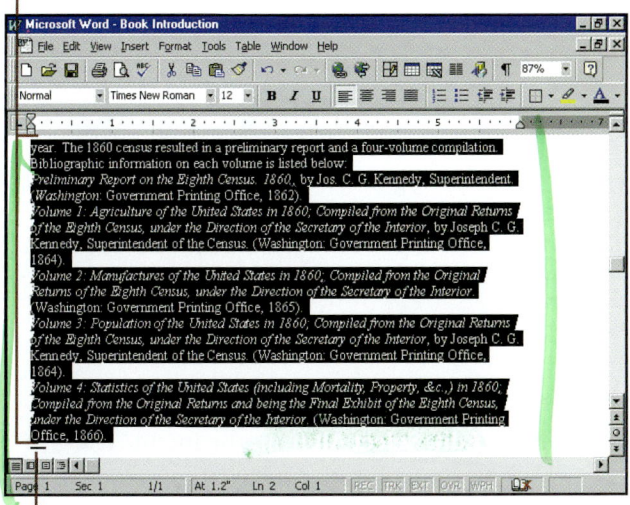

End of document marker

Quick Tip: On very long documents, scrolling to select a large portion of text can be cumbersome. A quick method is to click at the beginning of the text that is to be selected. Use the scrollbar to move to the end of the selection. Position the mouse pointer at the end of the selection, and then hold down ⇧Shift and click the left mouse button to mark the end of the selection. All of the text from the beginning marker to the end will be selected. Then you can apply the desired formatting to the selected text.

4 Click the **Justify** button on the Formatting toolbar, scroll to the top of the document, and click anywhere on the text to deselect it. All of the selected text is now justified.

3 Click to the left of the second line of the document and hold the left mouse button down. Drag down to the end of the document to select all but the first line.

Pothole: Make sure you go to the end of the document, not just to the end of the screen. When you go below the bottom of the text, the screen scrolls down. Don't stop until you see the end of document marker.

Justify button

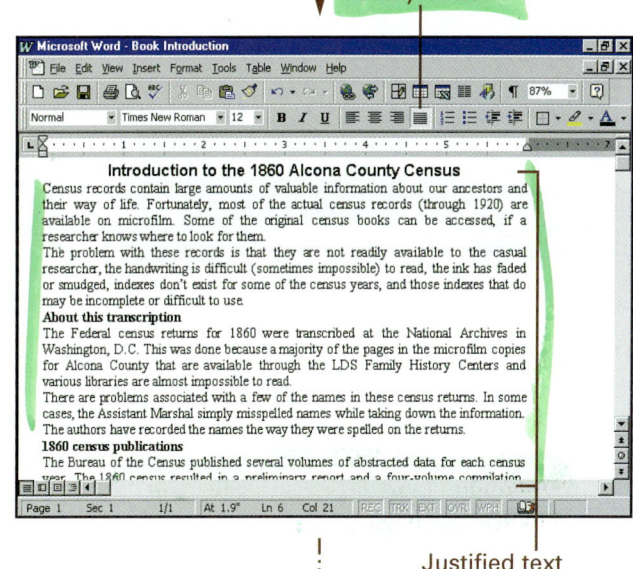

Justified text

5 Click the **Save** button on the Standard toolbar to save your work up to this point.

Lesson 3: Formatting Text 47

Task 3

Changing Line Spacing

Why would I do this?

In many cases, you type a document using single spacing but change the spacing to double spacing at a later time. Composing the document with single spacing enables you to see twice as much text on the screen as you would with double spacing. But if you change to double spacing before you print a copy of the document, the document is easier to edit. Double spacing also allows room for written comments between the lines.

In this task, you learn to change the line spacing in a document.

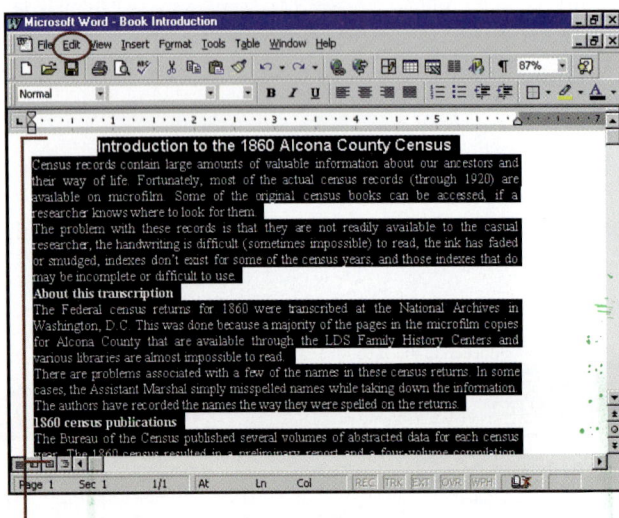

The whole document is selected.

1 With your **Book Introduction** file still active, choose **Edit, Select All** from the menu. The entire document is now selected.

2 Choose **Format, Paragraph** from the menu. The **Paragraph** dialog box opens. Click on the **Indents and Spacing** tab.

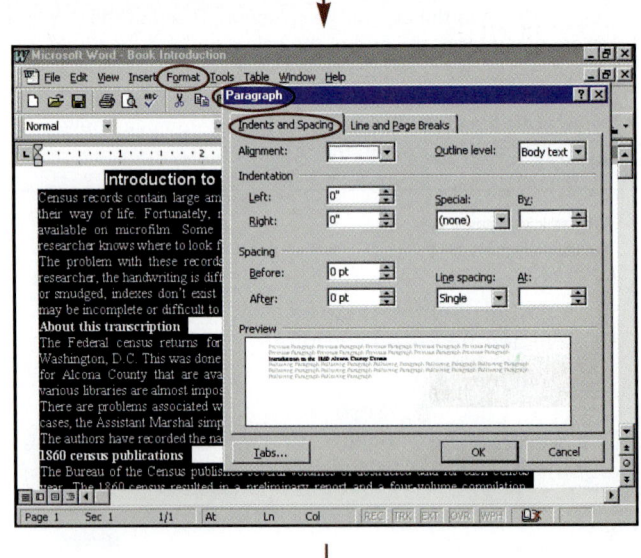

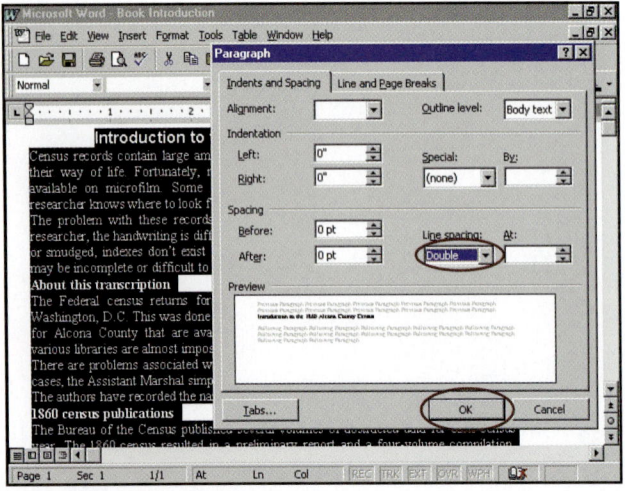

3 Select **Double** from the **Line spacing** drop-down menu.

48 Learn Word 97, Second Edition

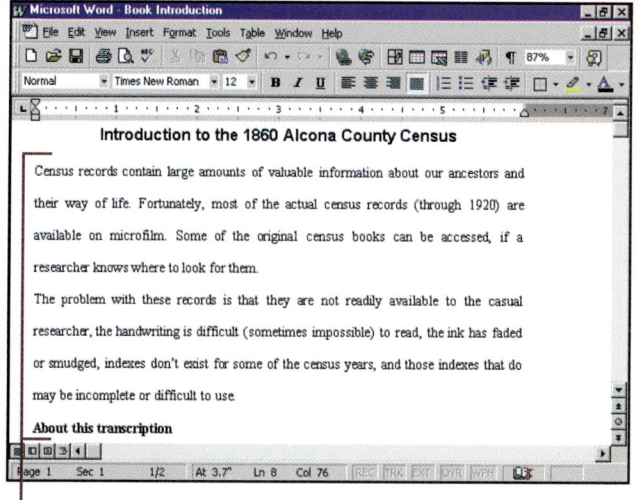

Double-spaced text

4 Click **OK** and then click anywhere in the document to deselect the text. Notice that the document is now double spaced.

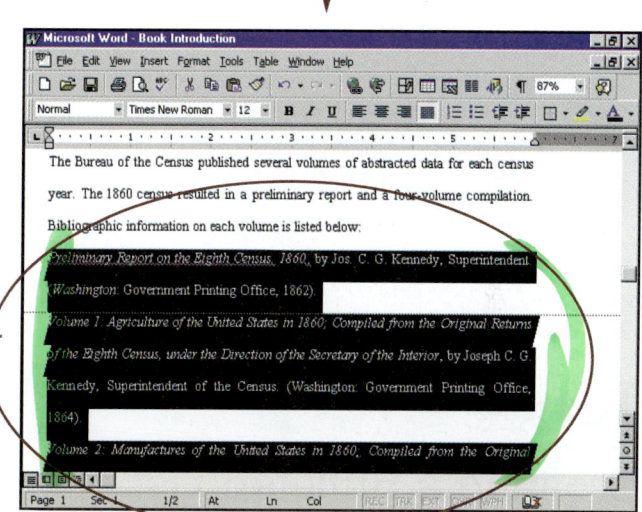

5 The bibliography at the end of the document should be single spaced. Select the text that extends from the first bibliographic entry to the end of the document.

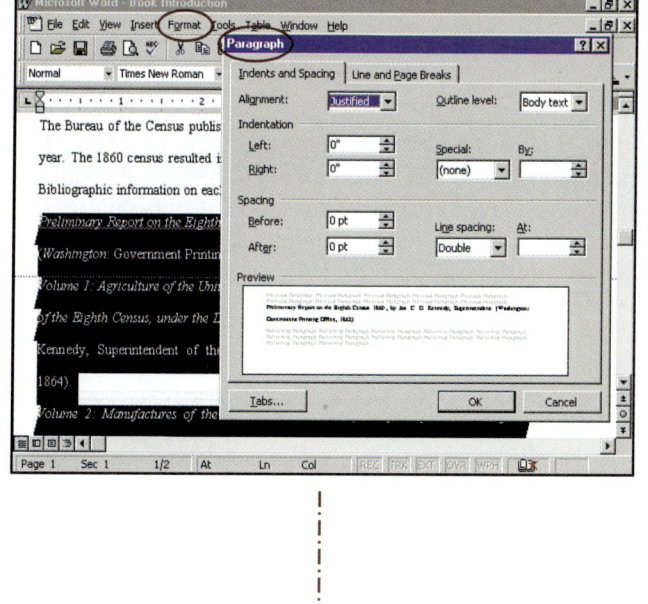

6 Choose **Format**, **Paragraph** from the menu. The **Paragraph** dialog box opens.

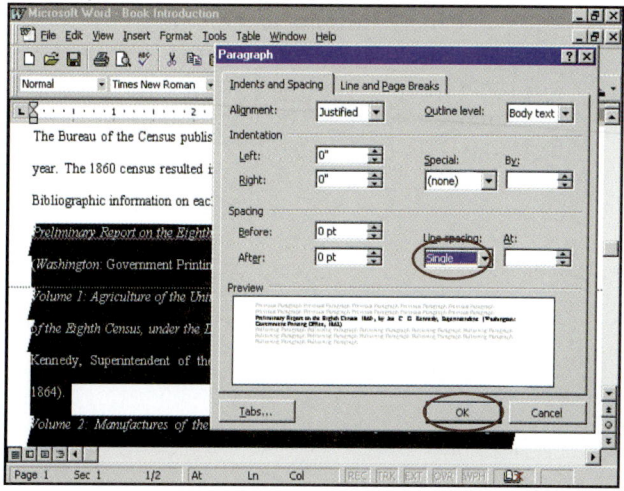

7 Select **Single** from the **Line spacing** drop-down menu.

Lesson 3: Formatting Text

8 Click **OK** and then click anywhere in the text to deselect it. The bibliographic entries are again single spaced.

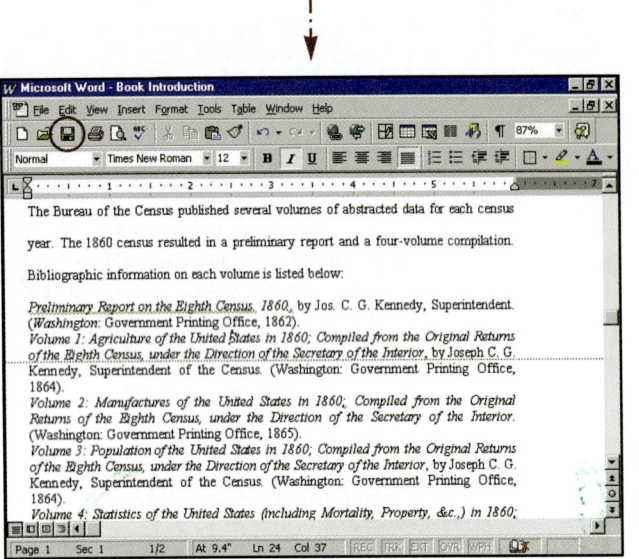

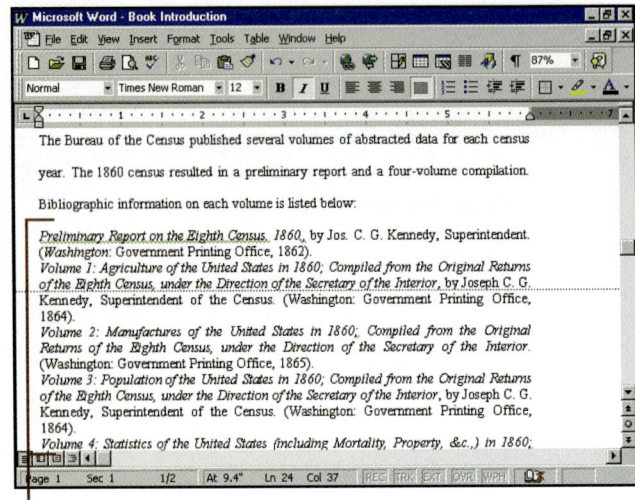

Bibliographic entries are single spaced.

9 Click the **Save** button on the Standard toolbar.

Task 4
Creating a Bulleted List

Why would I do this?

Lists of information can be handled in several ways. They can be listed using separate sentences. Alternatively, the items in the list can be included in the same sentence but separated by commas. Lists can also be styled as bulleted or numbered lists. Using a bulleted or numbered list helps draw the reader's attention to key points. Many people are busy and only glance at memos or letters they receive. The use of bulleted lists helps to ensure that the reader sees the most important points in a document. Word gives you the option of quickly creating effective, professional-looking lists.

In this task, you learn to create a bulleted list.

1 With your **Book Introduction** file still active, place the insertion point just to the right of the word **that** in the second full paragraph. Press [Del] and enter a colon (:). The insertion point should be to the right of the colon.

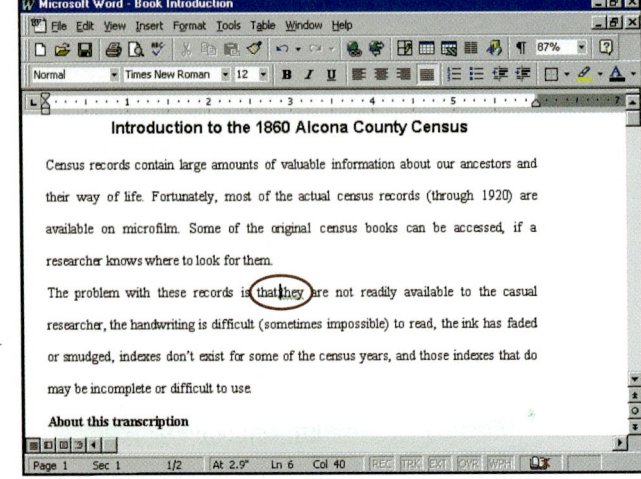

50 Learn Word 97, Second Edition

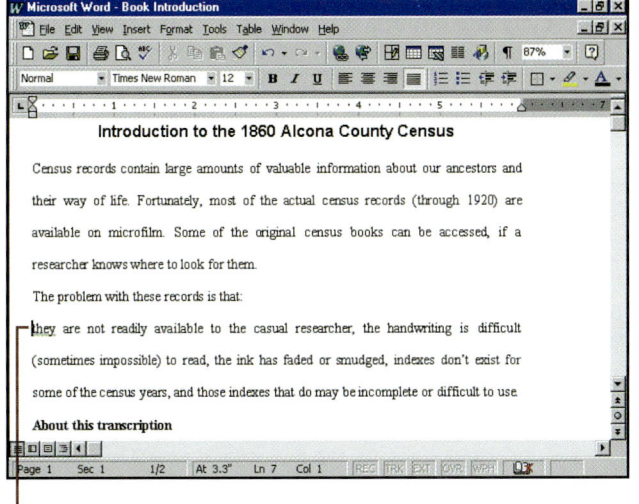

New paragraph

2 Press **Enter**. A new paragraph is created, which begins with the phrase **they are not readily available**. This paragraph will be the first item in a list of five items.

3 Select the comma and space after the word **researcher** and press **Enter**. A new paragraph is created.

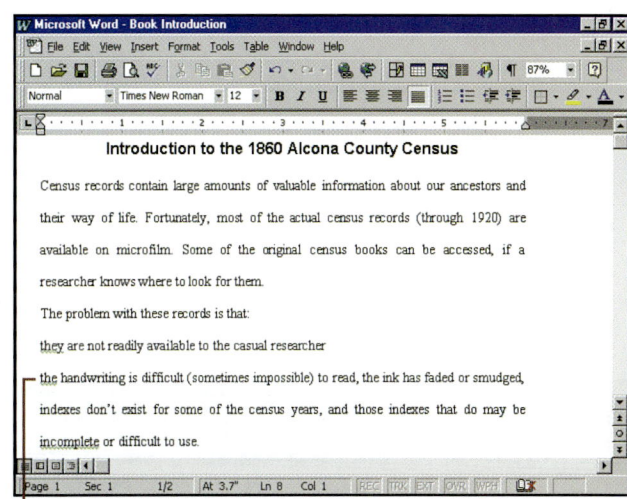

New paragraph

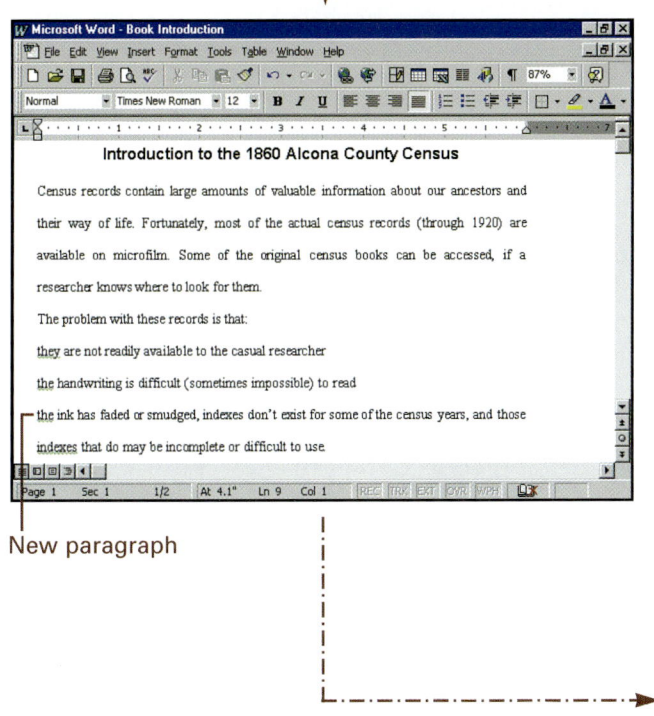

New paragraph

4 Select the comma and space after the words **to read** and press **Enter**. Another new paragraph is created.

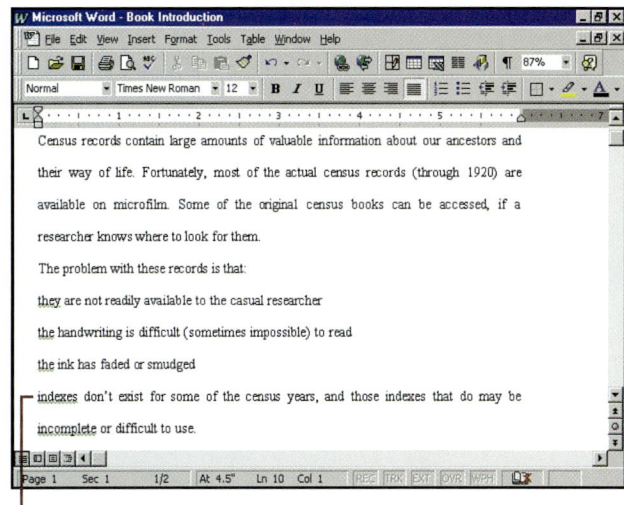

New paragraph

5 Select the comma and space after the word **smudged** and press **Enter**. Another new paragraph is created.

Lesson 3: Formatting Text 51

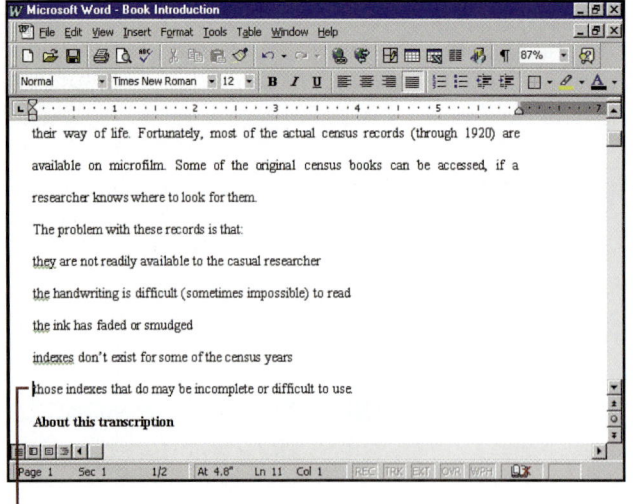

Final new paragraph

6 Select the comma and space after the words **census years** and press ←Enter. Another new paragraph is created. Delete the word **and** and the following space in this paragraph.

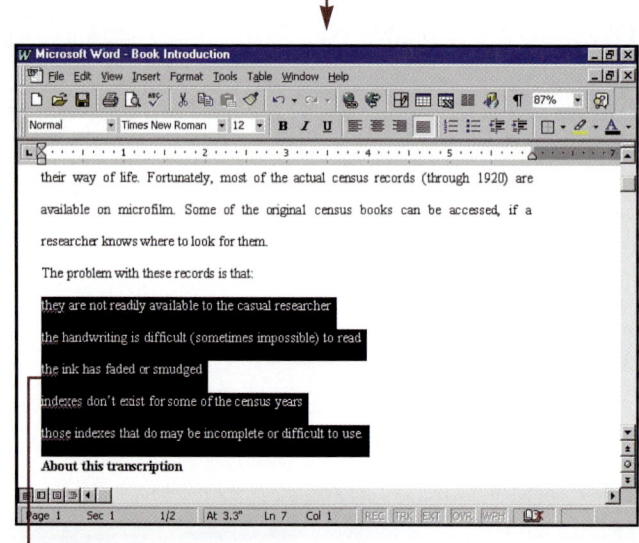

Five list items

7 Select all five items that are part of your list.

Bullets button

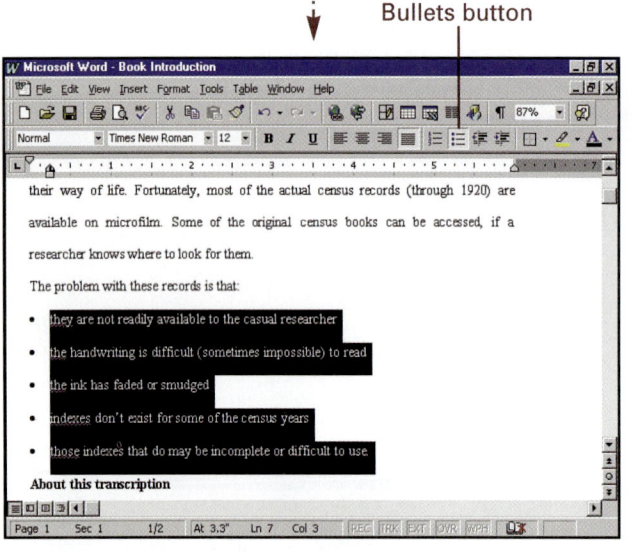

8 Click the **Bullets** button on the Formatting toolbar. Bullets are placed in front of the list items.

Increase Indent button

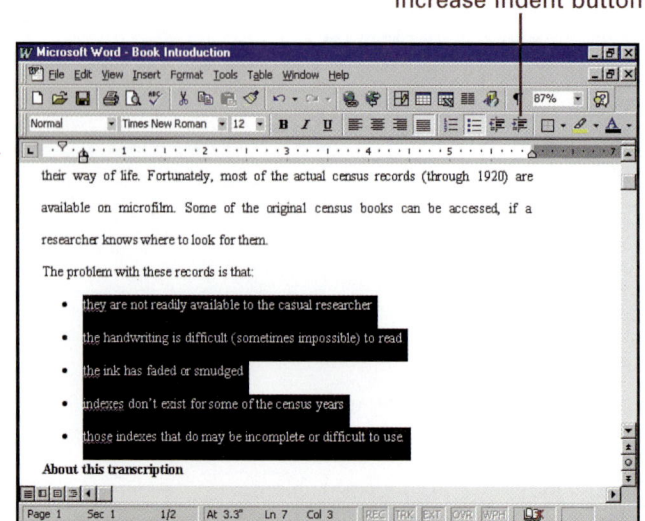

In Depth: If the information in a list is in some kind of sequential order, you might consider using the Numbering button, which is to the left of the Bullets button. If the information is in no particular order, it is best to use a bulleted list.

9 Click the **Increase Indent** button on the Formatting toolbar to move the text to the right.

10 With the list still selected, choose **Format, Paragraph** from the menu. The **Paragraph** dialog box opens. Select **Single** from the **Line spacing** drop-down menu.

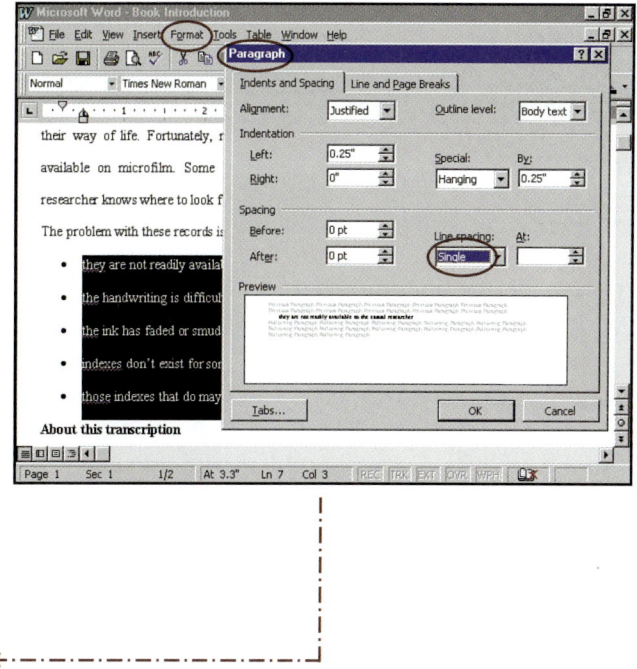

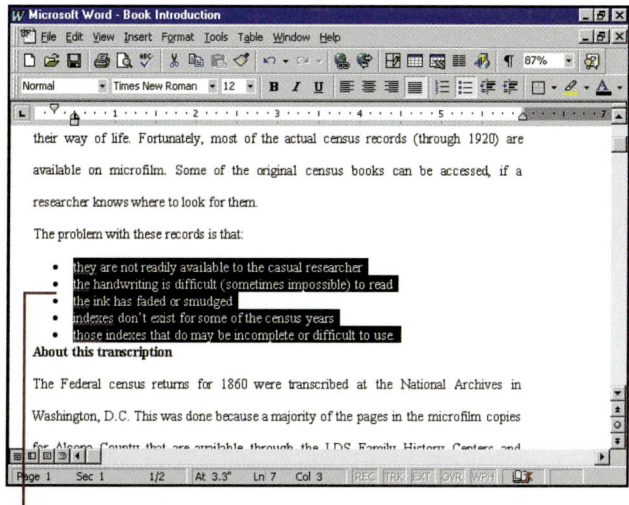

The bulleted list is single spaced.

11 Click **OK**. The bulleted list is now single spaced. In task 8, a line will be added after the fifth item.

Lesson 3: Formatting Text

Task 5

Indenting the First Line of a Paragraph

Why would I do this?

Whereas some writing styles call for the first line of each paragraph to be flush with the rest of the paragraph, others require that you indent the first line a certain distance. Many people indent the first line by typing five or six spaces. This method worked well on typewriters that always used the same size spaces, but it does not work well on computers that vary the size of spaces depending on the size of the paragraph's font.

Another method commonly used to indent the first line of a paragraph is to press Tab. This method works well, but it has two drawbacks. If no tabs have been set, Word assumes that you want to move .5 inches to the right each time you press Tab. If you try to edit this paragraph and set a tab for some other purpose, the indent lines up with the new tab. The real problem with using a tab to indent is evident when you try to use it to create hanging indents (paragraphs with all but the first line indented). Pressing Tab at the beginning of each subsequent line introduces tab characters that cause a lot of problems if you try to change the length of the line by editing the text or changing the font size.

If you use the **Format**, **Paragraph** menu options, you can specify the size of the indent in inches, set a standard that can be applied to more than one paragraph, and avoid later editing problems.

In this task, you learn to indent the first line of a paragraph.

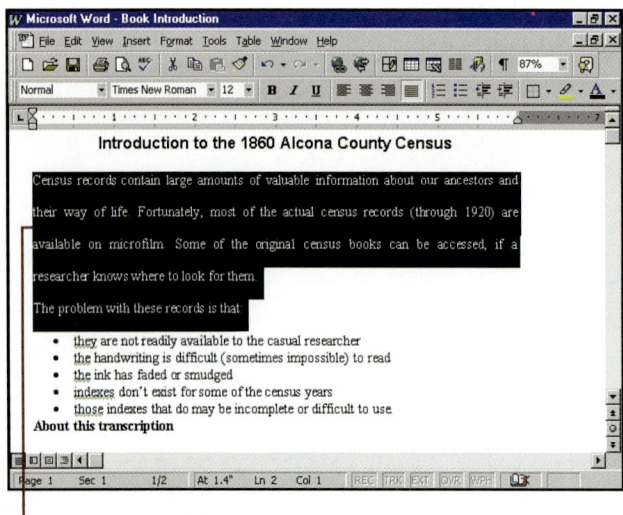

The first two paragraphs are selected.

1 With your **Book Introduction** file still active, select the first two paragraphs (but not the title), as shown in the figure. This text includes the introduction to the bulleted list you created in task 4 but not the list itself.

2 Select **Format**, **Paragraph** from the menu. The **Paragraph** dialog box opens. This is the same dialog box you used to change the line spacing in tasks 3 and 4. Click the **Indents and Spacing** tab.

Quick Tip: You can also open the paragraph dialog box by right-clicking on the selected paragraph. A shortcut menu opens. One of the options is Paragraph. Click the Paragraph option with your left mouse to open the Paragraph dialog box.

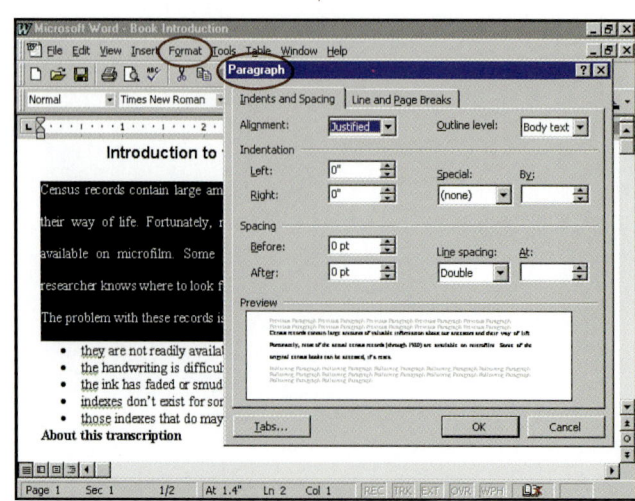

54 Learn Word 97, Second Edition

3 In the **Indentation** section, click the arrow on the right side of the **Special** drop-down menu. Choose **First line**.

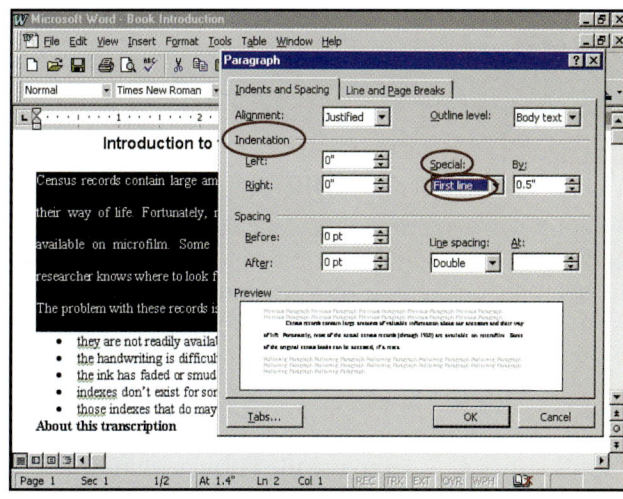

4 If necessary, click the up or down arrows on the right of the **By** box until you reach **0.5"**. This is the distance, in inches, that the first line of each selected paragraph will be indented.

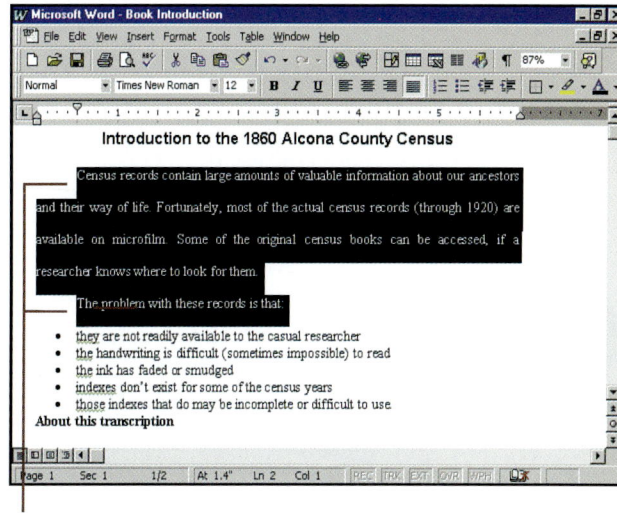

5 Click **OK**. The selected paragraphs are now indented half an inch.

First line indents

Lesson 3: Formatting Text   55

Task 6
Using the Format Painter

Why would I do this?

To apply a consistent look to your document, it is a good idea to have all of the paragraphs in the document formatted the same way. When you change the format of a paragraph, you usually will change the format of other paragraphs to match. If they are continuous, you can simply highlight all of the paragraphs and then do the formatting once. If the paragraphs are separated by lists, subtitles, or other text that requires different formatting, a different technique can be used. The *Format Painter* is a tool that enables you to copy the formatting of one paragraph and paint it onto another paragraph. This tool can help you apply formatting characteristics quickly and easily.

In this task, you learn to use the Format Painter.

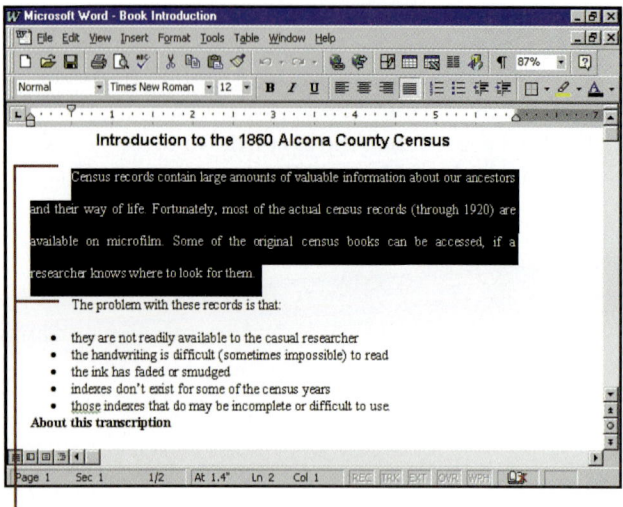

Paragraph format to be copied

1 With your **Book Introduction** file still active, select the first full paragraph (but not the title). The first line in this paragraph is indented. You will apply the format of this paragraph to several other paragraphs in the document.

In Depth: If the Format Painter is used to copy the format of a paragraph, the hidden paragraph mark must be included in the original selection.

2 Double-click the **Format Painter** button. The format of the first paragraph has been attached to the Format Painter. The pointer now includes a paintbrush.

In Depth: If you click once on the Format Painter button, you can change only one paragraph before the painter is turned off. By double-clicking, you have activated the Format Painter for as many uses as you want. It does not turn off until you click the Format Painter button again.

Format Painter button

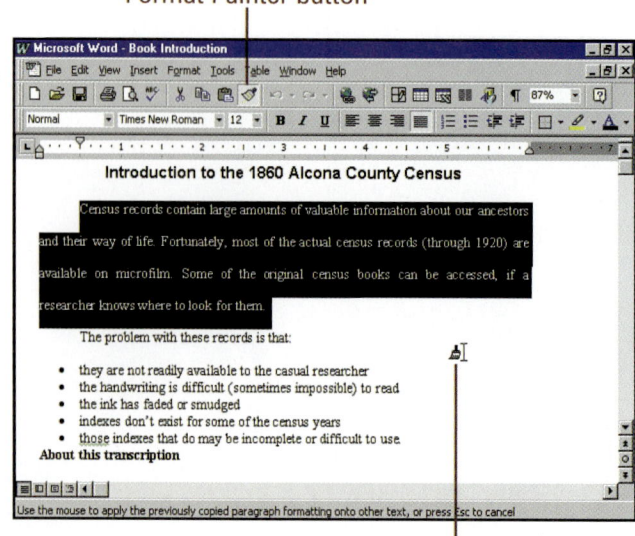

The Format Painter pointer

56 Learn Word 97, Second Edition

The paragraph is now indented.

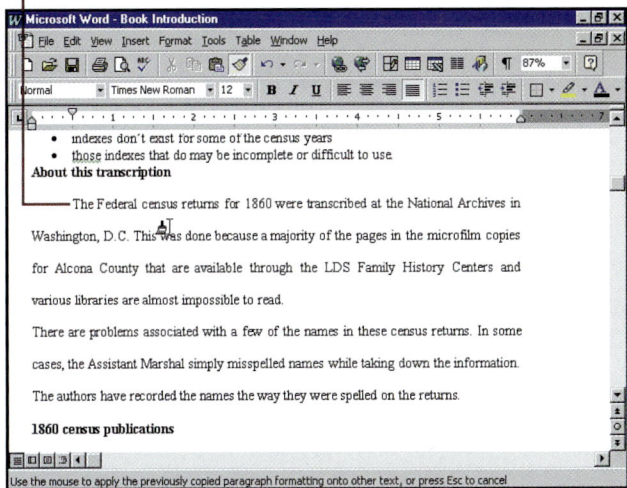

3 Use the vertical scrollbar to move the text until the paragraphs after the **About this transcription** subtitle are showing on your screen. Click anywhere in the first paragraph after the **About this transcription** subtitle. You do not need to select the whole paragraph for the Format Painter to work. Notice that the first line is now indented.

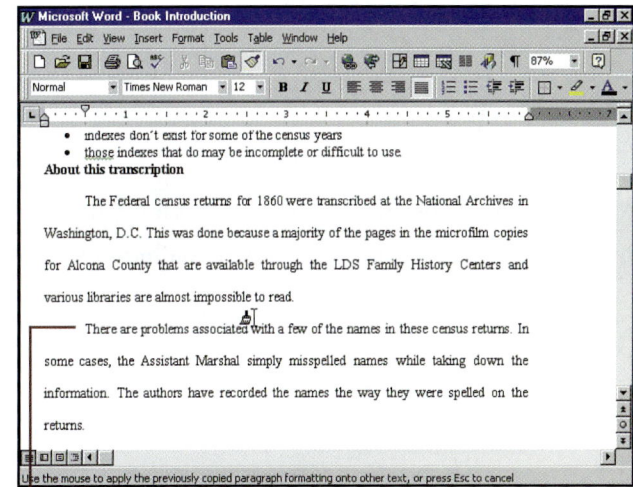

4 Click anywhere in the second paragraph after the **About this transcription** subtitle. This paragraph now exhibits the same formatting as the original paragraph.

The paragraph is now indented.

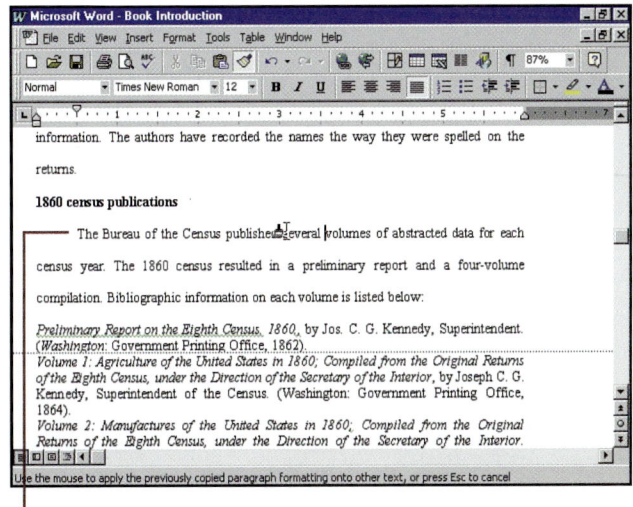

5 Click anywhere in the first paragraph after the **1860 census publications** subtitle. This paragraph is now indented. This is the last paragraph that needs a format change.

The paragraph is now indented.

Lesson 3: Formatting Text 57

6 Click the **Format Painter** button to turn this feature off. Click the **Save** button to save your changes.

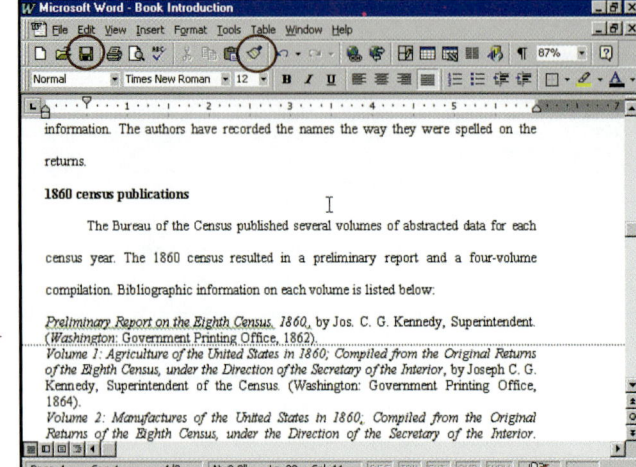

Task 7

Creating a Hanging Indent

Why would I do this?

Some styles use a *hanging indent*, which means that the first line of the text is to the left of the rest of the text. For example, it is common for bibliographic references to call for the first line of a bibliographic entry to be a half inch to the left of the rest of the entry. This is another formatting style that can be quickly applied using the options available in the **Format**, **Paragraph** menu.

In this task, you learn to create a hanging indent.

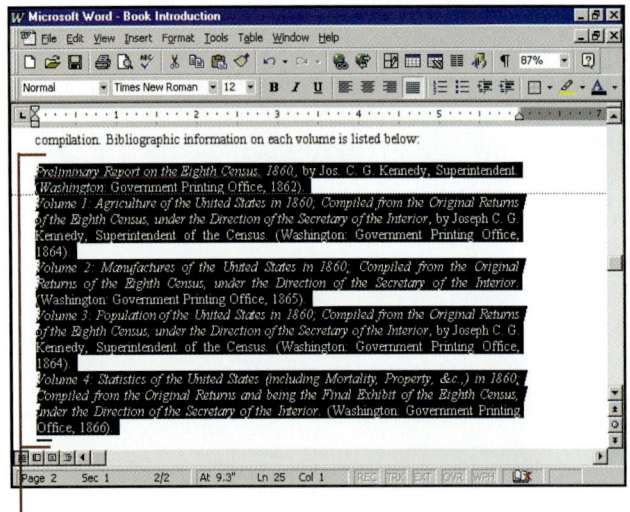

The bibliographic entries

1 With your **Book Introduction** file still active, select the last five paragraphs in the document. These are the bibliographic entries.

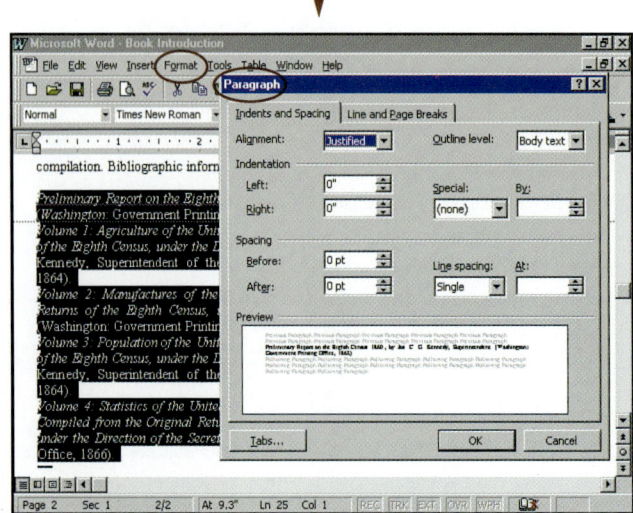

2 Select **Format**, **Paragraph** from the menu. The **Paragraph** dialog box opens.

58 Learn Word 97, Second Edition

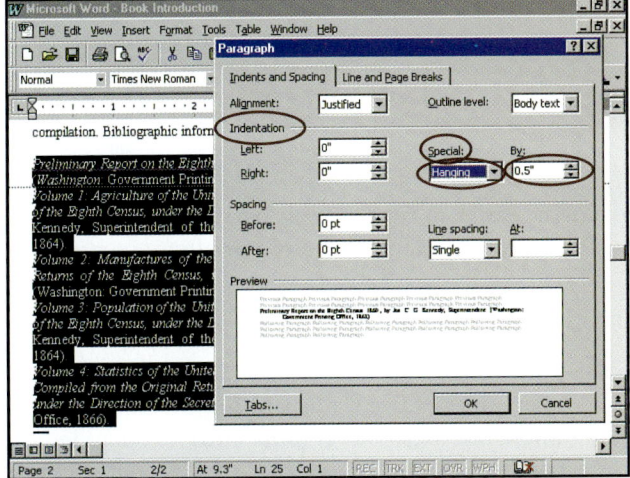

3 In the **Indentation** section, click the arrow on the right side of the **Special** drop-down menu. Choose **Hanging**. The **By** box should read **0.5"**, which means that the first line will be a half inch to the left of the rest of the paragraph. This structure is accomplished by indenting the rest of the text in each paragraph.

4 Click **OK**. The five bibliographic entries should now be formatted with hanging indents. Notice how much easier they are to read.

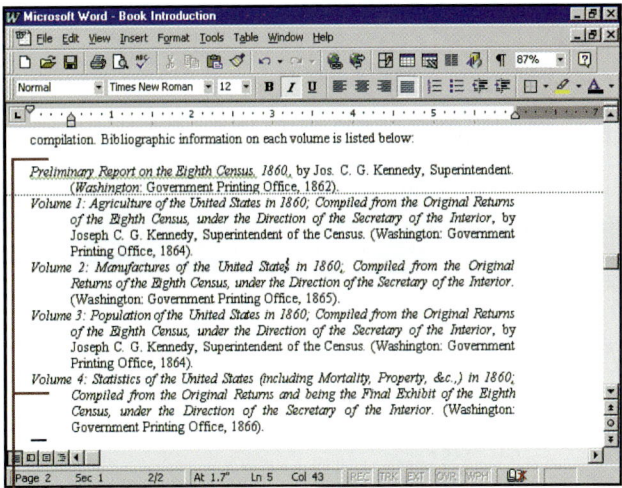

Hanging indents

Lesson 3: Formatting Text 59

Task 8

Adding Spaces After Paragraphs

Why would I do this?

In many cases, extra space between paragraphs makes the document easier to read. This is particularly true if the text is single spaced. You can set up your paragraphs to add extra space automatically before or after a paragraph.

In this task, you learn to add spaces of different heights after paragraphs.

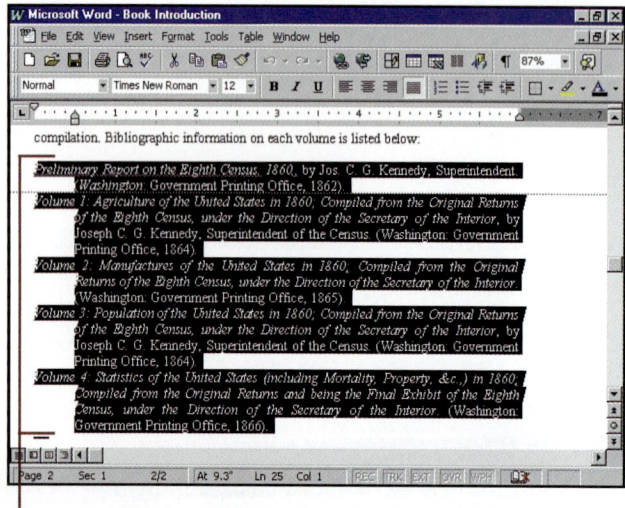

The bibliographic entries

1 With your **Book Introduction** file still active, select the last five paragraphs in the document. These are the bibliographic entries you added hanging indents to in task 7.

2 Select **Format**, **Paragraph** from the menu. The **Paragraph** dialog box opens.

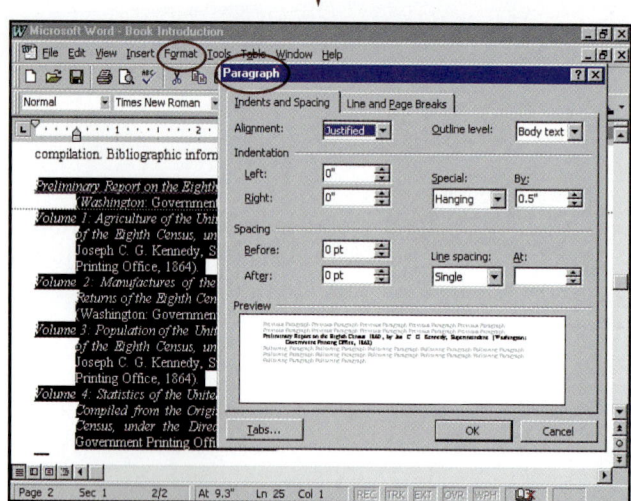

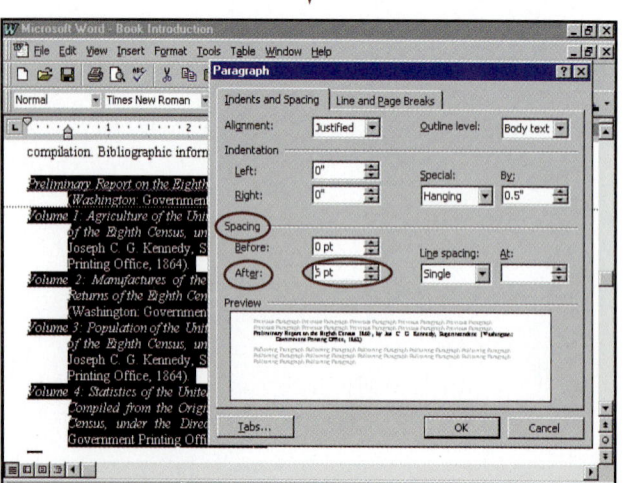

3 In the **Spacing** area of the dialog box, click the up arrow in the **After** box once, which changes the number to **6 pt**.

In Depth: When you see 6 pt in the After box, it means that a space equivalent to a line of 6-point text is added after each selected paragraph. A 6-point space is about the height of half a line when you are using 12-point type.

4 Click **OK** and then click anywhere in the document to deselect the text. A space is added after each selected paragraph, making the bibliographic entries even easier to read.

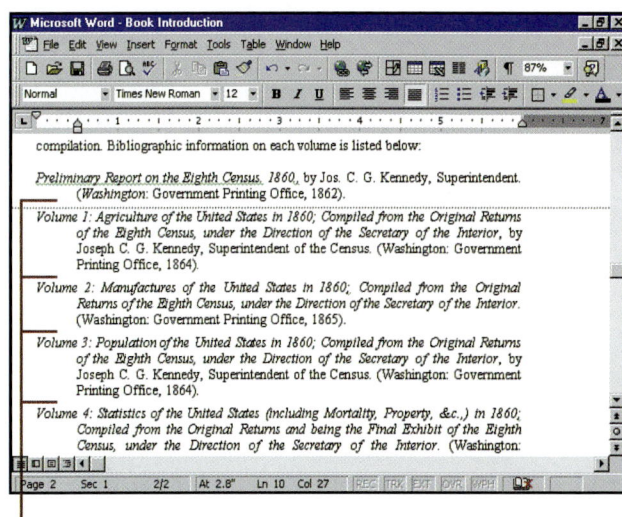

A 6-point space is added after each selected paragraph.

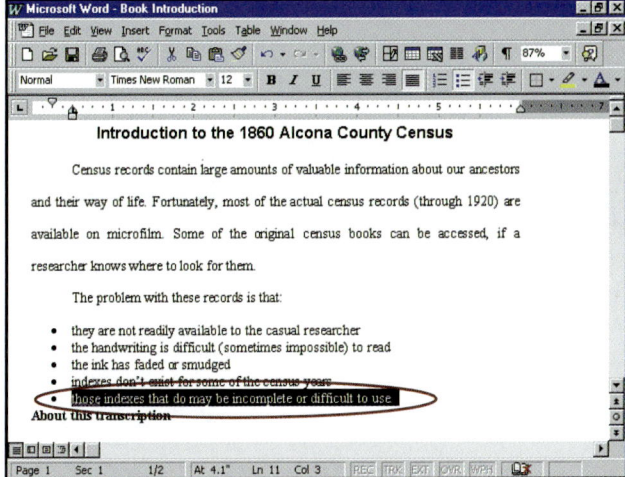

5 Select the last item in the bulleted list.

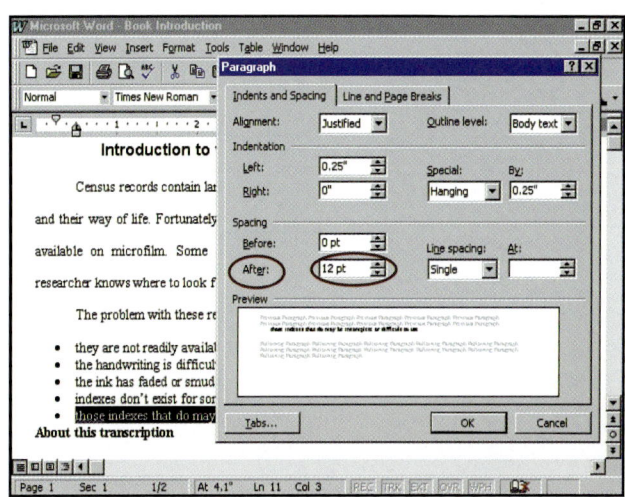

6 Select **Format**, **Paragraph** from the menu. The **Paragraph** dialog box opens. Click the up arrow in the **After** box twice to add a **12 pt** space.

Lesson 3: Formatting Text **61**

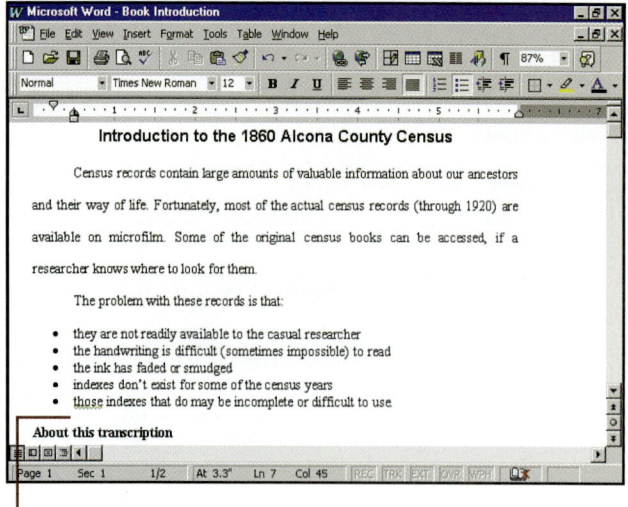

A 12-point space is added after the bulleted list.

7. Click **OK** and then click anywhere in the document to deselect the text. A 12-point space has now been added after the bulleted list. This space matches the other between-paragraph spaces in the surrounding area of the document.

> **In Depth:** You can also use the Before spacing option if you want to do so. It is usually a good idea, however, to use After if you are using anything but single spacing in the document because any other line spacing puts the extra space below the line rather than above it.

Task 9

Working with Tabs

Why would I do this?

Tabs have become less and less important in word processing documents in favor of other indenting techniques and tables. Sometimes, however, it is necessary to know how to use tabs. For example, it is often helpful to use a tab to line up the decimals in a column of numbers with decimal points. Tabs are also the only way to put regular dots or dashes, called *leaders*, between columns. Leaders are often used to separate chapter titles from page numbers in a table of contents. If you have a line of text with some words left aligned, other words centered, and still other words right aligned, you need to use tabs. Knowing how to use tabs increases your ability to create professional-looking documents.

In this task, you learn to use different kinds of tabs.

1. Place the insertion point at the end of the last item in the bulleted list. Press **←Enter**. A new bullet point is added below the last one.

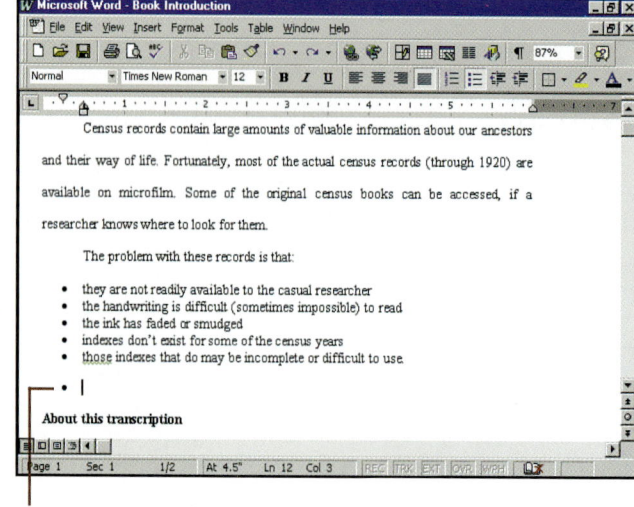

Blank bullet line

62 **Learn Word 97, Second Edition**

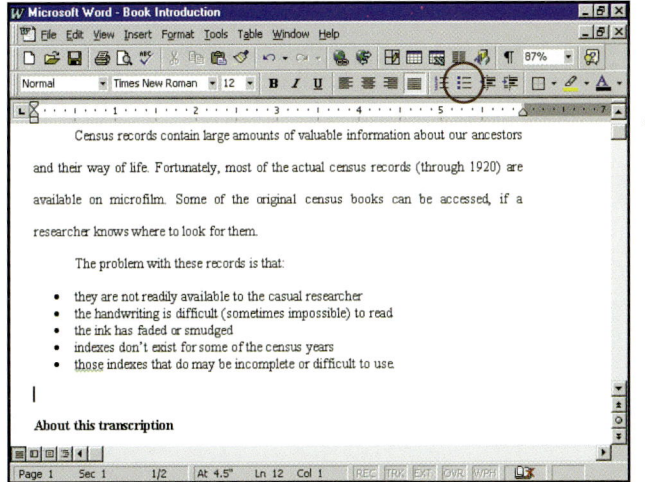

2 Click the **Bullets** button to turn off the bulleted list. The bullet is removed and the insertion point moves back to the left margin.

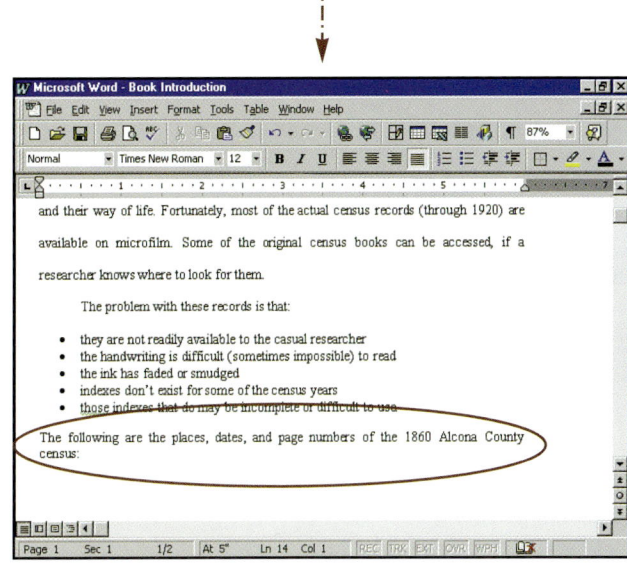

3 Type **The following are the places, dates, and page numbers of the 1860 Alcona County census:** and press ⏎Enter.

4 Select **F**ormat, **T**abs from the menu. The **Tabs** dialog box opens.

In Depth: The default for tabs in Word is a tab stop at every half inch. Rather than pressing the Tab key several times to reach the desired stop, you should set the tabs to the needed location before entering text. Doing so ensures that the text entered aligns properly regardless of differences in line length.

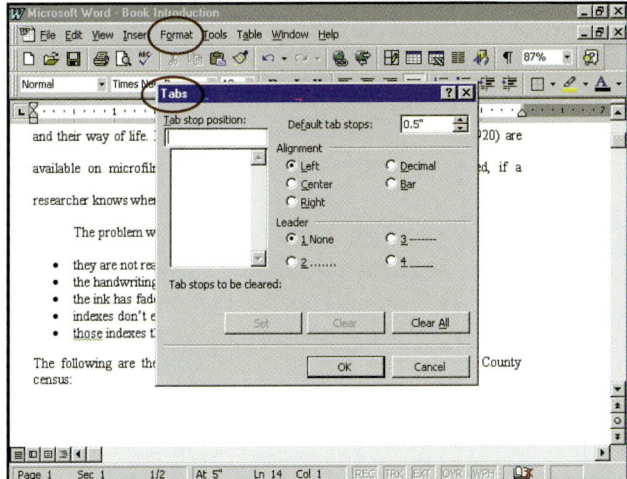

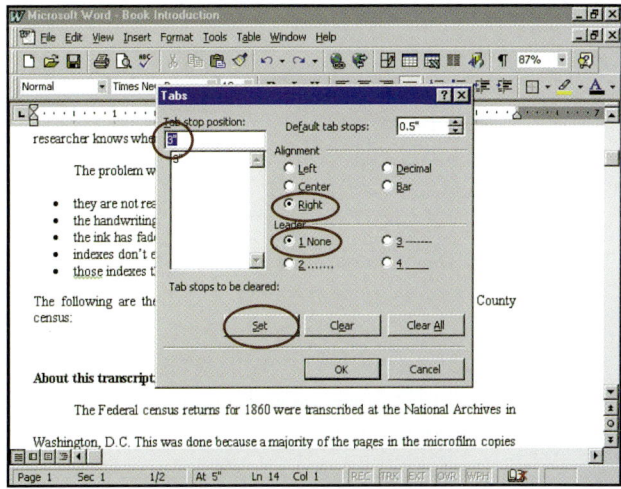

5 Type **3** in the **Tab stop position**, select **Right** in the **Alignment** area, and make sure **1 None** is selected in the **Leader** area. Click **Set** to enter the tab at the 3-inch mark.

Lesson 3: Formatting Text 63

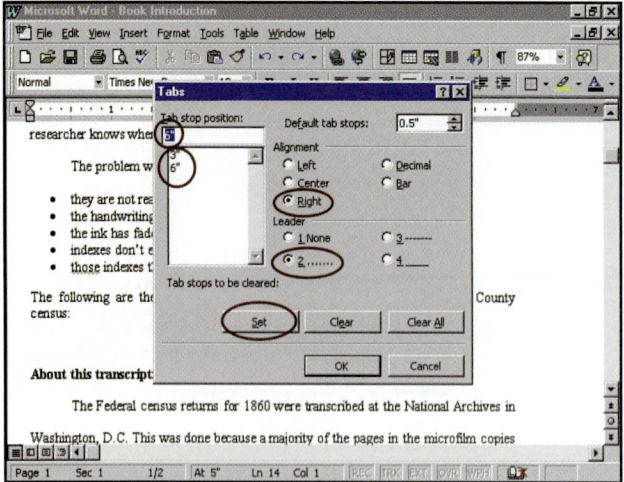

6 Type **6** over the measurement **3"** in the **Tab stop position**, select **Right** in the **Alignment** area, and select **2**...from the **Leader** area. Click **Set** to enter the tab at the 6-inch mark.

Tab markers set at 3" and 6"

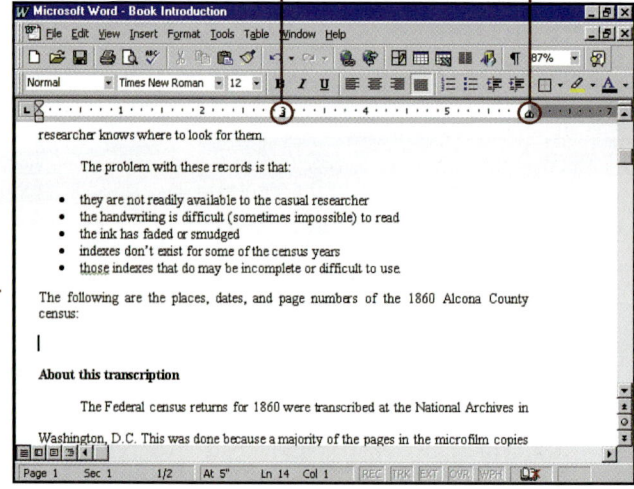

7 Click **OK**. The tabs you just added show up in the ruler at the top of the work area.

 **Pothole:** If the ruler is not showing on your screen, select **View**, **Ruler** from the menu.

In Depth: Different types of tabs can be selected by clicking the tab marker at the left end of the horizontal ruler. When the tab you want to use is displayed, add it to the horizontal ruler by clicking on the ruler at the position where you want the tab. A tab marker will be added to the ruler. To remove a tab, click in the paragraph where you want the tab deleted. Then click the tab marker on the ruler and drag it down and off the ruler. The tab is deleted from the selected paragraph.

8 Type in **Black River** and press Tab. This moves the insertion point to the right tab at the 3-inch mark.

64 Learn Word 97, Second Edition

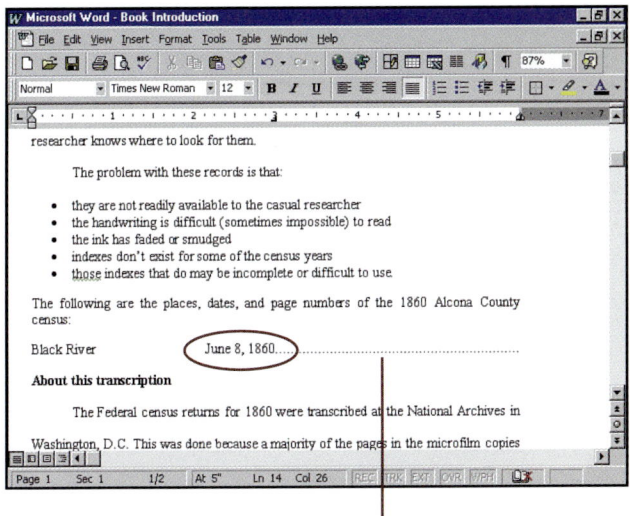

The dot leader

9 Type in **June 8, 1860** and press `Tab`. When you type the date, it moves to the left of the tab. The right tab allows the right edges of the dates to line up. Also, the dot leader appears when you press `Tab`.

10 Type in **10-11** for the page numbers and then press `Enter`. Notice that because the right tab is used, the numbers move to the left as they are typed—ensuring that the numbers line up on the right side.

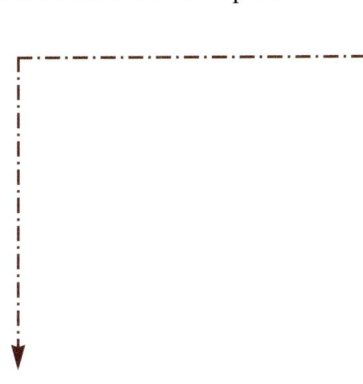

The right edges line up with the right tab.

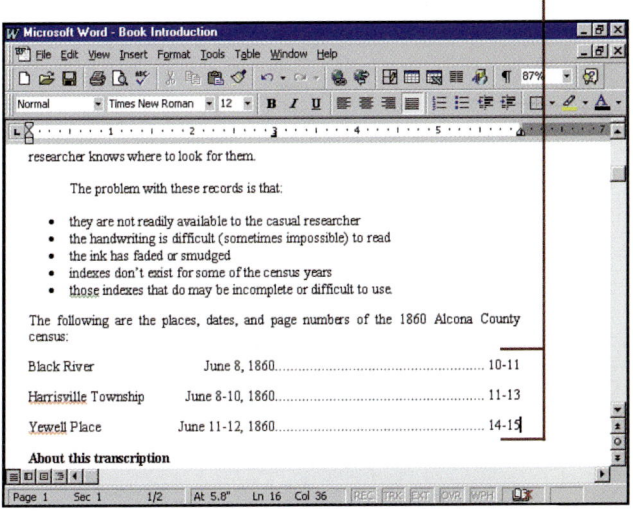

In Depth: Another useful type of tab is the decimal tab. When you use this tab, the numbers move to the left until you press the decimal point, at which point the numbers move to the right of the decimal as you type them. This ensures that the figures all line up on the decimal point.

11 Enter the following information using the same procedure:

Harrisville Township	**June 8-10, 1860**	**11-13**
Yewell Place	**June 11-12, 1860**	**14-15**

Lesson 3: Formatting Text 65

12 Click the **Save** button to save your work.

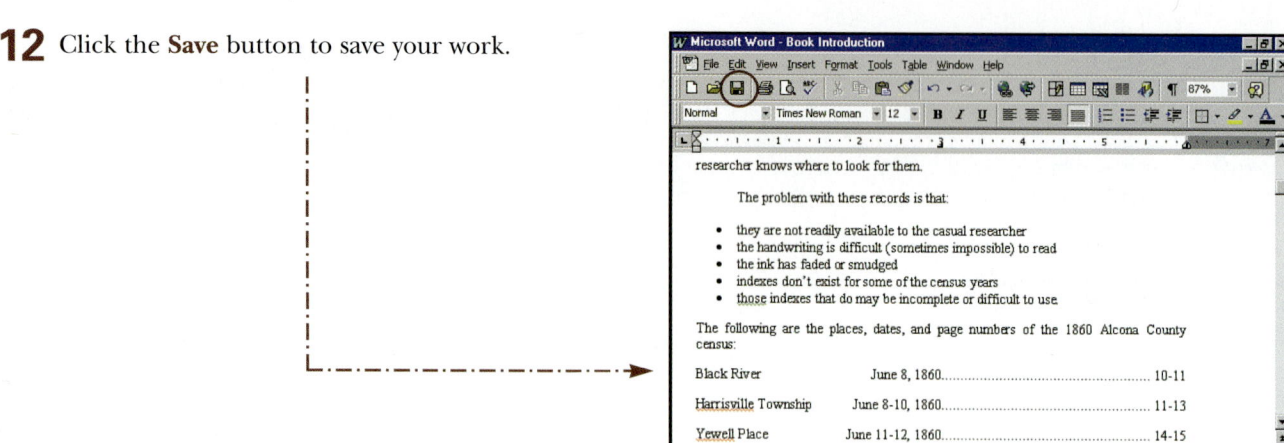

Task 10

Printing Selected Text

Why would I do this?

While you are working on a document, sometimes you will want to print out only a section of a document. Word has a feature that allows you to print selected portions of the text. This feature saves paper and enables you to print just the parts that you may want to use.

In this task, you learn to print only the text that you have selected.

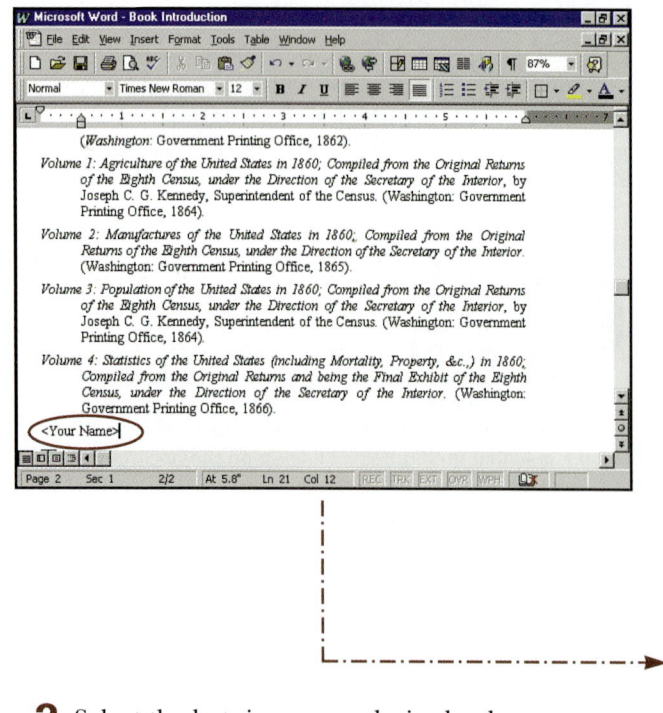

1 With your **Book Introduction** file still active, place the cursor at the end of the last paragraph of the document. Press ⏎Enter and type in your name. (Remove the italics from your name if necessary.)

Selected text to be printed

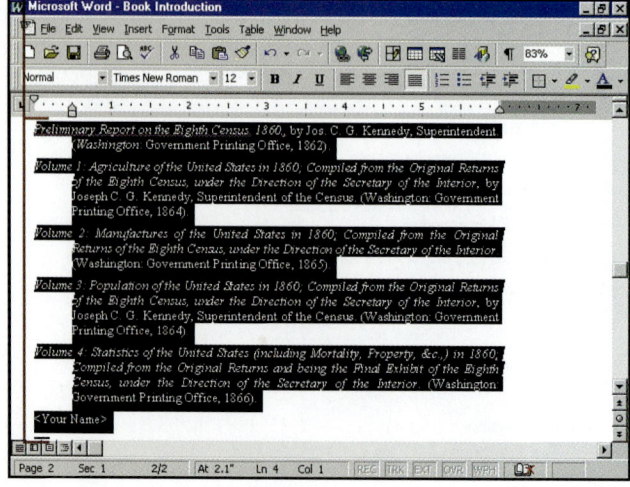

2 Select the last six paragraphs in the document. These are the five bibliographic entries, plus your name.

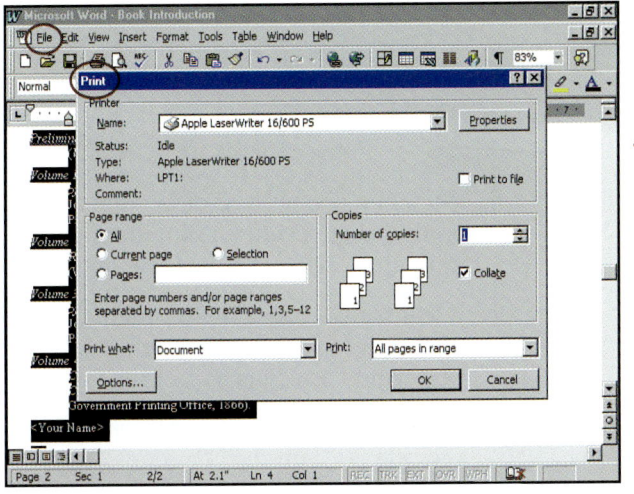

3 Select **File**, **Print** from the menu. The **Print** dialog box opens.

4 Choose **Selection** from the **Page range** area.

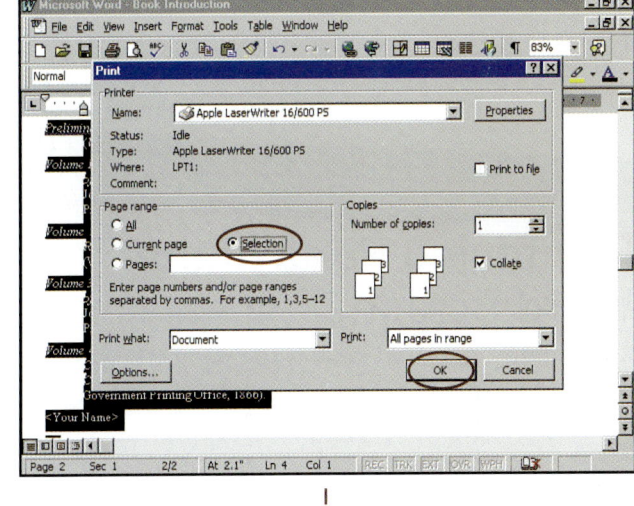

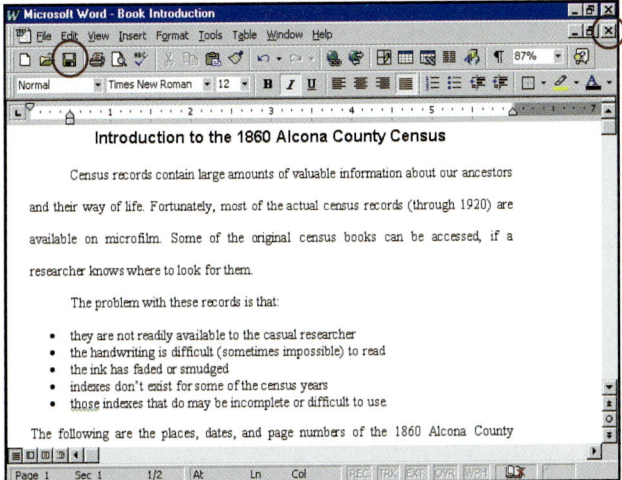

5 Click **OK**. Click anywhere in the document to deselect the text, scroll to the top, and click the **Save** button. Close the document.

Lesson 3: Formatting Text 67

Student Exercises

True-False

Circle either T or F.

T F 1. When you select text and change the font, the shape of the letters changes.

T F 2. If you change the size of the selected text to 36-point type, the text is about an inch high when it prints out.

T F 3. If a paragraph is formatted with a hanging indent, the first line begins farther to the right than the rest of the lines in the paragraph.

T F 4. To make the letters thicker and appear more important, you can select the text and then click the button on the toolbar that has a capital letter B on it.

T F 5. A first line indent created by pressing the Spacebar five times is the same as setting the first line indent to .5 inches.

T F 6. There is a certain type of tab that can be used to align a column of dollar figures so that the decimal points line up.

T F 7. If you want to apply the formatting of one paragraph to another, select **E**dit, **C**opy, and Paste **S**pecial from the menu.

T F 8. If you set up a tab with a dot leader, pressing Tab produces a series of dots between the previous text and the text at that tab.

T F 9. The only way to place extra space between paragraphs is to press Enter one or two extra times.

T F 10. If you only want to print one paragraph, you can select it and then choose **F**ile, **P**rint, **S**election, and **OK** from the menu.

Identifying Parts of the Word Screen

Refer to the figure and identify the numbered parts of the screen. Write the letter of the correct label in the space next to the number.

1. _____
2. _____
3. _____
4. _____
5. _____
6. _____
7. _____
8. _____
9. _____
10. _____
11. _____
12. _____
13. _____
14. _____

A. Additional space following a paragraph
B. Bulleted list
C. Buttons used for adding emphasis
D. Buttons used for aligning text

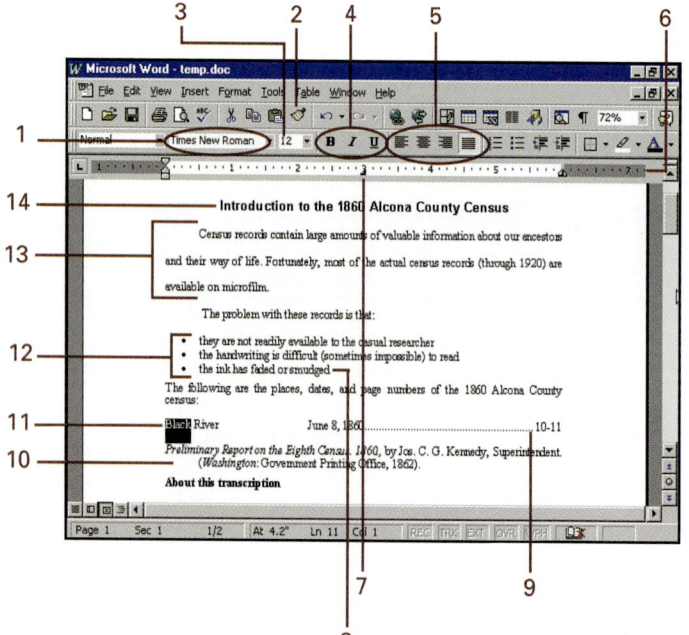

68 Learn Word 97, Second Edition

E. Centered text emphasized with bold
F. Dot leader
G. Double-spaced paragraph with the first line indented
H. Font size
I. Format Painter
J. Hanging indent
K. Name of font
L. Ruler displaying tabs for currently selected line
M. Selected text
N. Tab stop

Matching Questions

Match the following statements to the word or phrase from the list on the right. Write the letter of the matching word or phrase in the space provided next to the number.

1. ___ Rows of text preceded by round, black dots
2. ___ Automatically separates lines of text by an amount equal to the height of the text
3. ___ Paragraph whose first line begins to the right of the rest of the lines of text
4. ___ Paragraph whose first line of text is farther to the left than the rest of the lines
5. ___ Method of printing less than a whole page of text
6. ___ A feature that fills the space between tab stops with a character such as a dash or a dot
7. ___ Causes all of the lines of a paragraph to line up at both the left and right margins
8. ___ A line of text that has the same amount of space between its first character and the left margin and its last character and the right margin
9. ___ Tab that causes inserted text to move to the left as you type to ensure that the right side of the text stays aligned with the position of the tab
10. ___ Measurement used to describe the height of a line of text

A. Right alignment tab
B. Indent
C. Point
D. Double spaced
E. Bulleted list
F. Justified
G. File, Print, Selection
H. Leader
I. Centered
J. Hanging indent
K. Left alignment tab

Application Exercises

Exercise 1—Change the Font Type, Size, Alignment, and Emphasis

1. Launch Word. Open Less0302 from the student files. Save the file as **Distance Education Technologies**.

2. Select the first two lines of the document, which make up the title.

3. Change the font to Arial.

4. Change the font size to 14 point.

5. Change the emphasis to bold.

6. Change the alignment to centered.

7. Select the three lines that identify the author and date.

8. Change their alignment to centered.

9. Click on the line following the date. Type **Edited by: <Your Name>** (use your own name). Center this line. Press **Enter** to insert a blank line.

10. Select the section of text that you have been working on, which includes the title, the author information, the date of publication, and your name. Print this selection (see the figure).

11. Leave the document open for use in the next exercise.

Exercise 2—Use the Format Painter to Format Several Other Lines of Text

1. If the paragraph marks are hidden, click the **Show/Hide** button.

2. Select the subheading **Interactive Technologies** (it follows the first long paragraph). Make sure to include the paragraph mark at the end of the line.

3. Change its alignment to centered.

4. Double-click on the **Format Painter** button on the toolbar.

5. Scroll to the bottom of page 2 to find the next subheading, **Conclusion**.

6. Click on the word **Conclusion** to center it as well. Double-click the **Format Painter** button. It remains depressed to indicate that it may be used again.

70 Learn Word 97, Second Edition

7. Scroll down and find the subheading **Reference List**. Click on it to center it.

8. Click the **Format Painter** button to deselect it.

9. Leave the document open for use in the next exercise.

Exercise 3—Format Paragraphs

1. Scroll to the top of the document and select the paragraph that starts with **Distance education is**.

2. Choose **Format**, **Paragraph** to open the **Paragraph** dialog box.

3. Set the line spacing to **Double**.

4. Set the special indent to **First line** and click **OK**.

5. Double-click the **Format Painter** button on the toolbar.

6. Click in all of the following paragraphs except the subheadings that are underlined, the subheadings or titles that are centered, and the references at the end of the document.

7. Click the **Format Painter** button to turn it off.

8. Find the **Conclusion** section. Add your name at the end of the conclusion. Select the subheading and the next eight lines. Print the selected lines (see the figure).

9. Leave the document open for use in the next exercise.

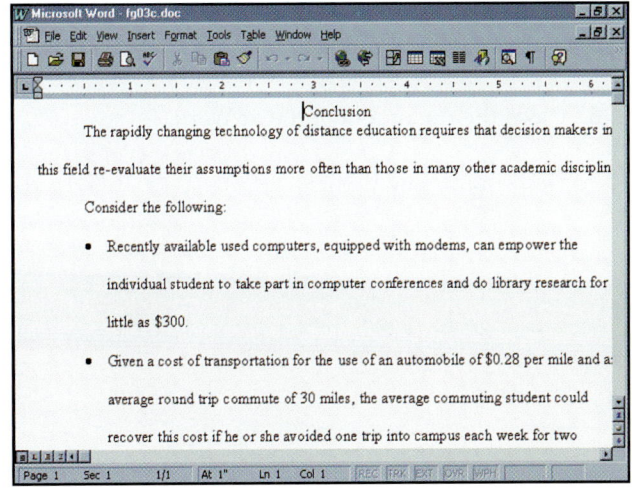

Exercise 4—Create a Bulleted List

1. Locate the **Conclusion** section.

2. Select the first four paragraphs that follow the phrase **Consider the following:** but come before the **Reference List**.

3. Click the **Bullets** button on the toolbar.

4. Add your name at the end of the last line in the bulleted list.

5. Select the text from **Consider the following:** through the four paragraphs that have been changed into a bulleted list, including your name.

6. Print the selected text.

7. Leave the document open for use in the next exercise.

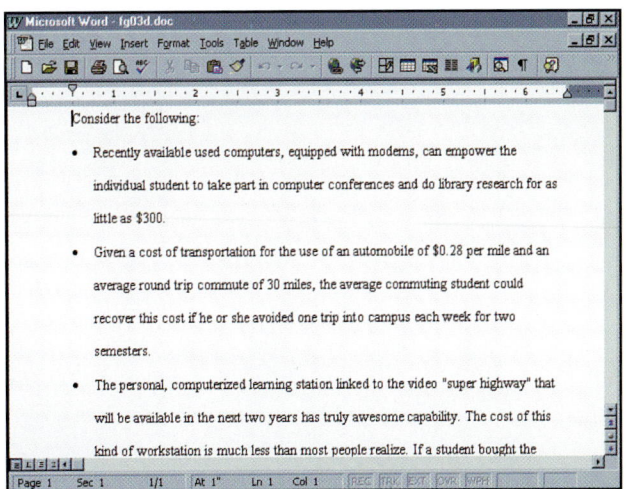

Exercise 5—Formatting a Hanging Indent and Following Spaces

1. Select all of the references at the end of the document.

2. Choose **Format**, **Paragraph** to open the **Paragraph** dialog box.

3. Set the special indent to **Hanging**.

4. Set the line spacing to **Single**.

5. Set the spacing after the paragraph to **6pt**. Click **OK**.

6. Type your name at the end of the **Reference List**.

7. Select the references portion of the text, starting with the subheading, **Reference List**, and ending with your name. Print the selected text (see the figure).

8. Close the document and exit Word.

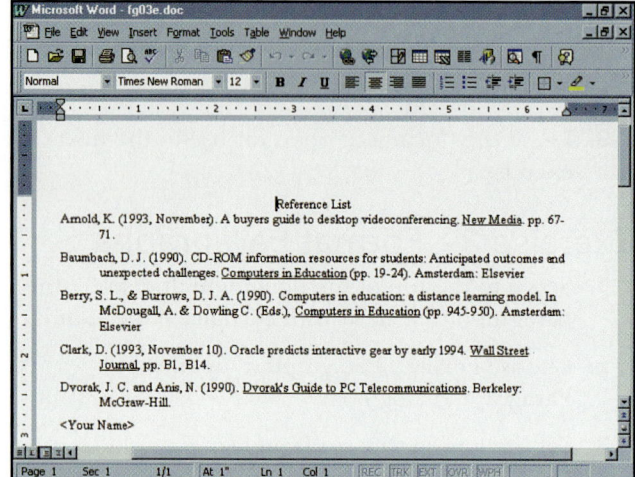

Lesson 4
Formatting a Document

Task 1: Setting Margins
Task 2: Inserting Page Numbers
Task 3: Entering Text in a Header or Footer
Task 4: Inserting the Date into the Header or Footer
Task 5: Formatting the Header and Footer
Task 6: Inserting Page Breaks
Task 7: Using Print Preview
Task 8: Printing a Range of Pages

Introduction

In Lesson 3, you learned how to use many important Microsoft Word text and paragraph formatting tools. Word also offers a wide range of formatting options that affect the way your overall document looks when it is printed.

Margins are the space between the text and the edge of the paper. Word allows you to set the left, right, top, and bottom margins independently. The top and bottom margins are also used for information that can be displayed on each page of a document. These areas, which are called *headers* and *footers*, can contain page numbers, dates, company logos, or general text. The top and bottom margins must be large enough to contain whatever text is placed in the header or footer.

When formatting your document, you can also insert *page breaks*. If there is space at the bottom of a page for the first few lines of the next topic but you want those lines to be at the top of the next page, you can insert a page break ahead of those lines. This feature enables you to control your document so that lines of text, images, or figures that should be displayed together can be shown on the same page. Word offers a print preview so that you can verify that the text of your document is placed on the pages exactly the way you desire.

In this lesson, you learn how to set margins, work with headers and footers, and insert page breaks.

By the time you have completed this lesson, you will have created a document that looks like this:

Visual Summary

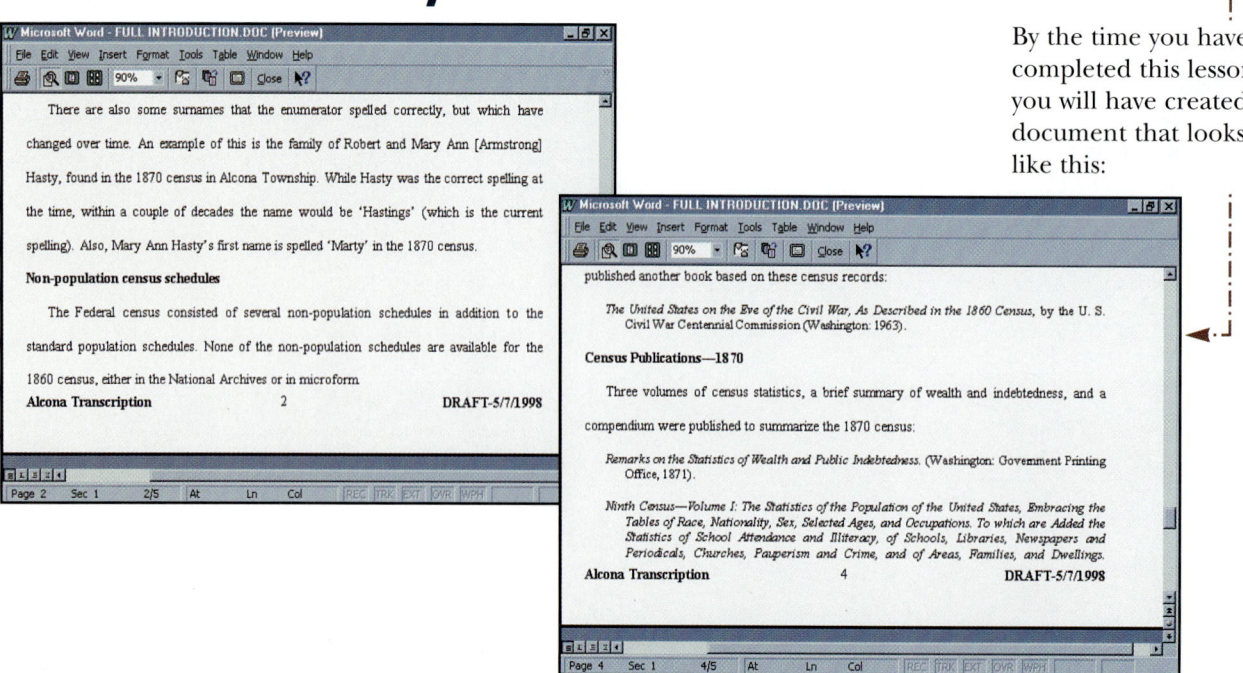

Task 1

Setting Margins

Why would I do this?

Margins are the empty space around the edge of your document—both on the top and bottom and on the sides. In Word, you can control the four margin settings individually. Specific margin settings are required for particular writing styles, such as research papers that use the APA or MLA style. Increasing or decreasing one or more of the margins can also make a document look better on a page or fit on fewer pages, depending on your need. Finally, you may want to increase the left side margin so that you can bind the document or punch holes in it. Knowing how to work with margins helps you create professional-looking documents.

In this task, you learn to change the margins of a document.

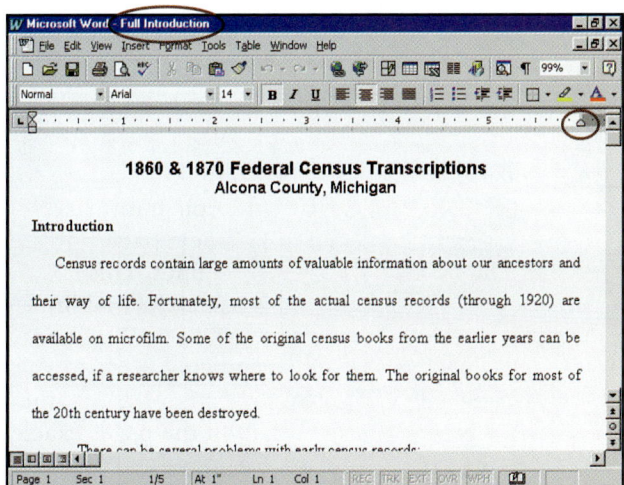

1 Launch Microsoft Word. Open **Less0401** from the student files. Save the file as **Full Introduction**.

Pothole: The ruler should be visible at the top of the screen. If not, choose **View**, **Ruler** from the menu bar. The width of the page on the ruler shows in white. The margin area on the right is dark gray. While 6 is not shown on the ruler, you can see that the measurement from 5 to the right margin is a full inch when you compare it to the measurements showing on the ruler.

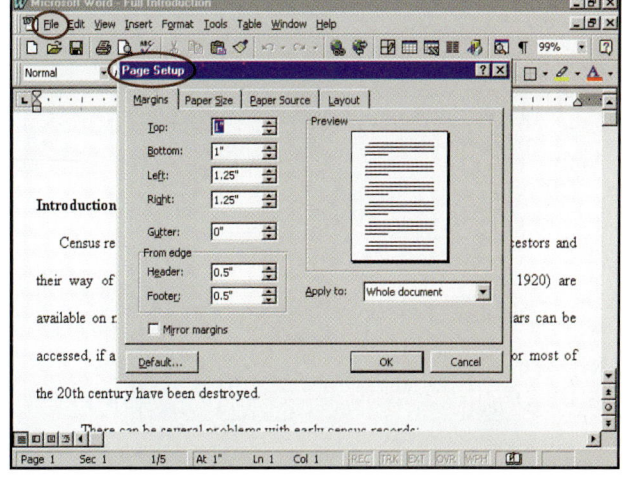

2 Select **File**, **Page Setup** from the menu. The **Page Setup** dialog box is displayed.

The Margins tab

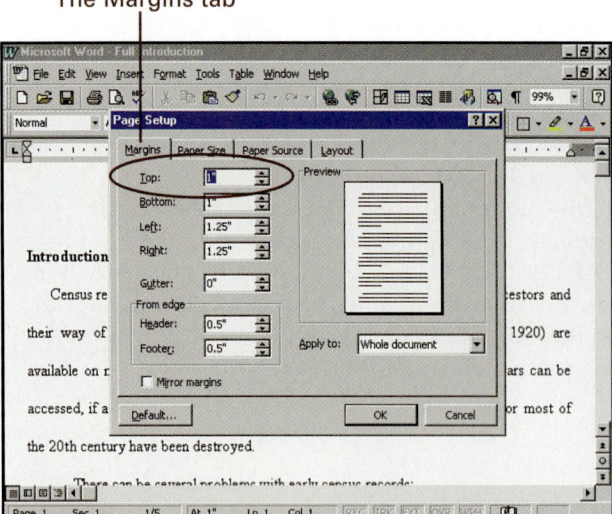

3 Make sure that the **Margins** tab is selected and then highlight the **Top** box if necessary. The number in this box controls the distance, in inches, from the top of the page to the top of the text on the page (excluding the header text).

In Depth: The margin settings are saved with the document. When you create a new document, the *default* margin settings are applied. The most common default margin settings are either an inch for all four sides or an inch at the top and bottom and an inch and a quarter on the left and right. You can change the default margin settings by setting new ones and then clicking the Default button in the Page Setup dialog box. You should only do this on your own computer.

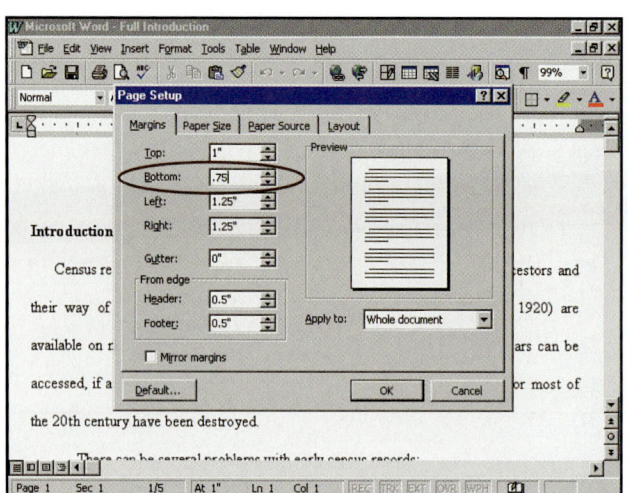

4 Leave the top margin at 1 inch and then press Tab to move to the **Bottom** margin. Type in **.75**. This leaves a three-fourth inch margin at the bottom of the document.

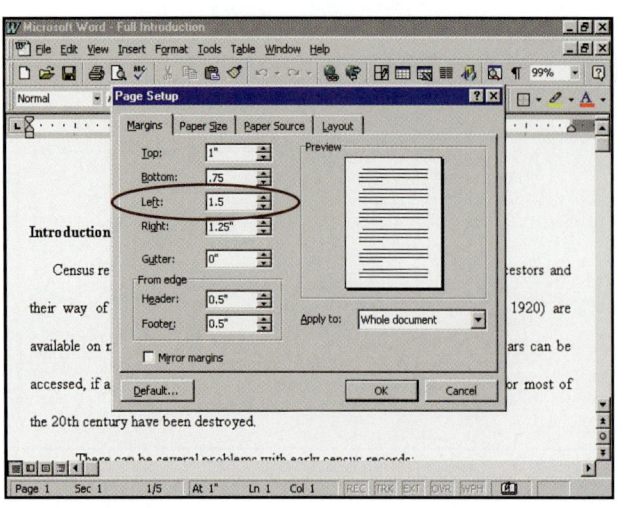

5 Press Tab to move to the **Left** margin. Type in **1.5**, which leaves enough room to bind the final document.

Learn Word 97, Second Edition

6 Press **Tab** to move to the **Right** margin. Type in **.75**. The right margin is now .75 inches. Make sure that the **Apply to** drop-down menu says **Whole document**.

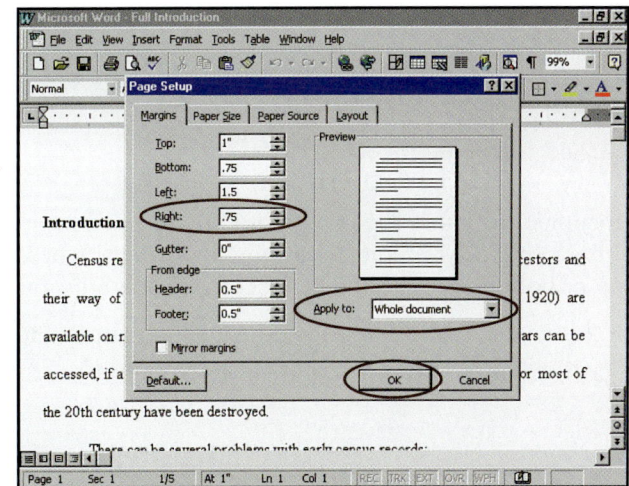

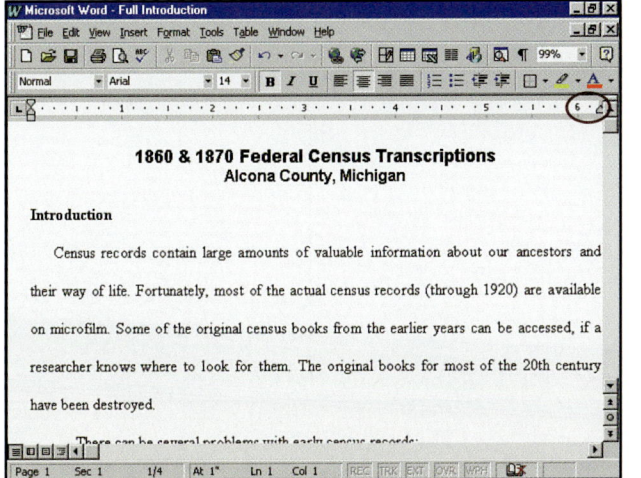

7 Click **OK**. Notice that the document is now 6.25 inches wide.

Lesson 4: Formatting a Document

Task 2

Inserting Page Numbers

Why would I do this?

Documents of more than two pages usually need page numbers. Page numbers help keep loose pages in order and provide easy reference for long documents. Word gives you a way to automatically insert page numbers at the top or bottom of a document. These numbers adjust themselves as necessary when you add or delete text.

In this task, you learn how to add page numbers to the document footer.

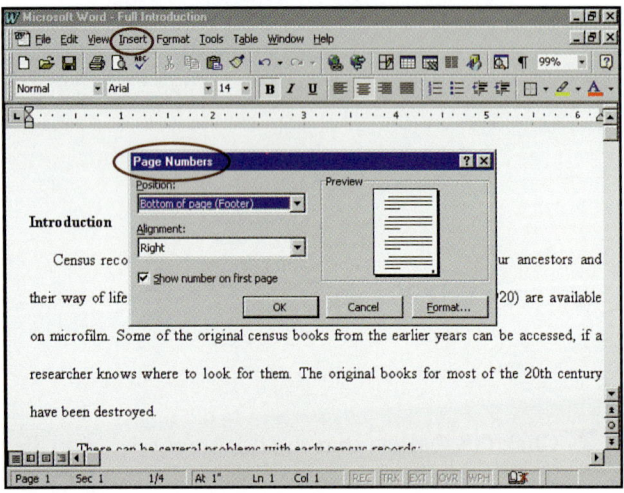

1 With your **Full Introduction** file active, choose **Insert**, **Page Numbers** from the menu. The **Page Numbers** dialog box is displayed.

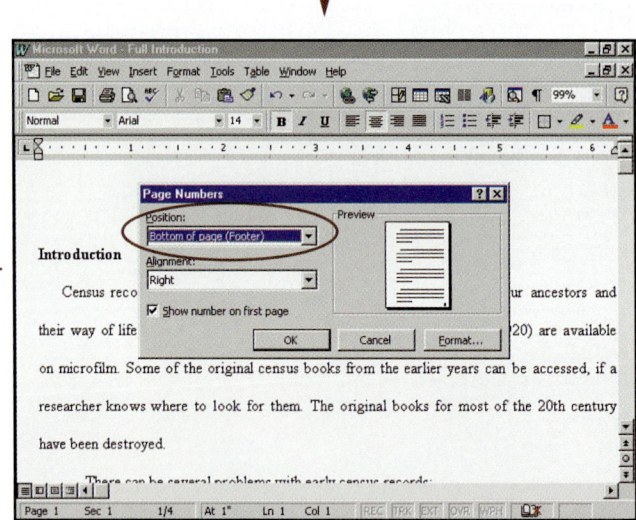

2 If necessary, select **Bottom of page (Footer)** from the **Position** drop-down menu. This places the page number at the bottom of each page.

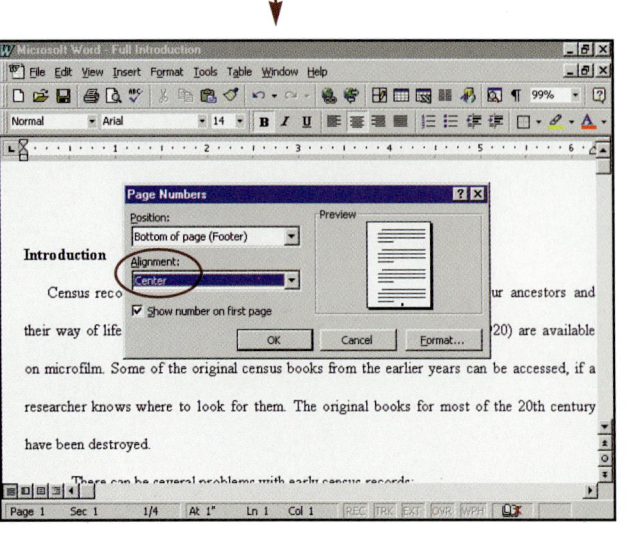

3 Select **Center** from the **Alignment** drop-down menu.

In Depth: You can center the page numbers or align them on the right or left side of the page. The other two options in the drop-down menu, inside and outside, refer to documents formatted for back-to-back printing.

4 Click the **Show number on first page** check box to turn on the check mark if necessary. This leaves the page number on the first page.

> **In Depth:** If you plan to add other text to the header or footer, add that text before you elect to turn off the page number on the first page. Otherwise, you end up with the header or footer text on the first page only and the page numbers on every page but the first. Therefore, make certain a check mark is in the **Show number on first page** check box in this dialog box. Later, you can elect to turn off the header and footer on the first page and both the page number and other text will not show.

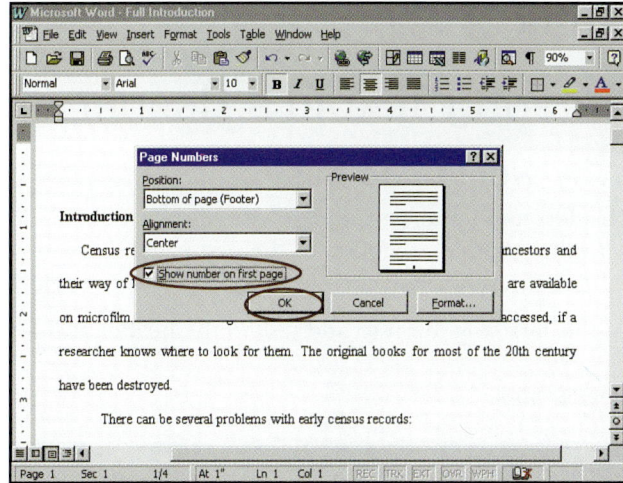

The top edge of the page is wider.

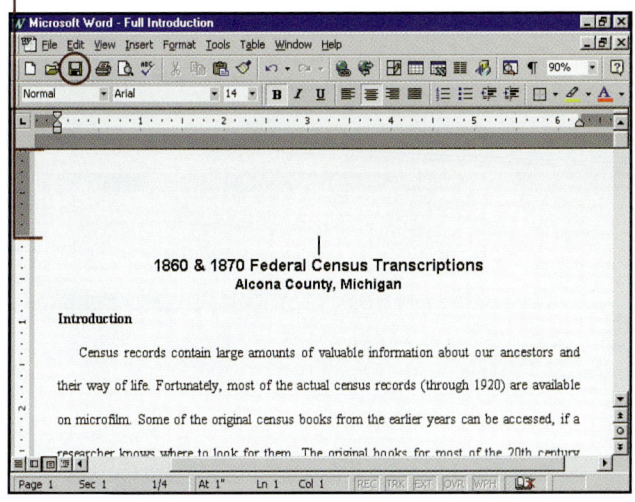

5 Click **OK**. The view of your document changes to the Page Layout view. Click the **Save** button to save your work.

> **In Depth:** The Page Layout view shows you the position of the document elements on the page. The edges of the page are displayed, and the document looks like it will when it is printed.

Lesson 4: Formatting a Document   79

Task 3

Entering Text in a Header or Footer

Why would I do this?

Headers and footers are designed to display information that needs to be shown on every page of a document, with the possible exception of the first page. You can add text to the header and footer areas to identify your document, its author, the current version, and other relevant information.

In this task, you learn to add text to the header and footer areas.

Header area

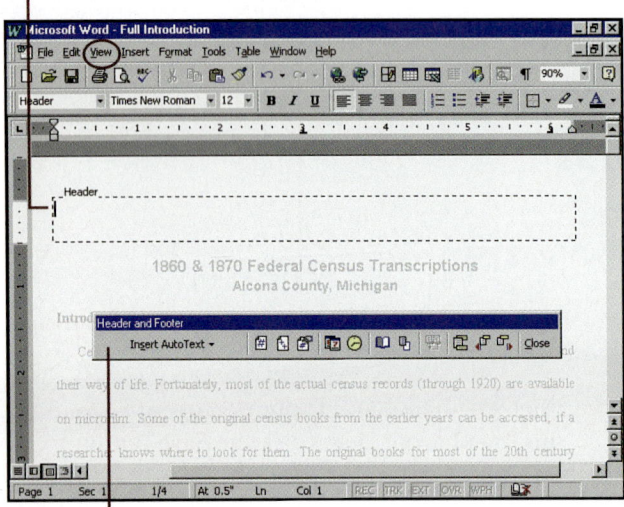

Header and Footer toolbar

1 With your **Full Introduction** file active, choose **View**, **Header and Footer** from the menu. The Header area is displayed, with the document text shown in light gray in the background. The Header and Footer toolbar is also displayed.

2 Type **Introduction** at the left edge of the Header area.

Switch Between Header and Footer button

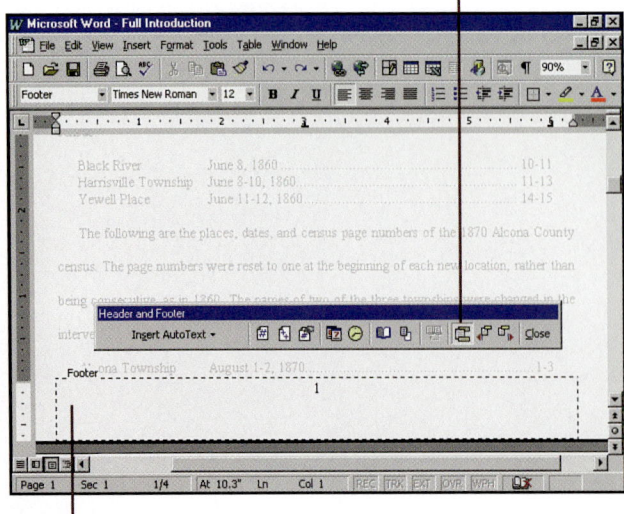

Footer area

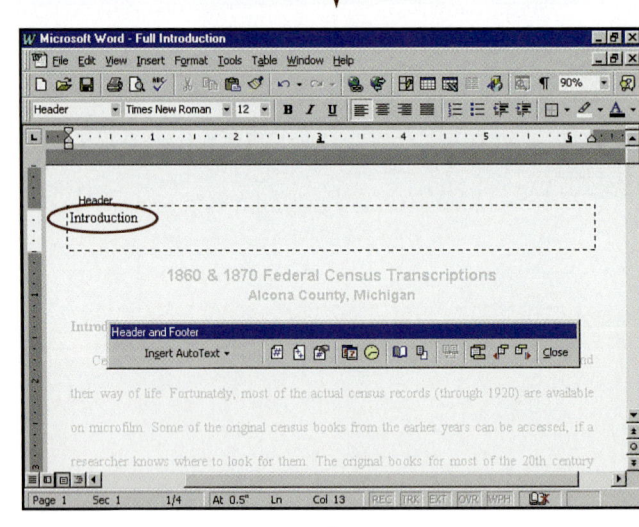

3 Click the **Switch Between Header and Footer** button in the Header and Footer toolbar. This takes you to the Footer area at the bottom of the page.

4 Type **Alcona Transcription** at the left edge of the Footer area.

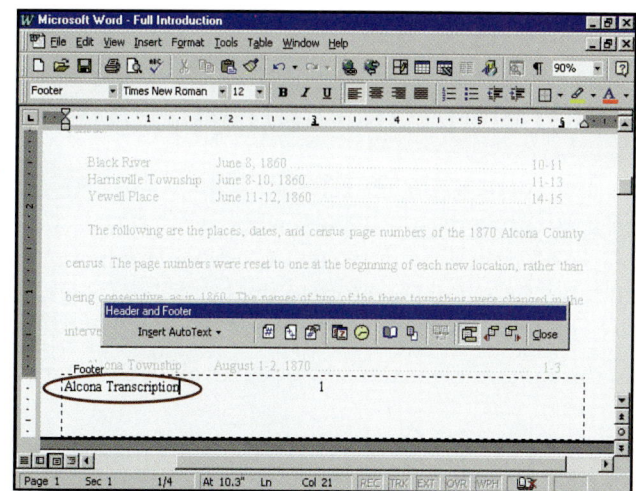

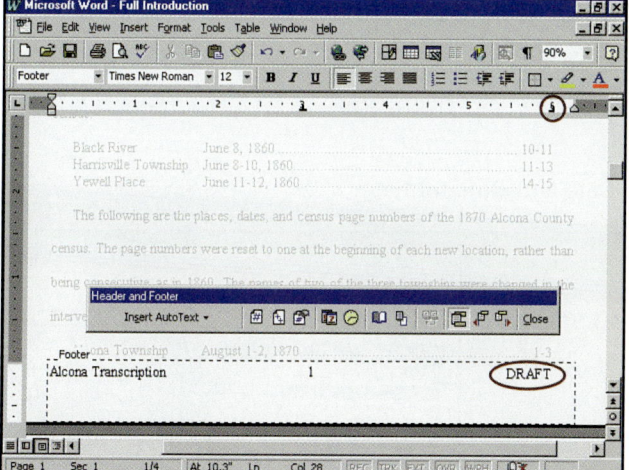

5 Press Tab twice to move to the right tab at the right edge of the Footer area. Type **DRAFT**. Leave the insertion point after the word **DRAFT** for the next task.

> **In Depth:** Notice that the page number you added earlier is showing in the page footer. This number could also be added by using the page footer options showing on the toolbar.

Lesson 4: Formatting a Document

Task 4

Inserting the Date into the Header or Footer

Why would I do this?

In many cases, documents that you work on are revised several times, often by more than one person. More than one version of a document may be around at the same time. It is easy to tell when a document was revised if you add the current date feature to the header or footer. With this feature, the current date appears on every page of the document whenever you make a revision and print it out.

In this task, you learn to add a date to all of the pages of your document.

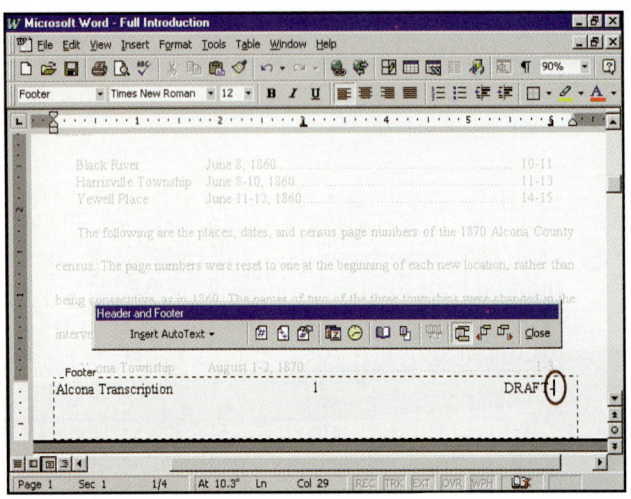

1 With the insertion point at the right of the word **DRAFT** in the **Page Footer** of your **Full Introduction** file, add a dash (-). You will add a date to show when the draft copy of your document is printed.

2 Select **Insert**, **Date and Time** from the menu. The **Date and Time** dialog box is displayed. This dialog box gives you formats for adding the current date, the current time, or both.

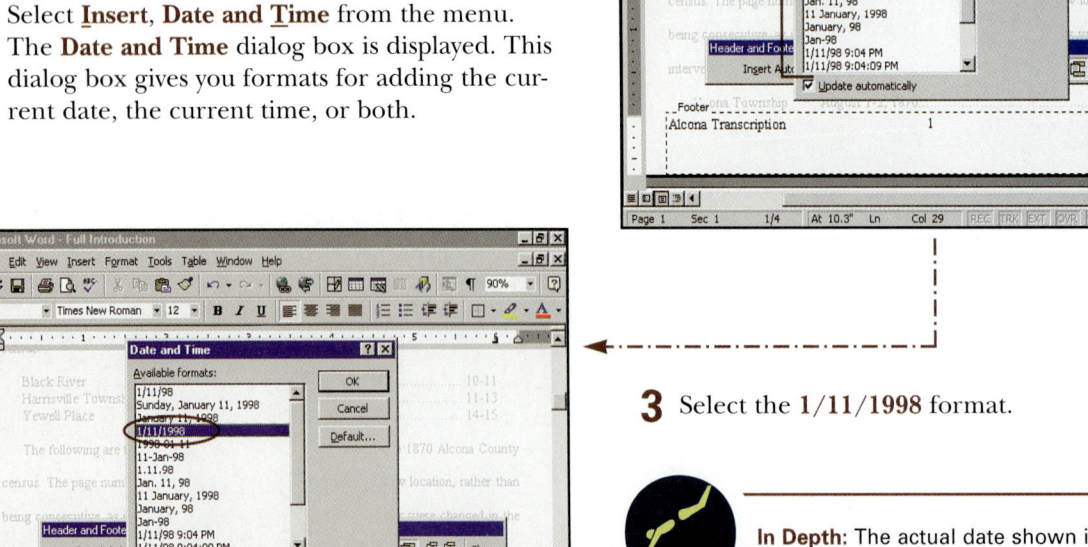

3 Select the **1/11/1998** format.

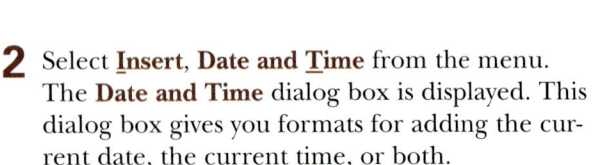

In Depth: The actual date shown in your dialog box is the date on which you are working on this task. By looking at the date in the figure, you can tell when this lesson was written, in much the same way the date you are adding to the footer tells you when your draft copy was written.

82 Learn Word 97, Second Edition

4 Click the **Update automatically** option box to turn on the check mark if necessary. This inserts the current date every time you print the document.

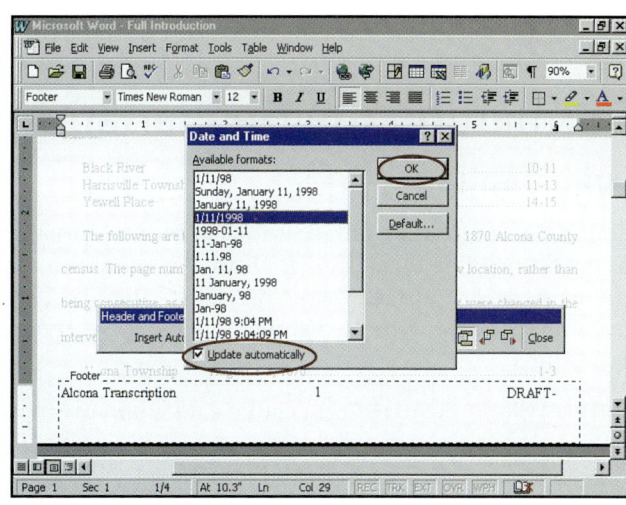

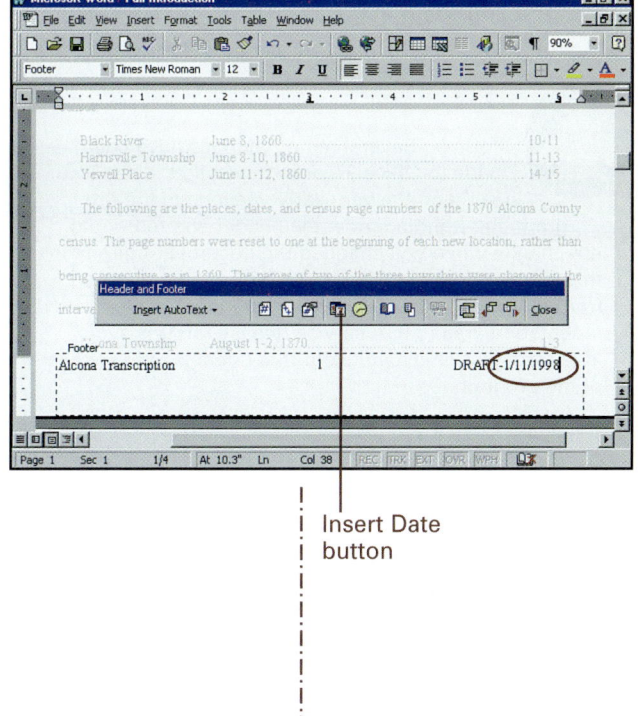

Insert Date button

5 Click **OK**. The date is inserted after the word **DRAFT** in the Footer area.

> **In Depth:** You can also add a date by clicking the **Insert Date** button on the Header and Footer toolbar. Using the **Insert, Date and Time** option from the menu enables you to select the formatting you prefer for your date.

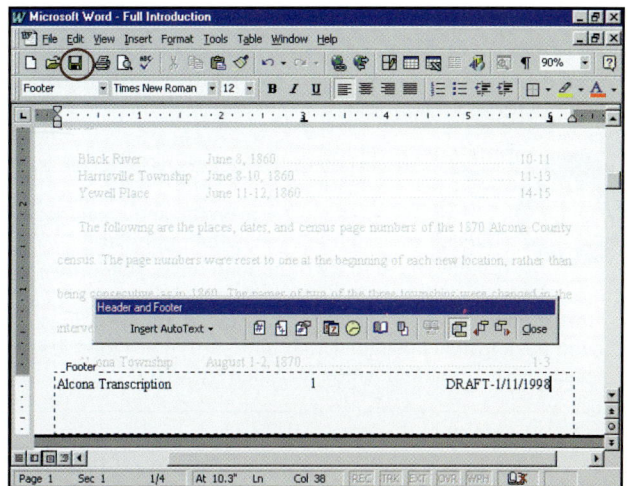

6 Click the **Save** button to save the changes to your document. Stay in the Footer area for the next task.

Lesson 4: Formatting a Document 83

Task 5

Formatting the Header and Footer

Why would I do this?

You may want to use a different format for the information in the header and footer than you used in the text. Many of the same formatting tools that work on the regular text in your document also work in the header and footer areas. For instance, you can change the font, font size, emphasis, or alignment of selected text. You can even use page setup tools. Therefore, you have a great deal of flexibility when you are working with header and footer text.

In this task, you learn how to center and emphasize text and adjust the tabs in the header and footer.

Right indent marker

Right tab marker

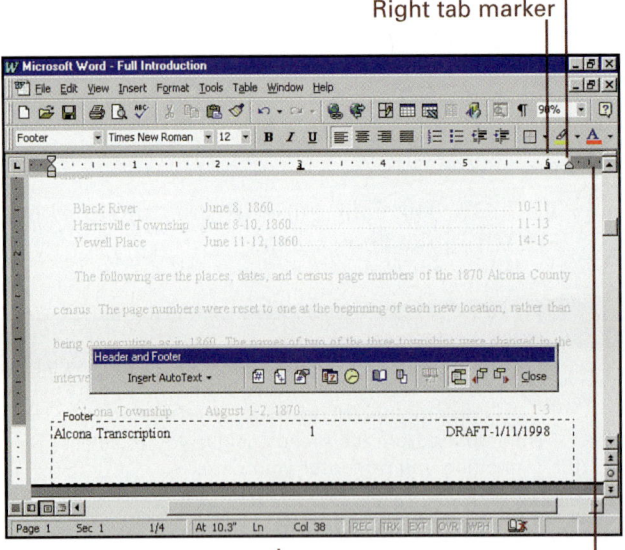

Right margin of document

1 Make sure the insertion point is to the right of the date in the Footer area. Notice that the right tab is still at the 6-inch mark, while the right indent and right margin are at 6.25 inches.

Pothole: Several minor changes have been made to Office 97 since it was first introduced. In some of the very early versions of the program, the right indent in the header and footer did not change when you changed the document margin. If this is true of your version, select **Format**, **Paragraph** from the menu and change the right indent in the Indentation area to 0. A service release (SR1) is available from www.microsoft.com that updates old versions of the program.

2 Click the right tab at the 6-inch mark, drag it to the **6 1/4**-inch mark, and release the mouse button. The date now lines up with the right margin of the document.

Pothole: The tab marker is small, and it can be difficult to drag it to exactly the right place. You may have to try more than once. This is an important skill to master because both tabs and indent markers on the ruler can be moved this way. If you have trouble, use the Undo button to return the tab back to the original position and then try again!

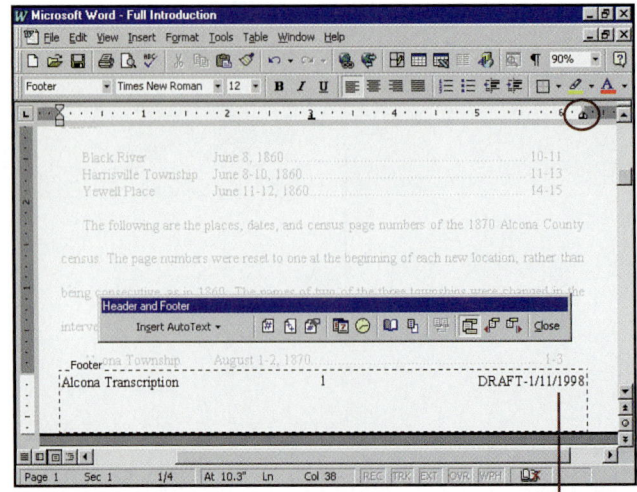

The date is aligned with the right margin of the document.

3 Click the **Switch Between Header and Footer** button in the Header and Footer toolbar. This takes you back to the Header area at the top of the first page. Notice that the right tab marker for the header is at the 6-inch position.

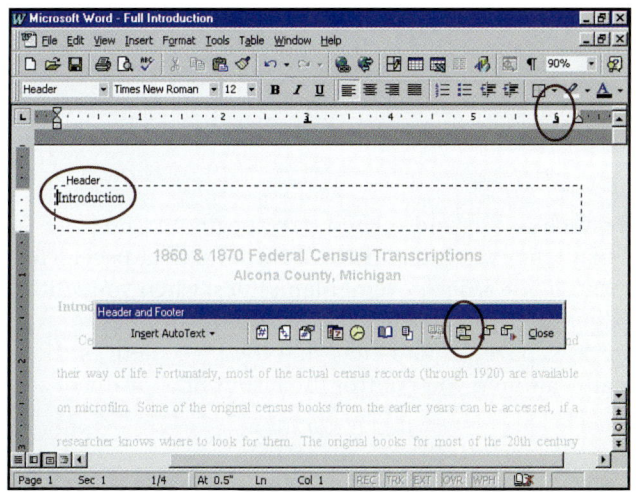

4 Click the **Center** button on the Formatting toolbar. The word **Introduction** is centered on the 6.25-inch width of the document.

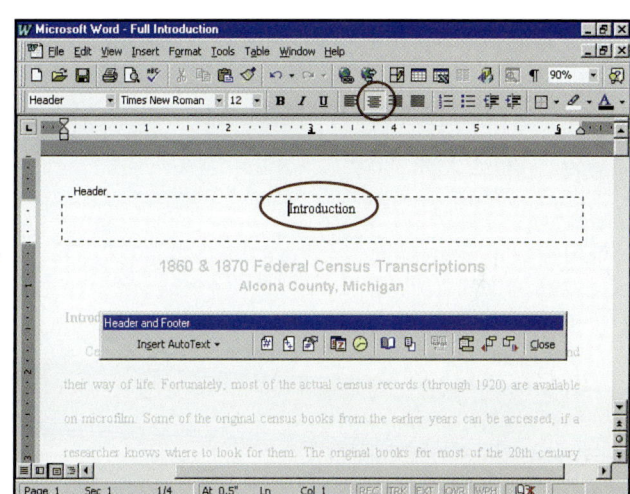

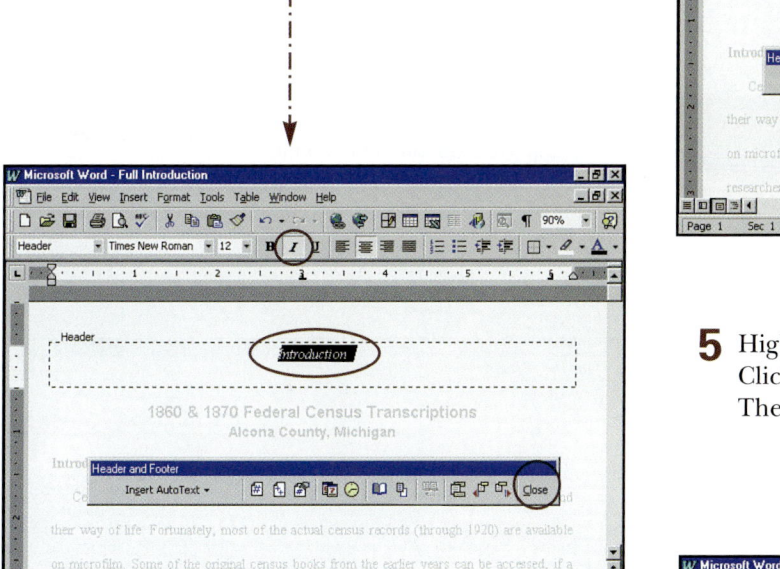

5 Highlight the word **Introduction** in the header. Click the **Italic** button in the Formatting toolbar. The word is italicized.

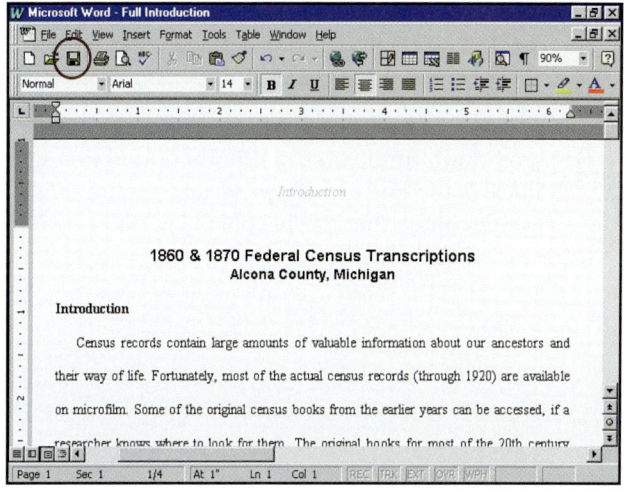

6 Click the **Close** button on the Header and Footer toolbar to return to the document. Click **Save** to save your changes.

Lesson 4: Formatting a Document 85

Task 6

Inserting Page Breaks

Why would I do this?

You will often find that elements that should be kept together, such as lists and related data, begin on one page and finish on the next. You may be tempted to insert several blank lines to force the text onto the next page. This practice can cause problems when you make changes to the text. If you insert several blank lines, when you edit the text you can end up with blank lines in the middle of a page. Inserting a page break is an effective way to resolve this problem. A page break enables you to edit the previous page without changing the placement of the text on the page following the break. Careful use of page breaks can help you control the layout of your document when it is printed.

In this task, you learn to insert a page break into a document.

1 With your **Full Introduction** file active, click the **Normal View** button to return to the Normal view.

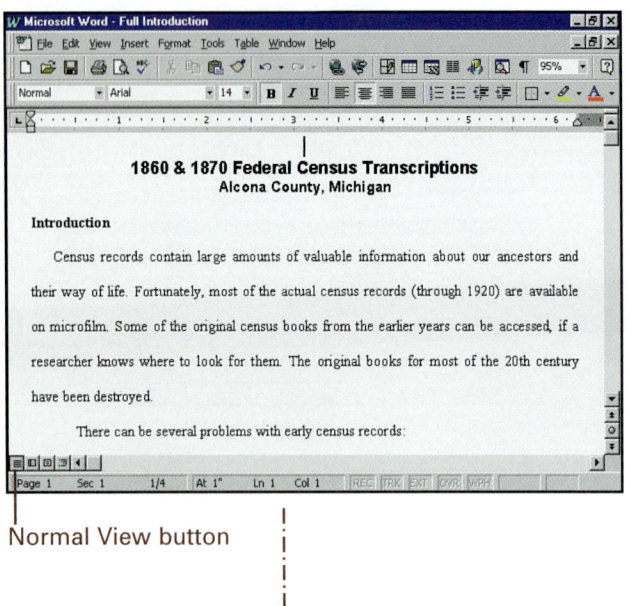

Normal View button

Pothole: If you accidentally click the **Online Layout View**, the View buttons are not displayed. You can change to any view by using the **V**iew option in the menu.

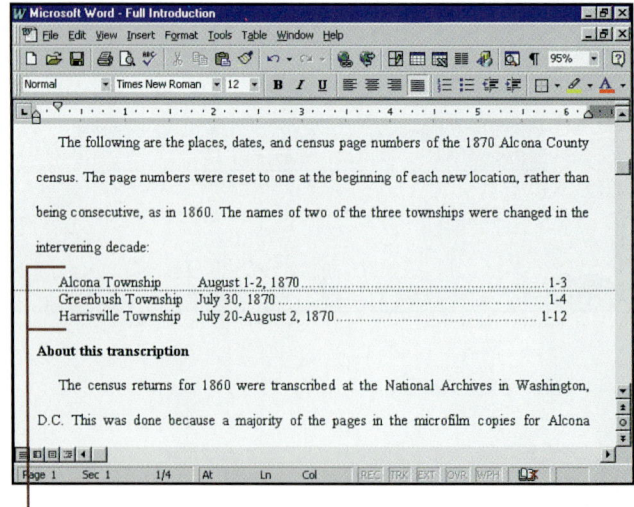

The list is split between two pages.

2 Scroll down until you can see the dotted line that indicates the bottom of page 1 and the top of page 2. Notice that the list of census dates is split between the two pages.

3 Place the insertion point to the left of the first item of the list, which begins with the words **Alcona Township**.

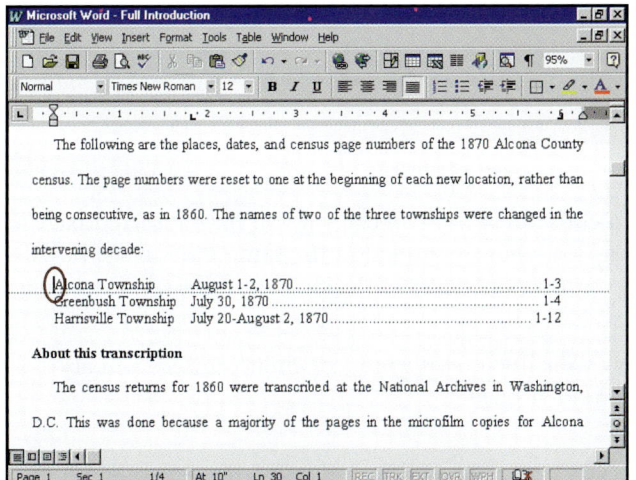

4 Select **Insert**, **Break** from the menu. The **Break** dialog box is displayed.

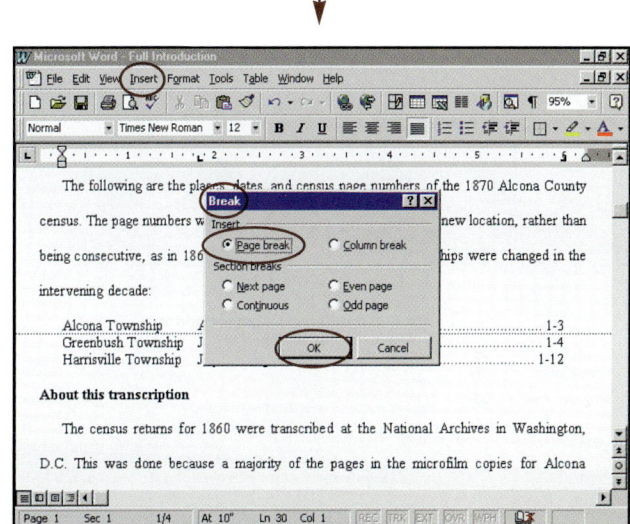

5 Select **Page break** from the **Insert** area of the dialog box if necessary. Then click **OK**. Notice that the page break dotted line now contains **Page Break** in the middle, which lets you know that the break has been inserted.

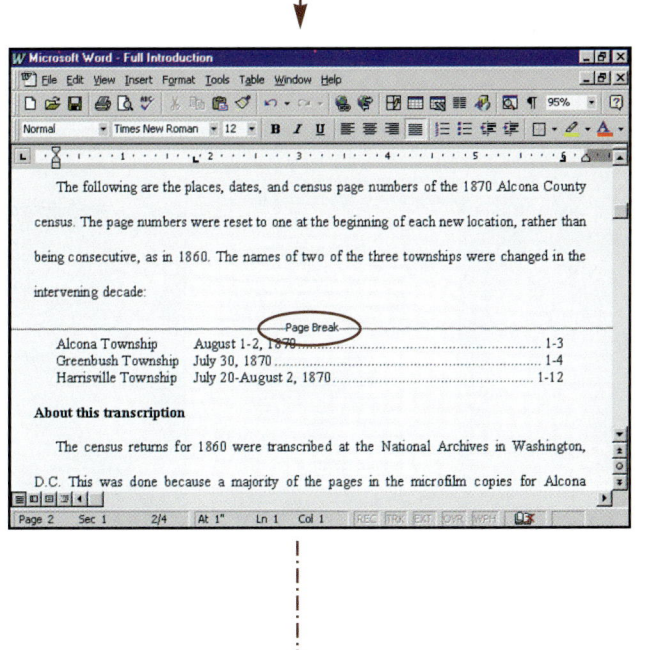

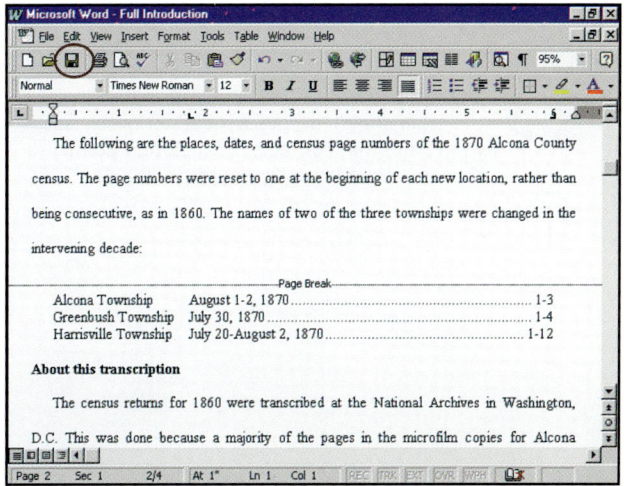

Quick Tip: You can also add a page break at the insertion point by holding down Ctrl and pressing Enter.

6 Click the **Save** button to save your changes.

Lesson 4: Formatting a Document   87

Task 7
Using Print Preview

Why would I do this?

Inserting or removing text on one page can have unexpected consequences, especially if you have inserted page breaks. Word gives you an easy way to look at one or more pages of your document at the same time to see how the text flows from one page to the next. *Print Preview* shows you what the layout of each page will look like when it is printed.

In this task, you learn to use Print Preview to examine the way your document will look when printed. You also learn how to turn off the header and footer information on the first page.

1 With your **Full Introduction** file active, scroll to the top of the document.

Print Preview button

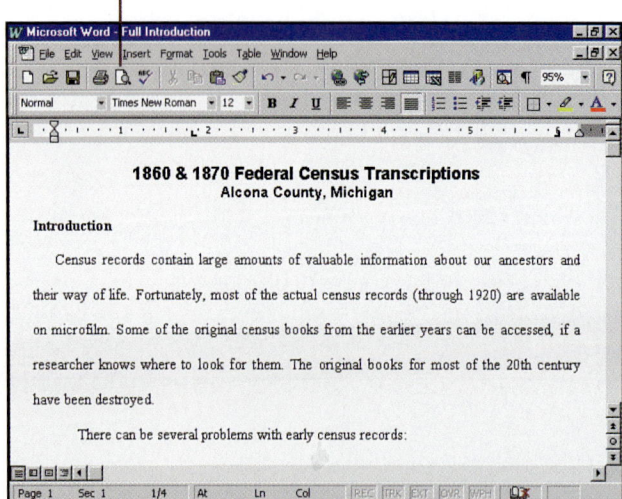

2 Click the **Print Preview** button. The full first page of the document is displayed. The text may be difficult or impossible to read, depending on your monitor, but the layout of the page is clearly displayed. If more than one page is displayed, click on the **First Page** button on the toolbar.

First Page button

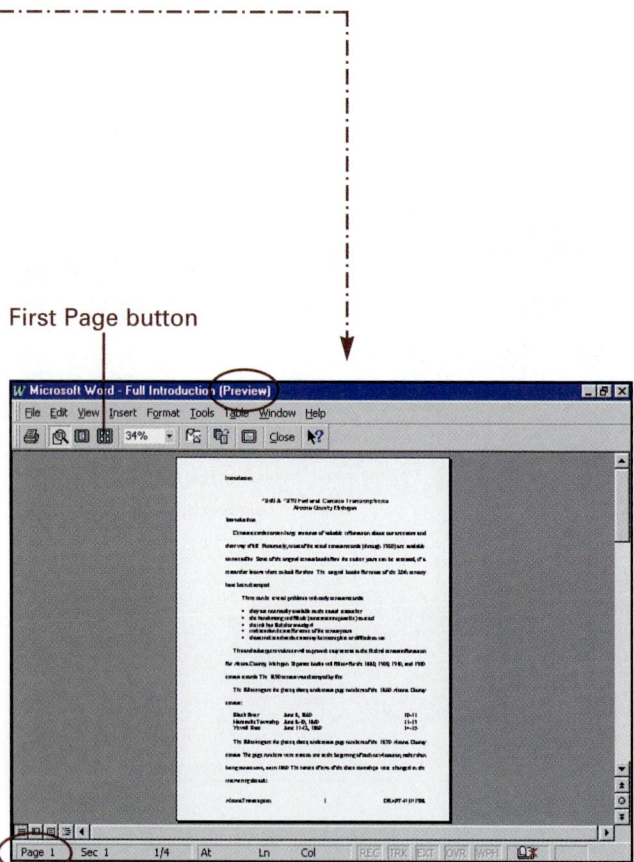

In Depth: The Print Preview button displays the page shown on the screen, not necessarily the page that contains the insertion point. Also, you can select **Print Preview** from the **File** menu.

88 Learn Word 97, Second Edition

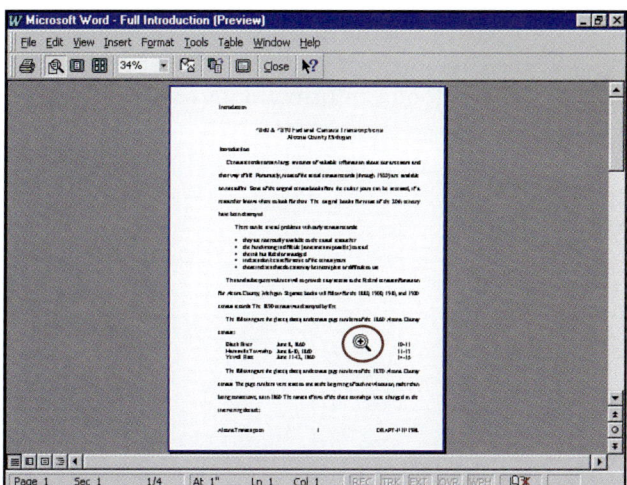

3 Click the pointer anywhere on the document. The pointer changes to a magnifying glass with a plus sign (+) in the middle.

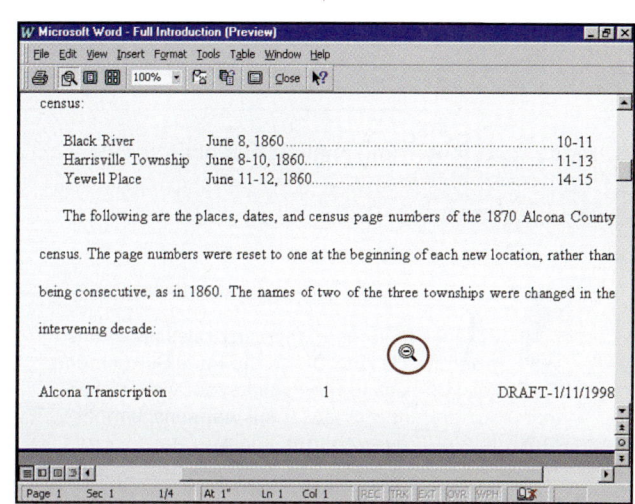

4 Click on the page number at the bottom of the page. You can now read the text at the bottom of the page and the footer information. The magnifying glass pointer now contains a minus sign (-).

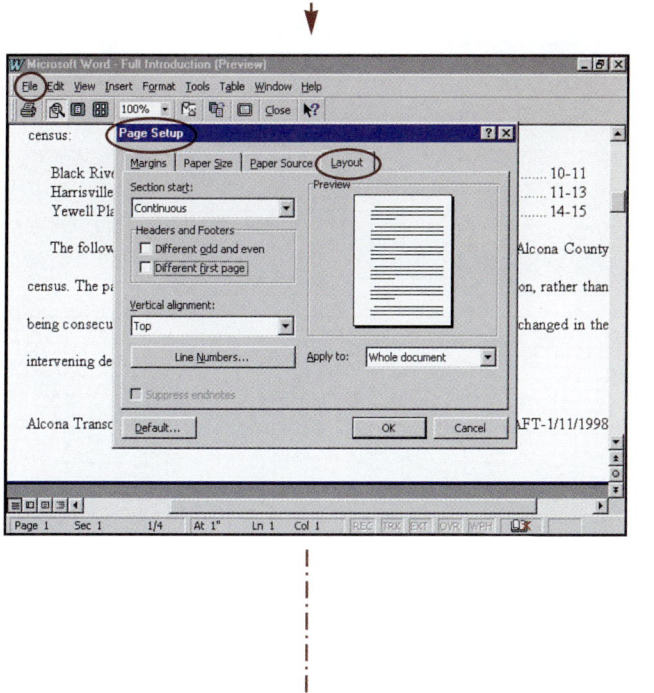

5 This footer information should not appear on the first page. Choose **File**, **Page Setup** and click the **Layout** tab in the **Page Setup** dialog box.

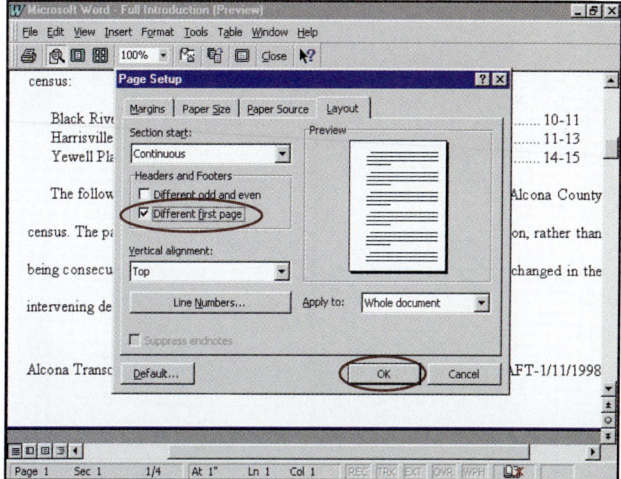

6 Click the **Different first page** option button in the **Headers and Footers** area. This option turns the header and footer information off on the first page of the document.

Lesson 4: Formatting a Document

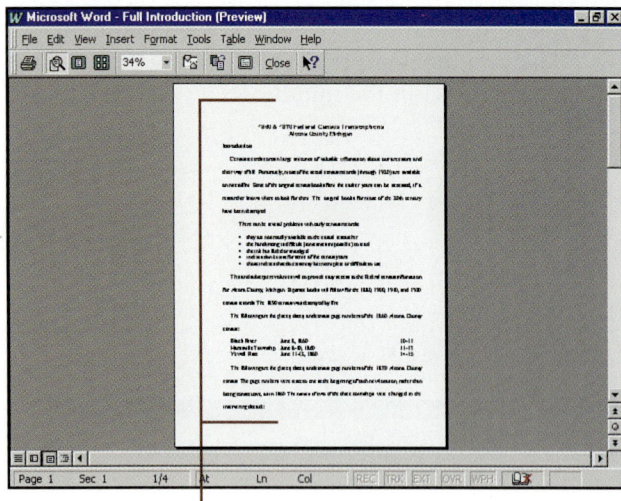

Header and footer information has been removed.

7 Click **OK**. Click the magnifying glass to fit the whole page back on the screen. Notice that no header or footer information is on the first page.

Pothole: In some of the early releases of this program, clicking OK on the Page Setup menu takes you back to the Page Layout view rather than back to Print Preview. If this happens, simply click on the Print Preview button again.

8 Click the **Multiple Pages** button on the Print Preview toolbar and move the pointer to one row and two pages.

Multiple Pages button

The one row, two pages option is selected.

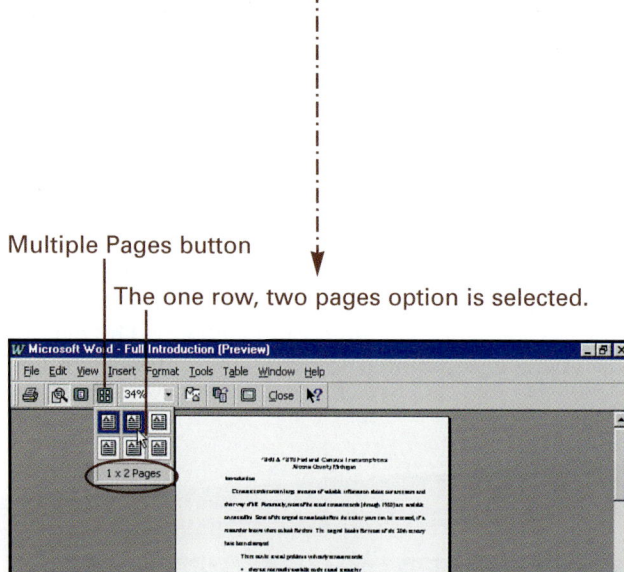

Pages 1 and 2 are displayed.

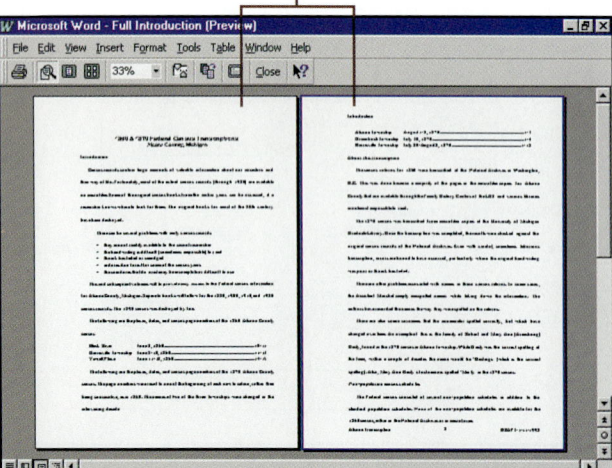

9 Click the **1x2 pages** option. Two full pages (pages 1 and 2) are displayed.

90 Learn Word 97, Second Edition

10 Click the **Next Page** button at the bottom of the vertical scroll bar. Pages 3 and 4 are displayed.

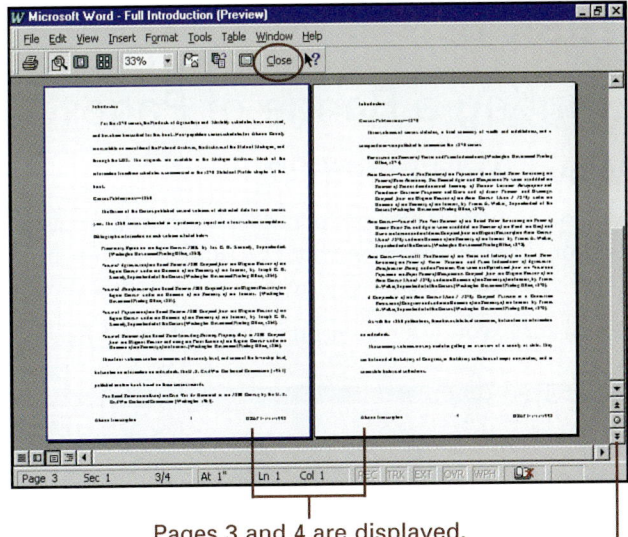

Pages 3 and 4 are displayed.

Next Page button

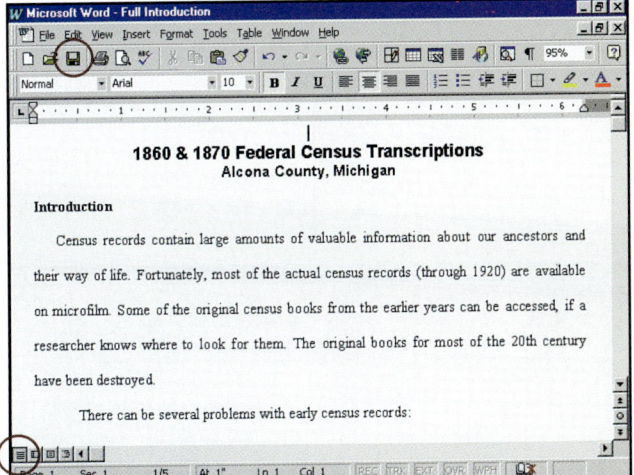

11 Click the **Close** button on the Print Preview toolbar and then click the **Normal View** button. Click the **Save** button to save your work.

> **In Depth:** It is a matter of personal preference whether you work in Page Layout view or Normal view. Either view can be used to enter and edit text. Some formatting, such as headers and footers, automatically changes your document to the Page Layout view. You can change views to suit your personal preference.

Lesson 4: Formatting a Document

Task 8

Printing a Range of Pages

Why would I do this?

When you have created a long document, you occasionally want to print out just a few pages to take with you to edit or to share with someone else. Rather than printing the entire document, you can print just the part that you need to review. This saves printer resources and time.

In this task, you learn to print a range of pages from a document.

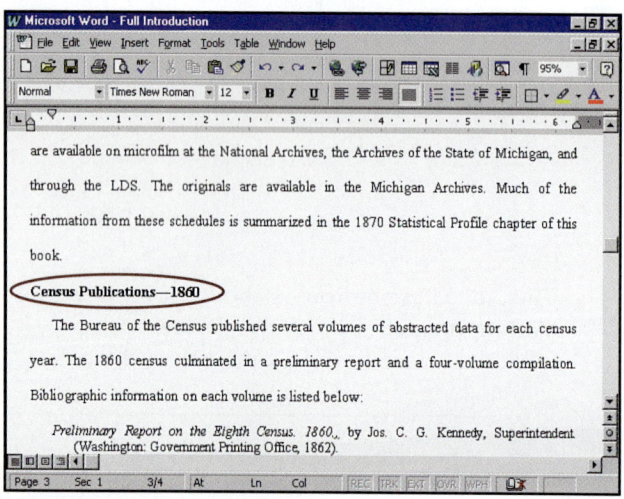

1 With your **Full Introduction** file active, scroll down to the subtitle **Census Publications—1860**, which is about a third of the way down page 3.

2 Place the insertion point to the left of the subtitle. You want to insert a page break at this point so that the bibliographic material is printed together.

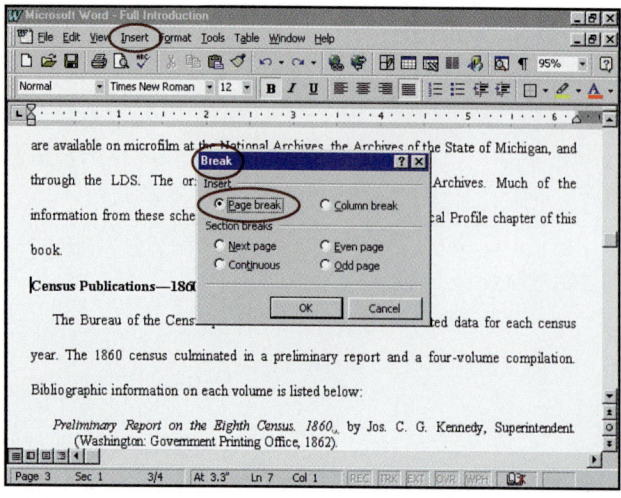

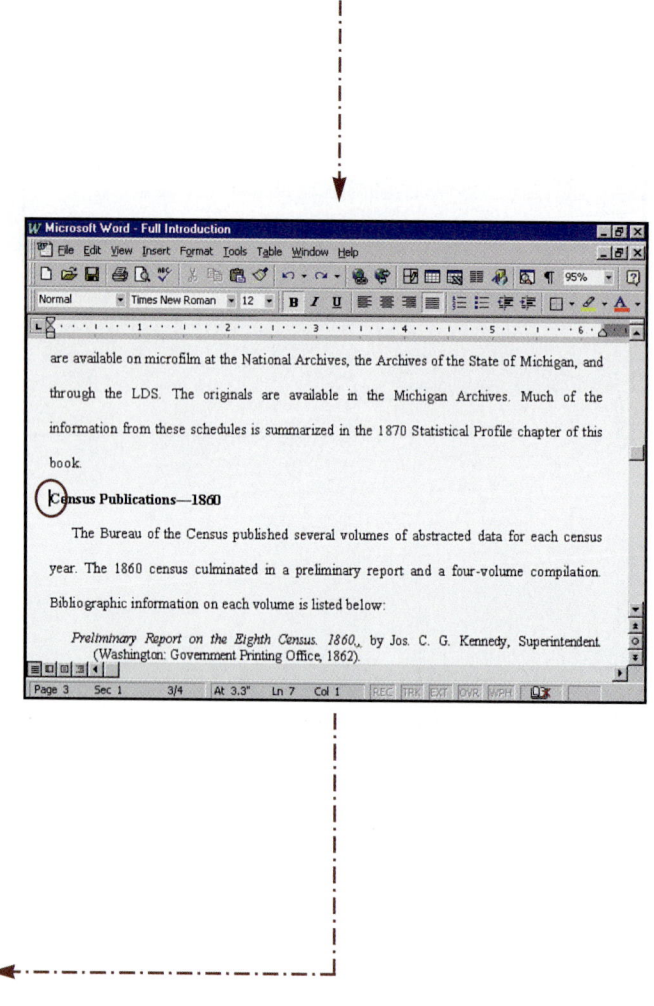

3 Select **Insert**, **Break** from the menu. The **Break** dialog box is displayed, with the **Page break** option selected by default.

92 Learn Word 97, Second Edition

4 Click **OK** to insert a page break. The **Page Break** dotted line shows where the break is inserted.

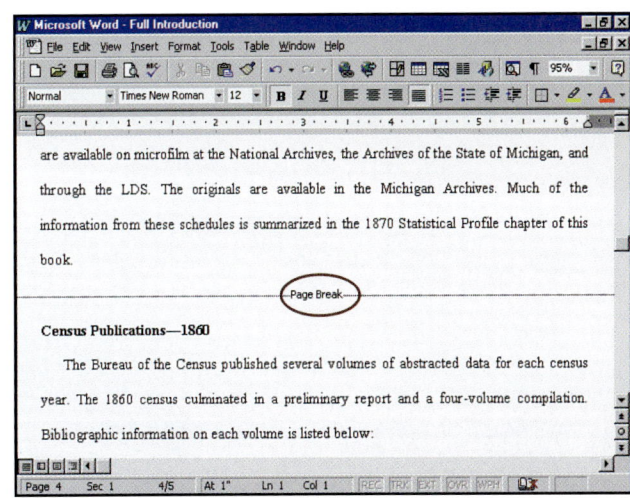

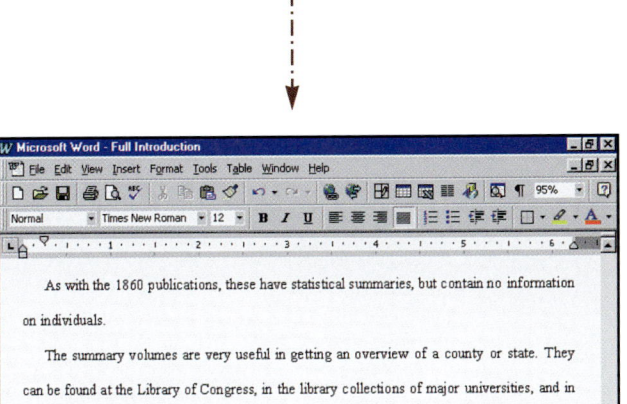

5 Scroll to the bottom of the document. Place the insertion point at the end of the last line of text, press ↵Enter, and then type in your name.

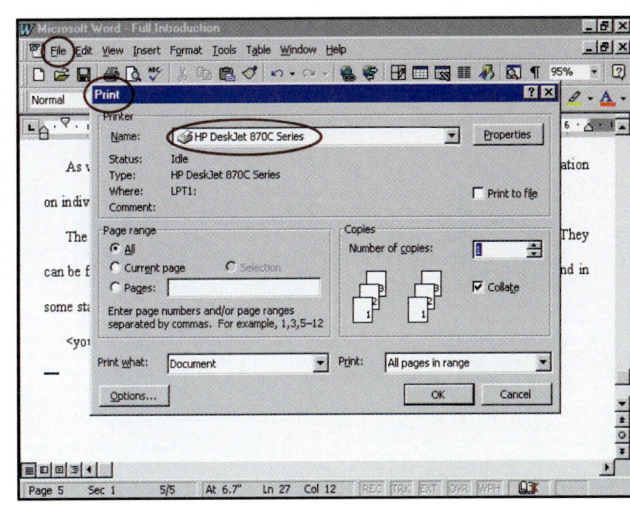

6 Choose **File**, **Print** from the menu. The **Print** dialog box is displayed. Make sure the printer you want to print to is turned on and connected.

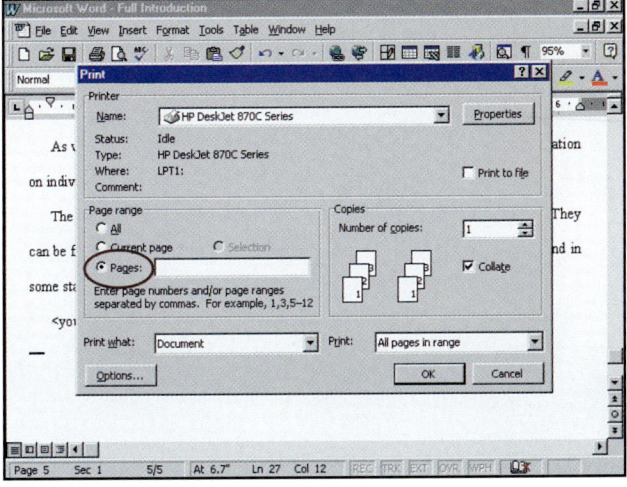

7 Click the **Pages** option button in the **Page range** area.

Lesson 4: Formatting a Document — 93

8 Type **4-5** in the Pages box. This tells the program to just print pages 4 and 5.

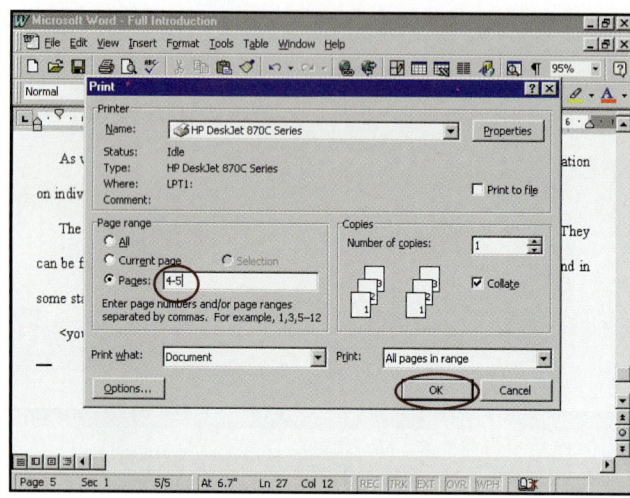

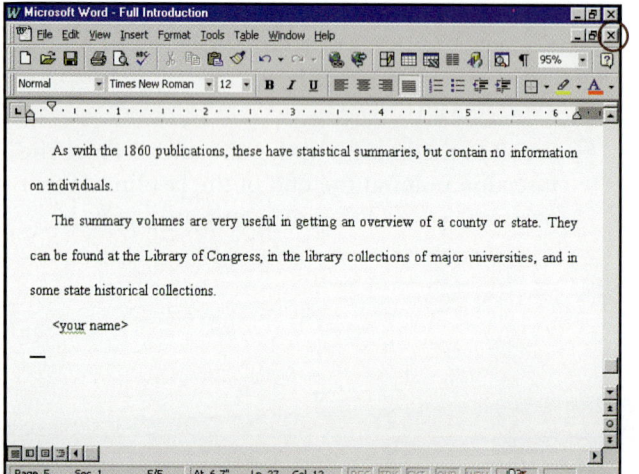

9 Click **OK** to print pages 4 and 5. Save your changes. Click the **Close Window** button to close the document. Exit Word.

Student Exercises

True-False

Circle either T or F.

T F 1. The margins may be set by using the Format option on the menu bar.

T F 2. The header is placed in the top margin.

T F 3. The text in the footer must be the same font as the text in the body of the document.

T F 4. It is possible to enter a special date field into the header that automatically updates to the current date every time the document is used or printed.

T F 5. If a new topic starts near the bottom of a page, it is best to insert several blank lines in front of it to force it to the top of the next page.

T F 6. Print Preview allows you to see several pages at once so that you can see how the text flows from one page to the next.

T F 7. If you only want to print pages 2 and 3 of a document, you can do so using the File, Print, Pages menu option.

T F 8. If you use automatic page numbering, you have to use the Recalculate Page Numbers command when you delete or add enough text to change the previous page numbers.

T F 9. Headers and footers appear at the top and bottom of each page (with the possible exception of the title page).

T F 10. Only one format is available for the automatic date in a header or footer. Dates must be in the dd/mm/yy format.

Identifying Parts of the Word Screen

Refer to the next two figures to identify the numbered parts of the screen. Write the letter of the correct label in the space next to the number.

1. _____
2. _____
3. _____
4. _____
5. _____
6. _____
7. _____
8. _____
9. _____
10. _____

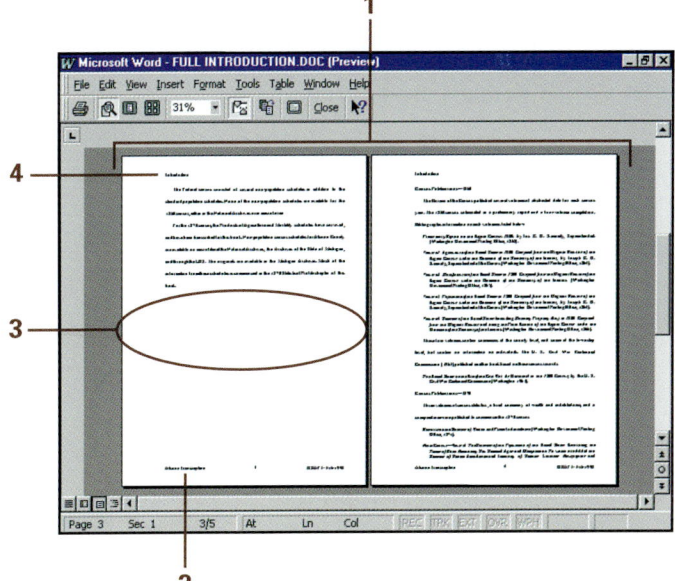

Lesson 4: Formatting a Document 95

A. Footer

B. Print Preview button

C. A page break has been inserted here

D. Automatic page number, centered

E. Header

F. Left alignment

G. Text in header, left aligned

H. Print Preview view

I. Switch Between Header and Footer button

J. Automatically updated date

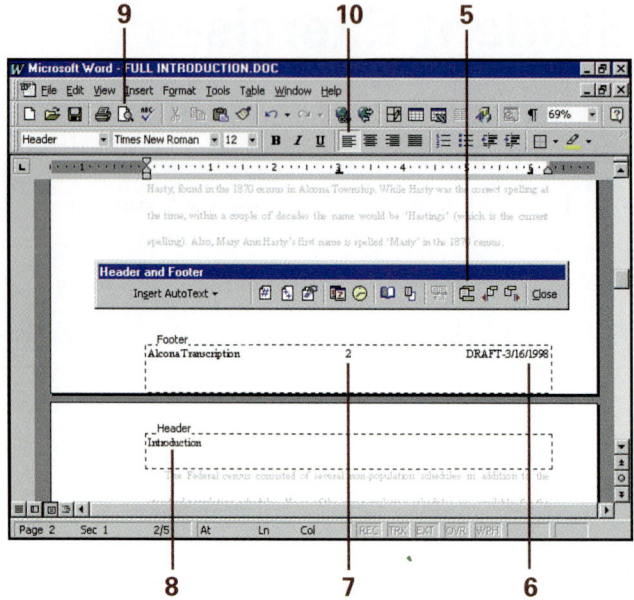

Matching Questions

Match the following statements to the word or phrase from the list at the right. Write the letter of the matching word or phrase in the space provided next to the number.

1. ____ Displays the current date

2. ____ Displays one or more pages as they appear if printed

3. ____ Contains text, page numbers, or dates that automatically print at the bottom of each page

4. ____ Dialog box used to set margins

5. ____ Automatically determines the current page number

6. ____ Contains text, page numbers, or dates that automatically print at the top of each page

7. ____ The white space between the edge of the paper and the text

8. ____ Forces text to the top of the next page

9. ____ Switches the view between the header and the footer even if they are not on the same screen

10. ____ May be used to align text in a header or footer if only one type of alignment is used

A. Automatic page number

B. Header

C. Page break

D. Alignment buttons on the toolbar

E. Footer

F. Switch Between Header and Footer button

G. Automatically updated date

H. Print Preview

I. Margin

J. Insert, Header and Footer

K. Page Setup dialog box

Application Exercises

Exercise 1—Change the Margins in a Document

1. Launch Word. Open **Less0402** from the student files. Save the file as **Distance Education 2**.
2. Select **File**, **Page Setup**.
3. Change the top and bottom margins to 1.0 inch.
4. Change the left margin to 1.50 inches and the right margin to .75 inches. Click **OK**.
5. Leave the document open for use in the next exercise.

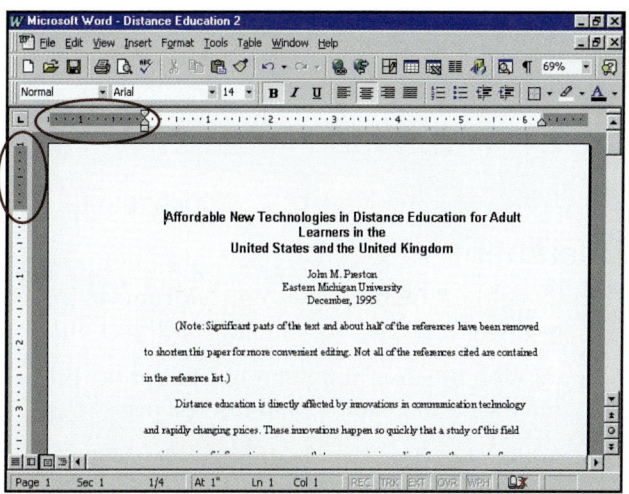

Exercise 2—Insert Page Numbers in a Document

1. Using the **Distance Education 2** document, insert page numbers.
2. Choose **Insert**, **Page Numbers** from the menu.
3. Insert page numbers at the top of the document on the right side. Click **OK**.
4. Leave the document open for use in the next exercise.

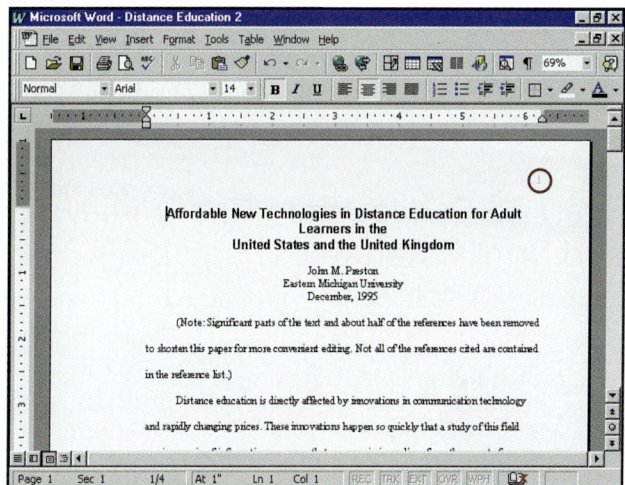

Exercise 3—Add a Header and Footer to a Document

1. Using the **Distance Education 2** document, add information to the header and footer.
2. Select **View**, **Header and Footer** from the menu.
3. In the Header at the left side type: **Affordable New Technologies**.
4. Switch to the footer. Use the **Insert, Date and Time** option from the menu to insert the date at the left side of the footer. Select the **January 16, 1998** format. Make sure that the **Update Automatically** option is deselected. Click **OK**.
5. On the right side of the Footer area, type your name.
6. Select your name and change the font to a style of your choice. Make it bold to add emphasis. If necessary, move the tab marker over so that your name in the footer lines up with the rest of the text at the .75-inch margin.

Lesson 4: Formatting a Document

7. Choose **File**, **Page Setup** and click the **Layout** tab in the Page Setup dialog box. Click the check box next to **Different First Page**. Leave the header and footer on the first page empty.

8. Save your work and leave the document open for use in the next exercise.

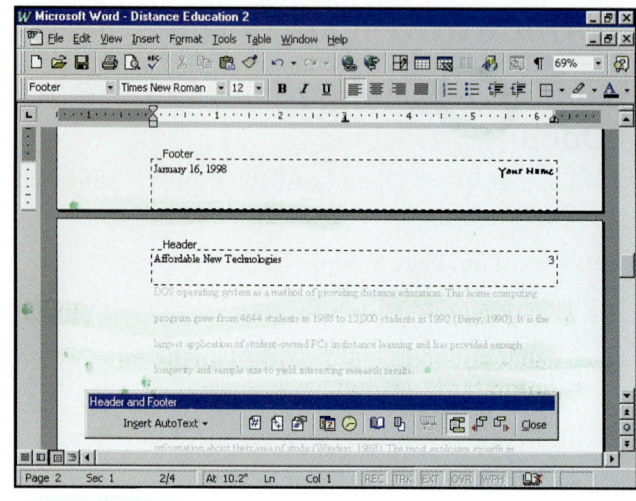

Exercise 4—Insert Page Breaks in a Document

1. Using the **Distance Education 2** document, insert page breaks at the beginning of each section.

2. Position the insertion point in front of the title **Interactive Technology** and insert a page break.

3. Add a page break so that the subtitle **Computer based conferencing** is on the same page as the rest of the text that follows that topic.

4. If necessary, add a page break in front of the **Conclusion** and **Reference List** sections of the paper. The paper should now have five pages.

5. Leave the document open for use in the next exercise.

Exercise 5—Use the Print Preview and Print a Range of Pages

1. Click on **Print Preview** to see how the document looks.

2. Switch to multiple pages if necessary.

3. Verify that the header and footer areas on the first page are empty and that the remaining four pages each show information in their headers and footers.

4. Make sure that each page begins with the title of a new section.

5. Go to the **Print** dialog box and select pages 1 and 2 to print.

6. Save your work and close the document. Exit from Word.

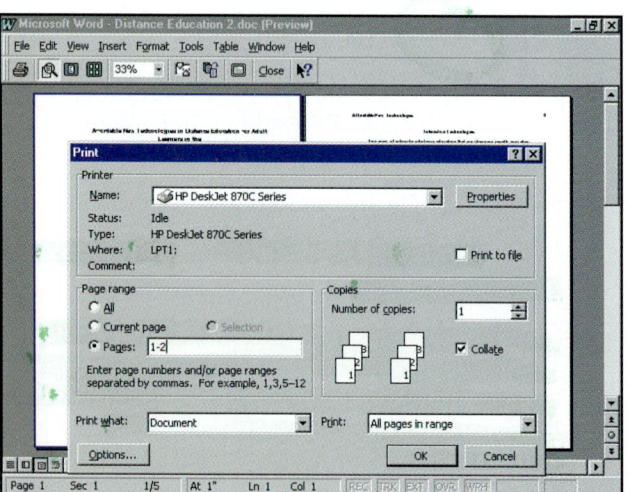

Lesson 5
Working with Tables

Task 1: Inserting a Table
Task 2: Entering Information into a Table
Task 3: Adding Rows to a Table
Task 4: Formatting Text in a Table
Task 5: Aligning Text in a Table
Task 6: Formatting Borders and Shading in a Table
Task 7: Using the AutoFormat and AutoFit Tools
Task 8: Centering a Table

Introduction

Tables are lists of information set up in a column-and-row format, somewhat like the layout of a spreadsheet. Each intersection of an individual row and column in a table is called a *cell*. The cells can contain text, numbers, or graphics.

Many formatting tools are available for tables. You can line up text in columns on the right or left sides or in the middle of cells. You can use all of the emphasis tools, such as bold, italic, and underline, on any text. You can also add borders and shading to the table. This formatting can be done on one or more cells at a time or on the whole table at once.

Tables can be used for many purposes. They can display numeric information, text, graphics, or a combination of the three. They are excellent for two-column tasks, such as résumés, in which the topic is on the left and the details are on the right.

In this lesson, you learn how to set up and edit a table. You also learn how to use a very powerful automatic formatting tool.

Visual Summary

By the time you have completed this lesson, you will have created a document that looks like this:

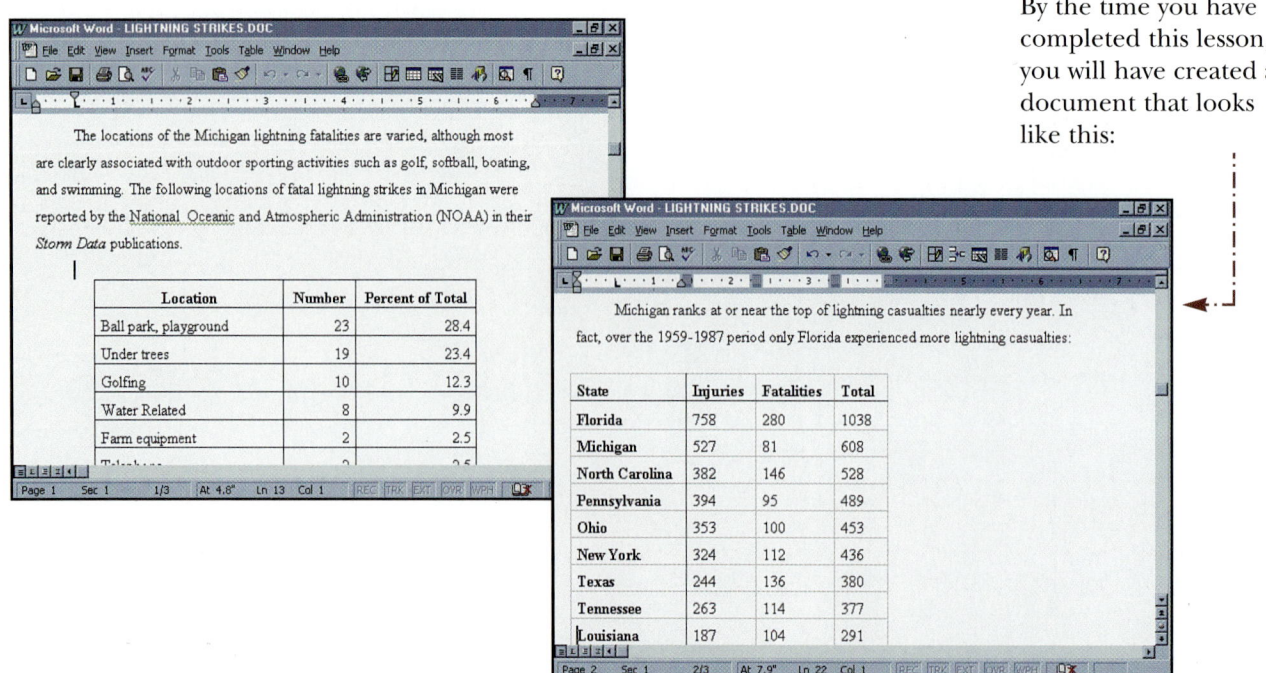

Task 1

Inserting a Table

Why would I do this?

Adding a table to a document is only one method of displaying lists of information in columns and rows. You can use tabs for many of the same functions. Tables are much easier to use than tabs, however, and they are far more powerful and flexible. After you have mastered the use of tables, you will find that you save a great deal of time and end up with a better-looking finished product.

In this task, you learn to insert a table into a document using the Insert Table button.

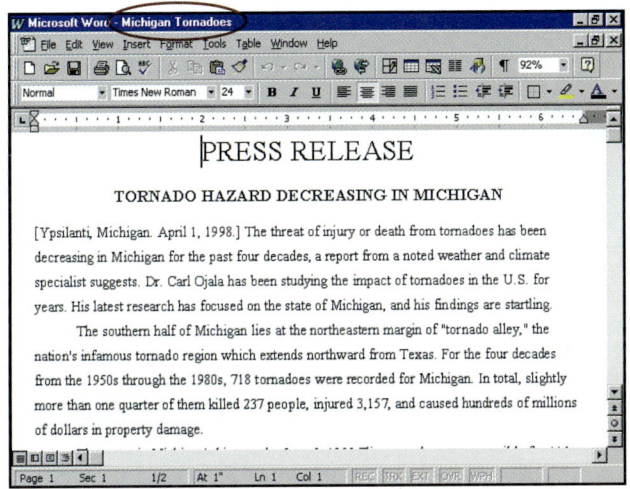

1 Launch Microsoft Word. Open **Less0501** from the student files. Save the file as **Michigan Tornadoes**.

2 Scroll down until you can see the paragraph that begins with the words **In the decades** on the screen. Place the insertion point at the beginning of that paragraph.

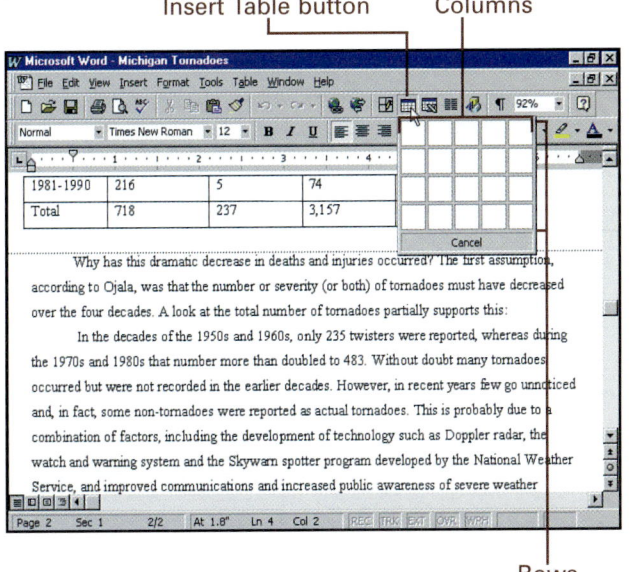

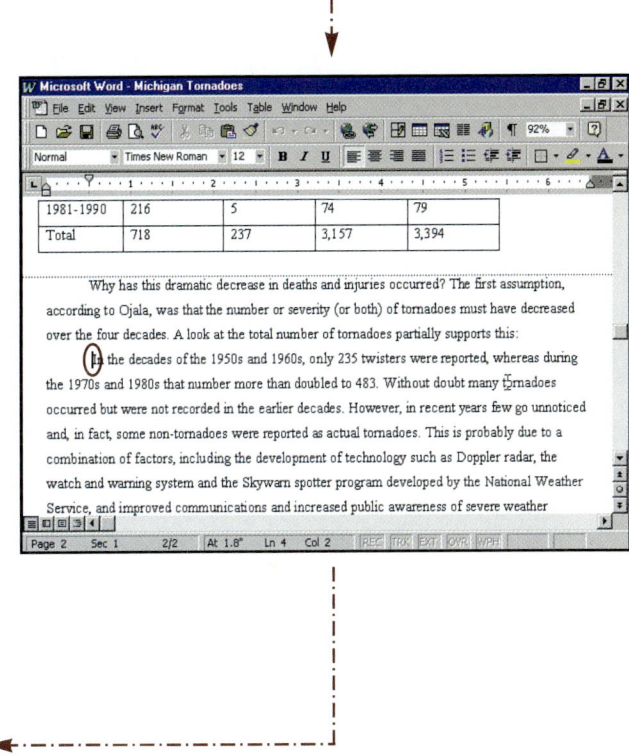

3 Click the **Insert Table** button on the Standard toolbar. A matrix is displayed that enables you to choose the number of rows and columns for your new table.

4 Move the pointer down and to the right until you have highlighted four rows and five columns. The table size appears at the bottom of the matrix.

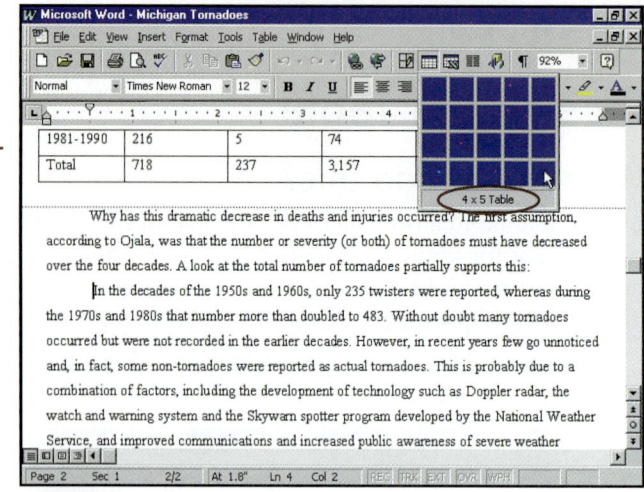

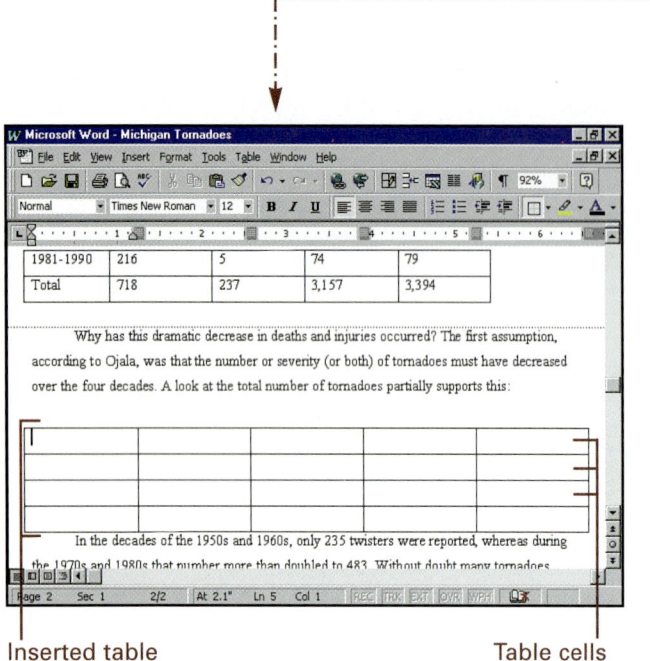

Inserted table   Table cells

In Depth: You can also add tables by using the Table, Insert Table menu command.

5 Click to insert a 4×5 table. The outlines of the table are displayed at the insertion point.

Task 2

Entering Information into a Table

Why would I do this?

After you have set up the rows and columns of your table, the next step is to enter information into the table cells. You can enter any kind of information you want. The most common table entries are text and numbers, but you can also enter graphics or even Internet locations if you want to do so.

In this task, you learn how to enter information into a table.

1 With the new table in the **Michigan Tornadoes** document on the screen, place the insertion point in the first cell.

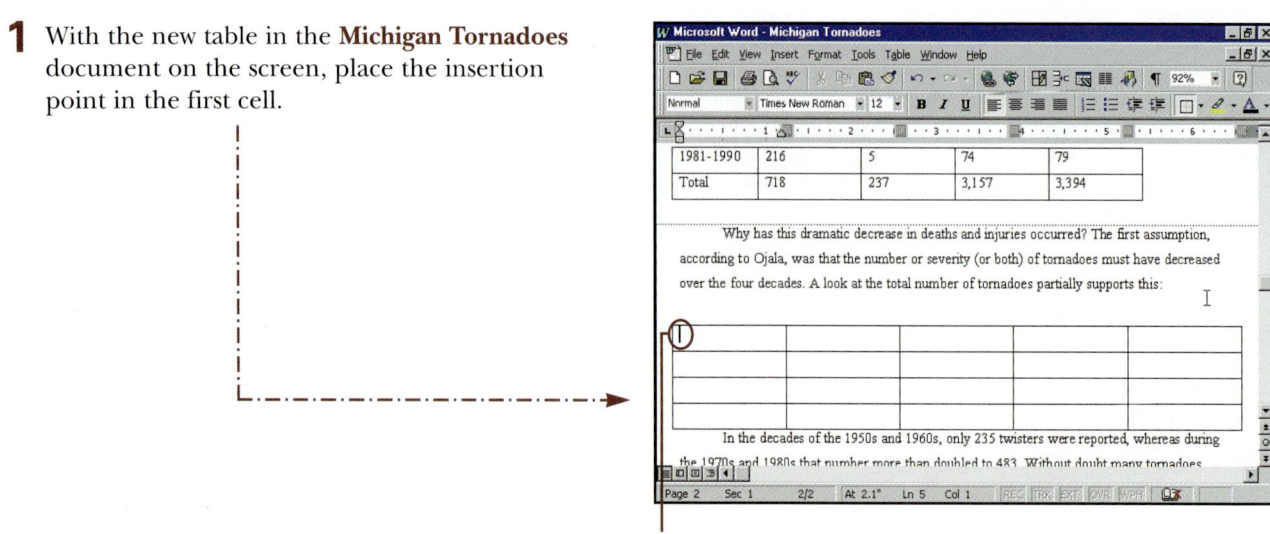

The first table cell

102 Learn Word 97, Second Edition

2 Type in **Decade**. This is the column heading for the first column of the table. Notice that the text is left aligned by default.

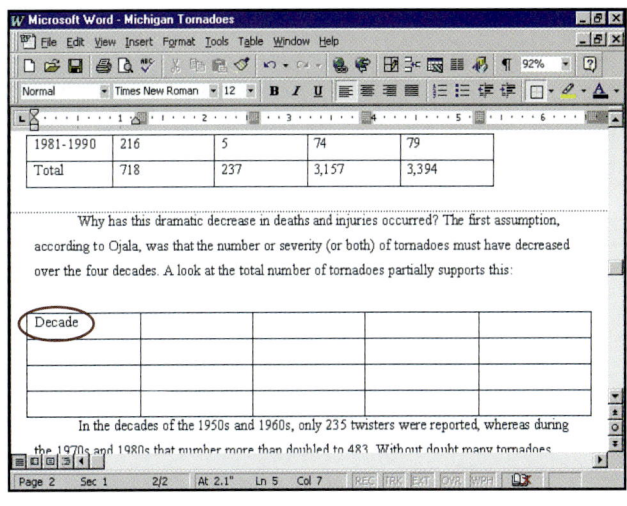

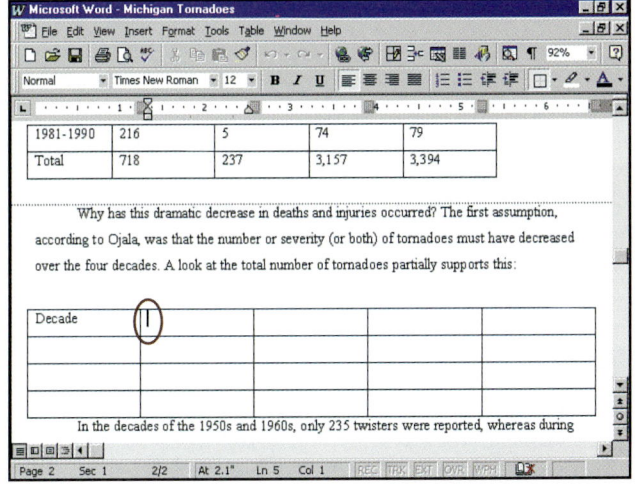

3 Press Tab. The insertion point moves to the second cell of the first row.

> **Pothole:** Many people automatically press Enter when they finish typing in a cell entry in a table. If you do so, the insertion point does not move to the next cell but instead creates a new line in the current cell. To recover from this error, press Backspace to remove the extra return marker in the cell and then press Tab to move to the next cell.

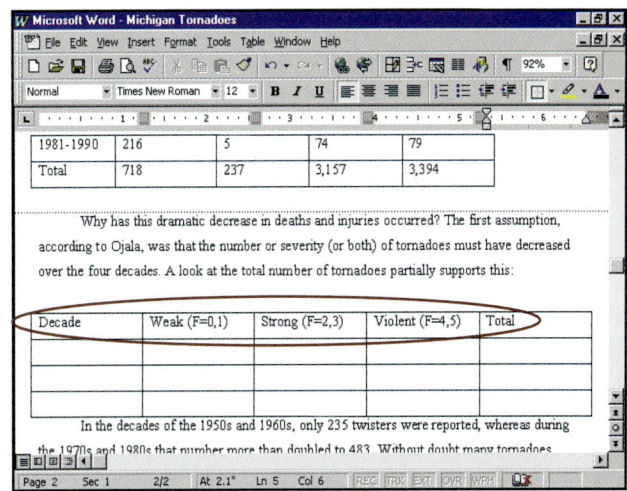

4 Type **Weak (F=0,1)** in the second cell in the top row and then type **Strong (F=2,3)** in the third cell in the top row. Finish the column headers by typing **Violent (F=4,5)** in the fourth cell and **Total** in the last cell of the first row.

Lesson 5: Working with Tables   103

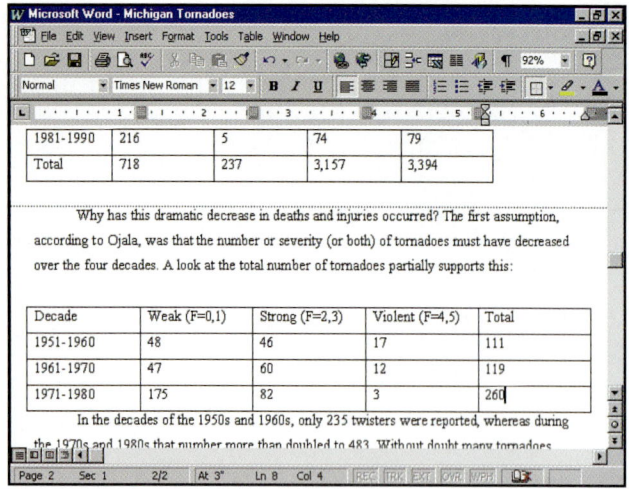

5 Fill in the next three rows with the following information:

Decade	Weak (F=0,1)	Strong (F=2,3)	Violent (F=4,5)	Total
1951-1960	48	46	17	111
1961-1970	47	60	12	119
1971-1980	175	82	3	260

Quick Tip: If you need to change information in a cell, you can move around in the table in faster ways than going across each row using Tab. You can use the mouse to click in the desired cell, or you can use the arrow keys to move up, down, left, or right one cell at a time. To move back one cell, you can press Shift plus Tab.

Task 3

Adding Rows to a Table

Why would I do this?

When you create a table, you may not always know ahead of time how many rows or columns you need. After a table is created, it is simple to add more rows at the end of the table.

In this task, you learn to add rows to a table.

1 If necessary, place the insertion point to the right of the entry in the last cell in the table.

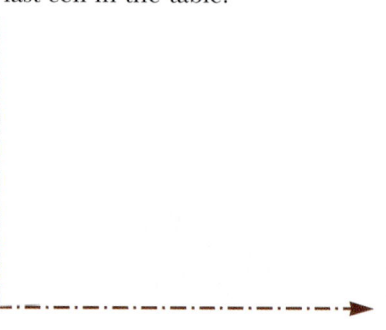
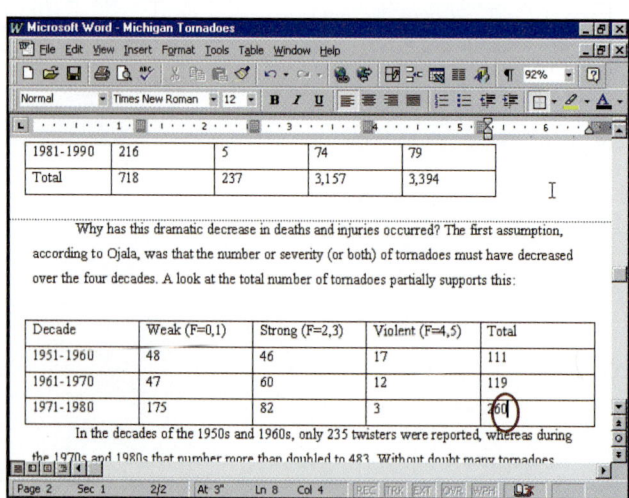

104 Learn Word 97, Second Edition

2 Press Tab. A new row is automatically added to the end of the table.

> **In Depth:** If you want to add rows to the middle of a table, highlight the row where you want the new row to appear and then choose Table, Insert Rows from the menu or use the Insert Row button on the toolbar. The highlighted row is moved below the new row.

Insert Row button

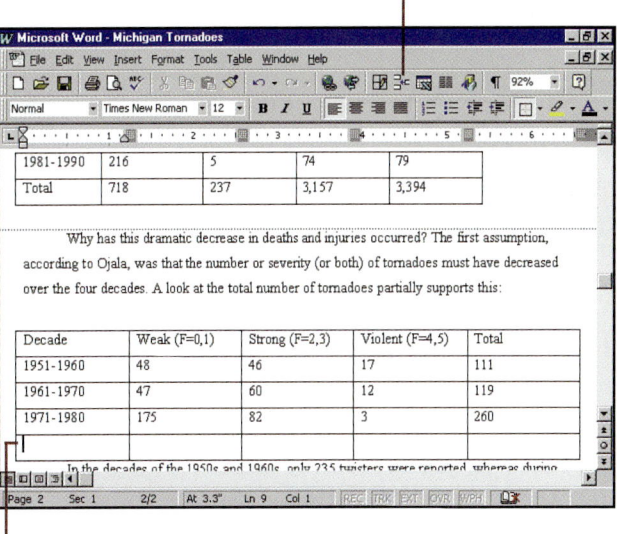

New row

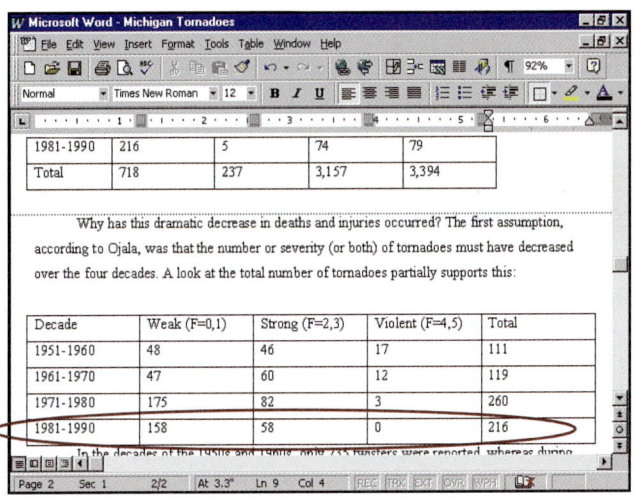

3 Add the following information to the last row of your table:

Decade   Weak (F=0,1)   Strong (F=2,3)   Violent (F=4,5)   Total

1981-1990   **158**   **58**   **0**   **216**

New row

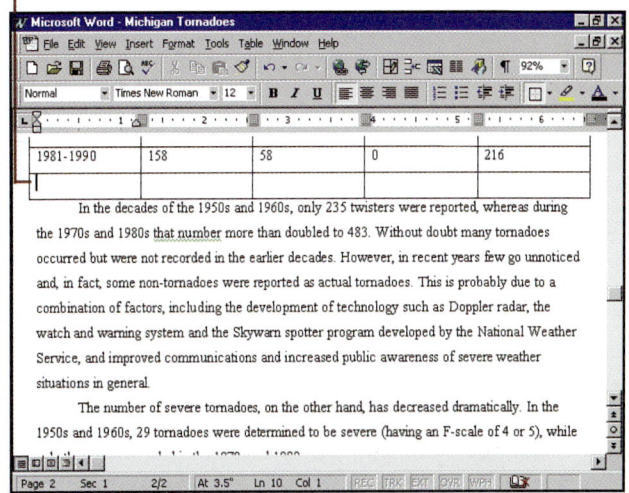

4 With the cursor at the end of the new row, press Tab again. Another new row is added to the end of the table.

> **In Depth:** Sometimes you want to insert a column in a table. This procedure is also relatively straightforward. To add a column, point to the very top of the column where you want the new one to appear. The pointer changes to a downward-pointing arrow. Click to select the column and then choose Table, Insert Columns from the menu or click the Insert Column button on the toolbar.

Lesson 5: Working with Tables 105

5 Add the following information to the new row:

Decade	Weak (F=0,1)	Strong (F=2,3)	Violent (F=4,5)	Total
Total	428	246	32	706

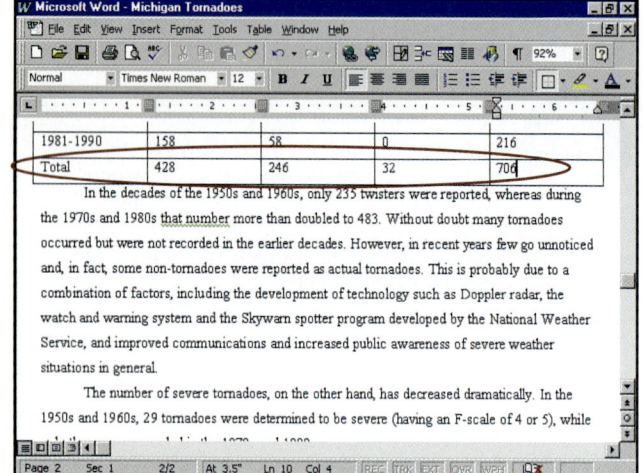

Task 4

Formatting Text in a Table

Why would I do this?

When you create a table, the text in the headings, the totals in the columns and rows, and the rest of the data all look the same. You can use standard formatting tools to emphasize important points, headings, and totals. This emphasis gives your table an easy-to-read, professional look.

In this task, you learn to format text in a table one cell at a time and several cells at once.

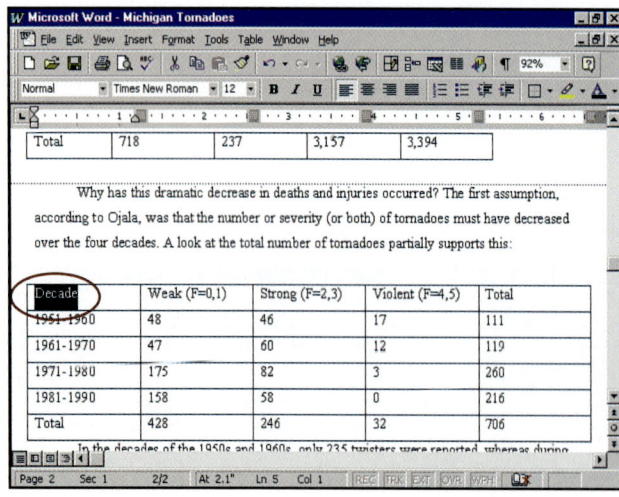

2 Click the **Bold** button. The word is now bold-faced.

1 With **Michigan Tornadoes** still open, select **Decade** in the first cell of the new table.

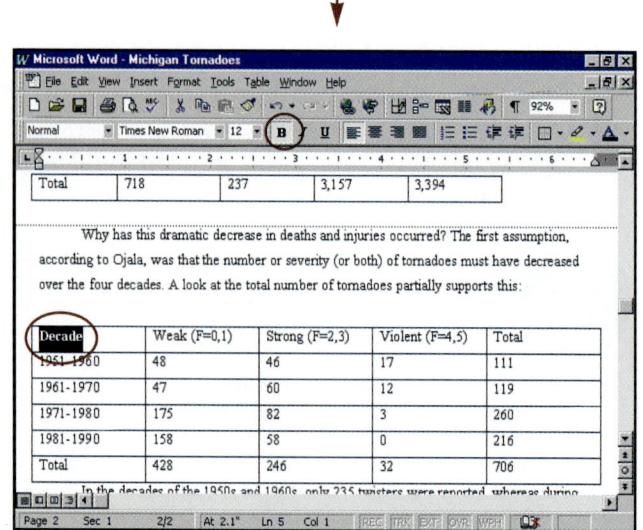

106 Learn Word 97, Second Edition

Highlighted cells

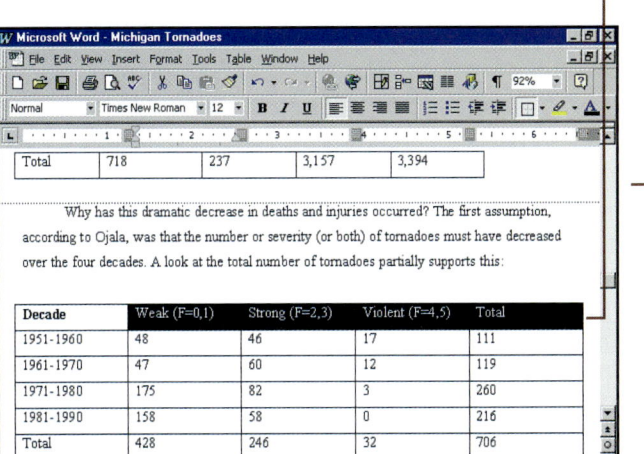

3 Place the insertion point to the left of the word **Weak** in the second cell of the first row and drag to the end of the row. Everything in the first row should be highlighted except the first cell.

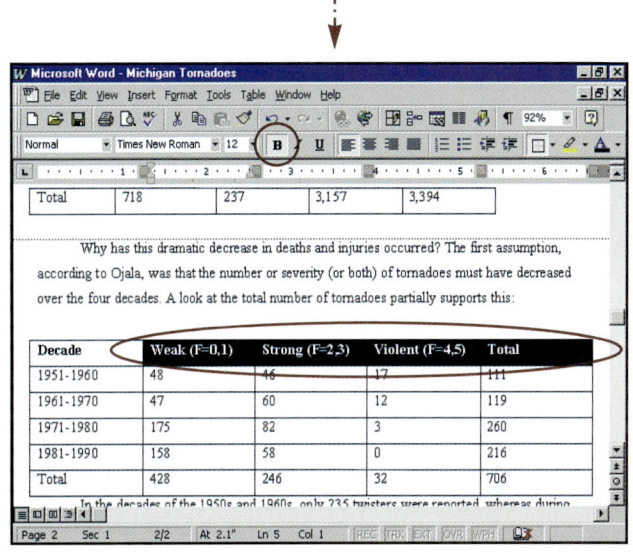

4 Click the **Bold** button. The rest of the row is now boldfaced.

5 Move the pointer to the left of the table next to the last row. The pointer becomes a right-pointing arrow.

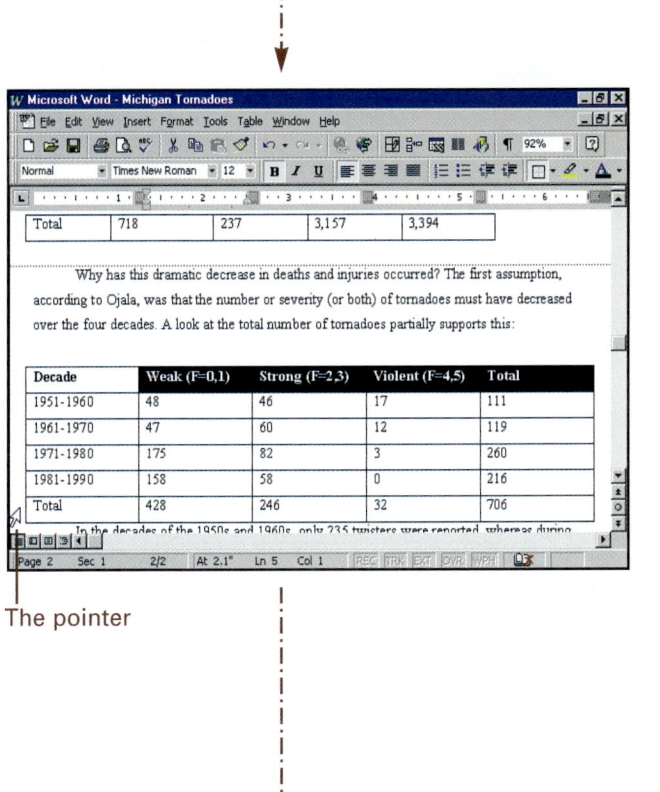

The pointer

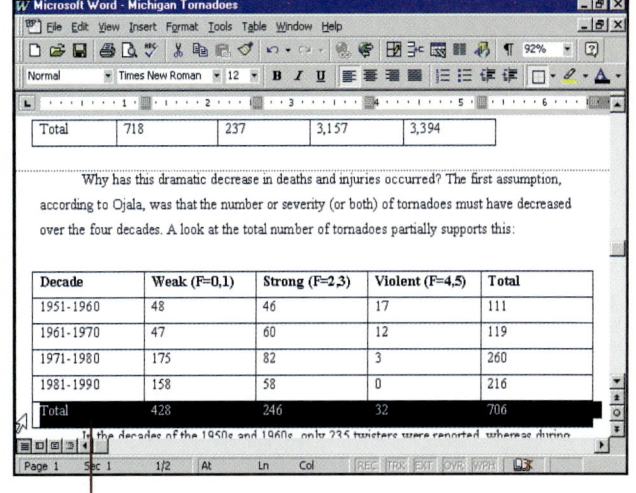

The whole row is selected.

6 Click the left mouse button one time. The whole last row is selected.

Lesson 5: Working with Tables   107

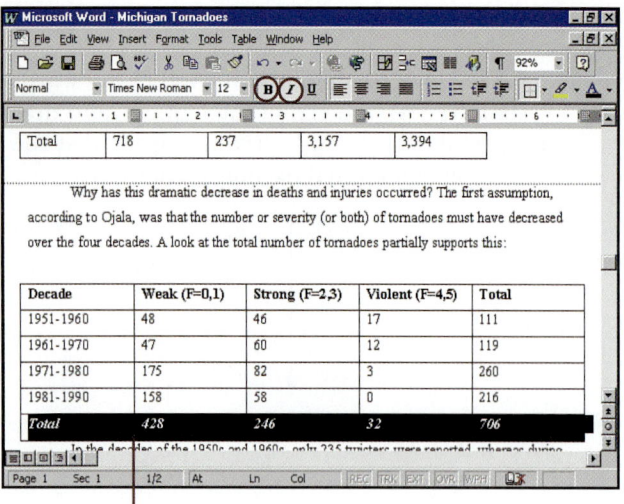

The whole row is boldfaced and italicized.

8 Move the pointer to the top of the first column. When the pointer is exactly over the top line, it turns into a black down arrow. Click once to select the first column.

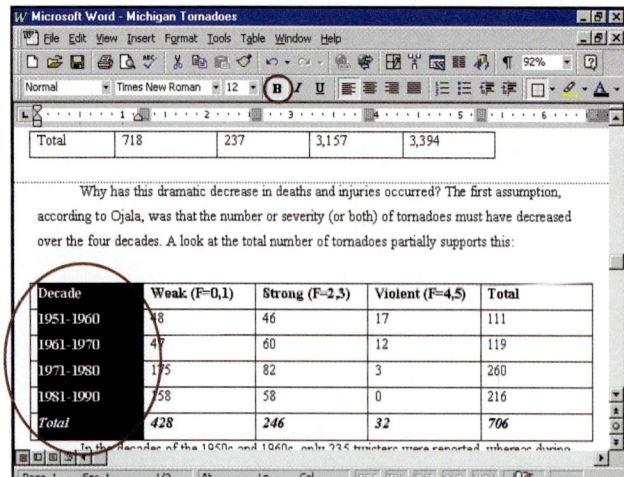

7 Click the **Bold** button and the **Italic** button. The entire row is now boldfaced and italicized.

The pointer changes to an arrow.

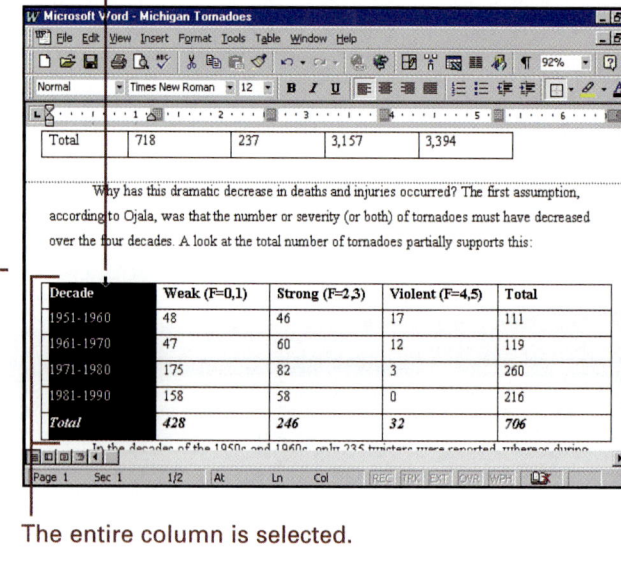

The entire column is selected.

9 Click the **Bold** button. Notice that the bold text is turned off in the first and last cells. Click the **Bold** button again. The entire column is now boldfaced.

In Depth: The formatting buttons only work on text entries that have the same attributes. If bold is on in the first cell selected, bold is turned off when you click the Bold button. If the first cell selected had not been boldfaced, clicking on the Bold button would have turned bold on for the entire selection.

Task 5

Aligning Text in a Table

Why would I do this?

Another way to make your table look more professional is to align the items in an attractive manner. Notice that your numbers do not line up on the right side in the table you just created. As a general rule, line up text on the left and numbers on the right. One exception to that rule is column headings, which should generally be right aligned if they are above numbers. To improve the appearance of this table, the numbers and text need to be properly aligned.

In this task, you learn how to right align numbers and text.

1 Select the second column of the new table in the **Michigan Tornadoes** document.

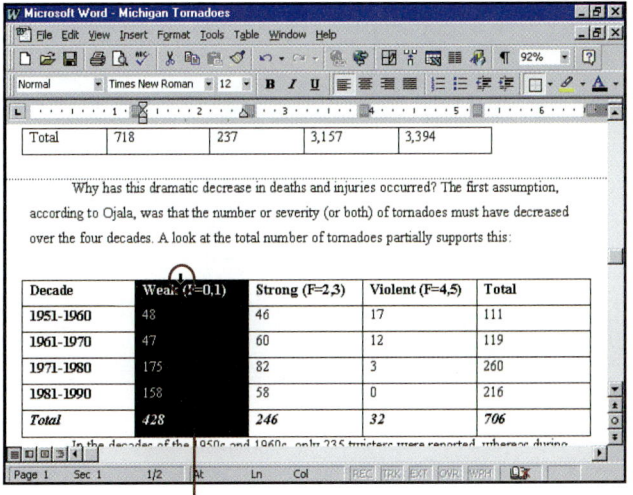

The second column is selected.

In Depth: Some people have trouble positioning the pointer at the very top of the column. When it is properly positioned, the mouse point changes into a small, thick, downward pointing arrow that is used to select a column in a table. You can also select a column by placing the insertion point to the left of the data in the top cell, clicking the left mouse button, and dragging down to the bottom of the column.

Align Right button

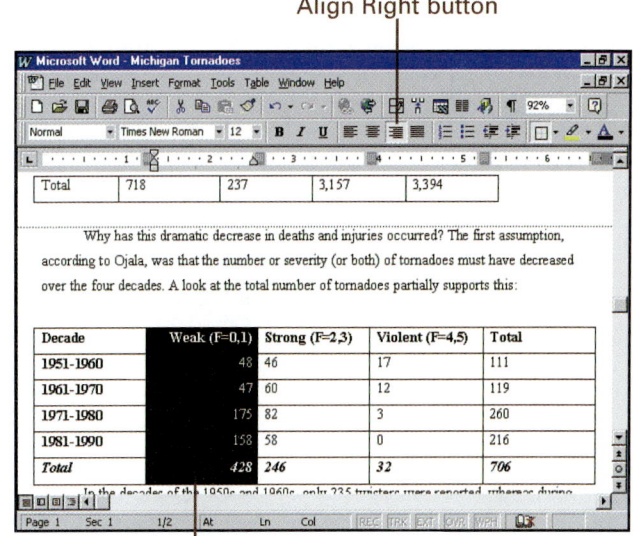

2 Click the **Align Right** button on the Formatting toolbar. The items in the second column are now right aligned.

The column is right aligned.

Lesson 5: Working with Tables   109

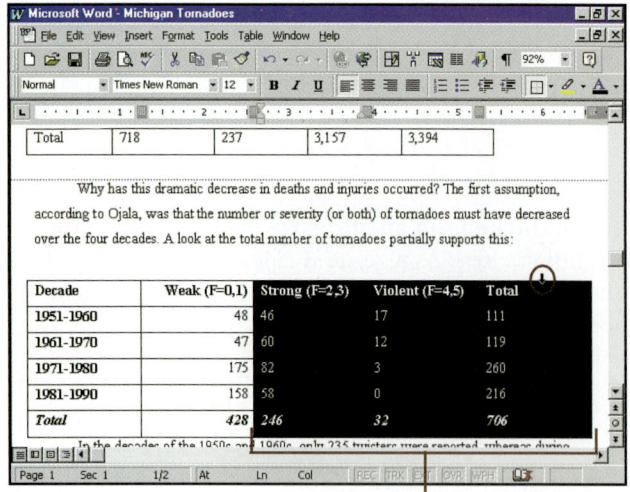

The last three columns are selected.

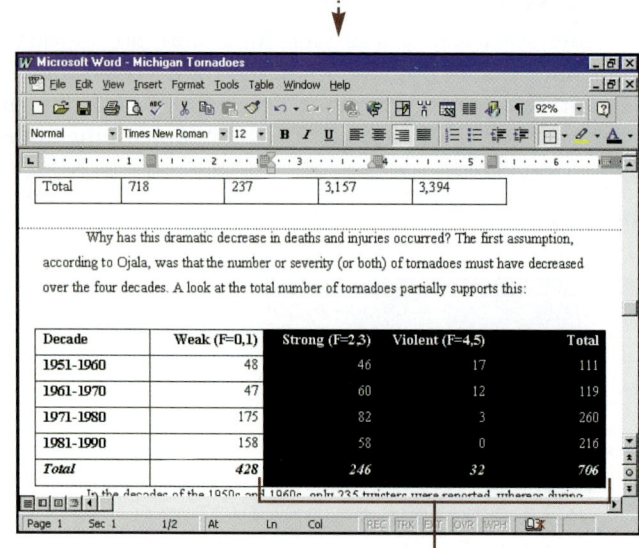

The last three columns are right aligned.

3. Move the pointer to the top of the third column until it turns into a black down arrow. Click and drag to the right until the last three columns are selected.

4. Click the **Align Right** button on the Formatting toolbar. The items in the third, fourth, and fifth columns are now right aligned.

Task 6

Formatting Borders and Shading in a Table

Why would I do this?

The sides of the cells in a table are called *borders*. These lines are usually the same thickness. You can visually highlight a group of cells by changing the thickness of the borders separating that group of cells from the others. Another way to visually identify a group of cells is to use a color or shade of gray as the background for a group of cells. Many other border and shading options are available to you, so you can make the final table look exactly the way you want it to look.

In this task, you learn to add lines and borders to a table and to shade cells.

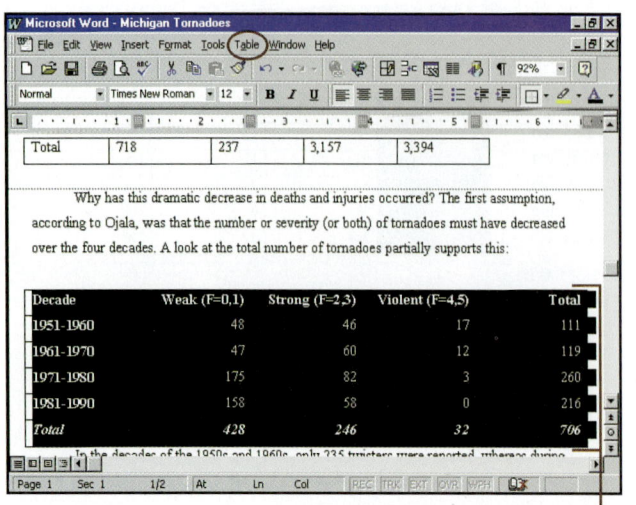

The whole table is selected.

1. Place the insertion point anywhere in your new table. Choose **Table**, **Select Table** from the menu. The whole table is now selected.

110 Learn Word 97, Second Edition

2 Click the down arrow on the **Border** button on the Formatting toolbar and move the pointer to the **No Border** option.

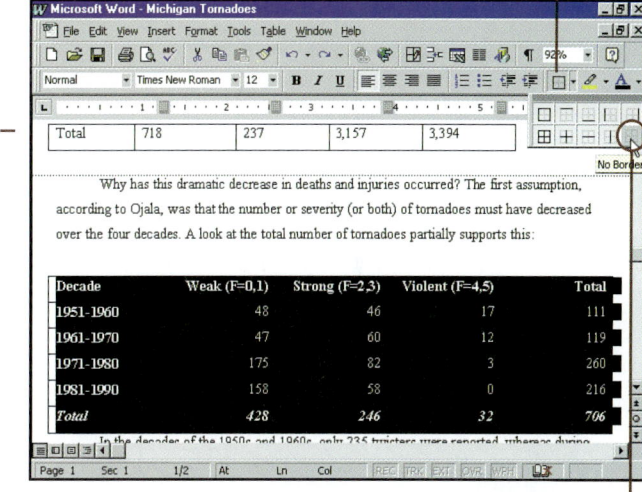

Border button

No Border option

3 Click the **No Border** option, which turns off the existing table borders. Gray lines are shown in place of the border. These would not show up if you printed the document at this point.

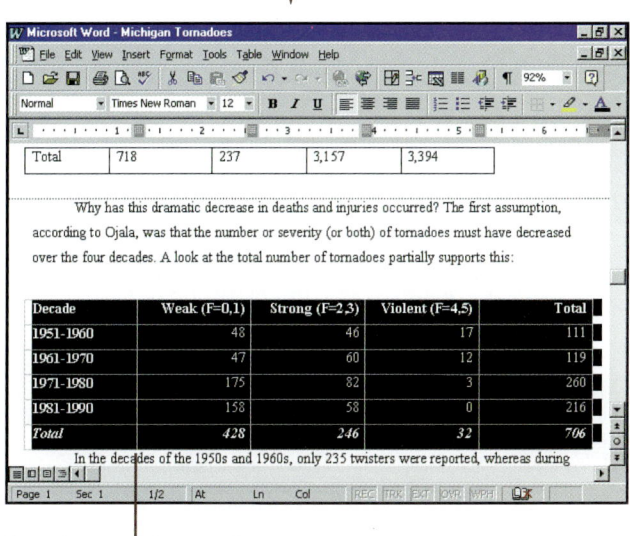

Gray lines will not print.

4 Select **Format, Borders and Shading** from the menu. The **Borders and Shading** dialog box is displayed. Select the **Borders** tab if it is not already selected.

Borders tab

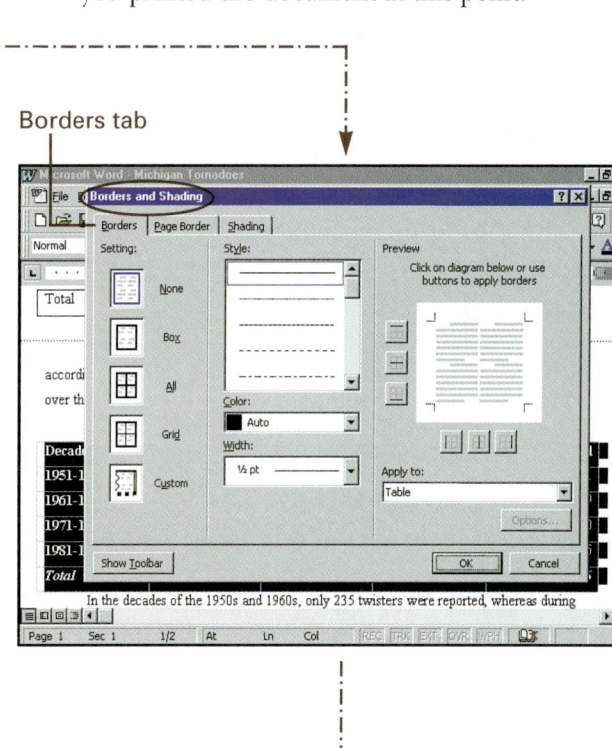

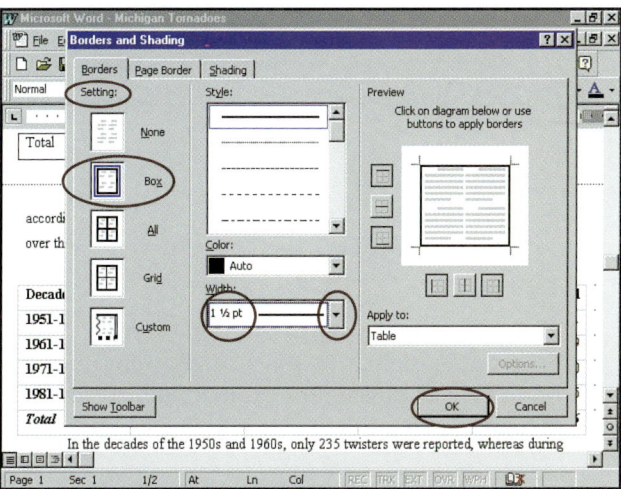

5 Click **Box** in the **Setting** area and then choose **1 1/2 pt** from the **Width** drop-down menu. This puts a 1.5-point border around the outside of the table.

Lesson 5: Working with Tables   111

6 Click **OK** and then click anywhere outside the table. Notice the box around the table.

Shading tab

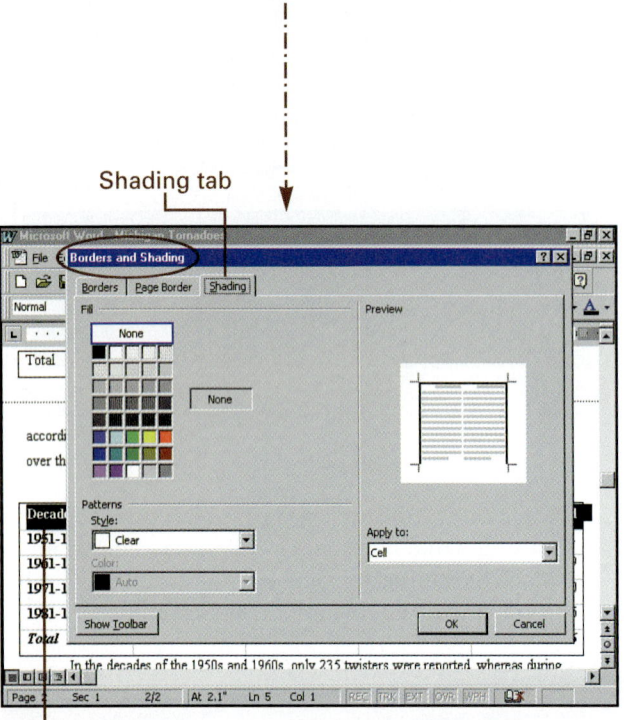

Row selected

8 Click the fourth box in the first row of the **Fill** area. The box to the right should say **Gray-10%**.

Gray-10% shading has been added to the column headings.

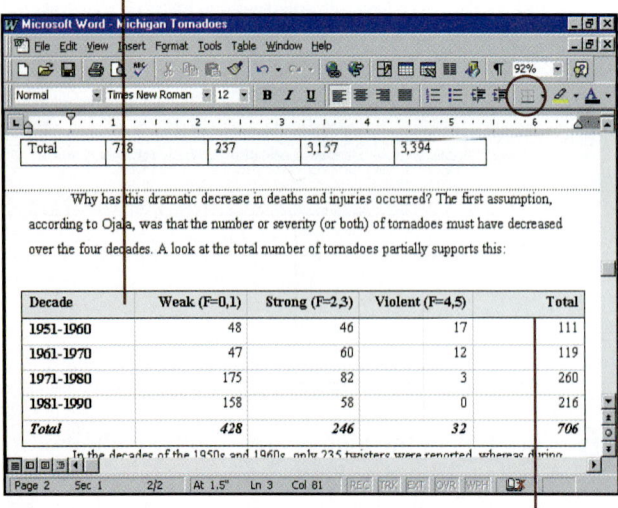

A bottom border has been added.

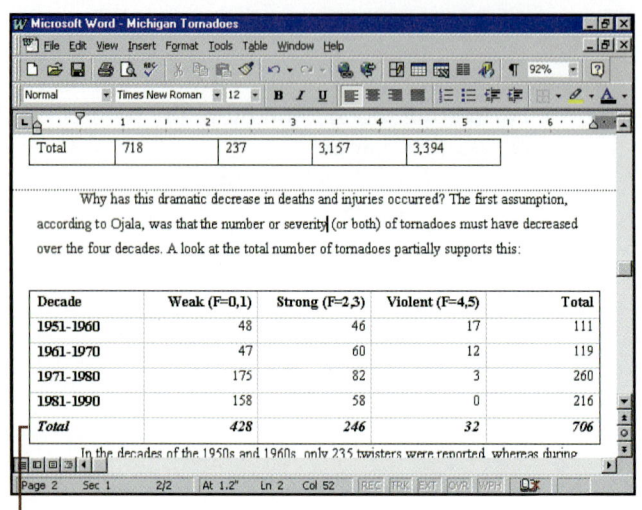

A border has been added.

7 Move the pointer to the left of the first row and click to select it. Select **Format**, **Borders and Shading** from the menu. Select the **Shading** tab from the **Borders and Shading** dialog box.

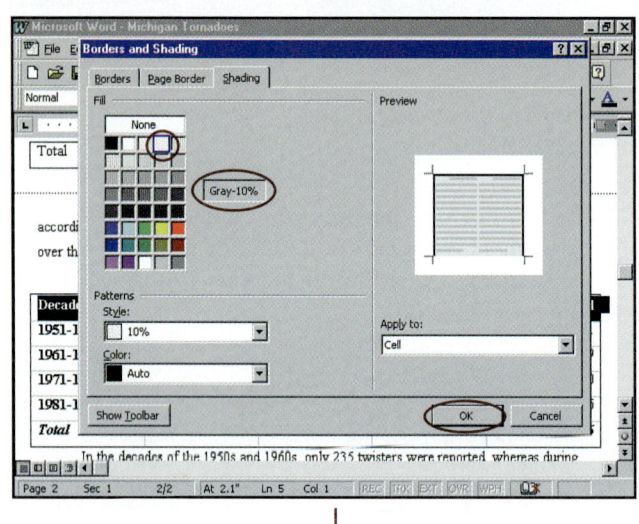

9 Click **OK**. Use the **Border** button on the Formatting toolbar to select the **Bottom Border** option. Click outside the table to look at your formatting changes.

112 Learn Word 97, Second Edition

Shading tab

10 Move the pointer to the left of the last row and click to select it. Select **Format**, **Borders and Shading** from the menu. Select the **Shading** tab from the **Borders and Shading** dialog box if necessary. Click the fourth box in the first row of the **Fill** area, as you did in step 8.

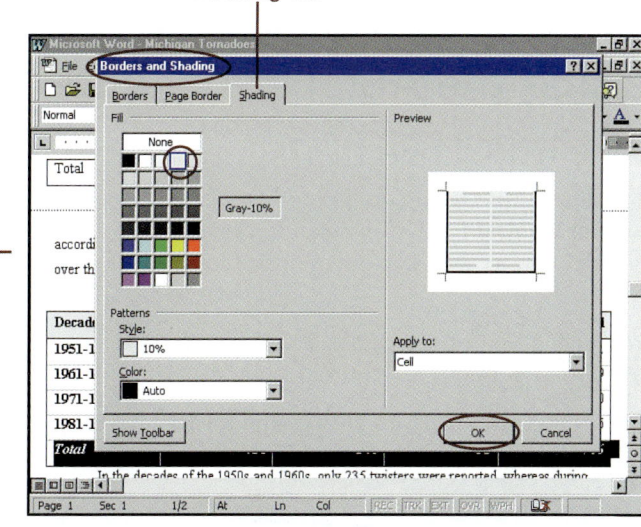

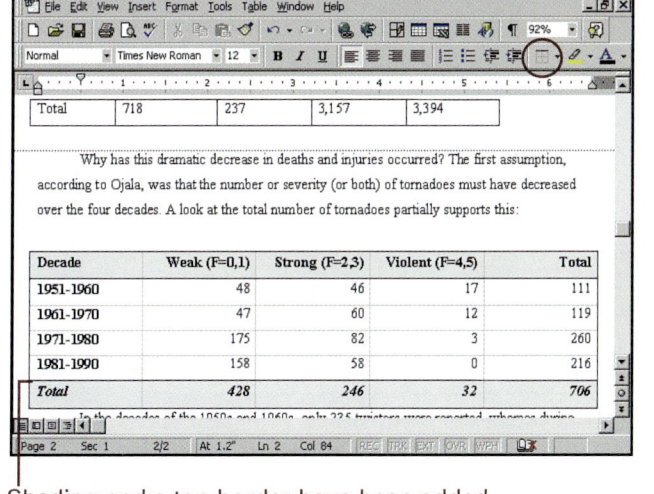

Shading and a top border have been added.

11 Click **OK**. Use the **Border** button on the Formatting toolbar to select the **Top Border** option. Click outside the table to look at your formatting changes.

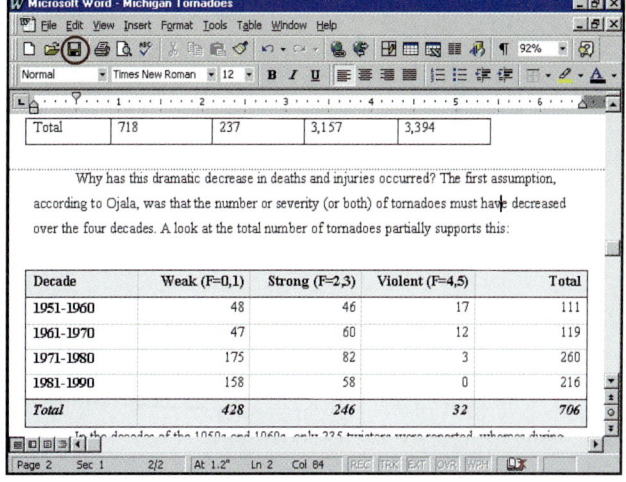

12 Click the **Save** button on the Standard toolbar to save your work.

Lesson 5: Working with Tables 113

Task 7
Using the AutoFormat and AutoFit Tools

Why would I do this?

The formatting tools you learned about in the earlier tasks in this lesson give you tremendous control over the look of your tables. Unfortunately, formatting your table can be time-consuming. The *AutoFormat* option, which enables you to choose from many different table styles, saves you a great deal of time if one of the styles fits your needs.

You may have noticed that the table you have created is wider than necessary. When you insert a table, it stretches from the left margin to the right margin. Another tool, called *AutoFit*, changes the width of the columns.

In this task, you learn to change the format of a table using the AutoFormat option and to optimize the column widths using the AutoFit tool.

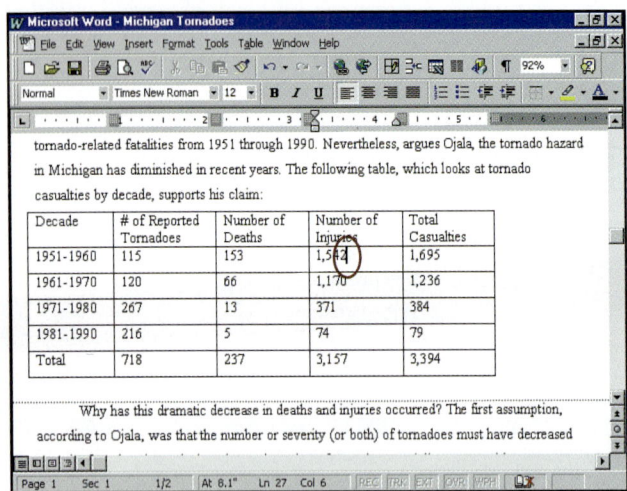

1 Scroll to the Tornado Casualties table located at the bottom of the first page. Place the insertion point anywhere in the table.

2 Choose **T**able, Table Auto**F**ormat from the menu. The **Table AutoFormat** dialog box is displayed. Scroll down the list of table types in the **Forma**t**s** area and click on several to see their appearance in the **Preview** box.

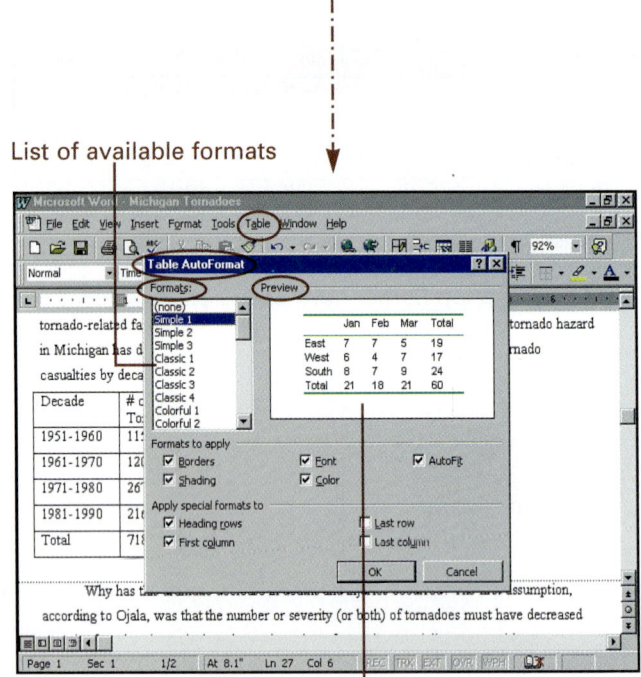

List of available formats

Table formats are previewed here.

Learn Word 97, Second Edition

Preview of the Grid 8 format

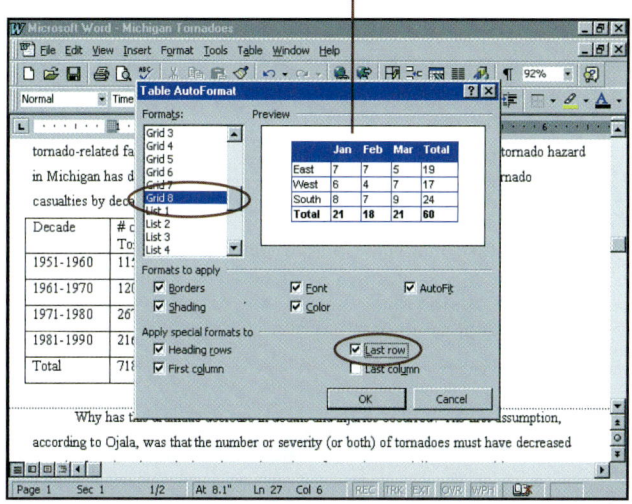

3 Select **Grid 8** from the **Formats** area. This format is different from the one you created for the new table. Click the check box for **Last row**. Notice that the last row is now boldfaced in the **Preview** area.

The AutoFormatted table

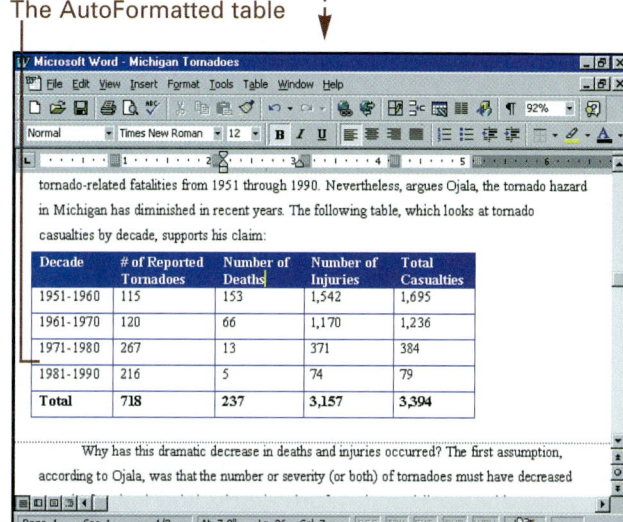

4 Click **OK**. The table in the document now looks like the sample you saw in the **Preview** area.

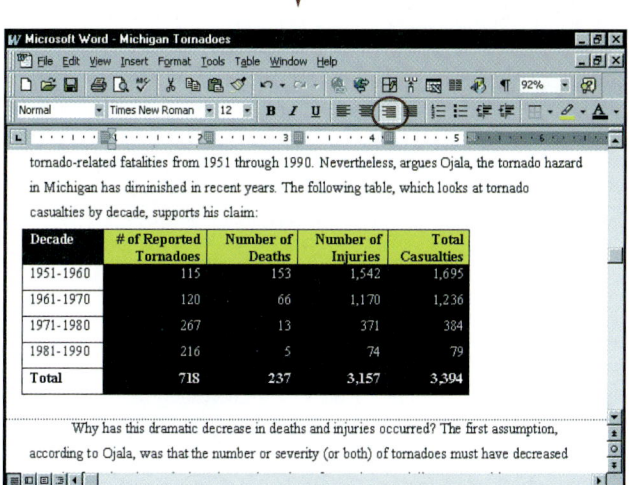

5 Select the last four columns and click the **Align Right** button to line up the numbers in this table.

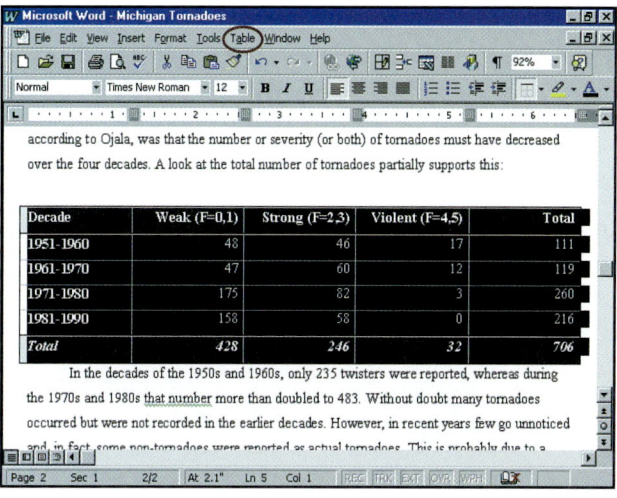

6 Place the insertion point in the table you created in Task 1 of this lesson. Choose **Table**, **Select Table** from the menu.

Lesson 5: Working with Tables   115

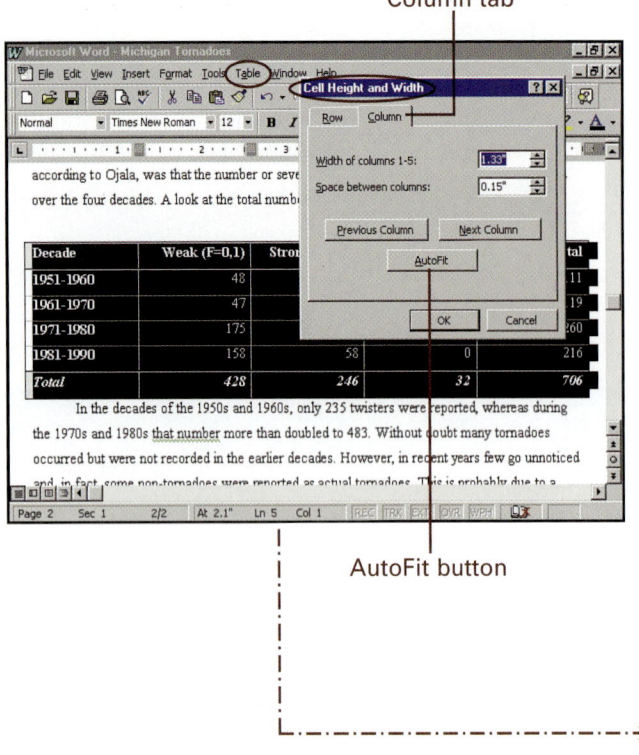

Column tab

AutoFit button

7 Choose **Table, Cell Height and Width** from the menu. The **Cell Height and Width** dialog box is displayed. Select the **Column** tab.

In Depth: The Cell Height and Width dialog box enables you to change the width of individual columns or to increase or decrease the height of individual rows. It also enables you to change the spacing between the columns.

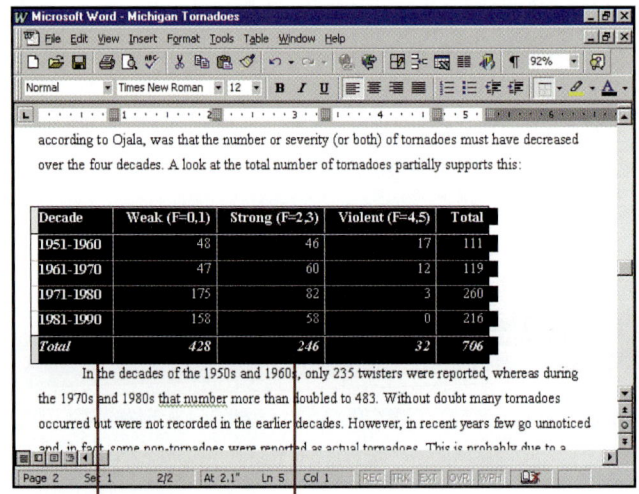

Each column has been resized.

8 Click the **AutoFit** button. This button automatically changes the column widths and takes you back to the table without your clicking **OK**. Each column is now the width of the widest object in that column (usually the column heading).

Task 8

Centering a Table

Why would I do this?

When you used the AutoFormat and AutoFit tools on the two tables in your document, both were shortened so that they no longer extended from the left margin to the right margin. The document would look more balanced if the tables were centered on the page rather than remaining on the left side of the page. You can use a tool to center tables between the left and right margins, which gives your document a more balanced and professional appearance.

In this task, you learn how to center tables on the document margins.

1 Place the insertion point anywhere in the second table in the document. Choose **Table, Select Table** from the menu.

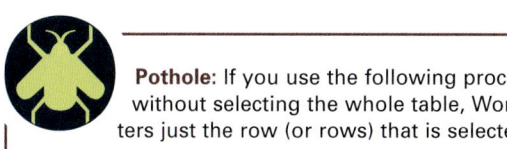

Pothole: If you use the following procedure without selecting the whole table, Word centers just the row (or rows) that is selected.

Row tab

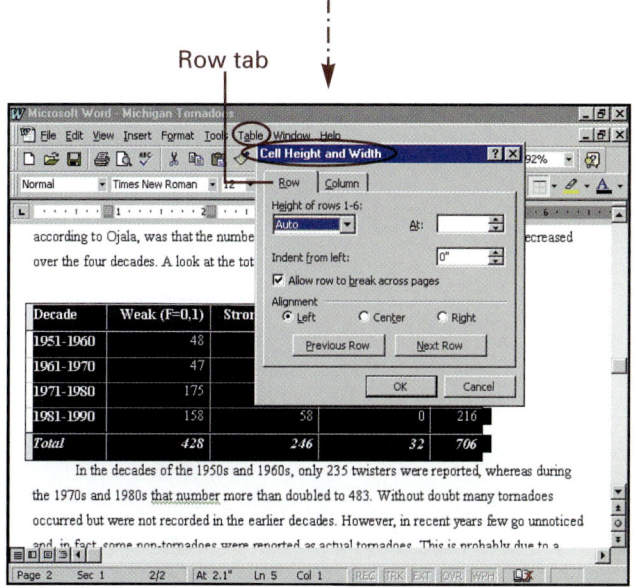

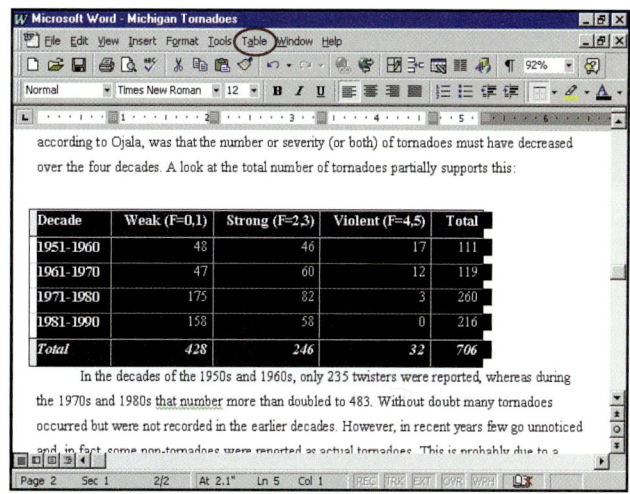

2 Choose **Table, Cell Height and Width** from the menu. The **Cell Height and Width** dialog box is displayed. Select the **Row** tab if it is not already selected.

3 Click the **Center** option button in the **Alignment** area.

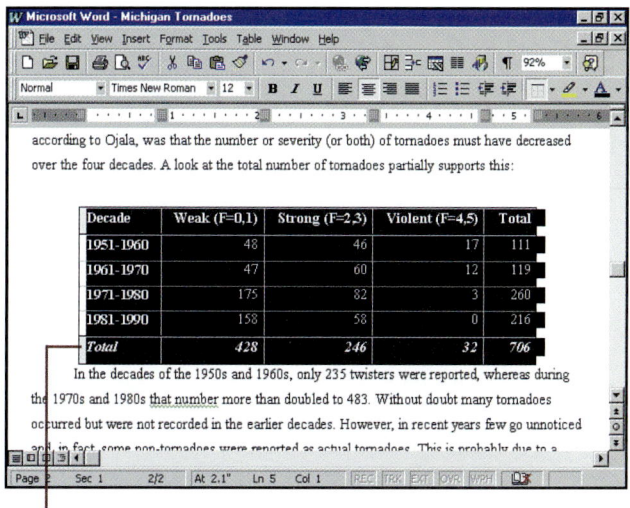

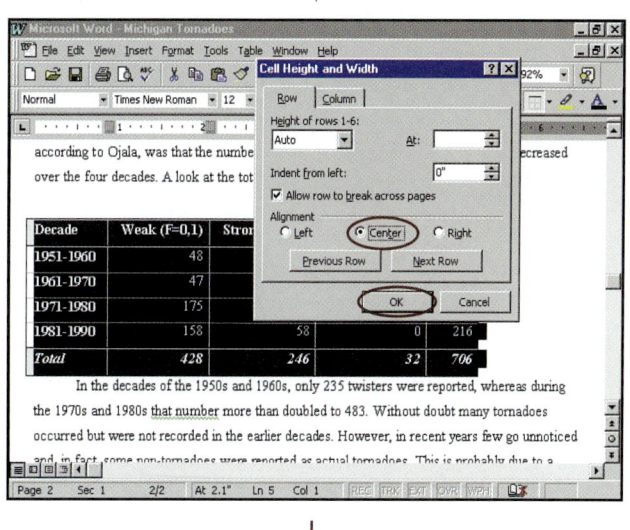

4 Click **OK**. The table is now centered on the document margins.

The table is now centered on the margins.

Lesson 5: Working with Tables

5 Place the insertion point anywhere in the other table. Choose **Table**, **Select Table** from the menu.

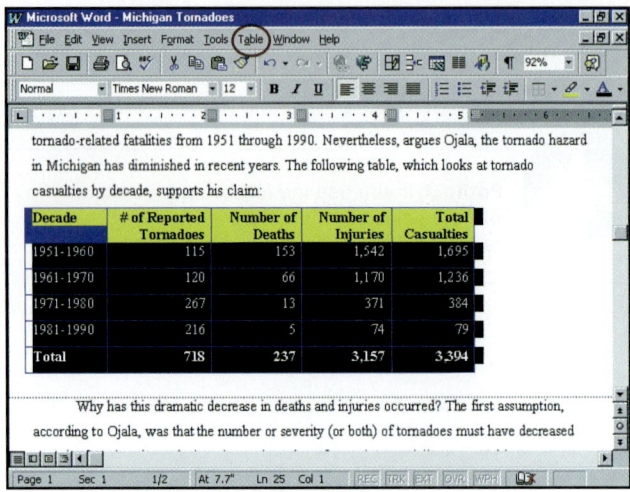

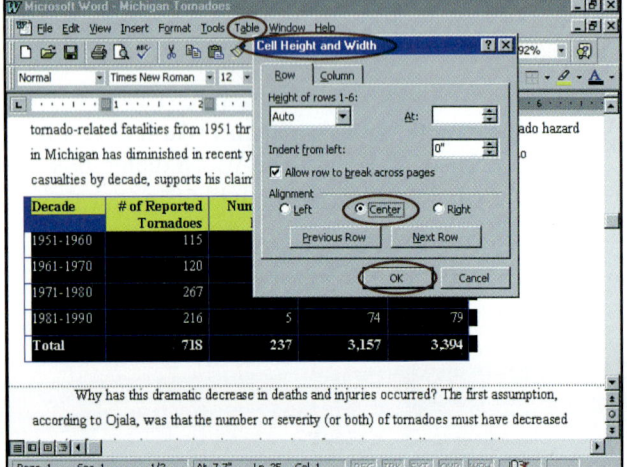

6 Choose **Table**, **Cell Height and Width** from the menu. The **Cell Height and Width** dialog box is displayed. Select the **Row** tab, if necessary, and then click the **Center** option button in the **Alignment** area.

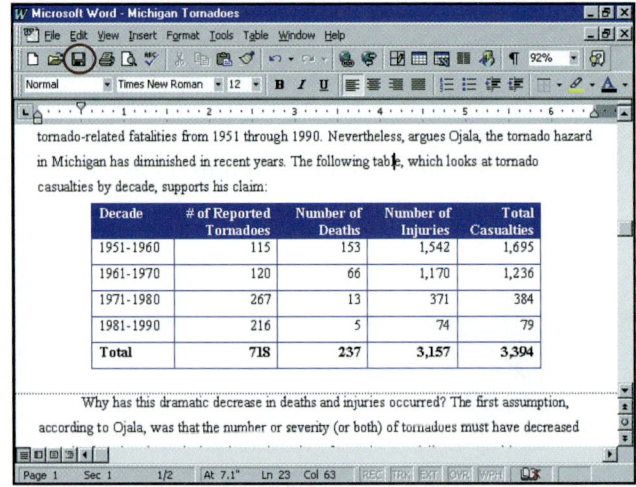

7 Click **OK** and then click outside the table to deselect the table. The table is now centered. Click the **Save** button to save your changes. Click the **Close Application** button to exit the document and exit Word.

118 Learn Word 97, Second Edition

Student Exercises

True-False

Circle either T or F.

T F 1. Tables consist of rows and columns of cells that resemble a worksheet.

T F 2. To create a table in a document, you enter the data, using tabs to separate the columns; select the rows and columns of data; and then choose Format, Table from the menu.

T F 3. When you enter text in a table, it is aligned to the left by default.

T F 4. To add an extra row when you reach the last cell at the bottom of a table, press Tab.

T F 5. When entering data into the cells of a table, you press Enter to move from one cell to the next.

T F 6. All the words in each row must have the same format.

T F 7. When you enter text in a table, it automatically aligns to the left. When you enter numbers, they automatically align to the right side of each cell.

T F 8. You can change the thickness of the line that makes up the outside edge of the table, but all of the lines making up the cells within the table must be of the same thickness.

T F 9. A group of cells—such as those at the top of each column—can be set apart from the others by using a 10-percent gray shade for their background color.

T F 10. The AutoFormat and AutoFit tools provide a faster way to produce a good-looking table that fits on your page.

Identifying Parts of the Word Screen

Refer to the figure and identify the numbered parts of the screen. Write the letter of the correct label in the space next to the number.

1. _____
2. _____
3. _____
4. _____
5. _____
6. _____
7. _____
8. _____
9. _____
10. _____

A. Left-aligned (boldfaced) text
B. Selected column
C. Right-aligned number
D. Select column pointer
E. Shaded background
F. Border line
G. Italicized and boldfaced text
H. Right Alignment button
I. Table centered left to right
J. Insert Column button

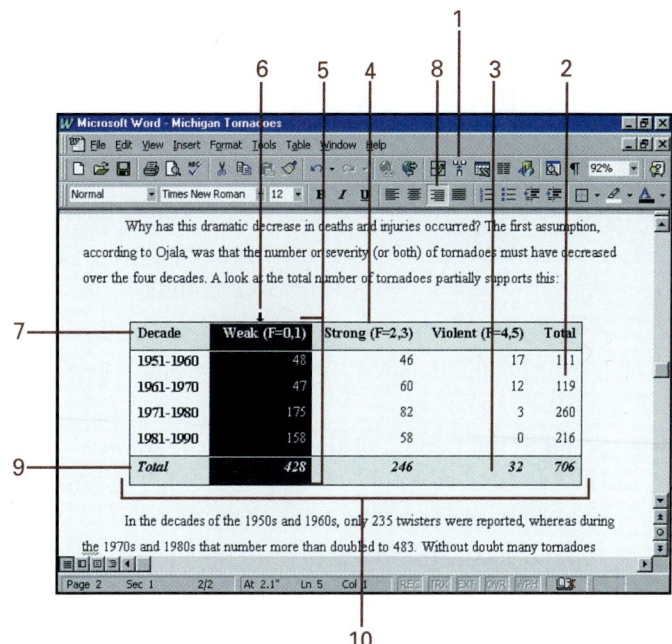

Lesson 5: Working with Tables 119

Matching Questions

Match the following statements to the word or phrase from the list on the right. Write the letter of the matching word or phrase in the space provided next to the number.

1. ___ Feature that automatically adjusts the width and height of the cells to accommodate the words or numbers in those cells

2. ___ Menu sequence that adds a table to the document

3. ___ Key you can press to add another row to the table if the pointer is in the lower-right cell (the last cell in the table)

4. ___ A good choice for shading the background of a cell

5. ___ Border setting used to remove the border line

6. ___ Font emphasis that is typically used to draw attention to words or numbers in a table

7. ___ Feature that automatically changes the borders and shading of a table

8. ___ Alignment typically used for numbers

9. ___ Alignment typically used for words

10. ___ Menu sequence that centers a table, left to right, on the page

A. [Tab] key
B. T<u>a</u>ble, <u>I</u>nsert Table
C. AutoFormat
D. AutoFit
E. T<u>a</u>ble, Cell Height and <u>W</u>idth, <u>R</u>ow, Cen<u>t</u>er
F. No Border
G. 10% Gray
H. Left aligned
I. Right aligned
J. Bold or italicized
K. [Enter] key

Application Exercises

Exercise 1—Insert a Table into a Document

1. Launch Microsoft Word. Open **Less0502** from the student files. Save the file as **Lightning Strikes**.

2. Type your name below the title in the space provided.

3. Scroll to the bottom of the second paragraph. Click in the blank space that has been left below the second paragraph.

4. Choose T<u>a</u>ble, <u>I</u>nsert Table from the menu.

5. Choose a table that has three columns and nine rows. Do not use the AutoFormat feature. Click **OK**.

6. Start at the upper-left cell and enter the following data:

Location	Number	Percent of Total
Ball park, playground	23	28.4
Under trees	19	23.4
Golfing	10	12.3
Water Related	8	9.9
Farm equipment	2	2.5
Telephone	2	2.5
Radios/transmitters/antennas	1	1.2
Other locations	16	19.8

7. Leave the document open for use in the next exercise.

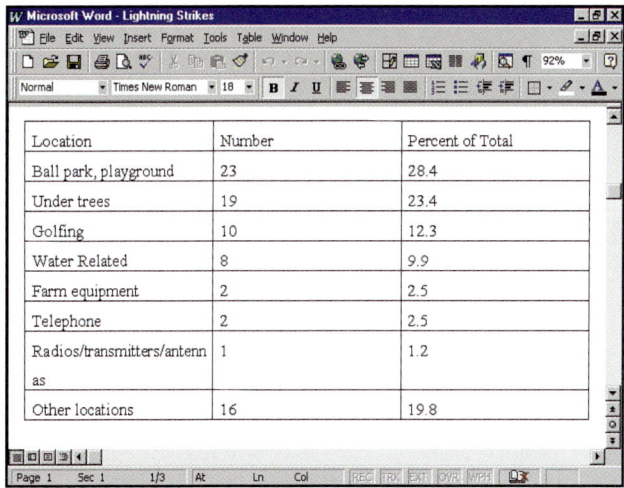

Exercise 2—Add a Row to a Table

1. Make sure that the cursor is located in the last cell in the bottom row of the table that was inserted in the previous exercise.

2. Press Tab to insert another row at the bottom of the table.

3. Add the following summary data to the three cells in the newly created row: **Totals**, **81**, **100.0**.

4. Leave the document open for use in the next exercise.

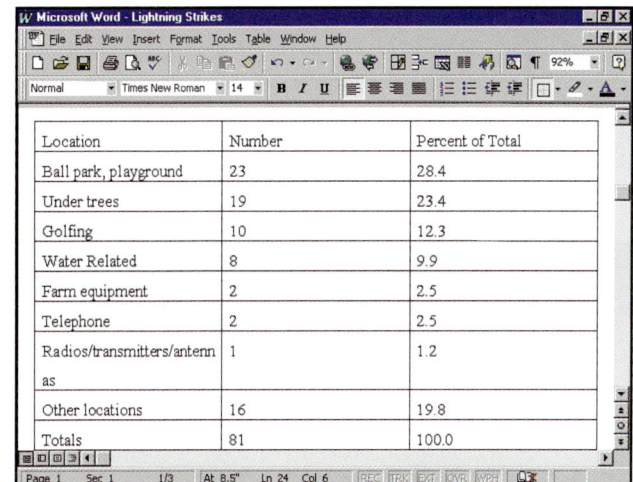

Exercise 3—Formatting Text in a Table

1. Select the first row of the table that you worked on in the previous exercises.

2. Change the font emphasis to Boldface.

3. Change the alignment to Centered.

4. Select all the cells that contain numbers.

5. Change their alignment to the right side of their respective cells.

6. Leave the document open for use in the next exercise.

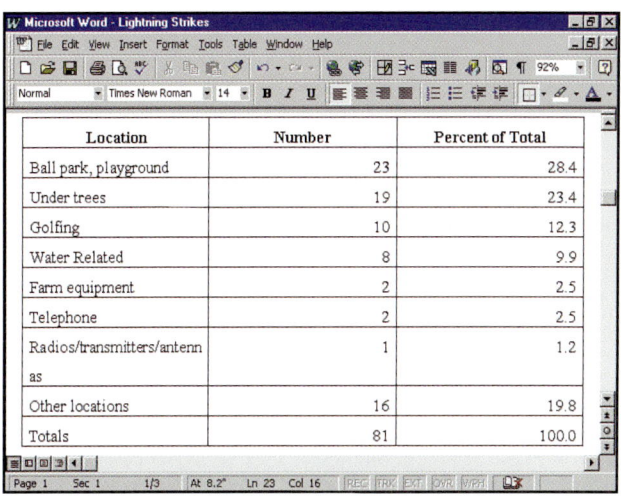

Lesson 5: Working with Tables

Exercise 4—Using AutoFit to Adjust Column Widths and Then Centering the Table

1. Make sure the cursor is located somewhere in the table and choose **Table**, **Select Table** from the menu.

2. Choose **Table**, **Cell Height and Width**, **Columns**, and **AutoFit** from the menu.

3. Click **OK**.

4. Choose **Table**, **Cell Height and Width**, **Row**, and **Center** from the menu. Click **OK** to center the table.

5. Leave the document open for use in the next exercise.

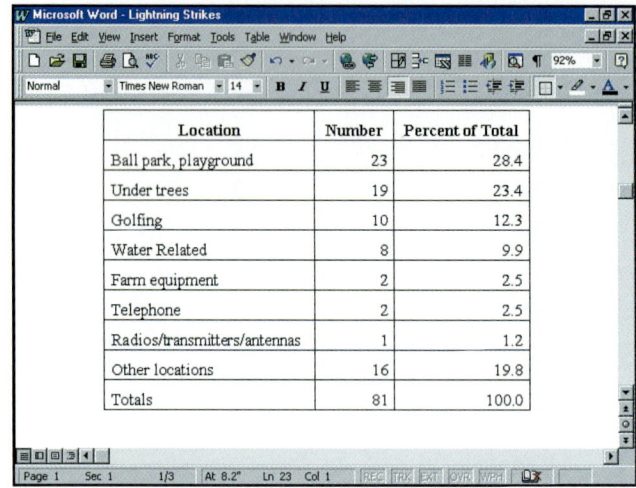

Exercise 5—Use AutoFormat to Apply a Predetermined Format to a Table

1. Click anywhere in the second table in the document.

2. Choose **Table**, **Table AutoFormat** from the menu.

3. Select **Simple 2** from the list of formatting designs.

4. Do not change any of the default settings. Click **OK**.

5. Print pages 1 and 2 of the document.

6. Save the document and then close it.

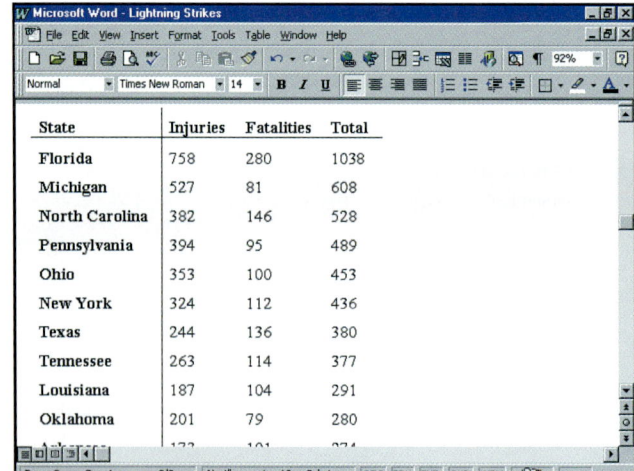

Lesson 6
Using Word Utilities

Task 1: Using the Shortcut Menu to Check Spelling and Grammar

Task 2: Using the Spelling and Grammar Checker

Task 3: Tracking Changes

Task 4: Using AutoCorrect

Task 5: Using AutoText

Task 6: Finding Text

Task 7: Finding and Replacing Text

Introduction

In the first five lessons of this book, you have dealt with putting text into a document and altering its appearance. Word contains features that help automate some of your regular text entries and can automatically correct words you commonly misspell. Word also offers a number of utility tools to help with the editing and proofing process.

The *AutoCorrect* tool corrects the most common spelling errors. It can be set to automatically capitalize the first letter of a sentence as well. An *AutoText* tool enables you to place boilerplate text, text that is used repeatedly, into your document with a short keyword or from a drop-down menu.

In addition to AutoText and AutoCorrect, Word offers other helpful tools that aid in the editing and proofing process. You can have the program track and display the changes that have been made to your document. You can correct spelling and grammar errors in two different ways. Finally, Word offers you a tool to enable you to quickly find and replace text either manually or automatically.

In this lesson, you learn how to use seven of the most important tools included in the Word program. (Note: The document used in this lesson contains a graphic, a topic explored in the next lesson.)

Visual Summary

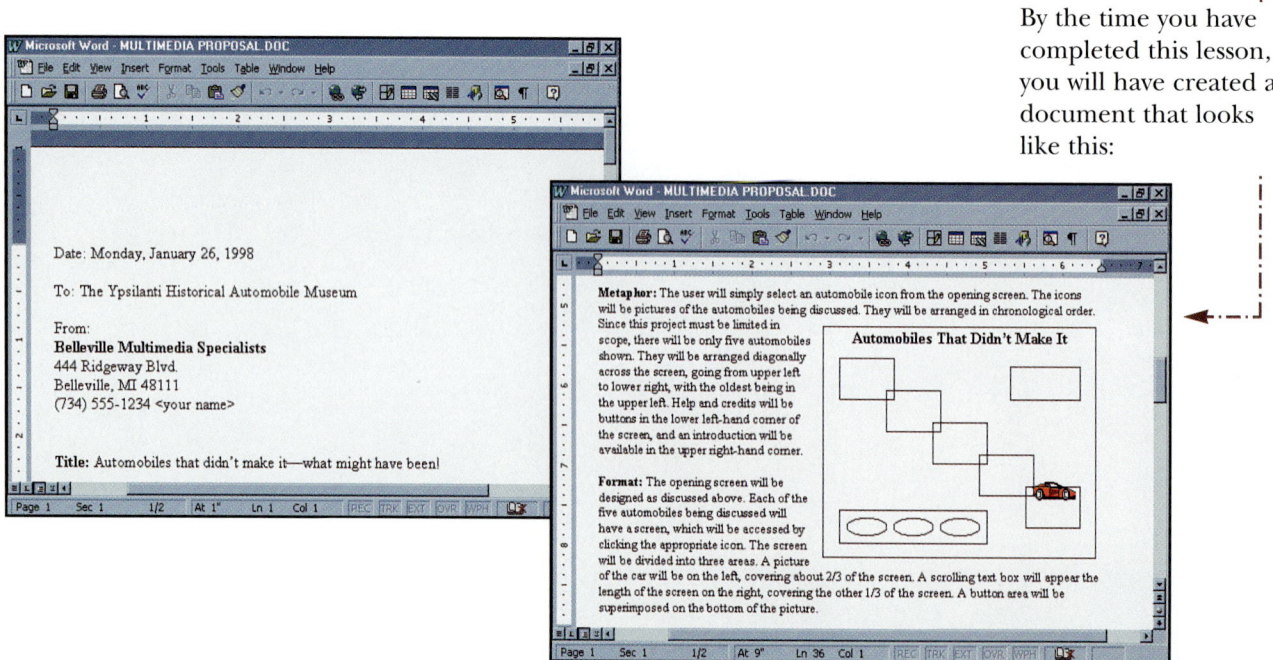

By the time you have completed this lesson, you will have created a document that looks like this:

Task 1

Using the Shortcut Menu to Check Spelling and Grammar

Why would I do this?

You can check the spelling and grammar in your document in two different ways. You can have the program check your spelling as you type, or you can check the spelling of a block of text or the whole document at one time. The shortcut menu allows you to make on-the-fly changes one word at a time.

One of the most useful features of the spelling shortcut menu is that it allows you to add words to the dictionary. With this feature, you can add unusual words or names that you type frequently.

In this task, you learn to check the spelling of a single word using the shortcut menu.

1. Launch Microsoft Word. Open **Less0601** from the student files. Save the file as **Multimedia Proposal**.

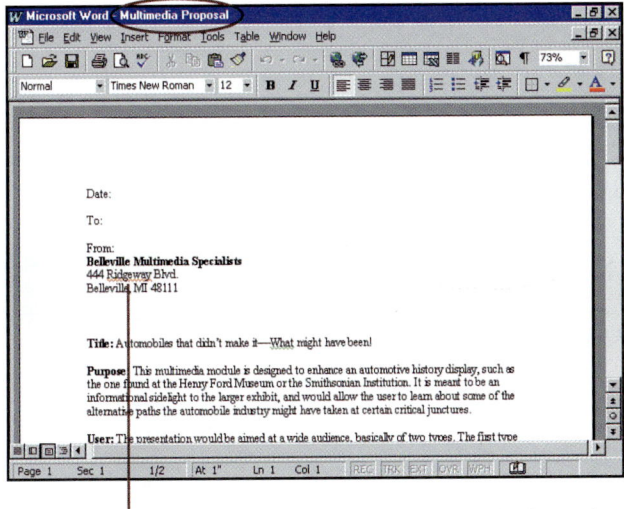

A wavy red line indicates a possible misspelled word.

In Depth: The wavy red line means that the word is not in the electronic dictionary that comes with Microsoft Office. If your screen does not display the wavy red line, select **Tools, Options** and then click on the **Spelling & Grammar** tab. Select **Check spelling as you type**.

2. Click the right mouse button on the word **Ridgeway**. The **Spelling** shortcut menu is displayed with spelling options for this word.

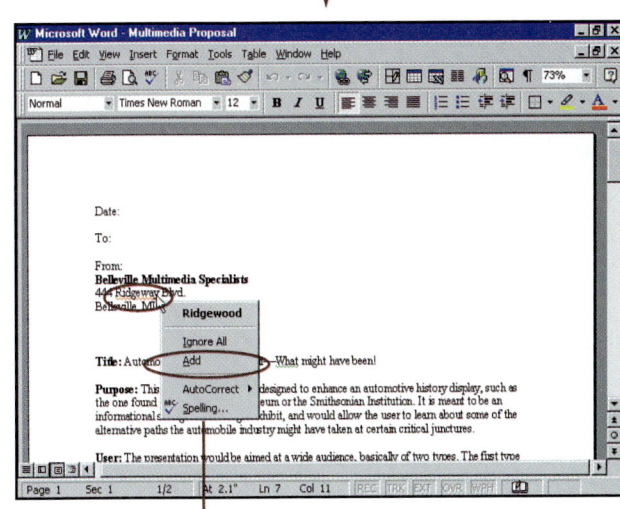

The Spelling shortcut menu

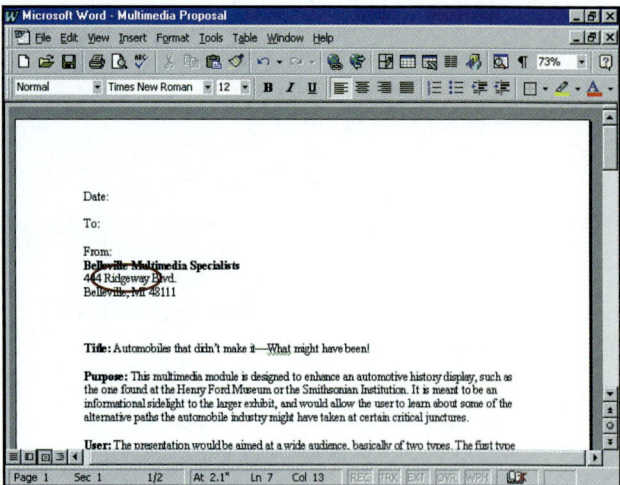

3 Click **Add**. The word has now been added to your dictionary. Notice that the wavy red line has disappeared from beneath the word.

4 Click the right mouse button on the word **What** in the title line. This line has a wavy green line under it, which means the program thinks it has detected a grammar mistake. The **Grammar** shortcut menu is displayed.

> **In Depth:** The shortcut menu shows possible changes and gives you the option of ignoring the sentence or going to the more detailed Grammar dialog box. The top line of the shortcut menu suggests that the word after the em dash (a long dash separating two parts of a sentence) should not be capitalized.

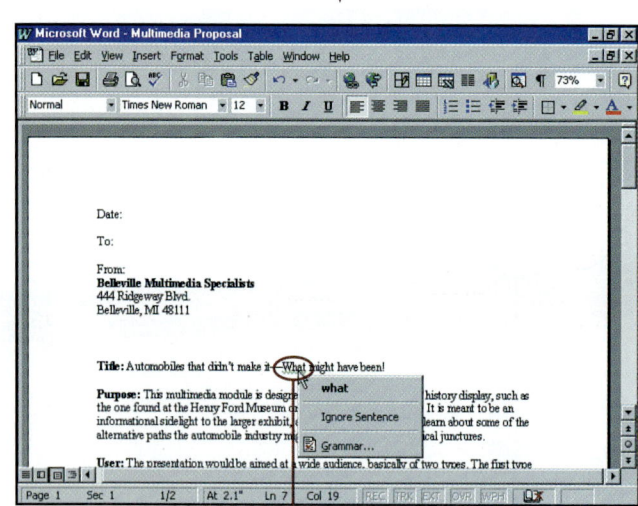

A wavy green line indicates a possible grammar error.

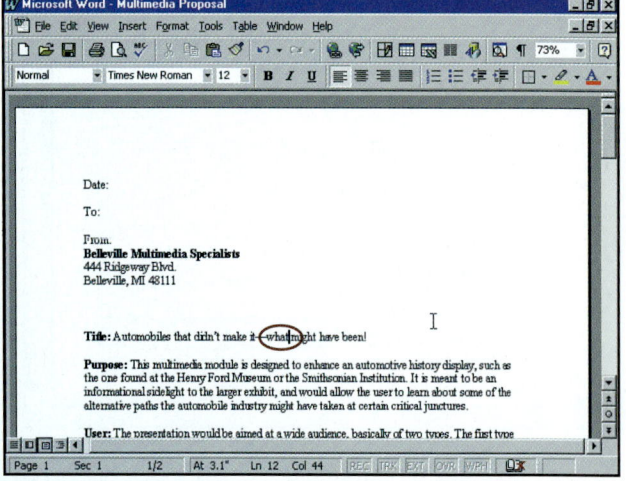

5 Click **what** in the shortcut menu to accept the recommended change. Notice that **what** is now lowercase.

126 **Learn Word 97, Second Edition**

Task 2

Using the Spelling and Grammar Checker

Why would I do this?

Sometimes you do not want to break your train of thought to correct errors as you type. You can wait until you have finished all or part of the document and then check all of the spelling and grammar problems at once. Using the Spelling and Grammar Checker, you can also type in the correct spelling of a word and then add it to the dictionary. You cannot do this using the shortcut menu.

In this task, you learn how to check the possible spelling and grammar errors in an entire document at one time.

1 Place the insertion point at the beginning of the document and then click the **Spelling** button on the Standard toolbar. The **Spelling and Grammar** dialog box is displayed, showing the first possible spelling or grammar error in the document—the word **notivated**.

> **In Depth:** The dialog box should display the sentence containing the misspelled word **notivated**. If your program stops at an earlier word, click the **Ignore** button until you reach this word.

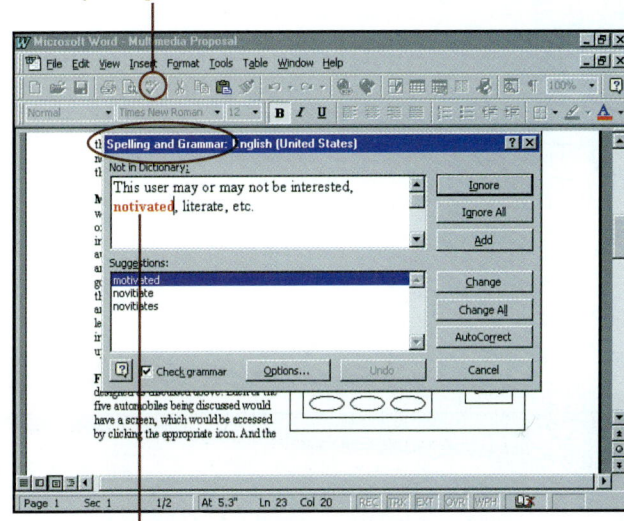

Spelling button

The unrecognized word is highlighted.

2 Click once on the word **motivated** in the **Suggestions** area if necessary. **Motivated** is the correct word for this sentence.

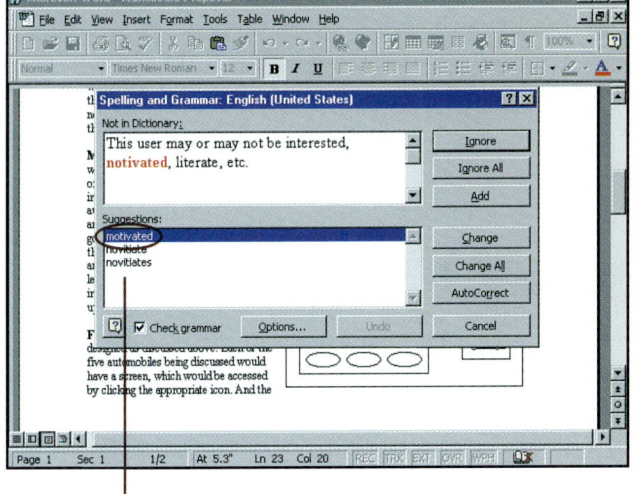

Suggested words to replace the misspelled word

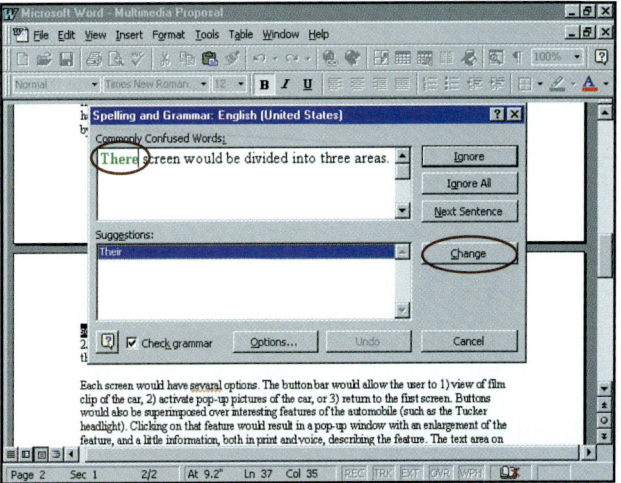

3 Click the **Change** button. The selected word replaces the misspelled word, and the Spelling and Grammar Checker moves to the next identified error—a sentence beginning with **There**.

Lesson 6: Using Word Utilities   127

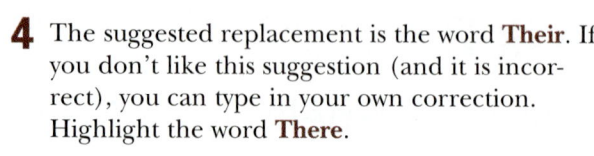

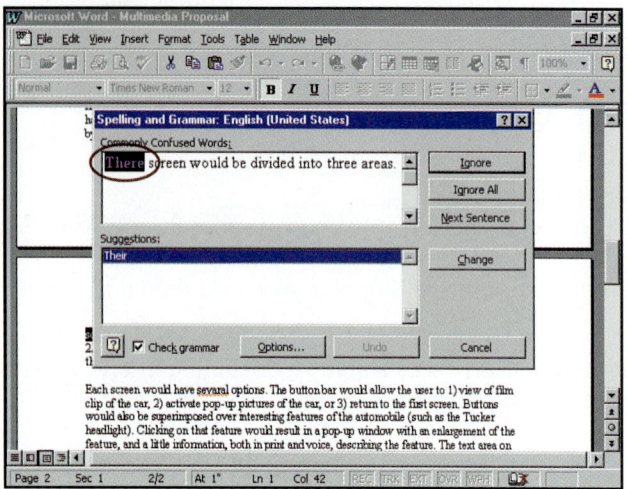

4 The suggested replacement is the word **Their**. If you don't like this suggestion (and it is incorrect), you can type in your own correction. Highlight the word **There**.

5 Type **The** to begin the sentence with the word **The**.

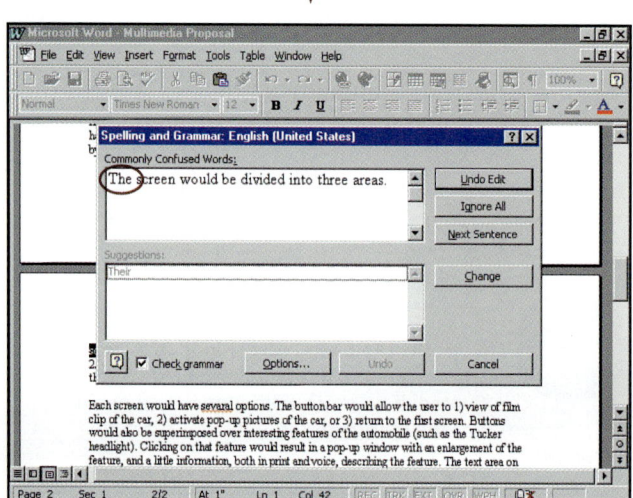

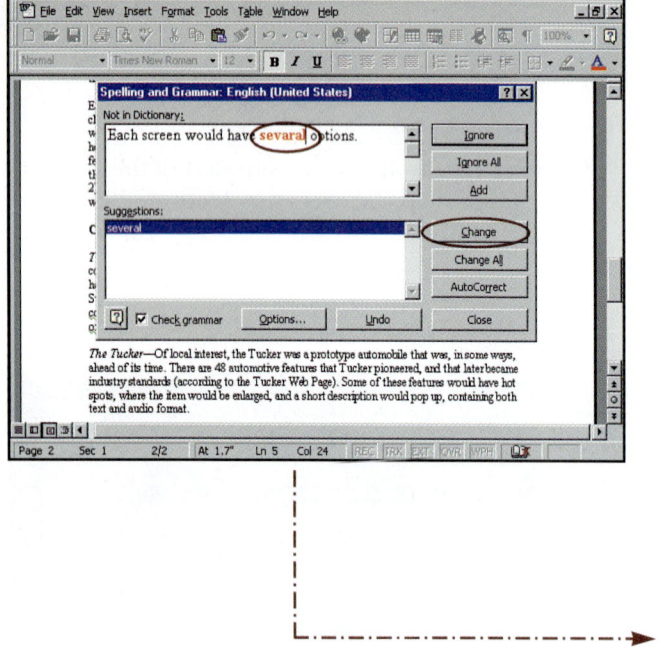

6 Click the **Change** button to replace the selected text with your correction. The program makes the replacement and moves to the next identified problem, the misspelled word **sevaral**.

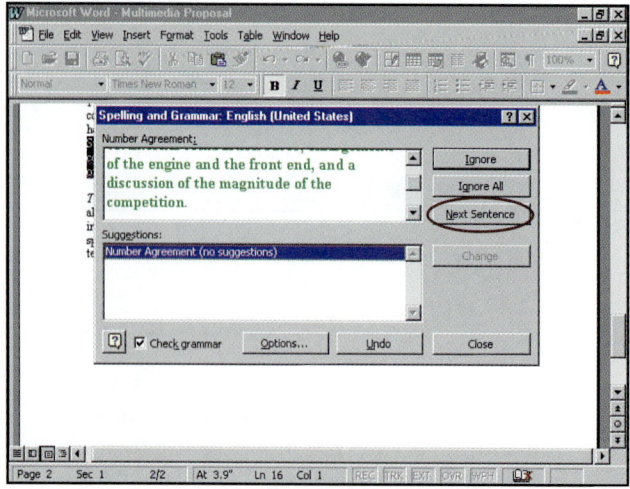

7 Choose **several** from the **Suggestions** area and click **Change**. The checker moves to a long sentence about the Stanley Steamer. That sentence is correct as it is. Click **Next Sentence** to move on without making any changes. The very next sentence in the paragraph is highlighted.

128 Learn Word 97, Second Edition

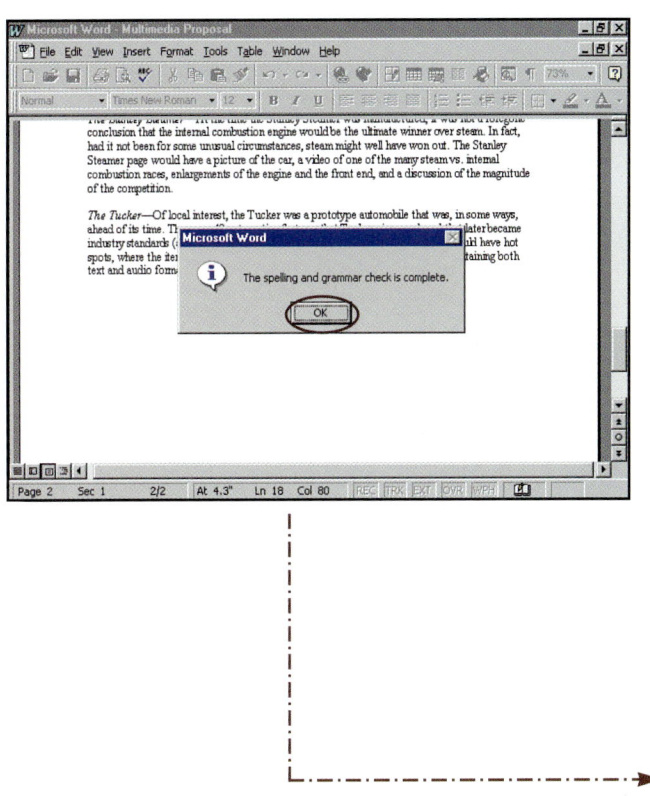

8 Choose **Next Sentence** to skip this sentence. A dialog box appears telling you that the spelling and grammar check is complete.

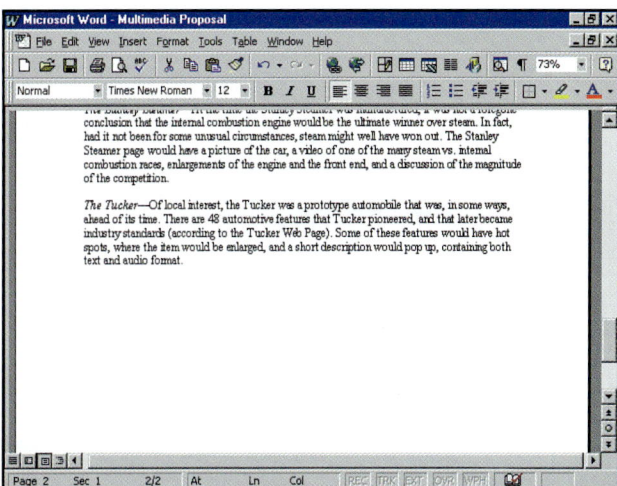

9 Click **OK** to return to the document.

Lesson 6: Using Word Utilities 129

...anges

...do this?

...both the business world and academia work with other people on the same document. Word offers a ... to see what changes have been made to a document and who made the changes. This feature can be enormously helpful to each person who has a hand in writing and editing the document.

In this task, you learn to track changes in a document and then accept the changes.

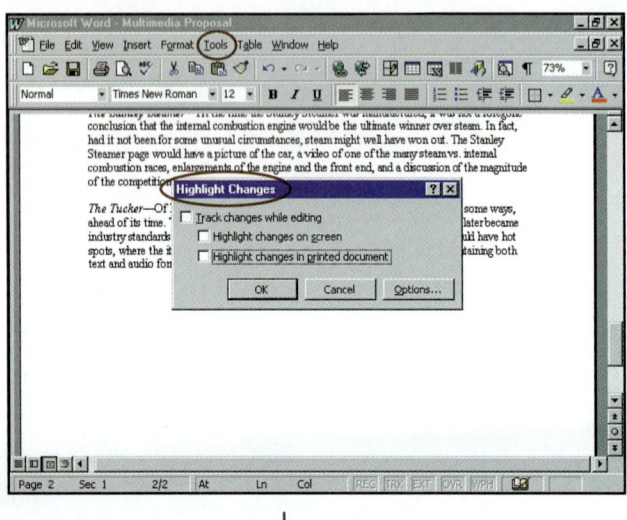

1 Choose **Tools**, **Track Changes**, **Highlight Changes** from the menu. The **Highlight Changes** dialog box is displayed.

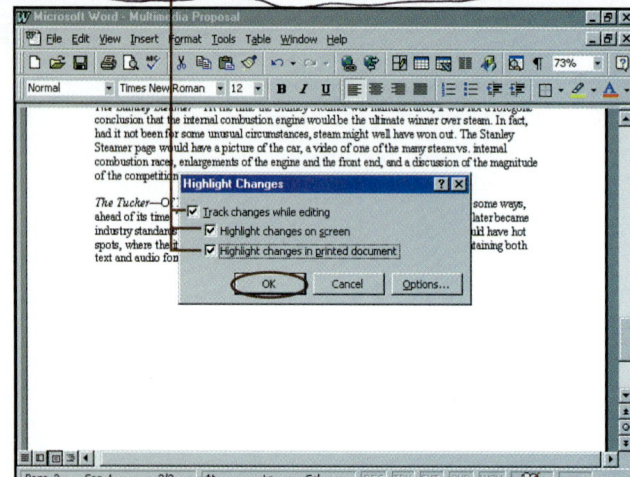

All three Highlight Changes options are selected.

2 Select the option boxes for **Track changes while editing**, **Highlight changes on screen**, and **Highlight changes in printed document** if they are not already selected.

Added text is underlined and in a different color.

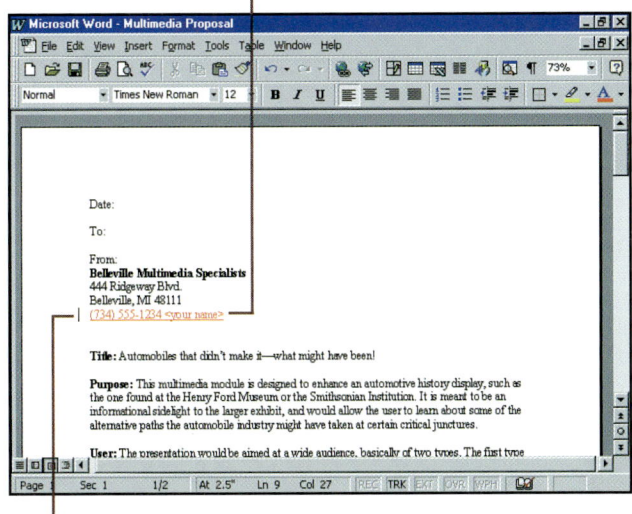

A line is shown in the margin next to the change.

3. Click **OK**. Place the insertion point in the line just after the address near the top of the document. Type **(734) 555-1234 <your name>**. (Type your name in place of <your name>.) Notice that the added text is displayed in red, and a line is added to the left side of the document area next to the change.

In Depth: The color displayed for changes may be different on your screen, depending on the settings used by the last person to use this feature. If you want to change the color, click the **Options** button when you are in the **Highlight Changes** dialog box. You might also want to change the color if you have problems seeing certain colors.

4. Scroll down and highlight **a wide audience, basically of two types** in the third paragraph. This phrase is awkwardly written and needs to be changed.

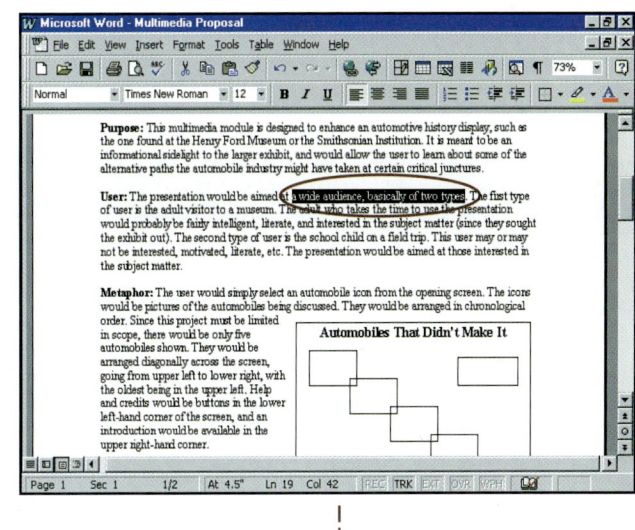

A line is shown in the margin next to the change.   Deleted text is still shown.

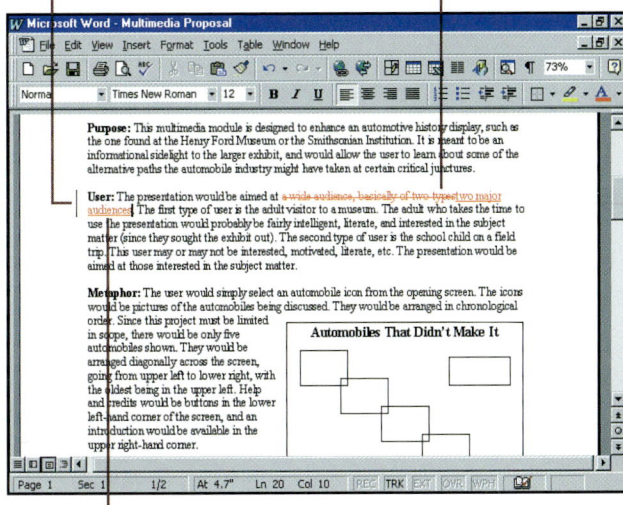

New text is underlined.

5. Type **two major audiences**. This text replaces the highlighted text, but the deleted text still appears with dashes through the words. Once again, a vertical line appears to the left of the changes. Your changes are now completed.

Lesson 6: Using Word Utilities   131

6 Click the **Print** button. Notice that all of the editing marks appear on the printout.

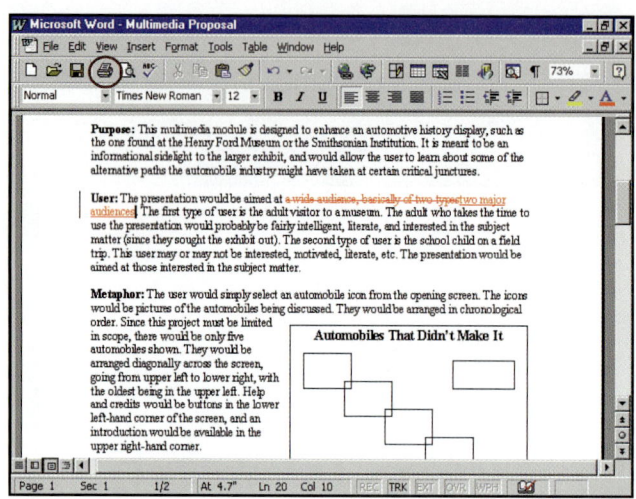

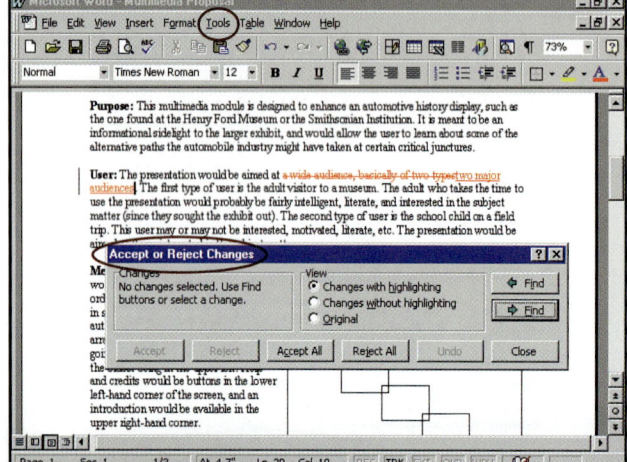

7 Choose **Tools**, **Track Changes**, **Accept or Reject Changes** from the menu. The **Accept or Reject Changes** dialog box is displayed.

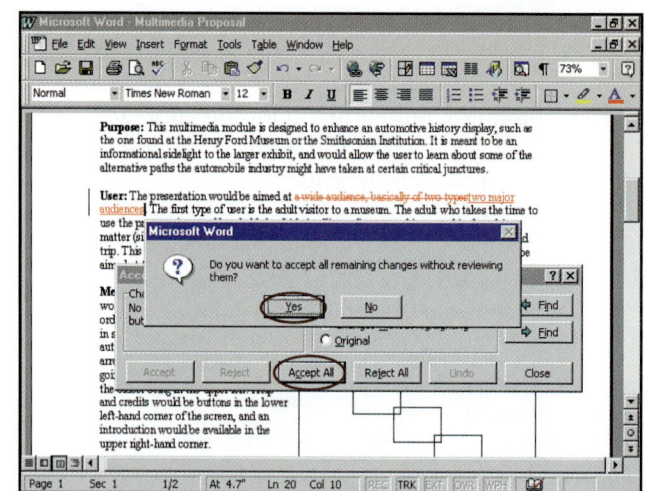

8 Choose **Accept All** to accept all of the changes. A dialog box is displayed asking whether you want to accept the changes without reviewing them.

Learn Word 97, Second Edition

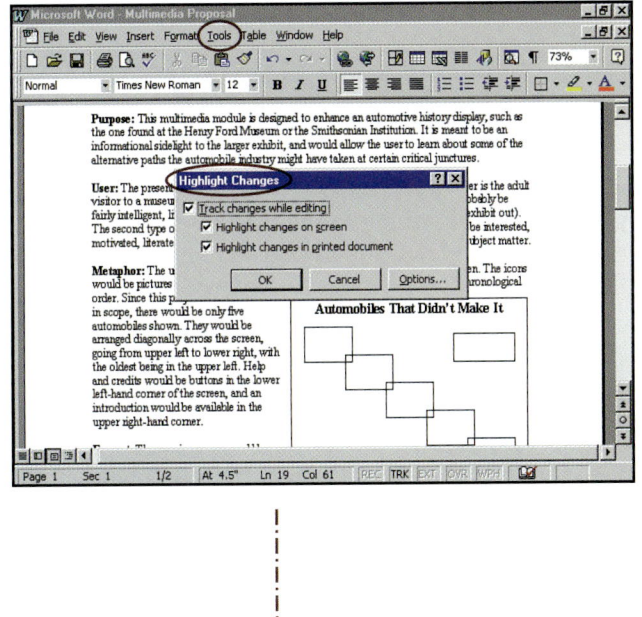

9 Click the Yes button to accept all chang[es]. [Click] Close to close the dialog box. To turn of[f track]ing, choose Tools, Track Changes, Highli[ght] Changes from the menu. The Highlight Cha[nges] dialog box is displayed.

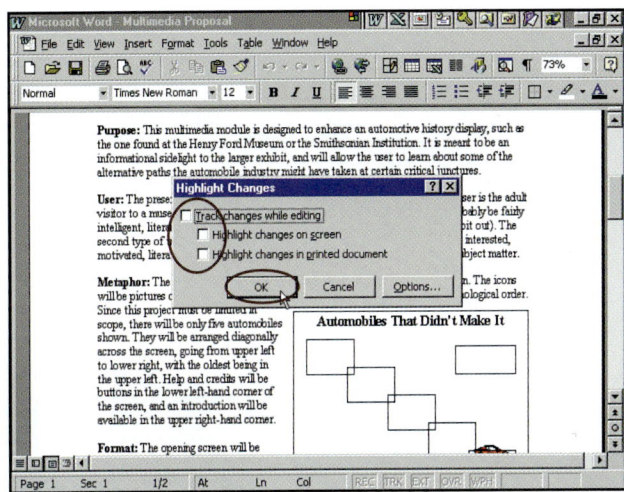

10 Turn off all three option boxes and click OK. This turns off the tracking option.

Lesson 6: Using Word Utilities 133

...ves you a great deal of time, even if you never add anything to the list of automatic correc-
...art adding words you commonly misspell (or type incorrectly), you save even more time. You
...the AutoCorrect tool to expand abbreviations into longer words or phrases. As you use this tool, it
...es second nature to you.

In this task, you learn to use the AutoCorrect feature to correct common typographical errors and misspelled words. You also learn how to add abbreviations that will expand into longer phrases.

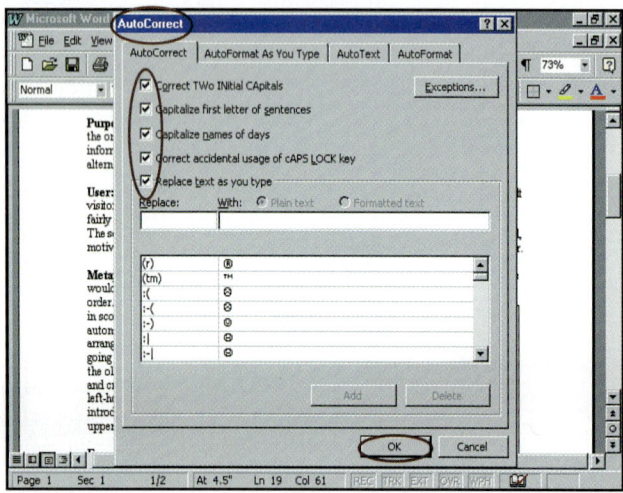

1 Choose **Tools**, **AutoCorrect** from the menu to activate the **AutoCorrect** dialog box. Click the **AutoCorrect** tab, if necessary, and make sure all five of the check boxes at the top of the dialog box are checked.

2 Click **OK** to close the dialog box. Scroll to the bottom of the **Multimedia Proposal** document and place the insertion point two lines below the bottom of the last paragraph.

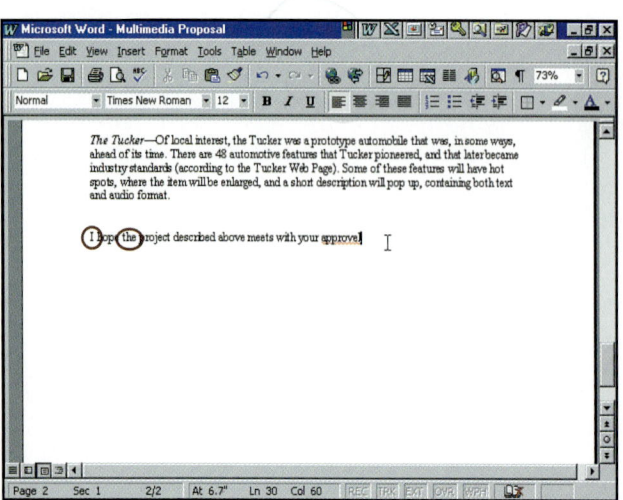

3 Watch the screen closely and type **i hope teh project described above meets with your approval.** exactly as shown. Notice that the first letter of the sentence is automatically capitalized and the word **teh** is corrected. The word **approval**, on the other hand, was not corrected.

134 Learn Word 97, Second Edition

4 Choose **Tools**, **AutoCorrect** from the menu to activate the **AutoCorrect** dialog box. Click the **AutoCorrect** tab if necessary.

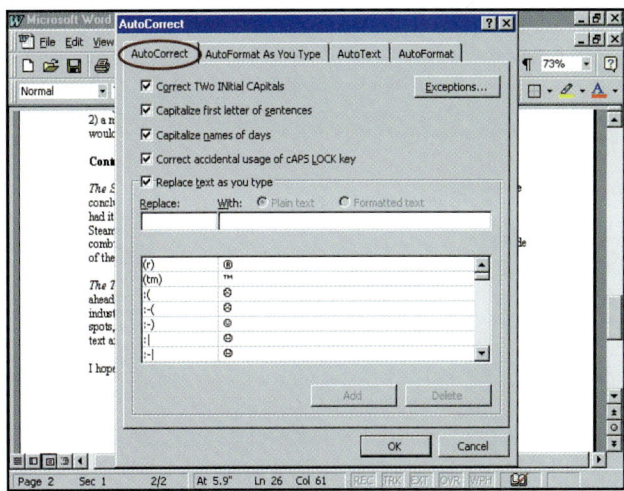

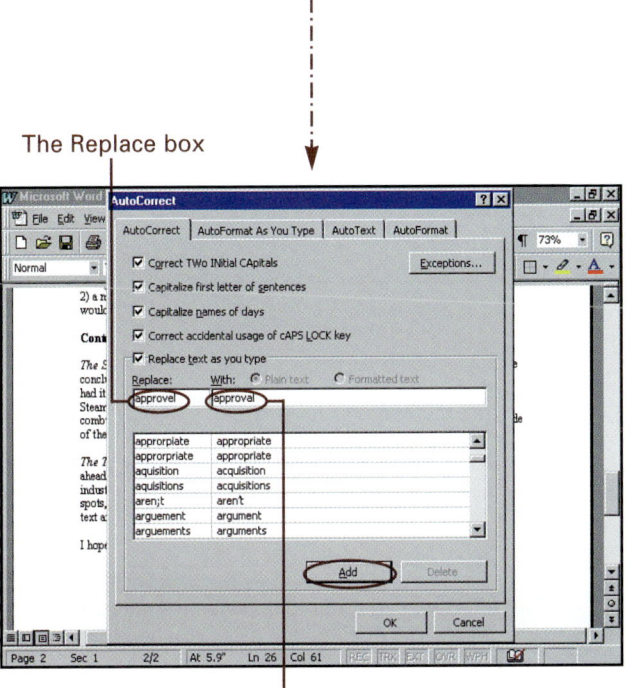

The Replace box

The With box

5 Type **approvel** in the **Replace** box and then type **approval** in the **With** box. Click the **Add** button to add this misspelled word to the **AutoCorrect** list. If approval is one of your commonly misspelled words, it will correct itself automatically each time you make this mistake.

6 Type **YHAM** in the **Replace** box, press Tab, and then type **Ypsilanti Historical Automobile Museum** in the **With** box. Click **Add**.

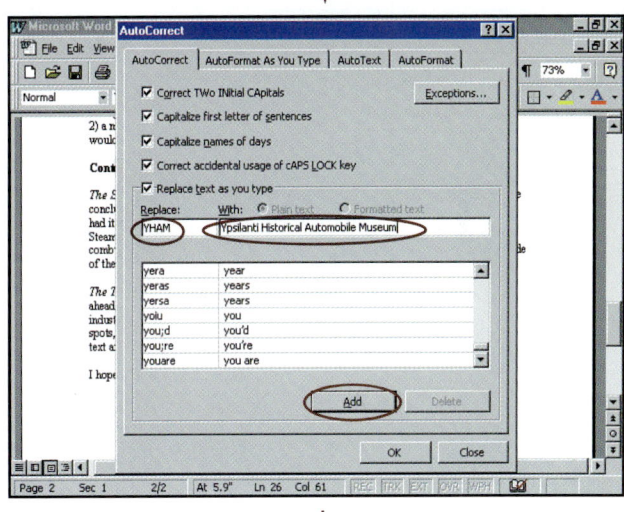

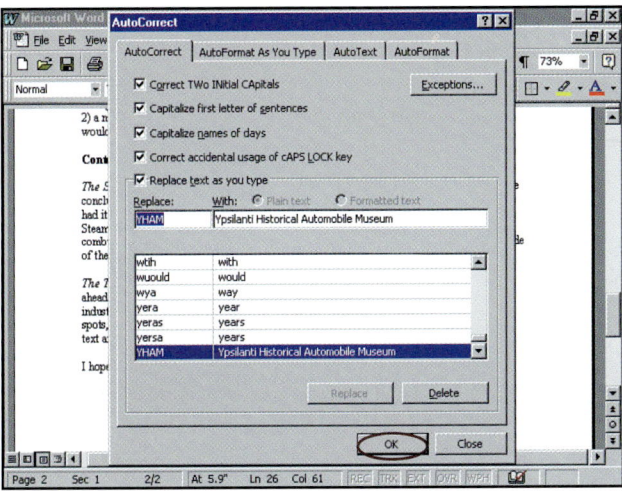

7 Click **OK**. This enables you to type in these initials and have Word expand them into the phrase you typed.

Lesson 6: Using Word Utilities

8 Scroll up to the top of the document, place the insertion point to the right of the **To:**, and press Spacebar to add a space after the colon.

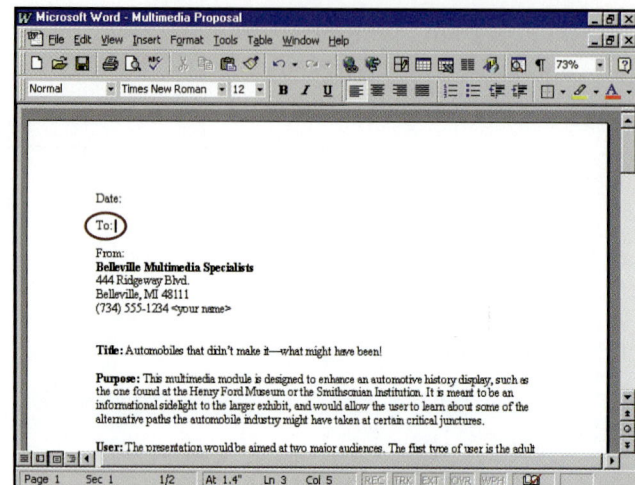

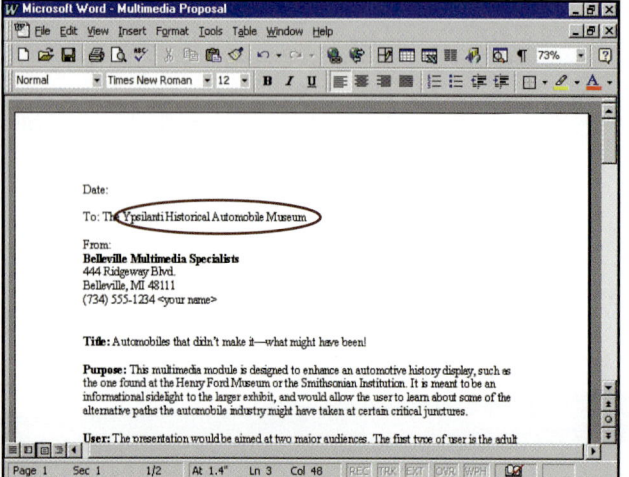

9 Type **The YHAM**, and then press Spacebar. The four initials were automatically expanded into the full name you entered in the **AutoCorrect With** box.

In Depth: In order to expand an AutoCorrect entry, you need to add a punctuation mark or press Spacebar or Enter.

Task 5

Using AutoText

Why would I do this?

For most simple expansions, such as the one you did in task 4, the AutoCorrect tool is sufficient. If you have multiple-line text that you use repeatedly, however, a feature called AutoText is more helpful. A subset of AutoText is the *AutoComplete* feature, which completes AutoText entries and commonly used words, such as the names of months or days of the week.

In this task, you learn how to insert AutoText and how to use the AutoComplete feature.

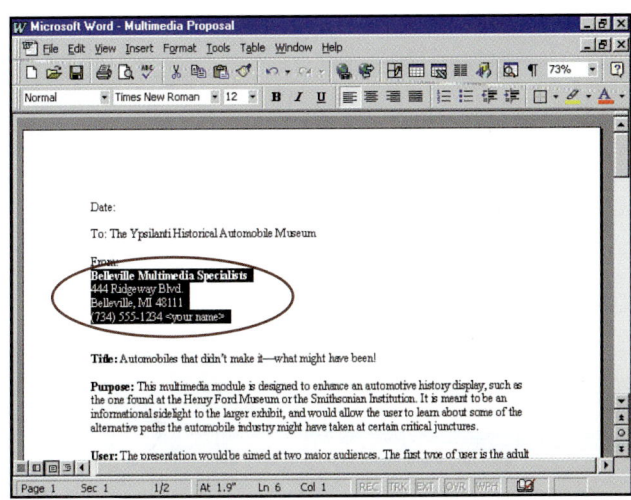

1 Highlight the address and telephone number near the top of the **Multimedia Proposal** document. You will use the **AutoText** tool for this text.

2 Choose **Tools**, **AutoCorrect** from the menu to activate the **AutoCorrect** dialog box. Click the **AutoText** tab. Notice that the full address is shown in the **Preview** area and that the first line is displayed in the **Enter AutoText entries here** area.

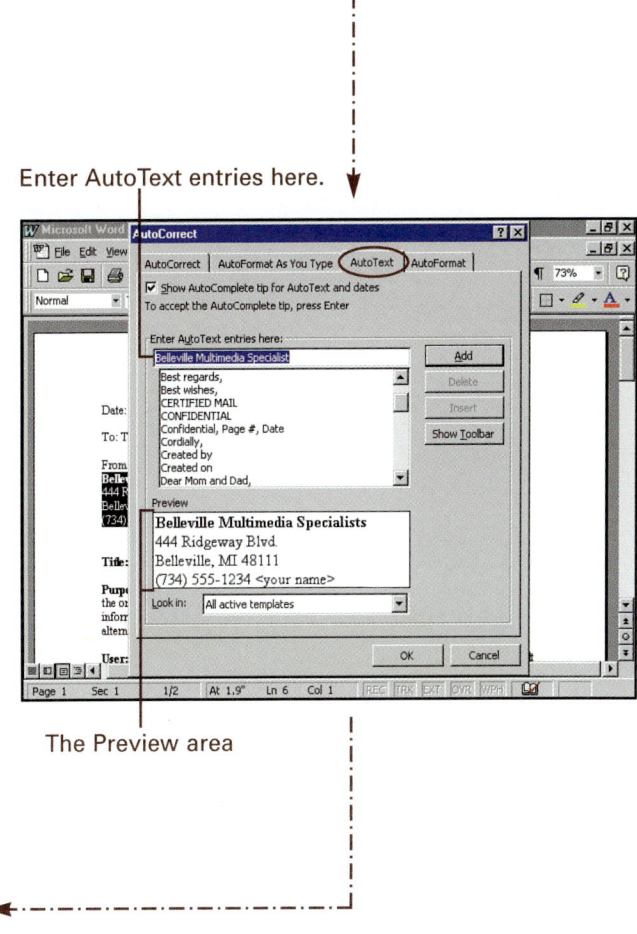

Enter AutoText entries here.

The Preview area

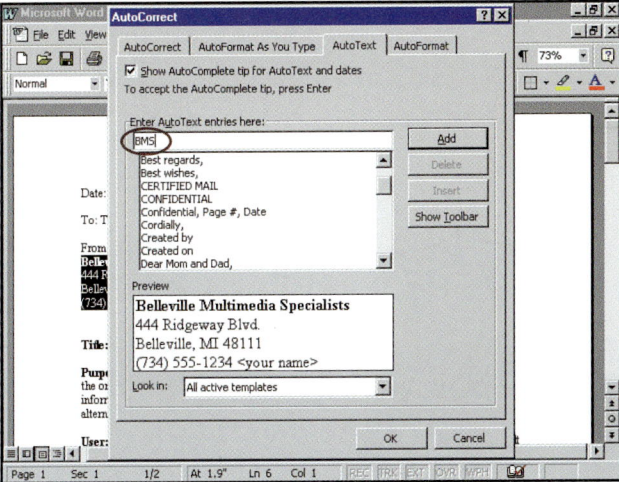

3 Type **BMS** over the entry in the **Enter AutoText entries here** area. Notice that the text in the **Preview** box remains the same.

Lesson 6: Using Word Utilities

4 Select **S**how AutoComplete tip for AutoText and dates if necessary. Choosing this option activates the **AutoComplete** tool if it has been turned off. Click **Add** to add the **AutoText** entry, and then click **OK** to close the dialog box.

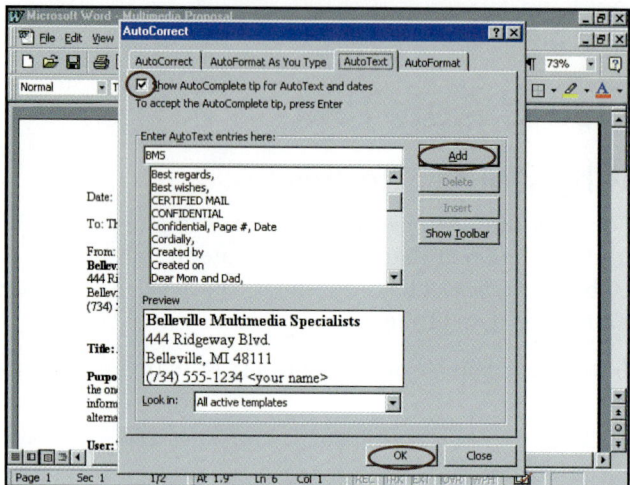

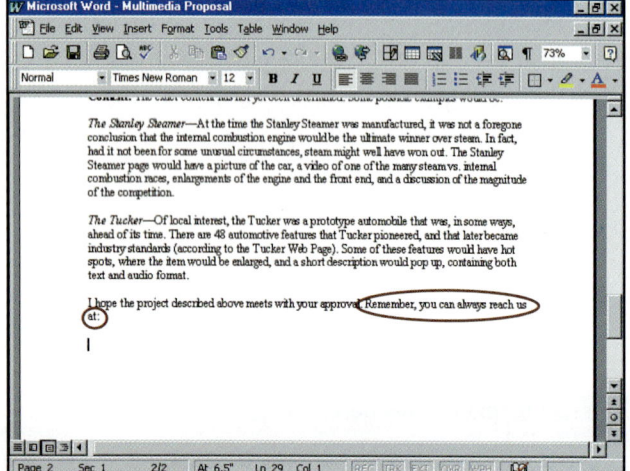

5 Scroll to the bottom of the document and place the insertion point at the end of the last sentence. Type **Remember, you can always reach us at:** and press ⏎Enter twice.

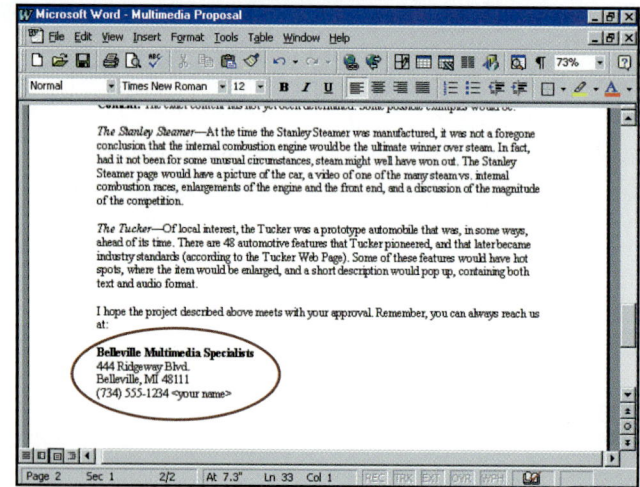

6 Type **BMS** and press F3. **AutoText** expands the entry into the full address.

Learn Word 97, Second Edition

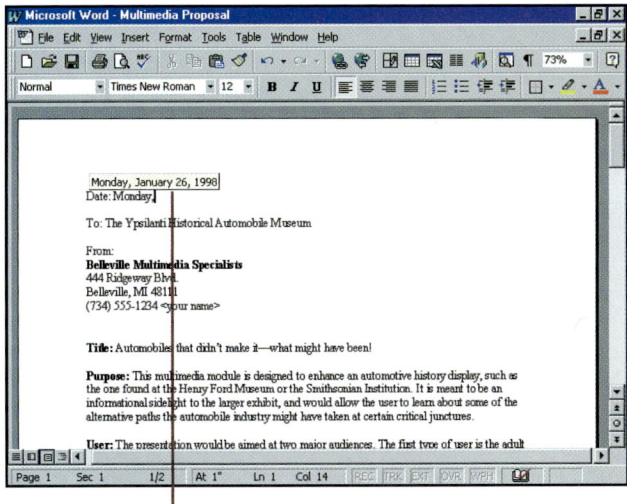

The ScreenTip shows the current date.

7 Scroll to the top of the document. Place the insertion point to the right of **Date:** in the first line. Press Spacebar and then type the current day of the week, followed by a comma. Today's full date is displayed in a *ScreenTip*. A ScreenTip is a box providing additional information, which pops up when you point to a button or hyperlink.

 **In Depth:** The day and date on your screen differ from the one shown in the figure.

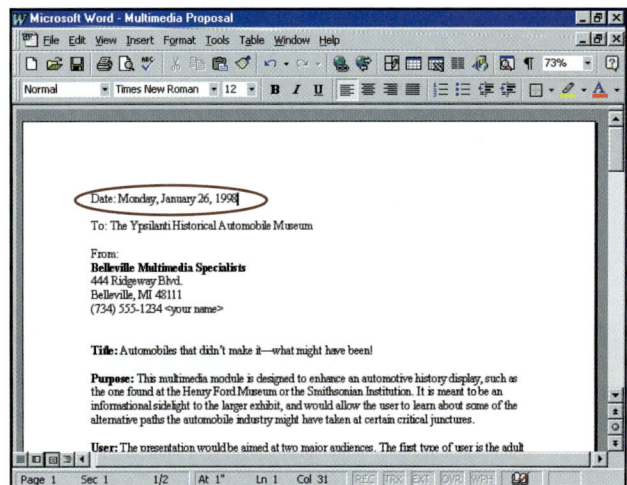

8 Press Enter. The **AutoComplete** tool inserts the full current date, but the Enter key does not send the insertion point to the next line.

Lesson 6: Using Word Utilities 139

Task 6

Finding Text

Why would I do this?

In long documents, you will sometimes want to go to a specific section but will not remember where that section is. If you can remember a unique word or phrase that occurs in the section you are searching for, you can use the Find command to go there quickly.

In this task, you learn to find text in a document.

1 Place the insertion point at the beginning of the document. Select **Edit**, **Find** from the menu. The **Find and Replace** dialog box is displayed.

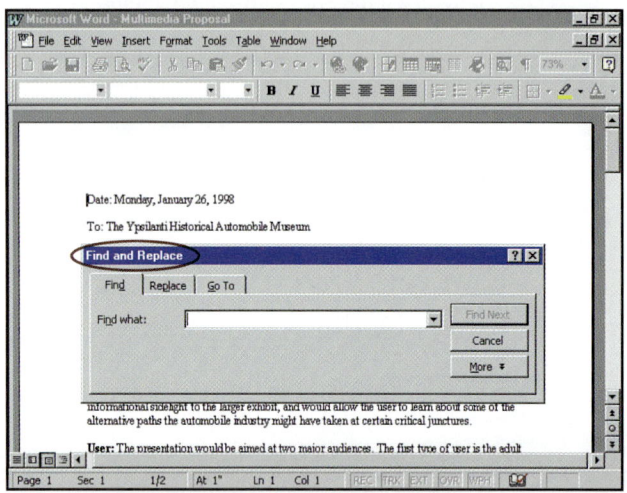

2 Type **opening screen** in the **Find and Replace** box. Because the insertion point is at the beginning of the document, the program finds the first appearance of this phrase in the document.

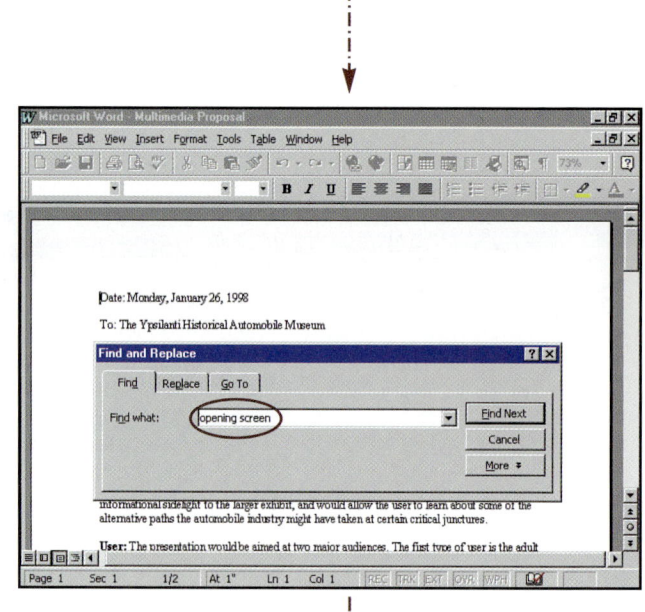

Matching text is highlighted.

3 Click the **Find Next** button. The first instance of the phrase is highlighted on the screen. The dialog box remains open.

> **In Depth:** If you see something that you want to change while using this dialog box, click on the document. Make your edit and then come back to the **Find and Replace** dialog box by clicking on it. This is one of the few dialog boxes that allows you to move back and forth between it and the document.

4 Click the **Find Next** button again. The next instance of the phrase is highlighted.

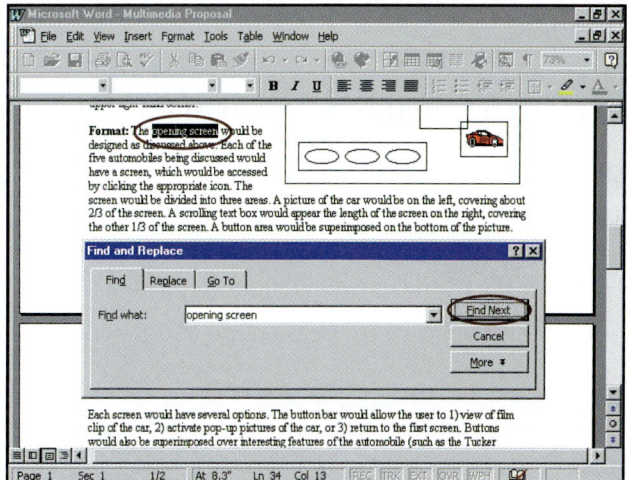

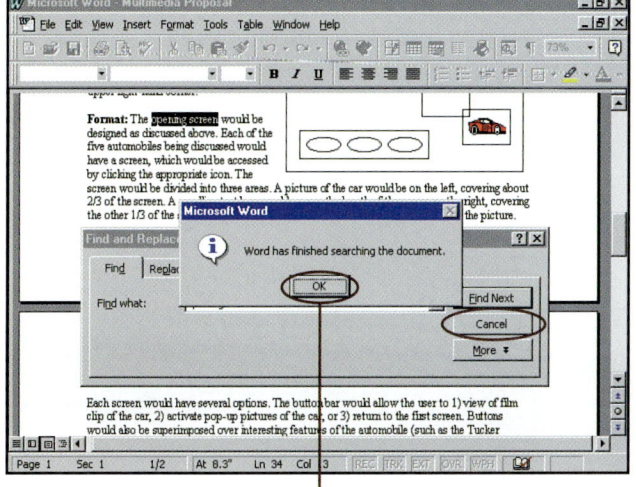

A dialog box tells you that the search is finished.

5 Click the **Find Next** button again. A dialog box tells you there are no more instances of the phrase in the document. Click **OK** to close the dialog box and then click **Cancel** to close the **Find and Replace** dialog box.

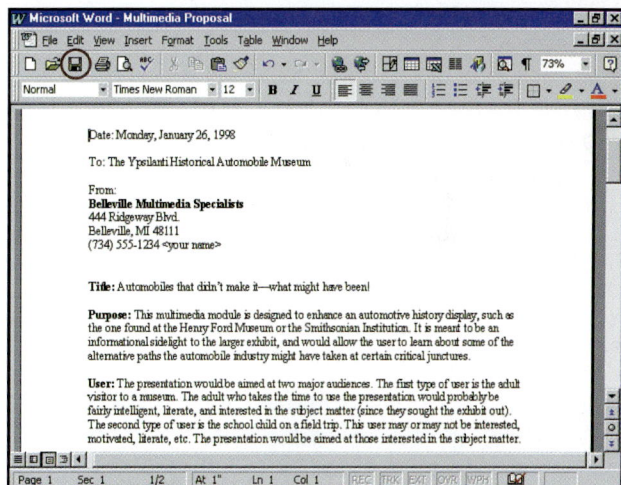

6 Click the **Save** button to save your changes.

Lesson 6: Using Word Utilities   141

Task 7

Finding and Replacing Text

Why would I do this?

Sometimes you want to find a word or phrase so you can replace it with something else. For example, you may misspell a name or find a word you like better than the one you chose before. Word gives you the option of replacing the words one at a time or replacing all of them at once.

In this task, you learn to use the Find and Replace tool.

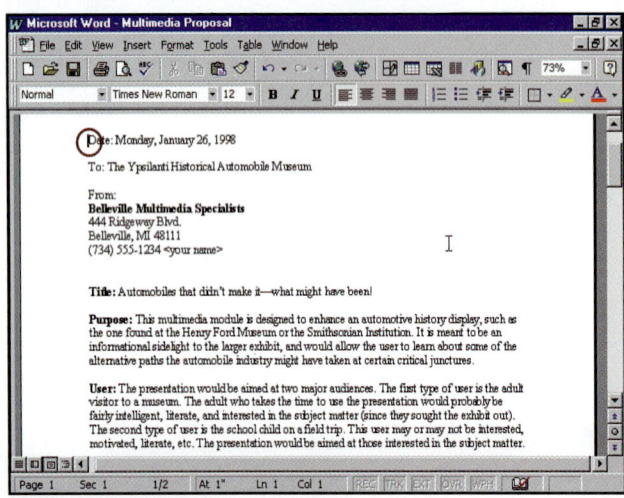

1 Place the insertion point at the beginning of the **Multimedia Proposal** document. You have decided to replace **would** with **will** throughout the document.

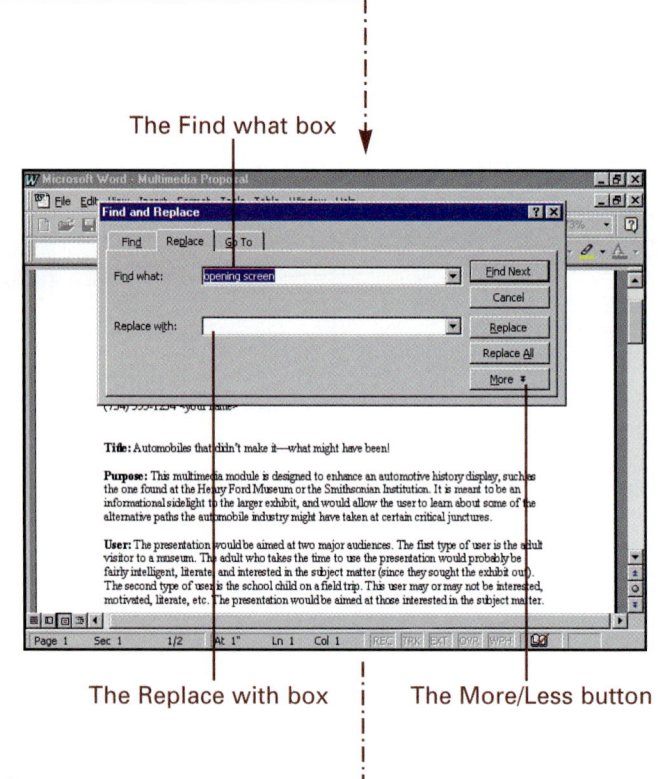

The Find what box

The Replace with box   The More/Less button

2 Select **Edit**, **Replace** from the menu. The **Find and Replace** dialog box is displayed, this time with a second input box. Click the **More** button to see the **Find and Replace** options. The More button becomes a Less button.

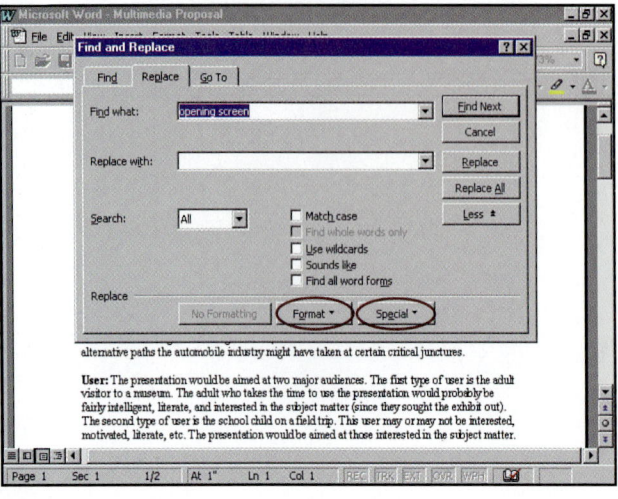

3 The **Find and Replace** dialog box extends to show special search options.

> **In Depth:** You can search for (and replace) more than just text. You can look for special font or paragraph formatting using the **Format** drop-down menu. You can also search for special characters, such as tabs, carriage returns, and line breaks, using the **Special** drop-down menu.

142 Learn Word 97, Second Edition

4 Type **would** in the **Find what** box. Press `Tab` to get to the **Replace with** box, or click in that box. Type **will** in the **Replace with** box.

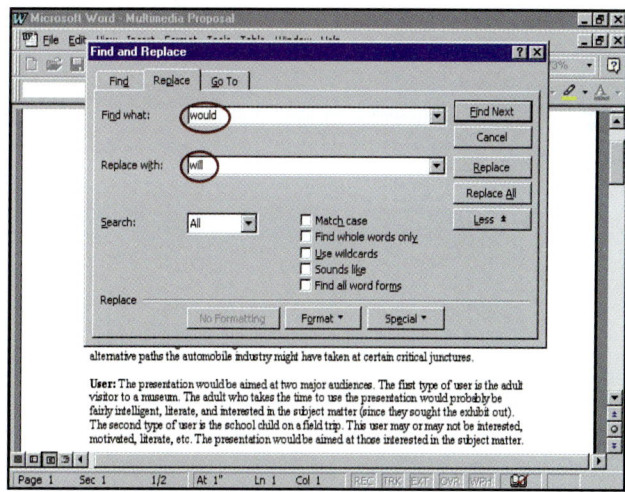

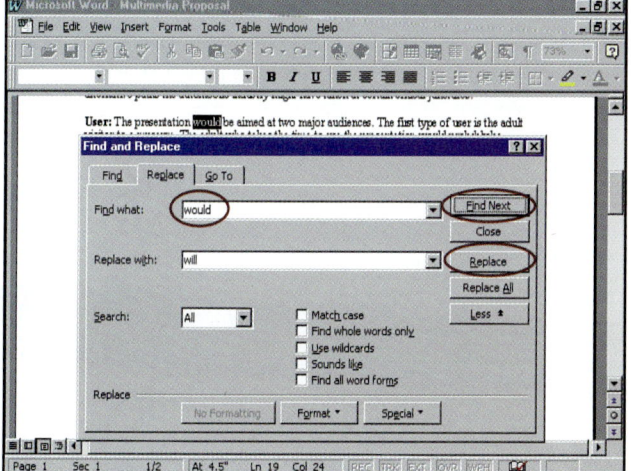

5 Click **Find Next**. The first instance of the word **would** is highlighted. Click **Replace** to substitute **will** for **would**. The program moves to the next instance of the word.

6 Select **Find whole words only**. Click **Replace All**.

Pothole: You have now replaced all of the instances of the word **would**. It is unlikely that this word is part of a larger word, but these things occasionally happen when using **Replace All**. For example, if you find out that a person's name is spelled **Smyth** and replace **Smith** with **Smyth** globally, you could end up with the Smythsonian Institution or a blacksmyth in your document. Sometimes it's safer to click on **Replace** instead of **Replace All** and do individual search and replaces. That way you won't inadvertently replace something that you shouldn't have.

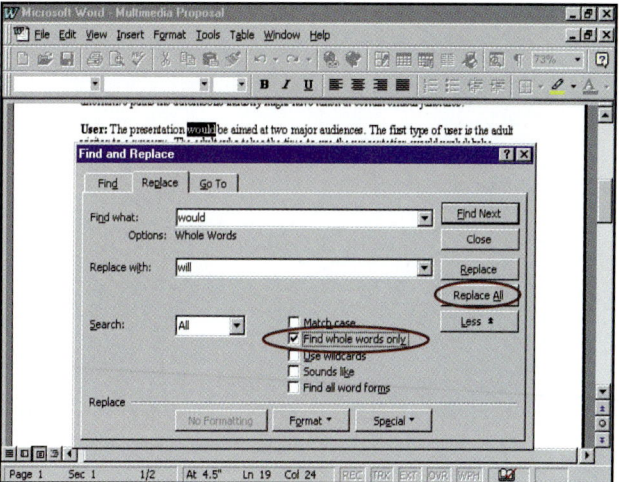

Lesson 6: Using Word Utilities

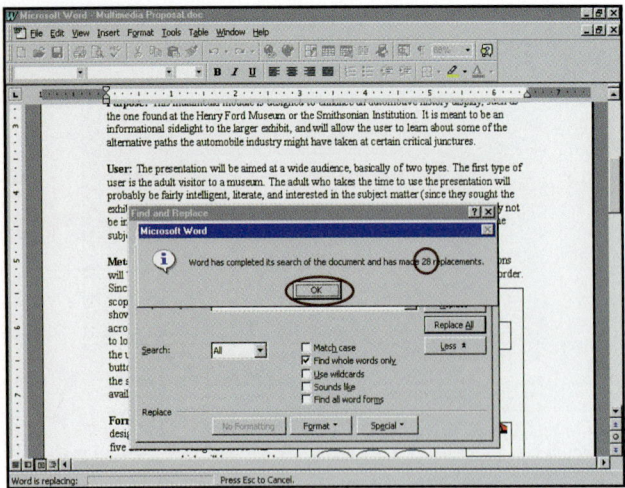

7 **Would** is now replaced with **will** throughout the document. A dialog box appears telling you the search is done and indicating how many substitutions were made—in this case, 28. Click **OK**.

8 Click the **Close** button to leave the **Find and Replace** dialog box. Click the **Save** button to save your work.

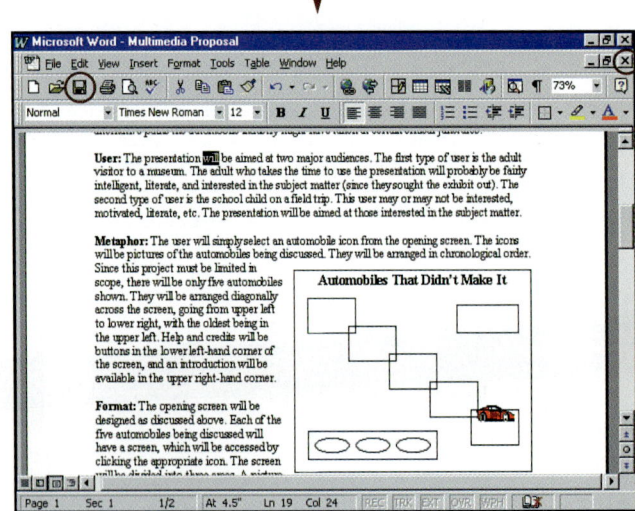

9 Click the **Close Window** button to close the document. Close Word.

144 Learn Word 97, Second Edition

Student Exercises

True-False
Circle either T or F.

T F 1. Each time you use the spell check feature, you have to check all the words in the whole document.

T F 2. The spell checker often assumes proper nouns (names) are misspelled words unless they happen to be spelled like an ordinary word, such as Baker. The only way to deal with proper nouns is to ignore the spell checker when it highlights names.

T F 3. If a word is marked with a red, jagged underline, you can right-click on it to correct its spelling.

T F 4. If you use "there" instead of "their," the spell checker does not catch it, but the grammar checker does.

T F 5. Several people can work on the same document, and each of their contributions can be identified separately.

T F 6. If Track Changes and Highlight Changes are both turned on and you replace one word with another, the original text is still shown next to the replacement.

T F 7. It is possible to print the document showing both the original and the substituted text.

T F 8. The AutoCorrect feature can be used to replace an organization's initials with its full name.

T F 9. If you start to type a commonly used word or phrase, the AutoComplete feature suggests the rest of the word(s) above the line, and it completes the word if you press ⏎Enter.

T F 10. If you are replacing one word with another, it is generally a good idea to examine each substitution individually rather than choosing Replace All. In this way, you avoid unexpected results.

Identifying Parts of the Word Screen

Refer to the figure and identify the numbered parts of the screen. Write the letter of the correct label in the space next to the number.

1. _____
2. _____
3. _____
4. _____
5. _____
6. _____
7. _____
8. _____
9. _____
10. _____

A. Suggested replacement

B. Button used to replace selected text with suggested text

C. Proper noun underlined as if it were misspelled

D. Acronym that is currently selected in the text because it should be capitalized

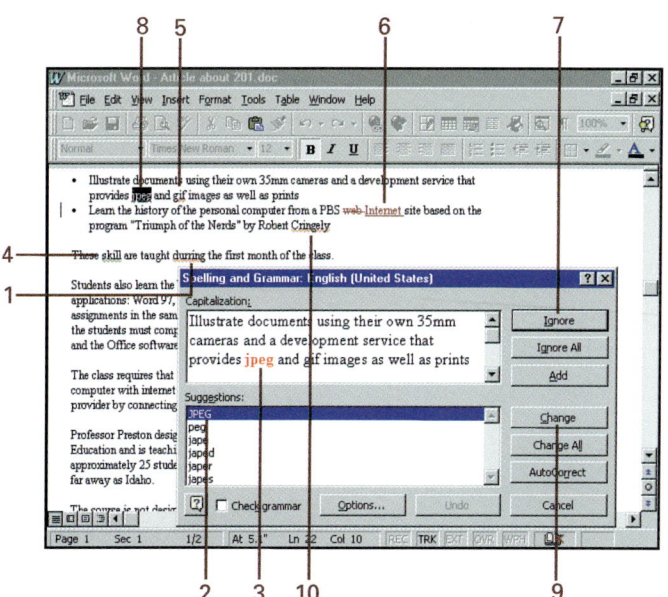

Lesson 6: Using Word Utilities

E. Another acronym that is underlined as if it were misspelled but is not currently selected

F. Misspelled word

G. Correctly spelled word that is used incorrectly

H. A change in the original text

I. Button used to skip the currently selected word without making any changes

J. Selected word displayed in the dialog box

Matching Questions

Match the following statements to the word or phrase from the list on the right. Write the letter of the matching word or phrase in the space provided next to the number.

1. ____ Method of indicating a word that is not in the program's dictionary

2. ____ Method of indicating a word or phrase that does not conform to the program's rules of grammar

3. ____ Names of places or things

4. ____ Feature that replaces a mistyped word such as "HEllo" with "Hello"

5. ____ Feature that completes a long phrase after the first few letters have been typed

6. ____ Method of preventing the program from identifying specialized words that are used in your profession

7. ____ Method of managing changes to a document

8. ____ Method that you would use if you were trying to find a particular paragraph in a legal document that dealt with penalties for overdue payment

9. ____ Feature you would use to make sure that all references to an old company had been replaced with the name of a new company

10. ____ A quick way to correct the spelling of a single word

A. Jagged green underline

B. AutoCorrect

C. Add to dictionary

D. Jagged red underline

E. Right-click on the word to bring up a shortcut menu of suggested replacement words

F. Edit, Find

G. Proper nouns

H. AutoText

I. Jagged blue line

J. Find and replace

K. Track Changes

Application Exercises

Exercise 1—Check Spelling and Grammar

1. Launch Microsoft Word. Open **Less0602** from the student files. Save the file as **Online Course**.

2. Right-click on the first misspelled word: **available**. Select the correct spelling from the shortcut menu.

3. Choose **Tools**, **Options**, **Spelling and Grammar** from the menu. Make sure that **Check grammar with spelling** is selected. Click **OK**.

4. Click the **Spelling and Grammar** button on the Standard toolbar to launch the **Spelling and Grammar** checking wizard.

5. Ignore the proper noun, **Cringely**, all of the occurrences of **Netmeeting**, and the capitalization suggestions for the words **Winter** and **Goes**. Change the other spelling and grammar mistakes as suggested.

6. Type **Edited by:**, followed by your name, on the line below the title.

7. Leave the document open for use in the next exercise.

Exercise 2—Using Find and Replace

1. Choose **Edit**, **Replace** from the menu.

2. Type **Netmeeting** in the **Find what** box.

3. Click the **Replace with** box and type **NetMeeting**.

4. Click **Replace All**, **OK**, and then **Close**.

5. Leave the document open for use in the next exercise.

Exercise 3—Track Changes

1. Choose **Tools**, **Track Changes**, **Highlight Changes** from the menu.

2. Select all three options in the dialog box: **Track changes while editing**, **Highlight changes on screen**, and **Highlight changes in printed document**.

3. Go to the last item in the list of bulleted points and change **personal computer** to **PC**. Your changes should be visible on the screen.

4. Print the first page of the document. The original term and its replacement should both be displayed on the printed page.

5. Close the document and save your changes.

Lesson 7
Working with Non-text Elements

Task 1: Adding Borders
Task 2: Adding Clip Art
Task 3: Resizing and Moving Clip Art
Task 4: Adding a Picture
Task 5: Wrapping Text Around an Image
Task 6: Using WordArt

Introduction

Microsoft Word enables you to create documents containing scanned pictures, *clip art*, borders, and even artistic-looking titles. These non-text elements are often used in the creation of flyers, posters, brochures, and newsletters.

Borders may be added around paragraphs or groups of paragraphs to set them off from the rest of the document. Word enables you to insert clip art images that come with the program and pictures from files that have been scanned in or captured with a digital camera to dress up a document. These graphics elements can be resized and repositioned, and the document text can be set to flow around the images. Word also has the capability to create interesting images using the letters from portions of text.

In this lesson, you learn how to add various non-text elements to a document.

Visual Summary

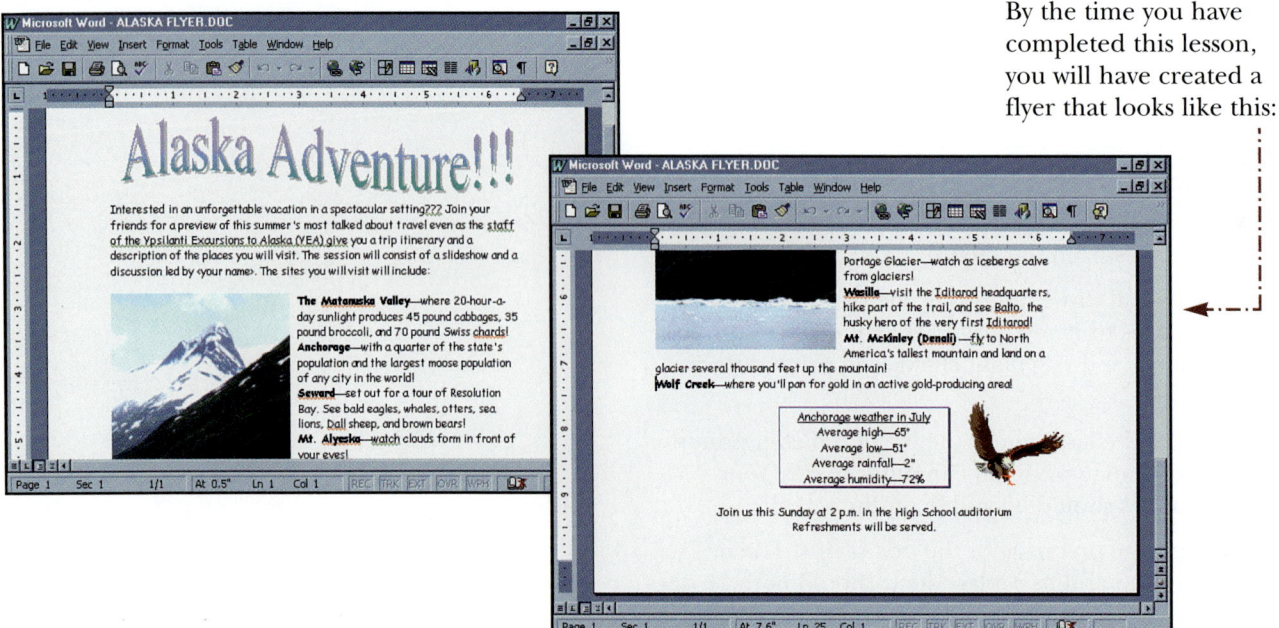

By the time you have completed this lesson, you will have created a flyer that looks like this:

Task 1
Adding Borders

Why would I do this?

Borders can be placed around text or graphics. They can be shown on one or more sides or on all four sides of the object. You can use borders to highlight important information that you want to stand out from the rest of the text.

In this task, you learn to add a border to several paragraphs of text.

1 Launch Microsoft Word. Open **Less0701** from the student files. Save the file as **Alaska Flyer**.

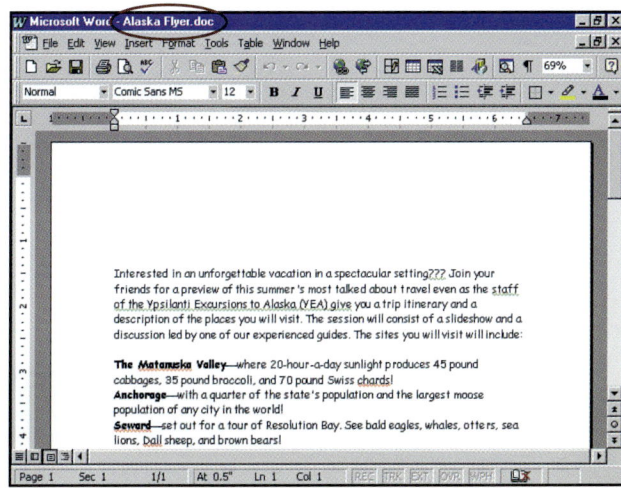

2 Scroll to the bottom of the flyer and select the five lines pertaining to Anchorage weather.

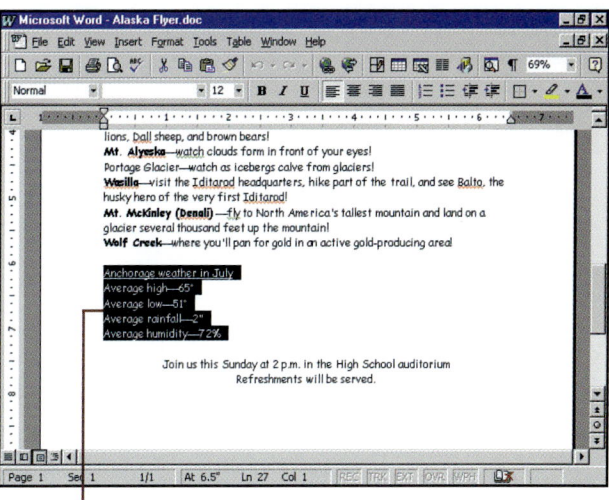

Selected text will have a border.

The Borders tab

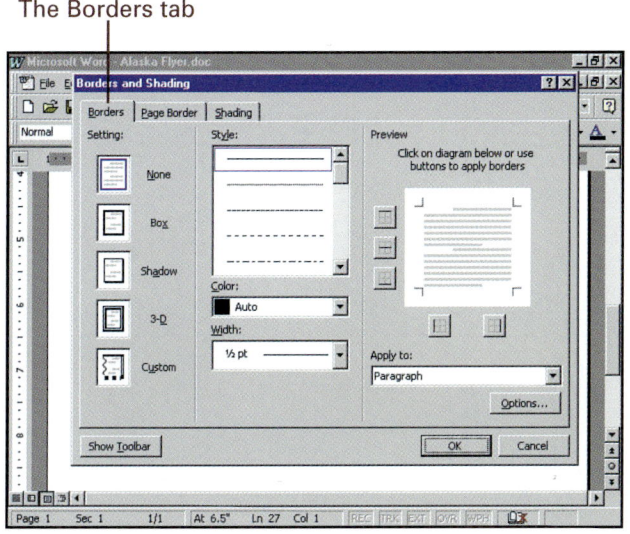

3 Select **Format**, **Borders and Shading** from the menu. Click the **Borders** tab if necessary.

4 Click the S**h**adow button in the **Setting** area, which gives the box a shadow effect.

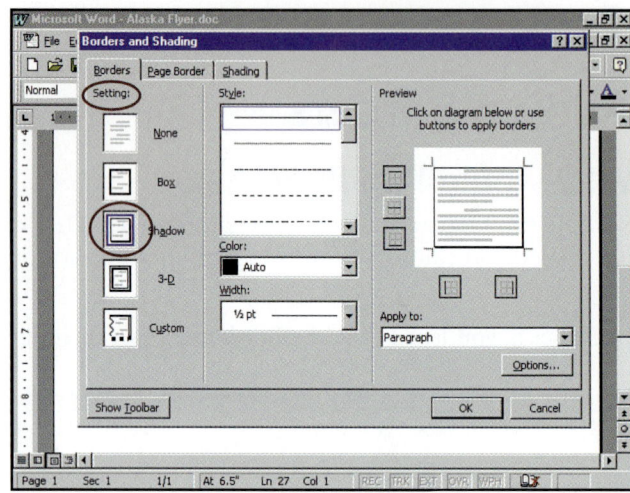

The Color drop-down menu

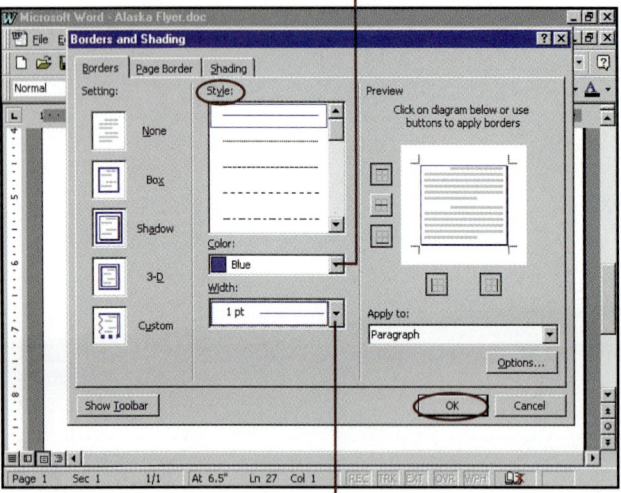

5 In the **Style** area, choose **Blue** from the **Color** drop-down menu and **1 pt** from the **Width** drop-down menu. Your border will be blue with a 1-point width. Look in the **Preview** area of the Borders and Shading dialog box to see what your box looks like.

The Width drop-down menu

The left margin marker   The right margin marker

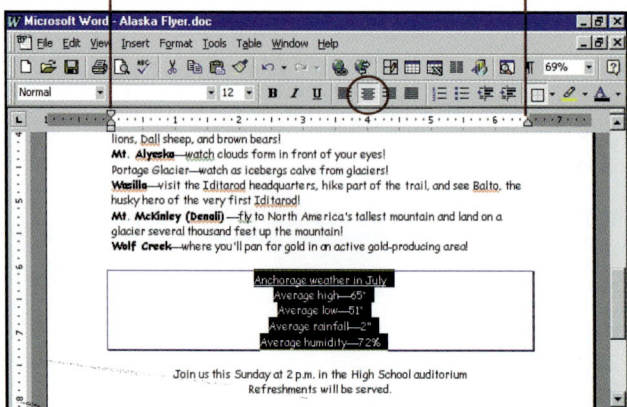

6 Click **OK** and then click the **Center** button in the Formatting toolbar. The box now extends from the left margin marker to the right margin marker.

Pothole: If you want a box to surround several paragraphs, the left and right margins must be the same. If they are different, you end up with multiple boxes.

150 Learn Word 97, Second Edition

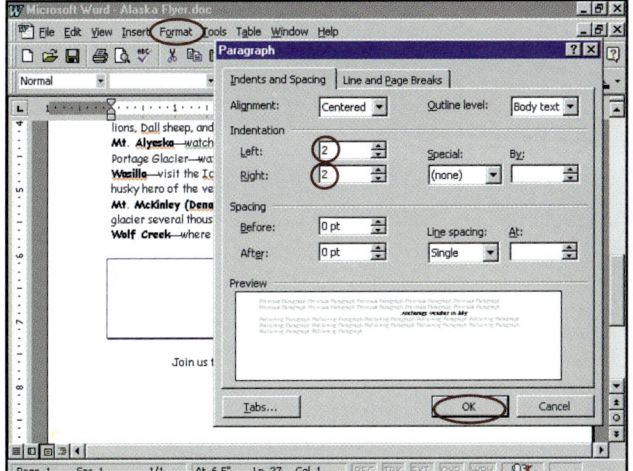

7 Select **F‌ormat**, **P‌aragraph** from the menu. Set the **L‌eft** and **R‌ight** indents to **2**. This leaves 2.5 inches for the selected text.

> **Quick Tip:** You can change the margins of the selected paragraphs without going to the menu. Grab the left indent marker on the ruler and drag it to the right, and then grab the right indent marker and drag it to the left.

The box now fits the selected text.

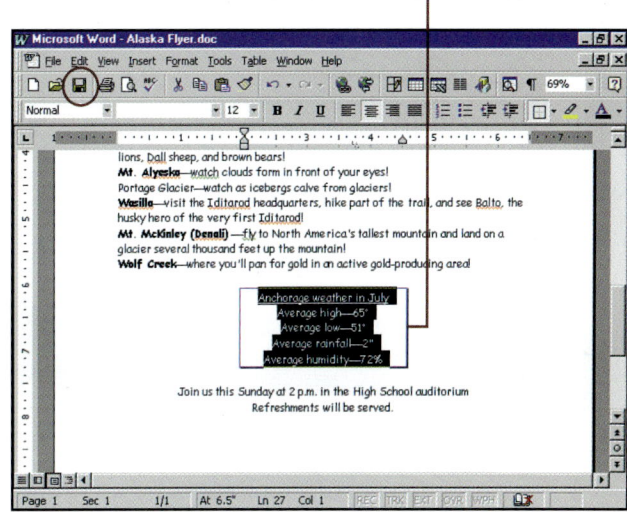

8 Click **OK**. The box now fits the text. Click the **Save** button to save your work.

Lesson 7: Working with Non-text Elements 151

Task 2
Adding Clip Art

Why would I do this?

Quite a few clip art images are included with Microsoft Word. These images cover a wide range of topics and styles, from black-and-white stick art to detailed color drawings. When you need an illustration for a flyer, poster, or brochure, you can usually find one that is appropriate.

In this task, you learn how to insert a clip art image into a document.

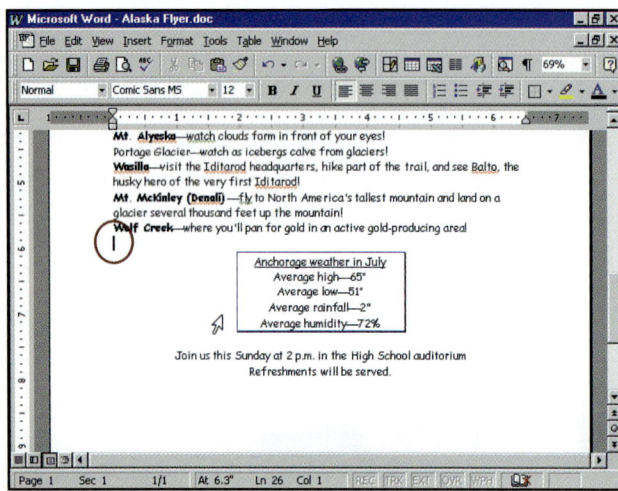

1 Place the insertion point in the blank line just after the words **Wolf Creek** in the **Alaska Flyer** document.

2 Select **Insert**, **Picture**, **Clip Art** from the menu. The **Microsoft Clip Gallery** is displayed. Make sure the **Clip Art** tab is selected.

> **Pothole:** If it has not been turned off, a dialog box is displayed that tells you more clips are available on the program CD. Click **OK** to close this box.

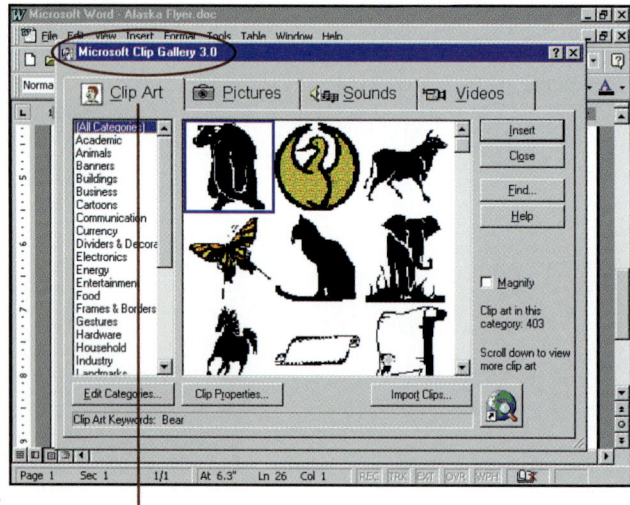

The Clip Art tab

152 Learn Word 97, Second Edition

The eagle will be placed at the insertion point.

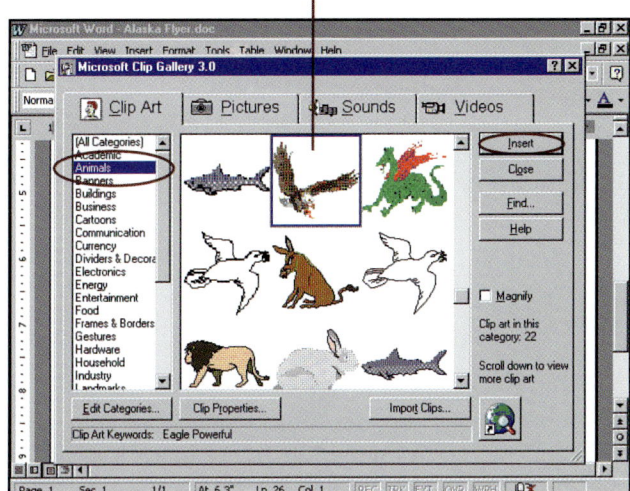

3 Select the **Animals** category. Scroll down and select the **eagle**.

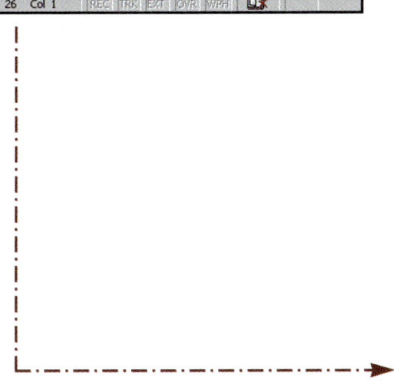

Pothole: The eagle may not be available on some installations. In that case, scan through the images and pick another appropriate one or go to the program CD and add the eagle to your Clip Art Gallery.

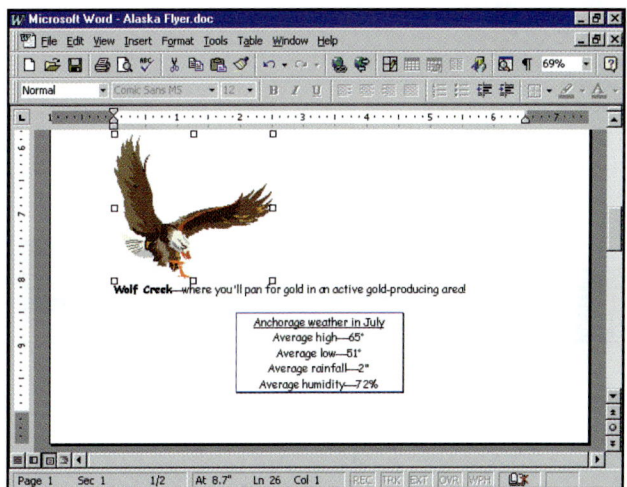

4 Click **Insert** to place the image in the document at the insertion point.

Lesson 7: Working with Non-text Elements   153

Task 3

Resizing and Moving Clip Art

Why would I do this?

Clip art is almost never the exact size you want when you insert it into your document, and it is seldom located exactly where you want it. Word allows you to resize and move the image so that it fits properly.

In this task, you learn to resize and move a clip art image in your document.

Handles indicate that the image is selected.

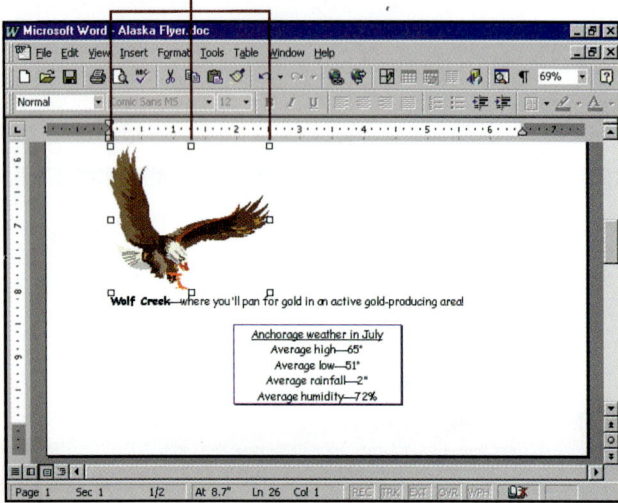

1 Click the clip art image of the eagle (or the other image you are using). *Handles* at the corners of and in the middle of the image's edges indicate that the image is selected.

> **Pothole**: On some setups, the clip art image is much larger, so the image is forced to continue on the next page. If this is the case, simply resize the image as instructed. The image should move back up to the proper location. On some systems, the resized image moves to the top of the first page. If this happens to you, use the Whole Page option in the Zoom box to show the whole page at one time. This makes it easier to move the image back to its proper location.

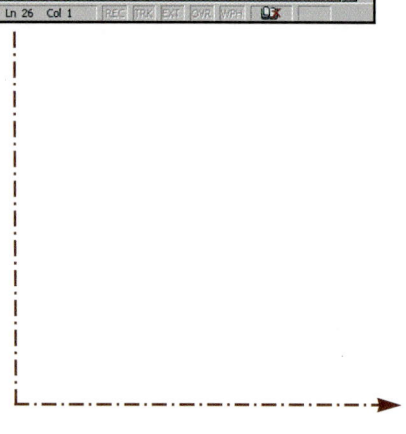

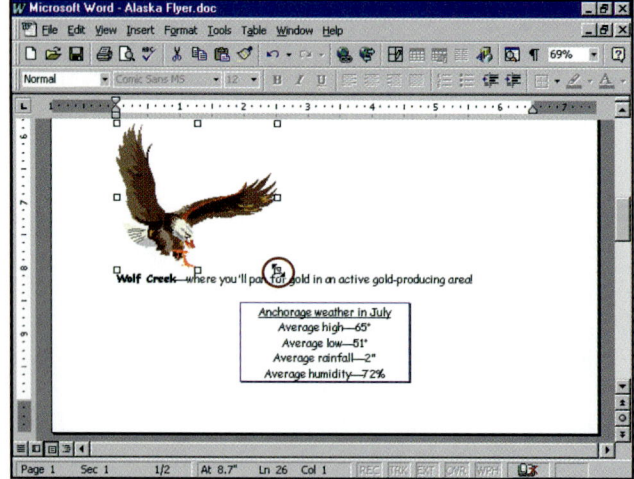

2 Move the pointer onto the handle in the lower-right corner. The pointer changes to a diagonal two-sided arrow.

154 Learn Word 97, Second Edition

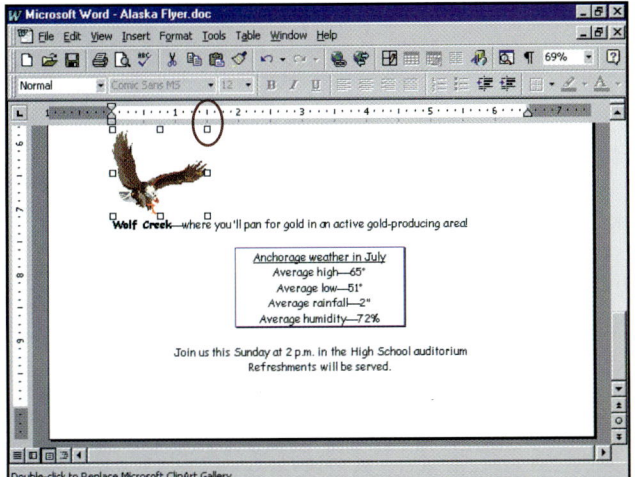

3 Click and hold down the pointer and drag the handle up and to the left until the image is about 1.5 inches wide and then release the mouse button. Use the top ruler to determine the width of the image.

Pothole: If you do not see the ruler at the top of your document, select **View**, **Ruler** to turn it on.

The eagle has been moved.

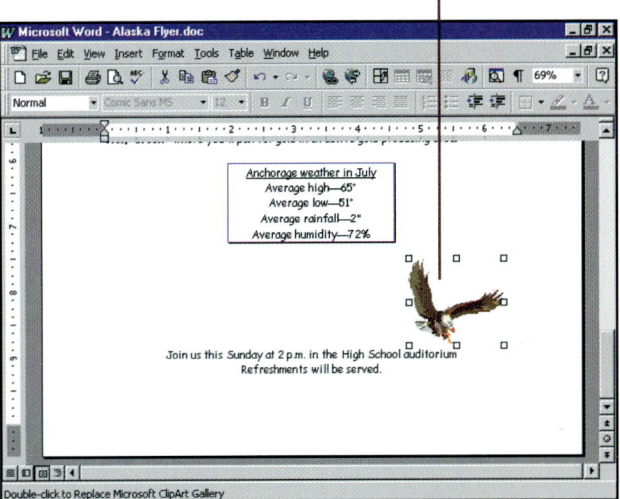

4 Click on the eagle, drag it to the right of the weather box, and let go of the mouse button. The image stays on the right side of the page but does not stay to the right of the box. This problem is corrected in a later task.

Lesson 7: Working with Non-text Elements

Task 4
Adding a Picture

Why would I do this?

Clip art is designed to convey an idea using a cartoon-like image. Clip art takes up much less disk space to store and transmits to other users in much less time than pictures. However, sometimes you will want to use digital photographs that you have taken with a camera (either film or digital) instead of clip art.

In this task, you learn to add a digital photograph to your document.

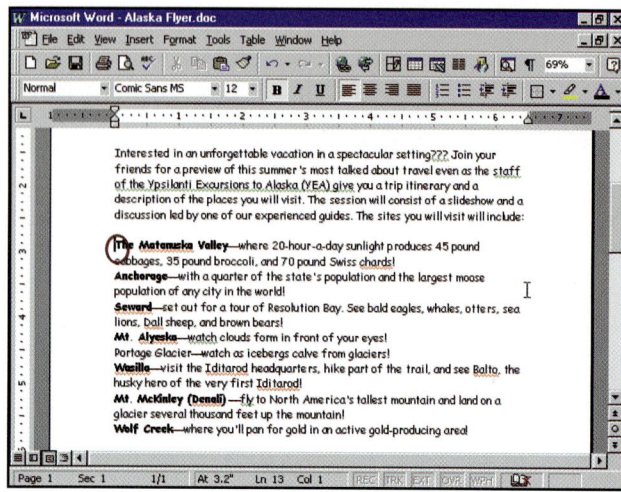

1 Scroll up in the **Alaska Flyer** document. Place the insertion point to the left of the paragraph about the Matanuska Valley.

2 Select **Insert**, **Picture**, **From File** from the menu. The **Insert Picture** dialog box is displayed. This dialog box works in much the same way as the **File**, **Open** dialog box.

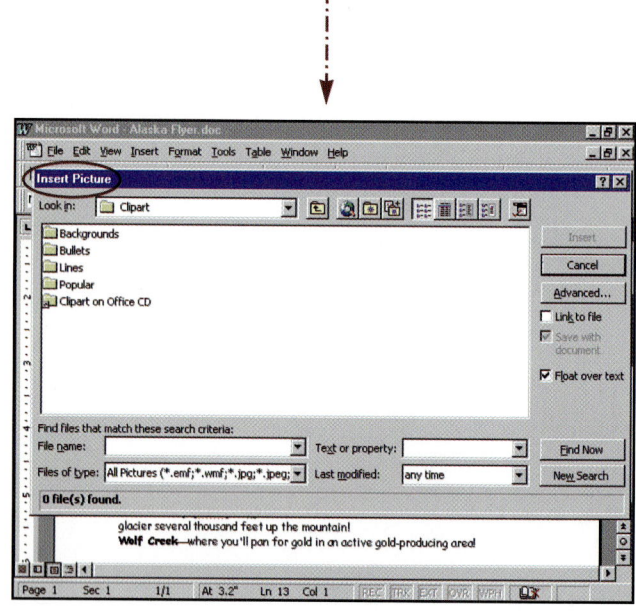

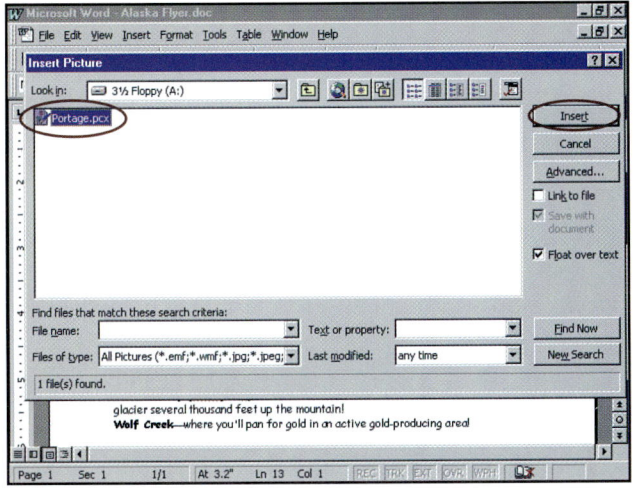

3 Find the **Portage** file that was included on your student disc. Highlight the **Portage** file.

The image is placed at the insertion point.

4 Click the **Insert** button. The image is placed at the insertion point. It pushes the text down past the bottom of the picture.

Lesson 7: Working with Non-text Elements

Task 5

Wrapping Text Around an Image

Why would I do this?

The clip art image and the photograph that you inserted are currently treated as (very large) characters in a line of text. In most cases, you want to be able to move these images around freely without displacing nearby text. Word allows you to wrap text around images and to free up images so that they can be placed anywhere (even behind the text) without disturbing the document layout.

In this task, you learn how to wrap text around an image and to free up another image so that it can be moved anywhere in the document.

Handles indicate that the object is selected.

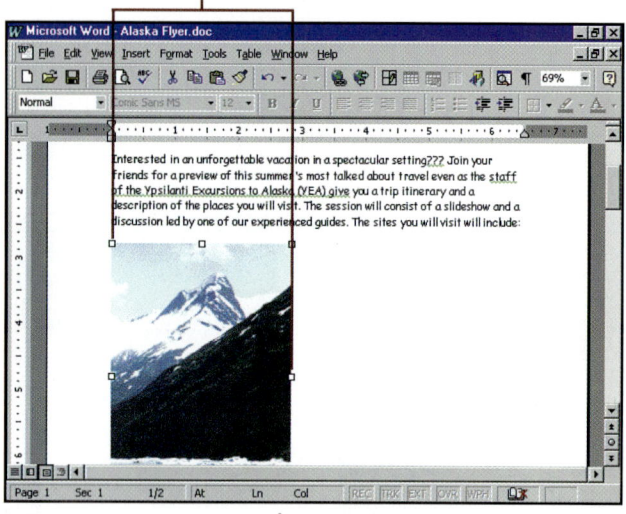

1 Click the photograph to select it. Handles appear around the outer edge to indicate that it has been selected.

The Wrapping tab

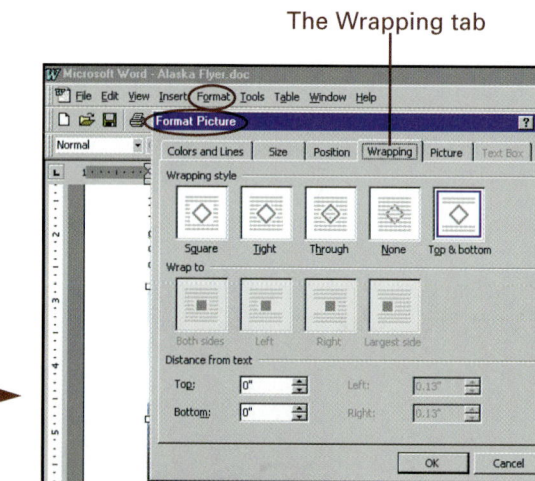

2 Select **Format**, **Picture** from the menu. The **Format Picture** dialog box opens. Click the **Wrapping** tab.

158 Learn Word 97, Second Edition

The Wrapping style area

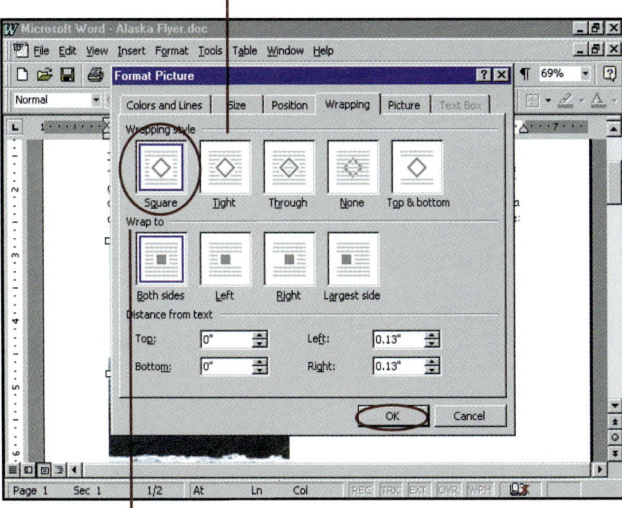

The Wrap to area

3 Choose **Square** in the **Wrapping style** area and then select **Both sides** from the **Wrap to** area.

> **Pothole:** Some of the settings in the **Format Picture** dialog box stay as they were set when last used. If the choices on the **Wrapping** tab are gray and won't work, go to the **Position** tab and select **Float over text** and **Move object with text**.

4 Click **OK**. The photograph is now embedded in the text. You could move this photograph anywhere in the document and the text would wrap around it.

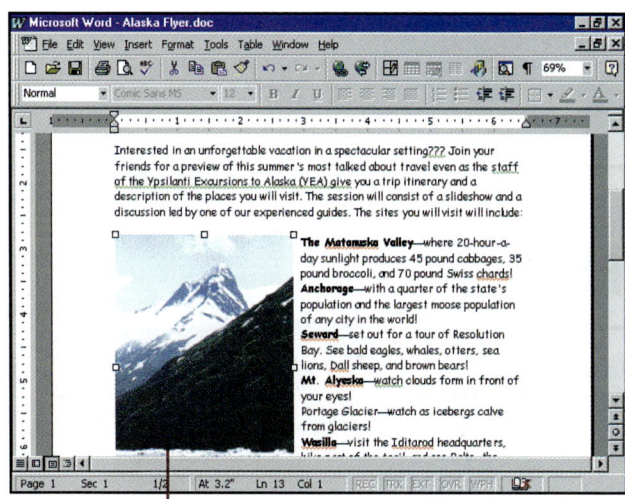

The photograph is embedded in the text.

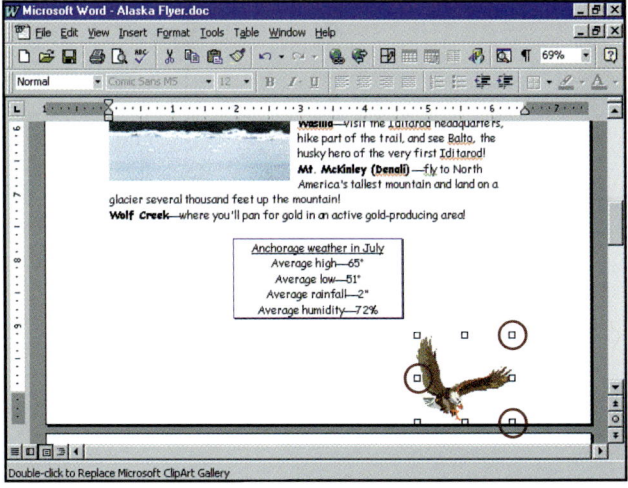

5 Click the eagle clip art image to select it. Handles appear around the outer edge to indicate that it has been selected.

Lesson 7: Working with Non-text Elements   159

6 Select **Format**, **Picture** from the menu. The **Format Picture** dialog box opens. Click the **Wrapping** tab.

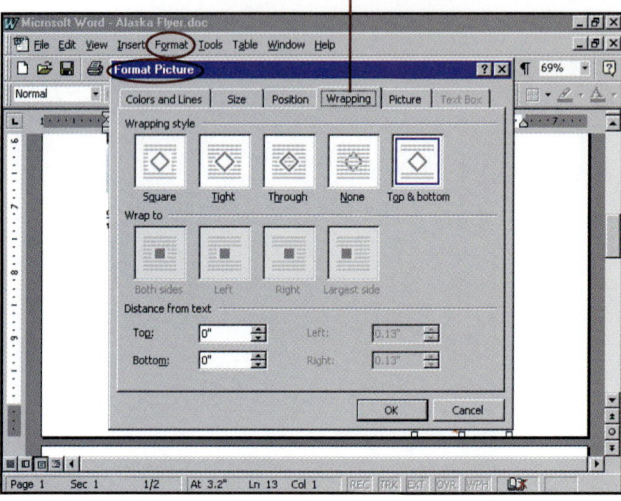

The Wrapping tab

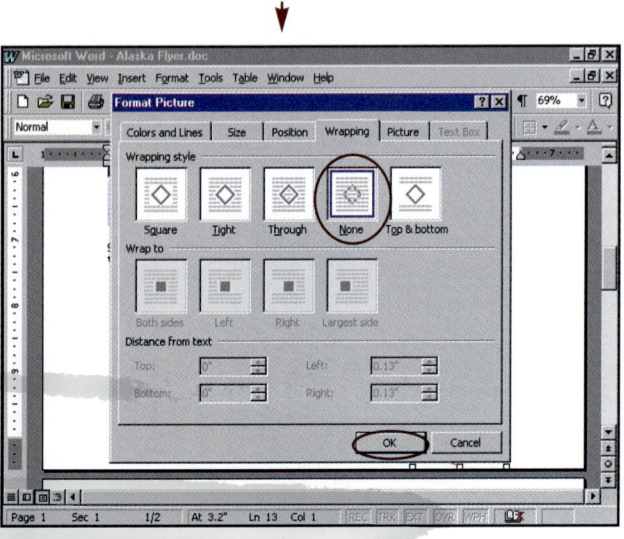

7 Choose **None** in the **Wrapping style** area.

In Depth: If you choose None in the Wrapping style area, the text does not wrap around the image; the image coexists with the text—even in the same location. With None selected, you can put a graphic behind the text.

8 Click **OK**. Place the pointer over the **eagle** and then click and drag it up to the right of the weather box. Keep the right edge of the image inside the right margin of the document.

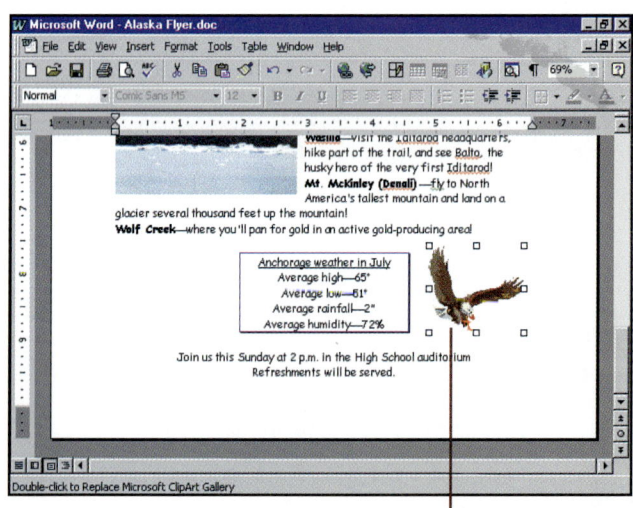

Keep the image inside the document margins.

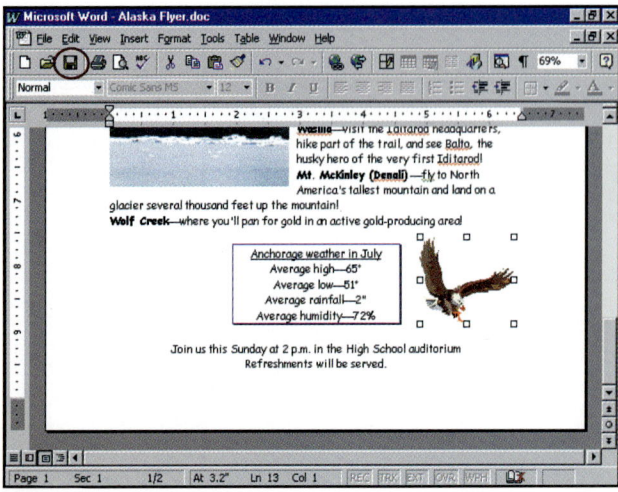

9 Click the **Save** button to save your work up to this point.

160 Learn Word 97, Second Edition

Task 6
Using WordArt

Why would I do this?

Your options for creating a title with text are limited. You can use emphasis (bold, italics, underline), a larger font size, or an unusual font to make your title stand out, but you are limited to straight lines of text. *WordArt* is a Word subprogram that turns text into graphics. It gives you great flexibility in creating very artistic titles.

In this task, you learn to create an artistic title using WordArt.

1 Place the insertion point at the top of the document. Select **View**, **Toolbars**, **WordArt** from the menu. The **WordArt** toolbar is displayed.

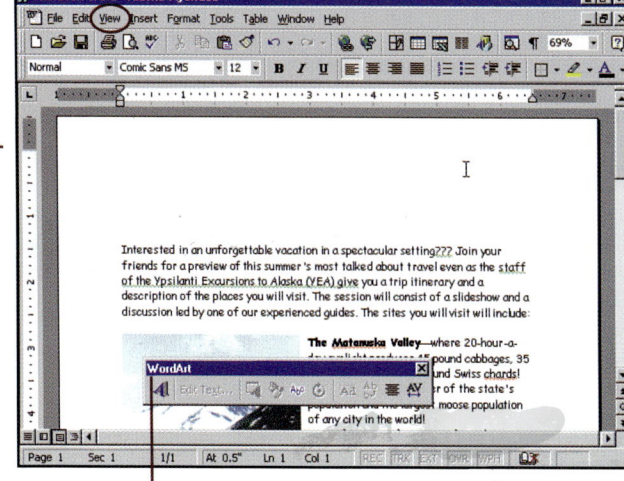

The WordArt toolbar

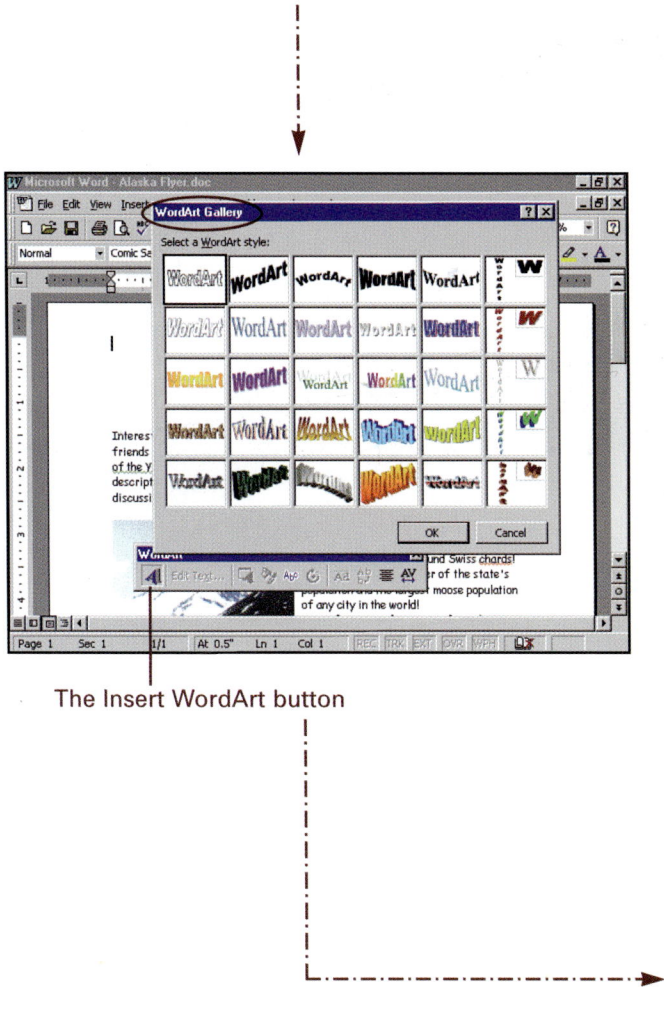

The Insert WordArt button

2 Click the **Insert WordArt** button. The **WordArt Gallery** is displayed.

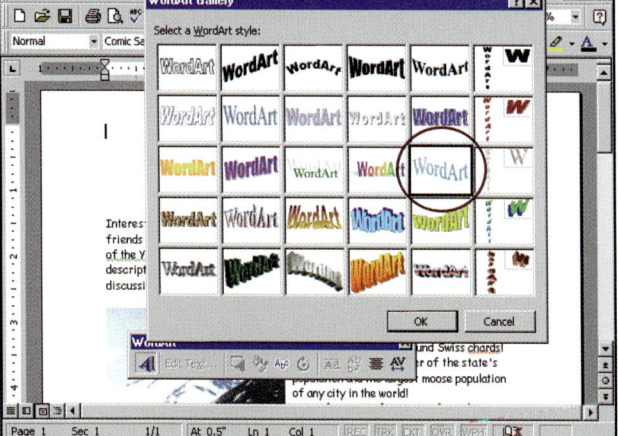

3 Select the fifth **WordArt** style in the third row.

Lesson 7: Working with Non-text Elements

This will be the flyer title.

4 Click **OK**. The **Edit WordArt Text** dialog box is displayed. Type **Alaska Adventure!!!**, which will be the title for your flyer.

5 Choose **54 pt** from the **Size** drop-down menu.

Do not drag the title above this point.

6 Click **OK**. The new **WordArt** title is near the top of the document, but it's not quite in the right place. Click on the title and drag it up so that it is centered and near the top of the document.

Pothole: You must click on one of the letters to drag the WordArt text. If you click between letters, you highlight text when you move the pointer. If this happens, go back and try again.

162 **Learn Word 97, Second Edition**

7 Highlight **one of our experienced guides** in the first paragraph. Substitute your name for this line. Click the **Print** button to print the flyer.

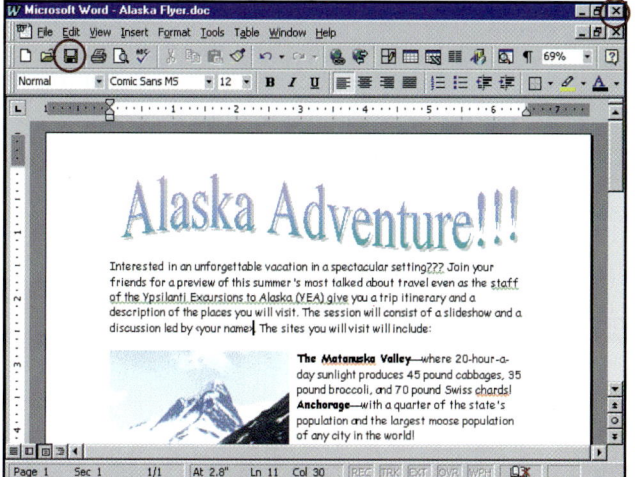

8 Click the **Save** button to save your work and then click the **Close** button on the **WordArt** toolbar. Click the **Close** button to exit Microsoft Word.

Lesson 7: Working with Non-text Elements   163

Student Exercises

True-False

Circle either T or F.

T F 1. You can't add borders around several paragraphs at the same time.

T F 2. Word allows you to specify the color and width of the border lines.

T F 3. You can place the same box around several paragraphs even if the margins for the selected paragraphs are different.

T F 4. If you don't find a clip art image you like, you can find more on the program CD-ROM.

T F 5. Clip art takes up as much disk space as a photograph for the same size image.

T F 6. Images cannot be placed behind text.

T F 7. If the buttons on the Wrapping tab are unavailable (gray), it could mean that you need to alter the settings on the Position tab.

T F 8. WordArt text is edited in the Edit WordArt Text dialog box.

T F 9. When a WordArt image is inserted into a document, handles around the edges indicate that it is selected and that it can be resized and moved.

T F 10. You can change the font size of the text in WordArt.

Identifying Parts of the Word Screen

Refer to the figure and identify the numbered parts of the screen. Write the letter of the correct label in the space next to the number.

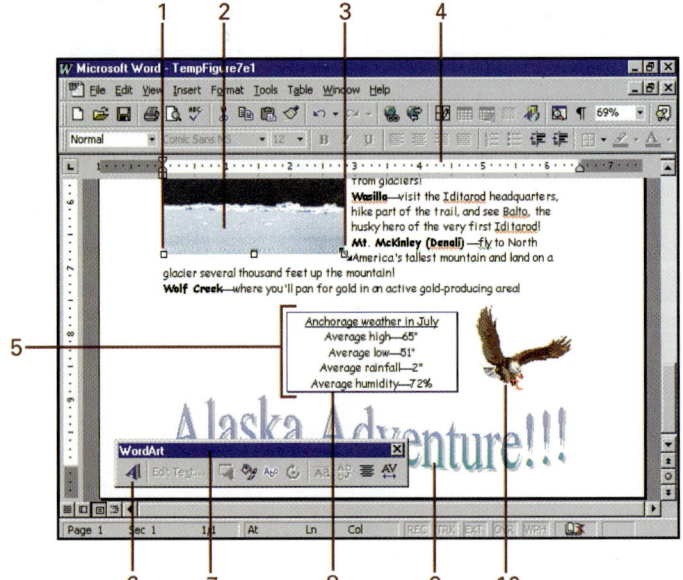

1. ____
2. ____
3. ____
4. ____
5. ____
6. ____
7. ____
8. ____
9. ____
10. ____

A. Insert WordArt button
B. Border
C. Clip art image
D. Horizontal ruler
E. Resizing cursor
F. Shadow
G. WordArt image
H. Handle
I. Image from a file
J. WordArt toolbar

Matching Questions

Match the following statements to the word or phrase from the list on the right. Write the letter of the matching word or phrase in the space provided next to the number.

1. _A_ Quick way to adjust the width of a border box
2. ____ Opens the Microsoft Clip Gallery
3. ____ Contains controls for how text and images interact
4. ____ A method of making artistic images out of text
5. ____ Markers that indicate an image is selected
6. ____ Wrapping tab option allowing images and text to coexist
7. ____ Works in much the same way as File, Open
8. ____ The menu option that allows you to turn rulers on or off
9. ____ Dependent on the left and right margin of the paragraph(s)
10. ____ Gives choices of text image shapes

A. Handles
B. Wrapping tab
C. WordArt Gallery
D. Width of border box
E. Insert Picture dialog box
F. WordArt
G. Insert, Picture, Clip Art
H. Clip Art Gallery
I. Left and right indent markers
J. None button
K. View

Application Exercises

Exercise 1—Add a WordArt Title to the Poster

1. Launch Microsoft Word. Open **Less0702** from the student files. Save the file as **Benefits Day**.
2. Choose **File**, **Page Setup** and set the document margins to **1"** all the way around. Click **OK**.
3. Choose **Edit**, **Select All** and then choose **Format**, **Paragraph**. Indent the left margin by **1.5"**, which allows room for a vertical WordArt title. Click **OK**.
4. Choose **View**, **Toolbars** and activate the WordArt toolbar. Click the **Insert WordArt** button.
5. Select the sixth button in the fourth row (it shows a vertical title). Click **OK**.
6. Type **Benefits Day** in the **Edit WordArt Text** dialog box. Change the font size to **60** points and click **OK**.

Lesson 7: Working with Non-text Elements

7. Use the **Zoom** drop-down box to see the whole page. Move the title between the text and the left margin. Place the top of the title even with the top of the text. Your document should look like the figure you see here. You can also click **View**, **Zoom**, **Whole Page**, and **OK**.

8. Leave the document open for use in the next exercise.

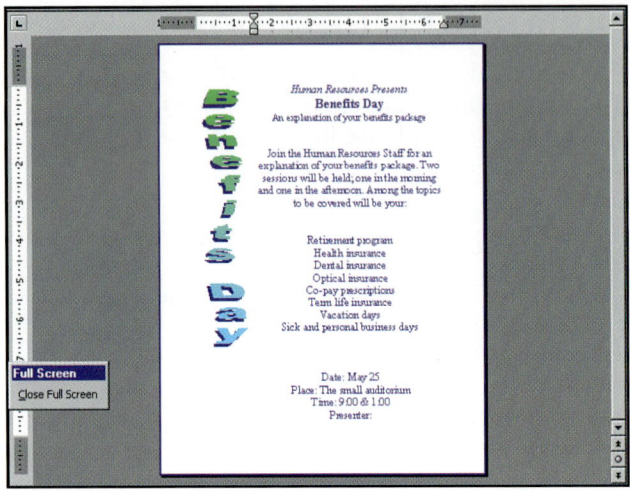

Exercise 2—Add, Resize, Move, and Wrap a Clip Art Image

1. Place the insertion point to the left of the date line near the bottom of the poster.

2. Choose **Insert**, **Picture**, **Clip Art**, go to the **People** category, choose the image with the group of people and a blackboard in the background, and insert it into your document. If this image is not available, choose another one with people in it.

3. Resize the clip art image so that it is as wide as the WordArt title (about 1.25 inches or so).

4. With the clip art image selected, select **Format**, **Picture**. Select the **Wrapping** tab.

5. Select **None** from the **Wrapping style** area of the **Wrapping** tab. Click **OK**.

6. Move the clip art image below the WordArt title, which makes the left side of the poster look like an exclamation point. Your document should look like the figure you see here.

7. Leave the document open for use in the next exercise.

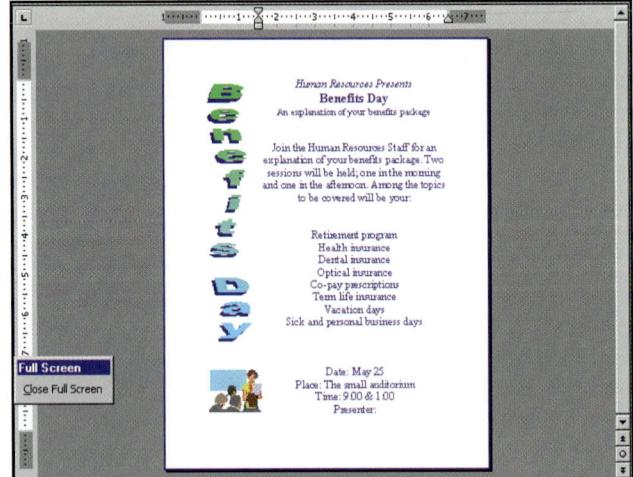

Exercise 3—Add Borders to Text

1. Select the first three lines of text. Choose **Format**, **Borders and Shading**.

2. Choose the **Box** shape, **Blue** as the color, and **1 1/2 pt** as the width of the line. Click **OK**.

3. Type your name after the word **Presenter:** on the last line.

4. Select the last four lines of text.

5. Repeat the borders procedure from steps 1 and 2.

6. Select **Format**, **Paragraph** and reset the margins for the selected lines to **2.25"** on the left and **.75"** on the right. If your name is too long and wraps to the next line, adjust these numbers accordingly. Your document should look like the figure you see here.

7. Click the **Print** button to print the poster.

8. Save your document and close Word.

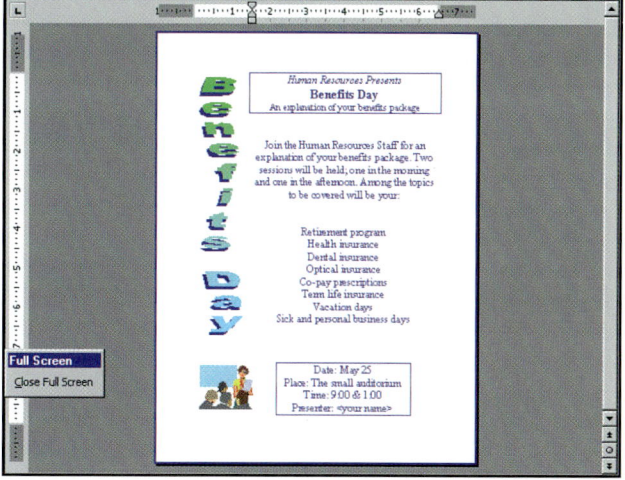

Lesson 8
References to Other Documents and Getting Help

Task 1: Moving Information Between Documents
Task 2: Adding Bookmarks
Task 3: Linking Word Documents Together
Task 4: Linking to Pages on the Internet
Task 5: Using the Office Assistant
Task 6: Using the Help Menu
Task 7: Getting Help on the Internet
Task 8: Finding Reference Books and Self-help Textbooks

Introduction

Improvements in technology have made it increasingly easy to communicate with others, whether they are in the same building or on another continent. This ease of communication can have profound effects on the way we manage documents. If you have a list of prices or product descriptions that changes often, it is easier to update a single copy and have other people connect to that copy than to distribute multiple paper copies that quickly become out-of-date. If someone in your company has written a document that contains sections you need to use, you can locate that document on a shared drive on a local area network, copy the section, and paste it into your document. You can also label sections of a document electronically and then link to these sections from other documents.

Now that the Internet has provided us with a global information network, you can enrich your documents with references to Web sites. Help with all of these new features is also available. You can use the Office Assistant to analyze a question that you enter in a normal sentence, or you can look up topics using more conventional indexes or tables of contents. For unusual problems or more advanced training materials, you can link to special sites on the Internet.

In this lesson, you learn how to use this connectivity to share the results of your work and to get help when you need it.

Visual Summary

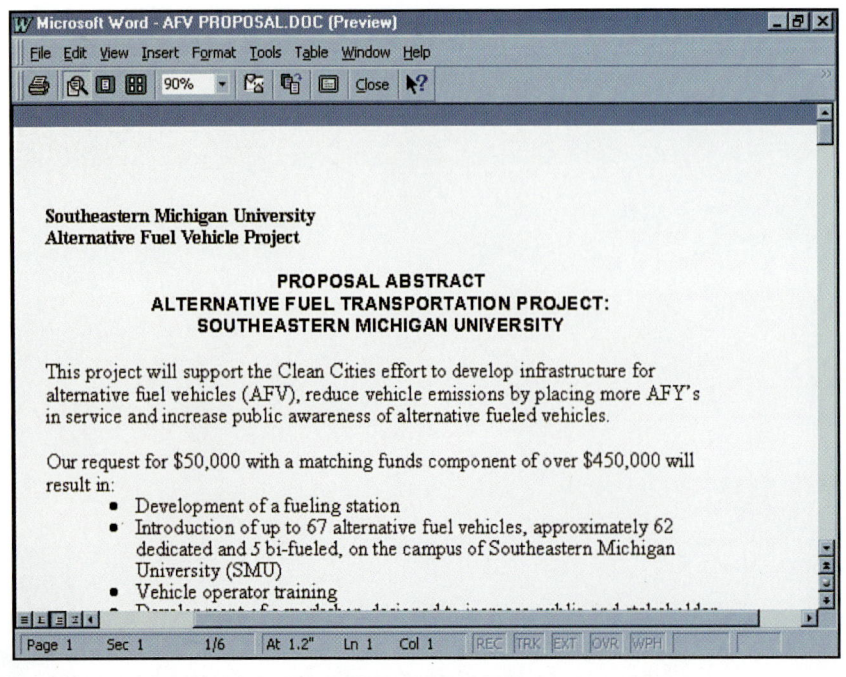

By the time you have completed this lesson, you will have added hyperlinks to a document that can connect to bookmarks in other documents or to Web pages on the Internet, such as this one shown:

Task 1

Moving Information Between Documents

Why would I do this?

If you or someone else has already written a portion of a document, you do not have to write it again if you need to use that same portion in another document. You can copy a portion of one document and paste it into another. In this lesson, you learn how to manage two documents that are open at the same time and to copy sections from one to the other.

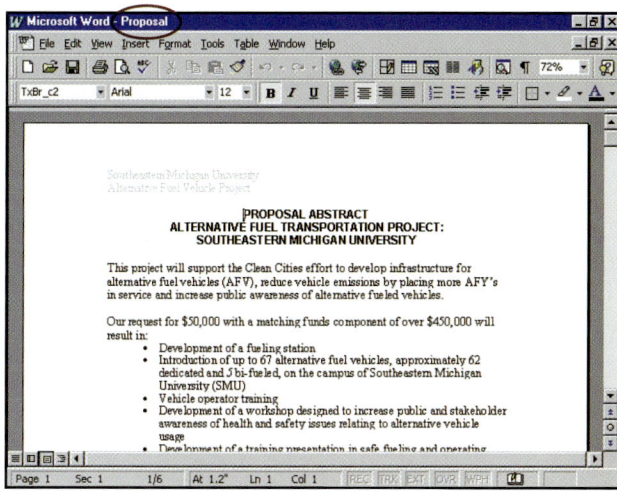

1. Launch Word. Open **Less0801** from the student files. Save the file as **Proposal**.

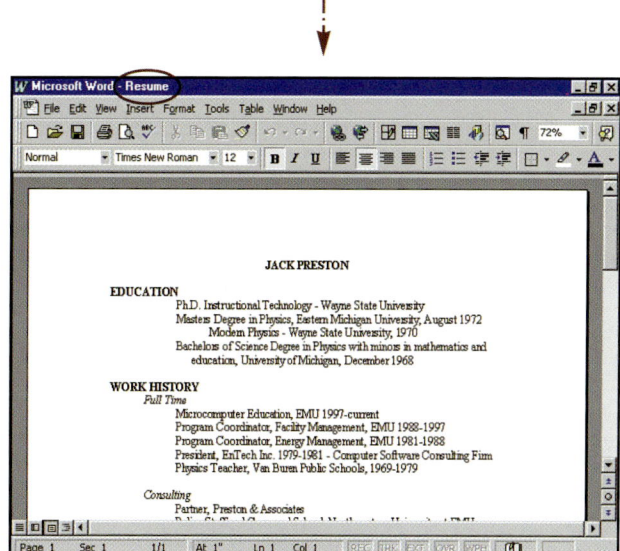

2. Open **Less0802** from the student files. Save the file as **Resume**. The **Proposal** and **Resume** files are now both open.

3 Choose **Edit**, **Select All** from the menu. All of the text is selected. Click the **Copy** button on the Standard toolbar.

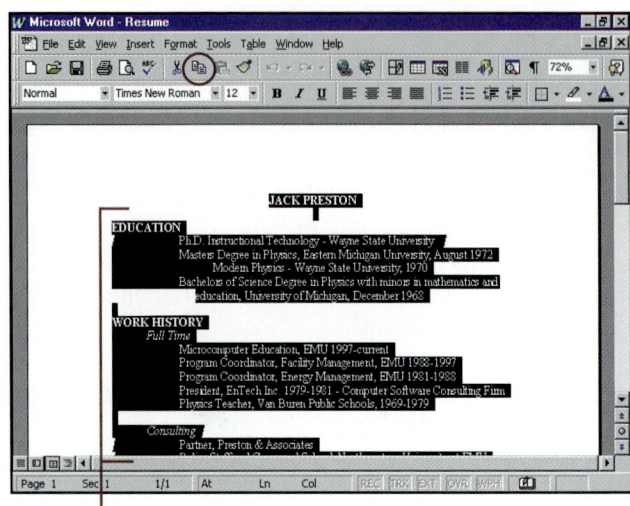

Selected text

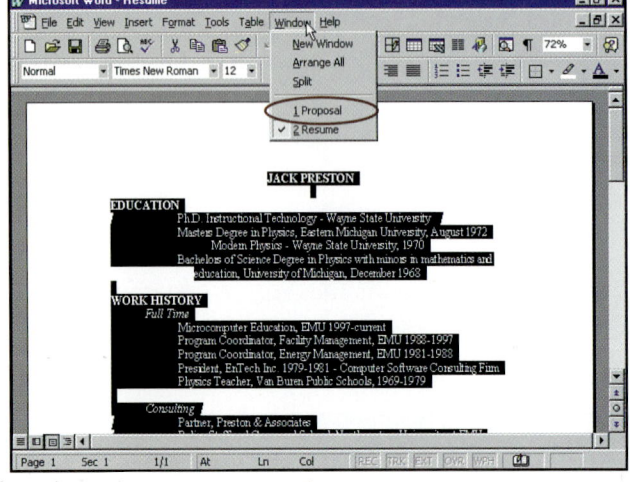

4 Click the **Window** menu option to display a list of open documents. The active document has a check mark, while the other open document, **Proposal**, does not.

5 Click **Proposal** to switch to the **Proposal** document.

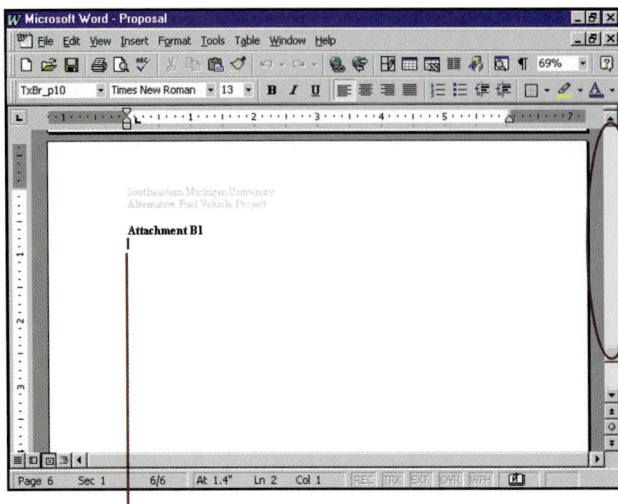

Insertion point

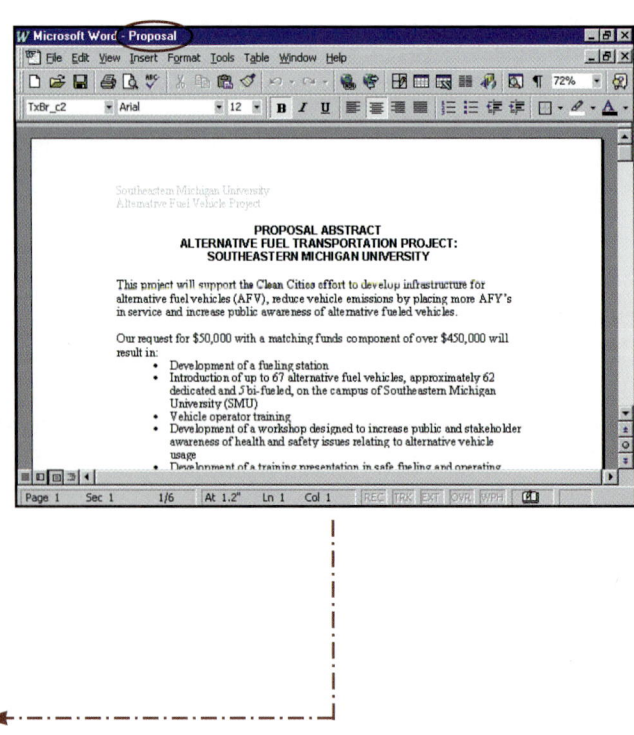

6 Scroll to the last page of the **Proposal** document and place the insertion point on the line below **Attachment B1**.

170 Learn Word 97, Second Edition

7 Click the **Paste** button on the Standard toolbar. The text copied from the **Resume** document is added to the **Proposal** document.

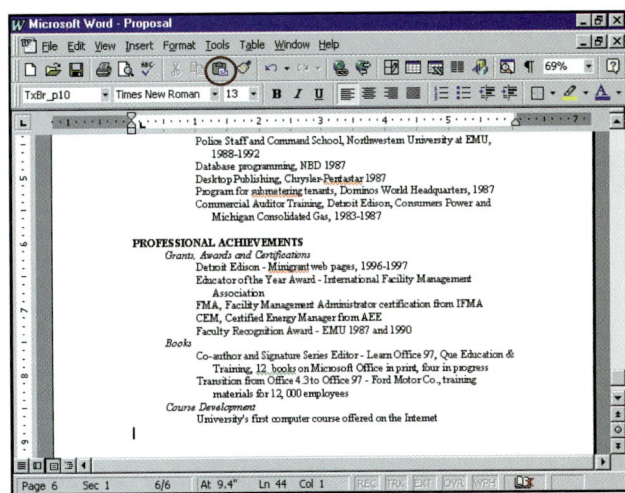

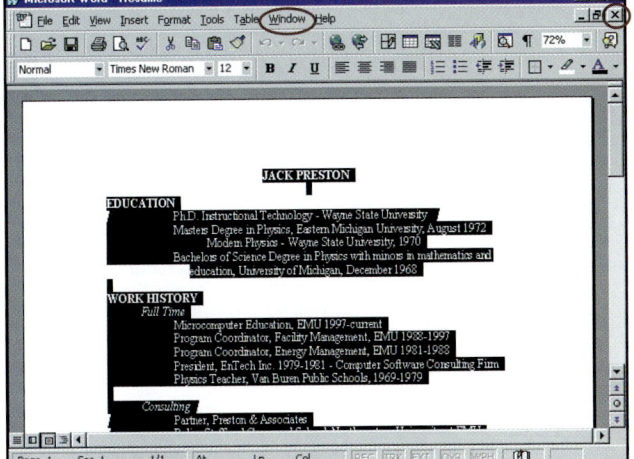

8 Choose **Window**, **Resume** from the menu. The **Resume** document is displayed.

9 Click the **Close Window** button to close the **Resume** file.

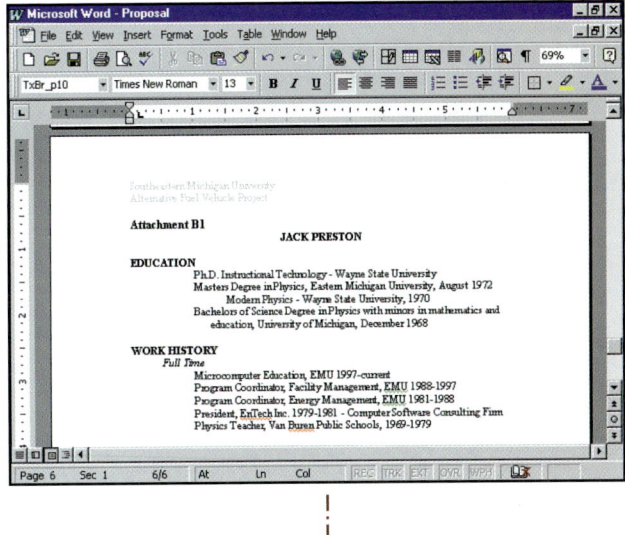

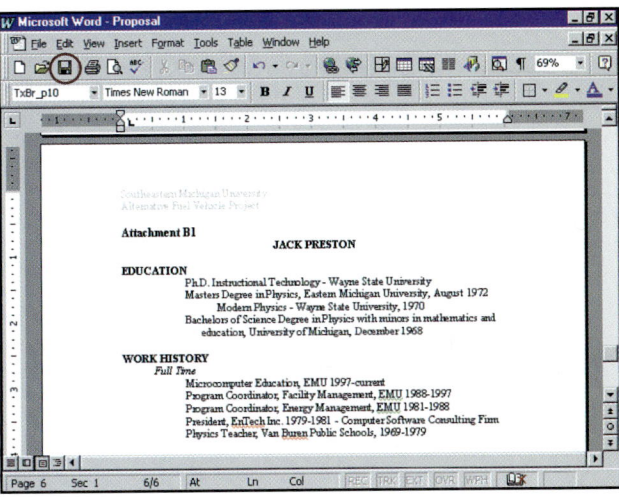

10 Click the **Save** button to save the changes you have made to the **Proposal** file. Leave the document open for use in the next task.

Lesson 8: References to Other Documents and Getting Help — 171

Task 2
Adding Bookmarks

Why would I do this?

A bookmark is an electronic reference point that you can place anywhere in a document. If you need to find particular sections of a long document on a regular basis, using bookmarks helps you find those places in the document much more readily.

1 Scroll to the first page of the **Proposal** document and locate the section entitled **General Information**.

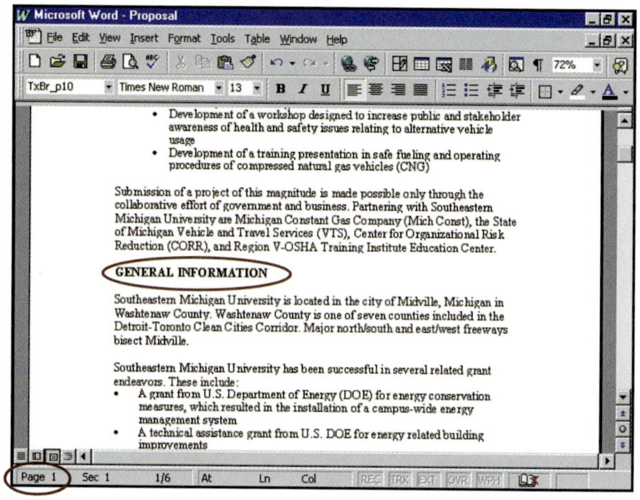

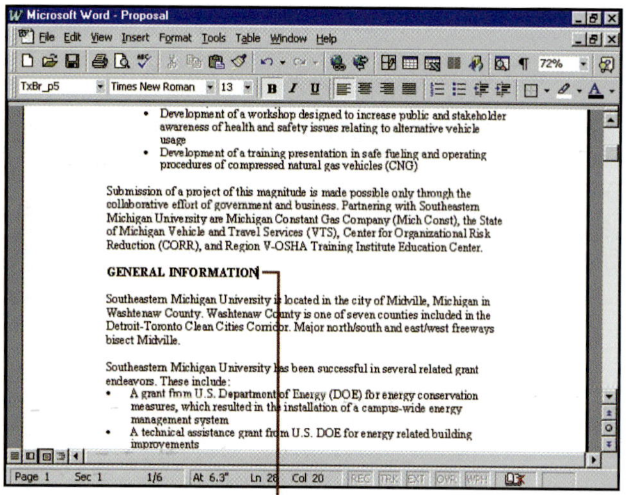

2 Place the insertion point to the right of the title.

3 Choose <u>I</u>nsert, Boo<u>k</u>mark from the menu. The **Bookmark** dialog box is displayed.

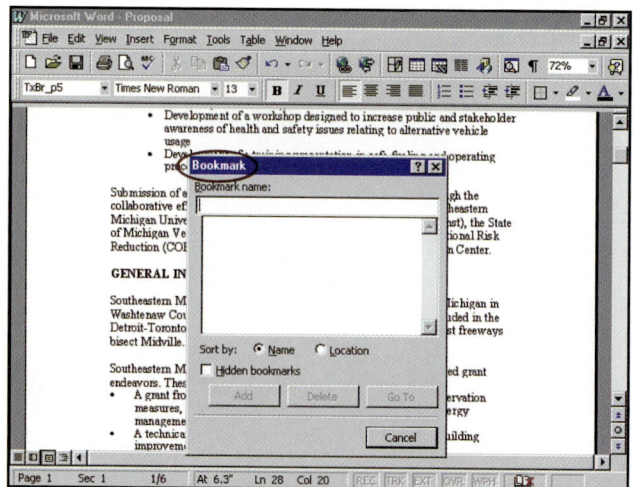

Learn Word 97, Second Edition
172

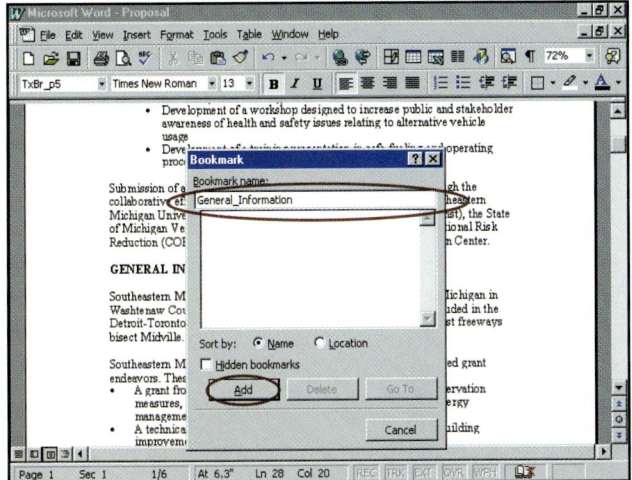

4 Type **General Information** in the **Bookmark name** box.

Pothole: The name you choose for the bookmark does not have to match the word or words next to the insertion point. The bookmark name must be a continuous string of characters without spaces or punctuation. In this example, the underscore character is used to create a single, long string of characters with the appearance of a space—General_Information.

5 Click **Add** to finish placing the bookmark.

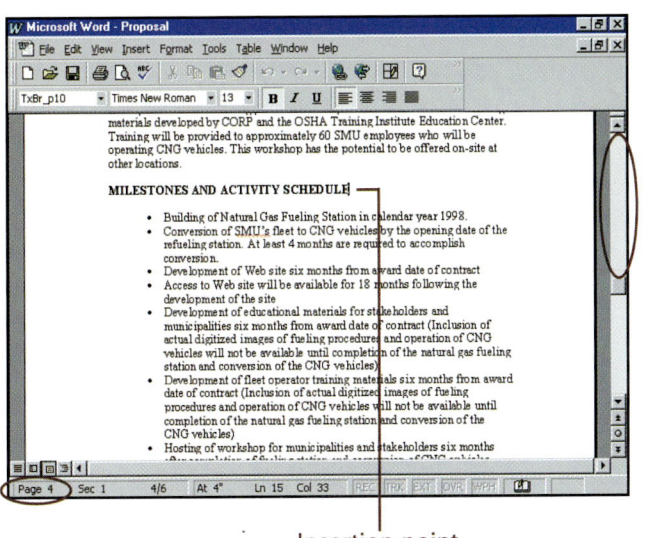

Insertion point

6 Scroll to page 4 and locate the section entitled **MILESTONES AND ACTIVITY SCHEDULE**. Place the insertion point to the right of the word **SCHEDULE**.

Lesson 8: References to Other Documents and Getting Help   173

7 Choose **Insert**, **Bookmark** from the menu. The **Bookmark** dialog box is displayed. The previously created bookmark is shown in the **Bookmark name** box.

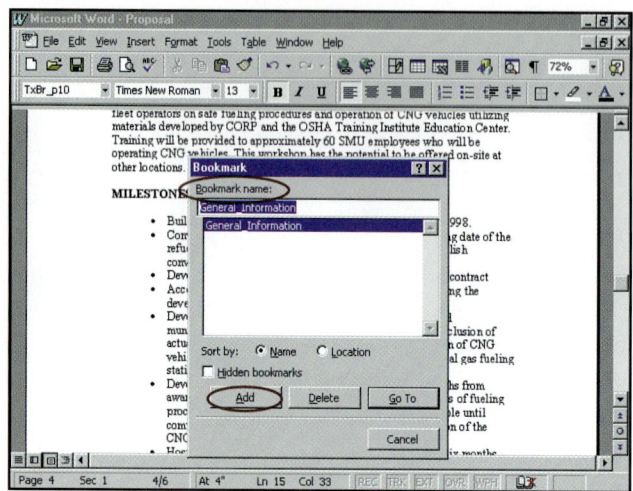

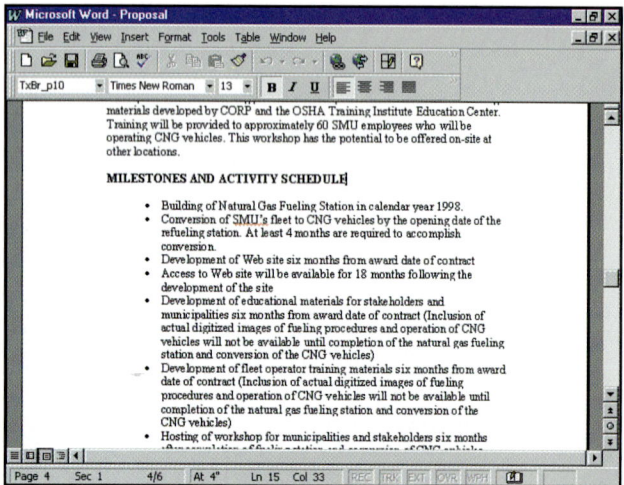

8 Type **Schedule** in the **Bookmark name** box and click **Add**.

9 Choose **Edit**, **Go To** from the menu. The **Find and Replace** dialog box is displayed with the **Go To** tab selected.

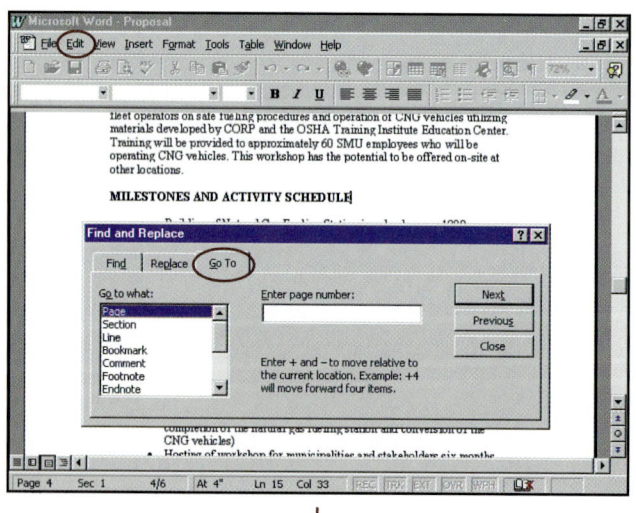

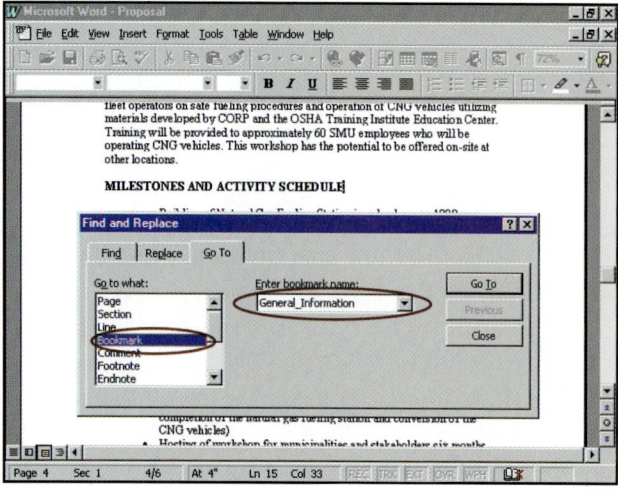

10 Click **Bookmark** in the **Go to what** box. The name of the list box in the center of the dialog box changes to **Enter bookmark name**. The first in a list of bookmarks is shown in the **Enter bookmark name** box.

174 Learn Word 97, Second Edition

11 Confirm that the bookmark, **General_Information**, is displayed in the **Enter bookmark name** box and click the **Go To** button. You now view the position of that bookmark in the document.

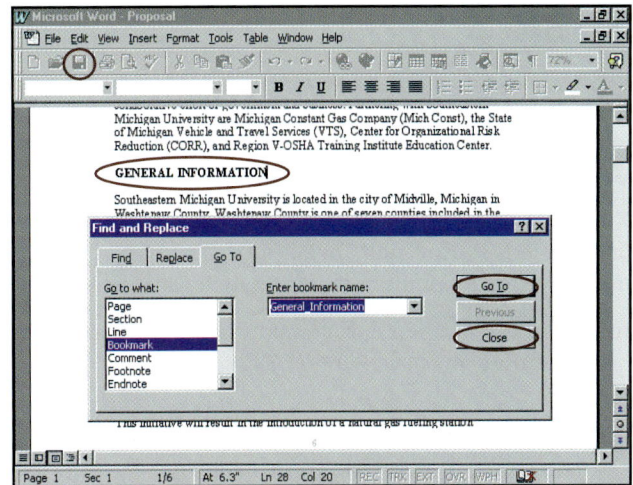

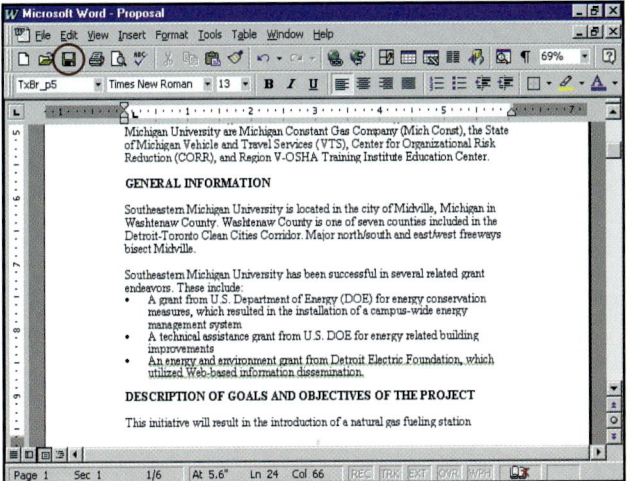

12 Click **Close** to close the dialog box. Click the **Save** button to save the changes that you have made and leave the document open for use in the next task.

Lesson 8: References to Other Documents and Getting Help 175

Task 3

Linking Word Documents Together

Why would I do this?

It is often easier to manage documents created as modules that are linked together than to manage one large document. This is especially true if more than one person is responsible for maintaining and updating these documents or if the documents reside on separate computers that are connected on a network.

In this task, you open a document that is used to track several projects and create a *hyperlink* between it and the proposal that you have been working on.

1 Launch Word. Open **Less0803** from the student files. Save the file as **List of Projects**. Select the subheading **Introduction and General Information**. This heading will be hyperlinked to the corresponding bookmark in the **Proposal** document.

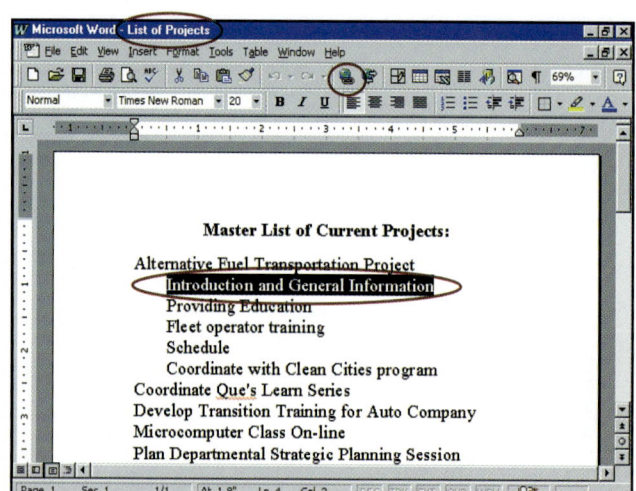

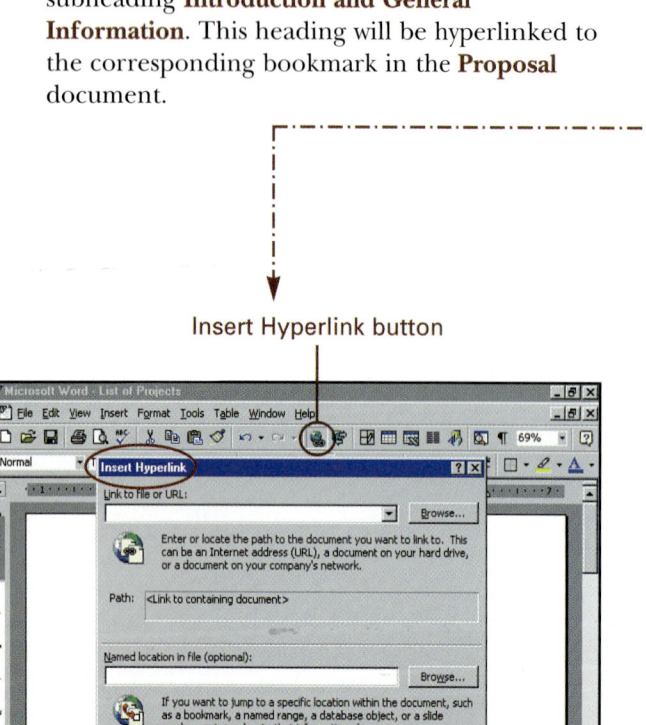

Insert Hyperlink button

2 Click the **Insert Hyperlink** button. The **Insert Hyperlink** dialog box opens.

176 Learn Word 97, Second Edition

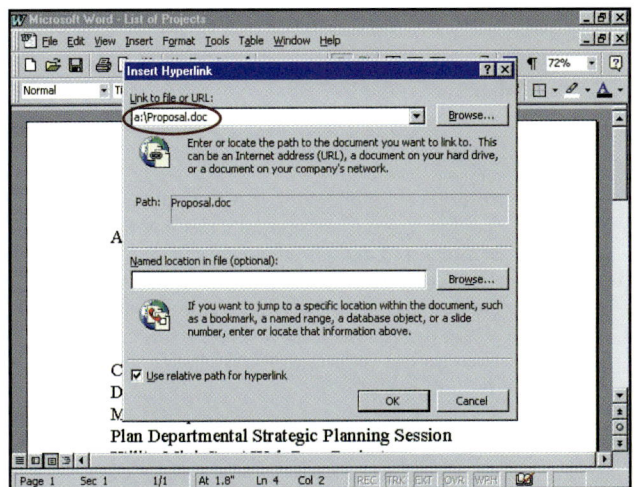

3 Type **a:\Proposal.doc** in the **Link to file or URL** box. (If you are saving your documents in another drive or folder, substitute that drive and folder for a:\.)

Existing bookmarks

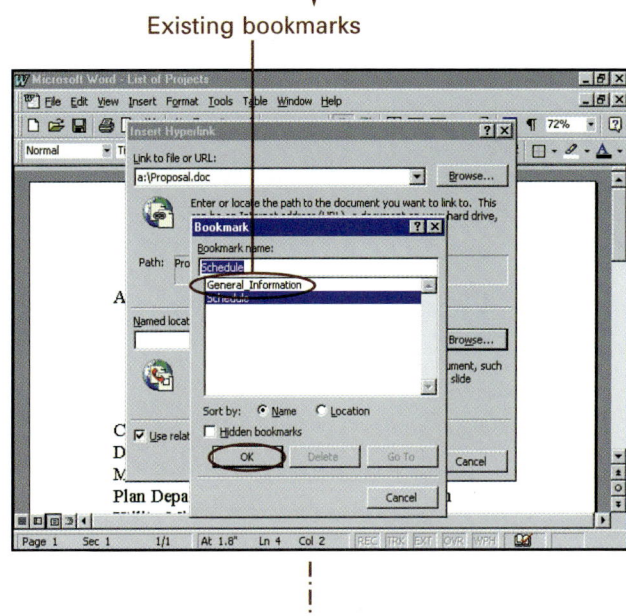

4 Click in the **Named location in file (optional)** box and click the **Browse** button. The **Bookmark** dialog box opens and displays the available bookmarks in the **Proposal** document.

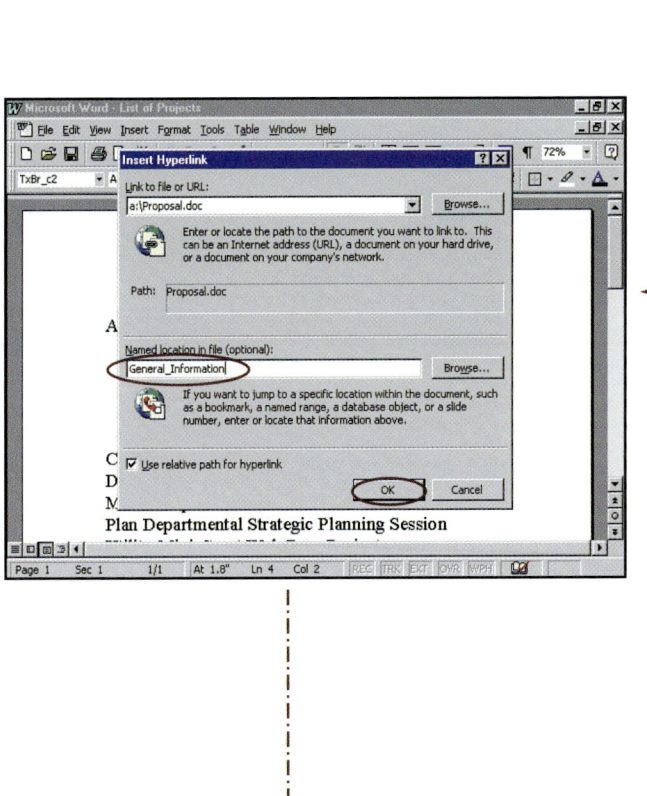

5 Select the **General_Information** bookmark and click **OK**. The bookmark is displayed in the **Named location in file (optional)** box.

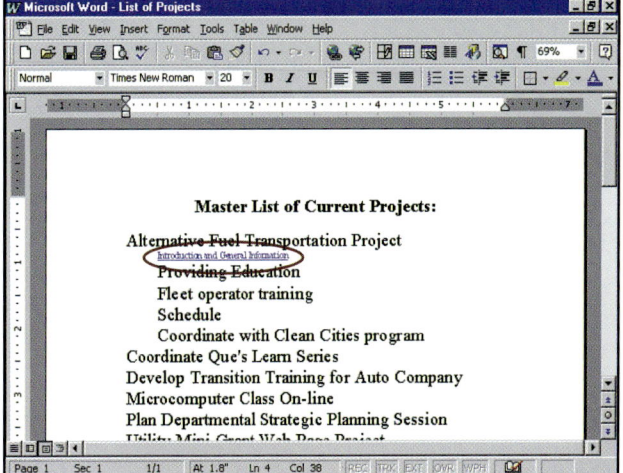

6 Click **OK**. The selected text in the **List of Projects** document is displayed in a smaller, blue font, which is used to indicate hyperlinks.

Lesson 8: References to Other Documents and Getting Help 177

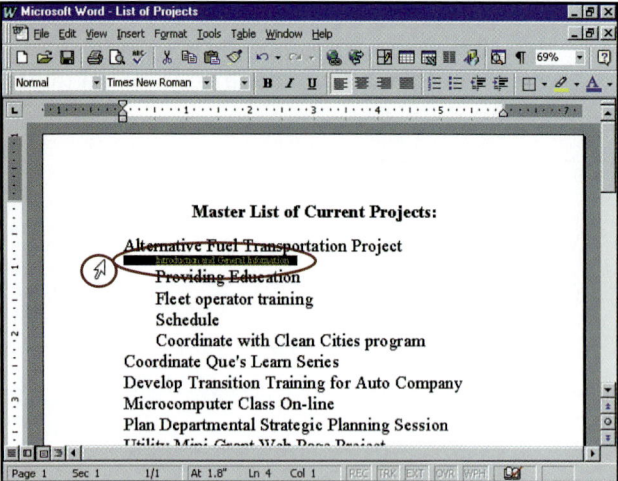

7 Move the pointer to the left of the line of text that displays the hyperlink and click to select that line of text.

> **Pothole:** Hyperlinked text is hard to edit because the pointer changes to the small hand that is used to activate the link whenever the pointer is placed over the text. If a single word in a line is used as a hyperlink, you can place the insertion point in the text to the left or right of the word and use the arrow keys on the keyboard, `Backspace`, and `Del` to edit the hyperlinked word.

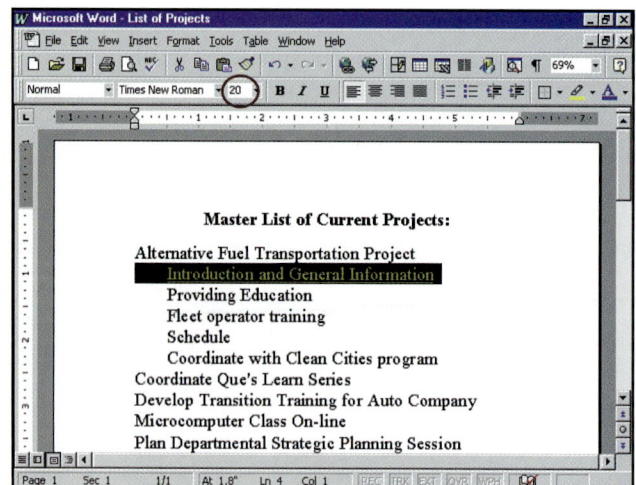

8 Click the list arrow next to the **Font Size** display on the Formatting toolbar and change the font size back to 20.

Web toolbar   Location of bookmark

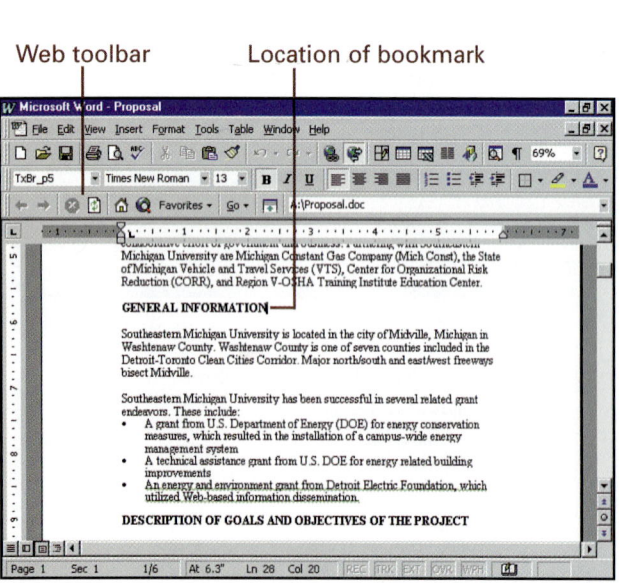

9 Move the pointer over the hyperlinked text (the pointer now changes into a small hand) and click. The program opens the file and goes to the selected bookmark. The *Web toolbar* automatically displays.

10 Click the *Back* arrow on the Web toolbar to return to the **Master List of Current Projects** document.

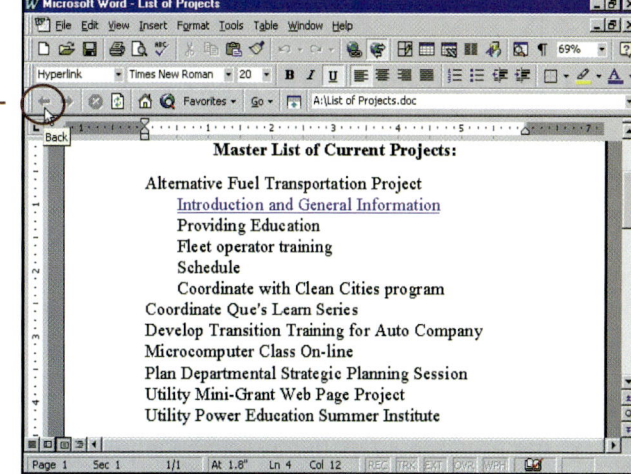

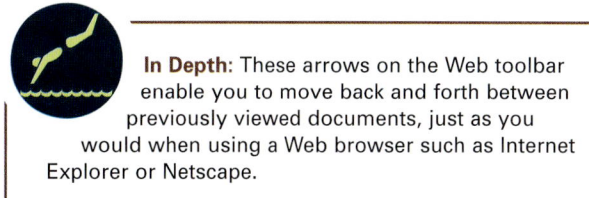

11 Click the *Forward* arrow on the Web toolbar to return to the previously selected document.

In Depth: These arrows on the Web toolbar enable you to move back and forth between previously viewed documents, just as you would when using a Web browser such as Internet Explorer or Netscape.

12 Click the **Close** button to close the document. The proposal is closed and the **Master List of Current Projects** is displayed on your screen.

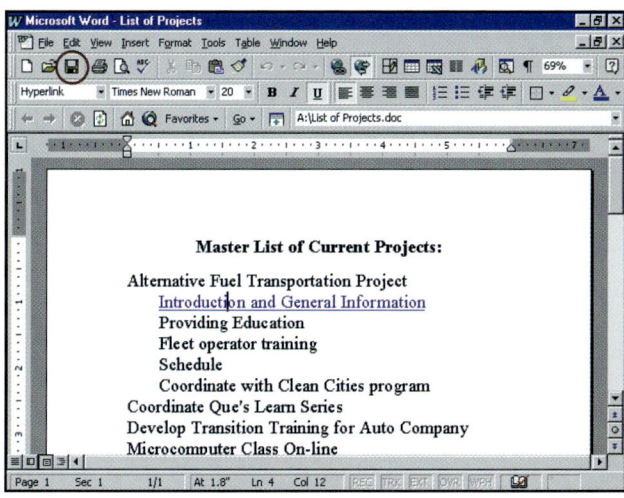

13 Click the **Save** button to save your changes. Leave the **Master List of Current Projects** document open for use in the next task.

Lesson 8: References to Other Documents and Getting Help   179

Task 4

Linking to Pages on the Internet

Why would I do this?

Many organizations now have Web pages that provide a great deal of pertinent information that you may want to reference in your documents. You can use hyperlinks to connect to these Internet Web pages if your computer is connected to the Internet and has the appropriate browser software installed. If the computer you are working on does not have such a connection, you can create a hyperlink in the document. The hyperlink in the document can be used if the document is transferred to a computer that does have such a connection.

1 Select the subheading **Coordinate with Clean Cities program**. Click the **Insert Hyperlink** button on the Standard toolbar. The **Insert Hyperlink** dialog box opens.

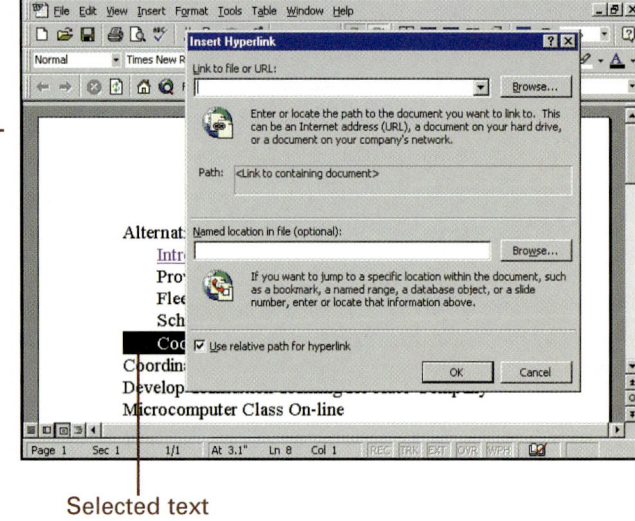

Selected text

2 Type **http://www.ccities.doe.gov/** in the **Link to file or URL** box.

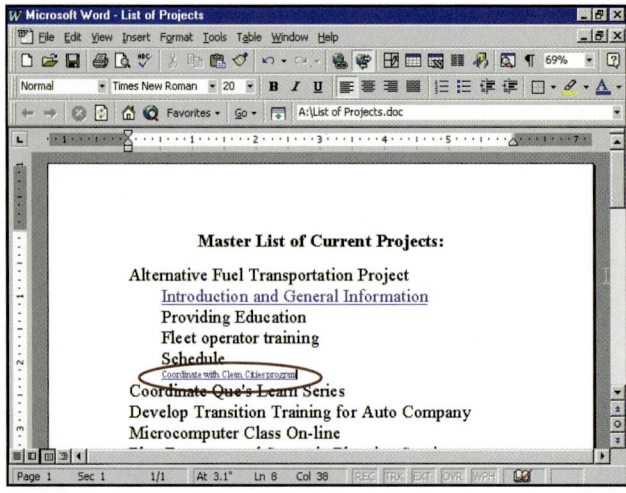

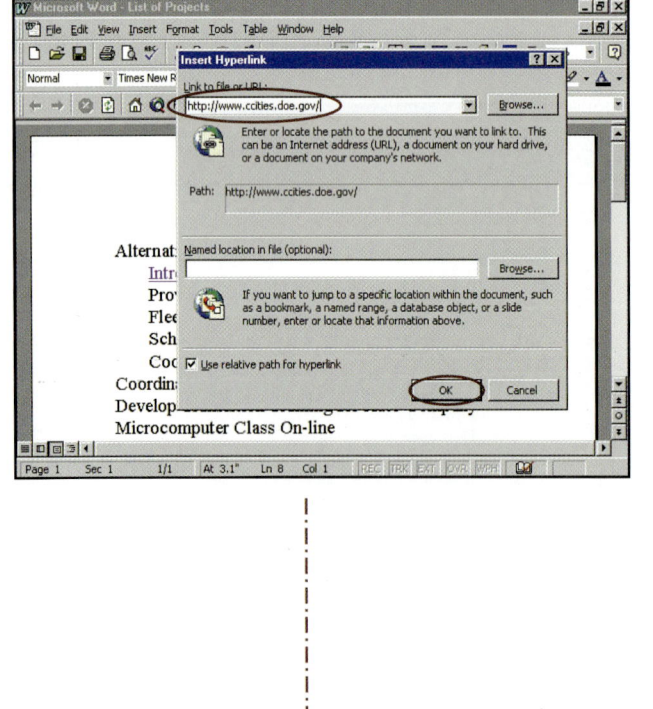

3 Click **OK**. The text is displayed in a blue, smaller font.

180 Learn Word 97, Second Edition

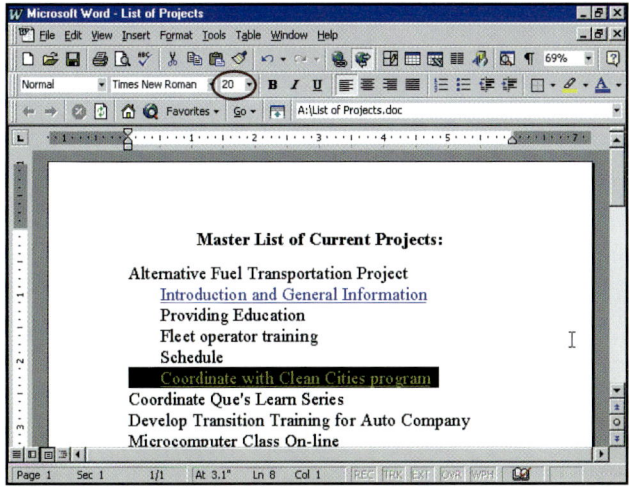

4 Select the whole line of text that contains the new hyperlink. Use the list arrow next to the **Font Size** box on the Formatting toolbar to change the font size back to 20.

5 Move the pointer onto the hyperlinked text (the pointer now changes into a small hand) and click. If you have an Internet link and a Web *browser* installed, the browser opens automatically and uses the Internet to locate this government Web site.

Pothole: Web sites change often. The sites shown in this book may have changed or may be inoperable when you do this assignment. If that is the case, use your browser to find an appropriate alternative site and use its location instead of the one given.

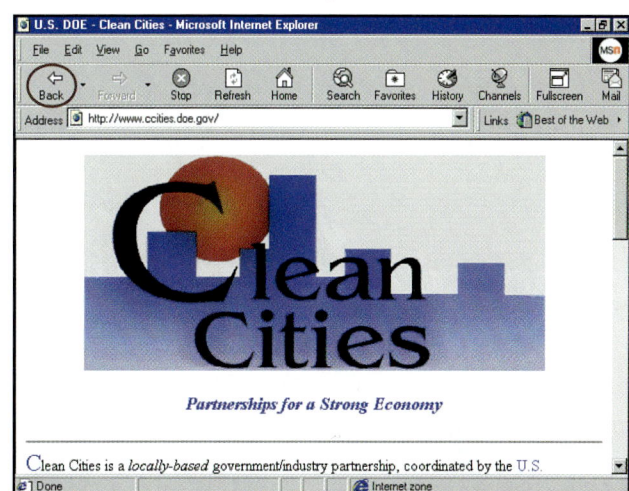

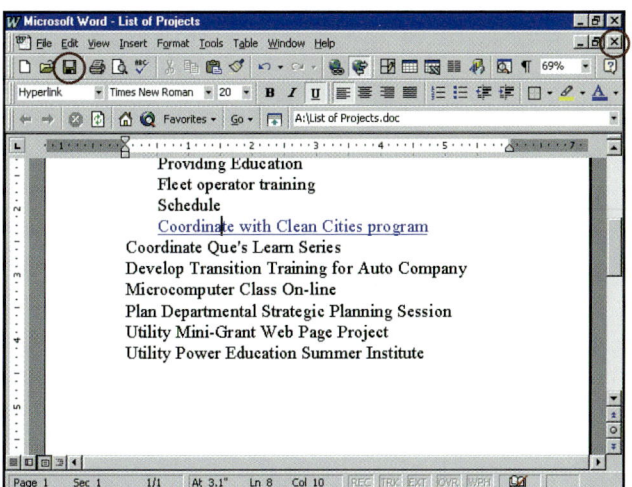

6 Click on the **Back** arrow in the Web toolbar to return to the **List of Projects** document. Click the **Save** button to save your changes. Click the **Close** button to close the document.

Lesson 8: References to Other Documents and Getting Help   181

Task 5

Using the Office Assistant

Why would I do this?

This book provides you with introductions to many topics. Word contains more options and topics than can be included in this book, however, so you need to know how to expand your knowledge to meet your specific needs. Fortunately, you have several very powerful tools at your disposal. An entire manual on disk comes with Word, which can be searched electronically. In this task, you learn how to use the *Office Assistant* to find out more about using tables.

1. Select **Help, Microsoft Word Help**. The Office Assistant is displayed.

   Quick Tip: You can also use the F1 key on your keyboard or click the Office Assistant button on the right end of the Standard toolbar.

Enter question here.

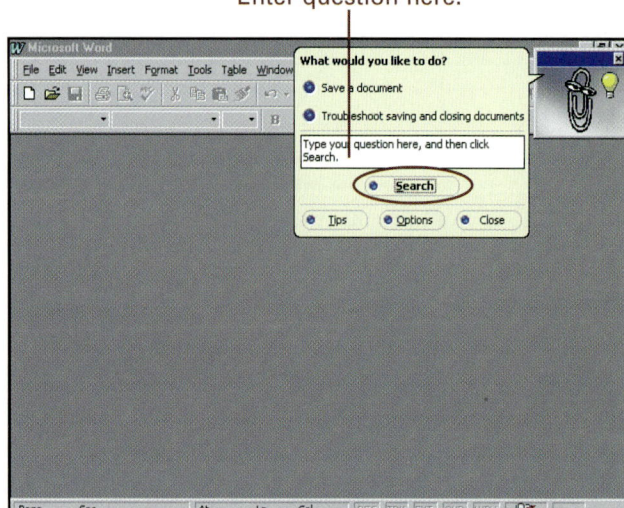

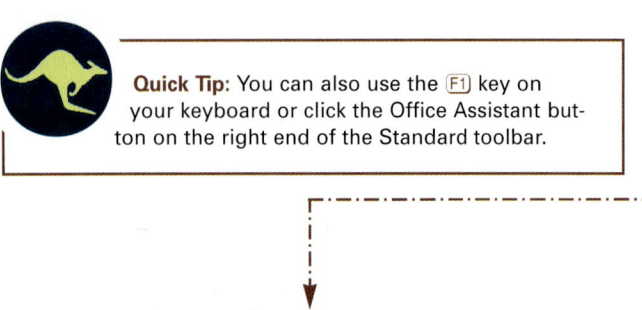

2. Type **How do I use a table?** and then click the **Search** button. The Office Assistant scans your sentence for key words, looks up topics that may be related to your request, and displays them.

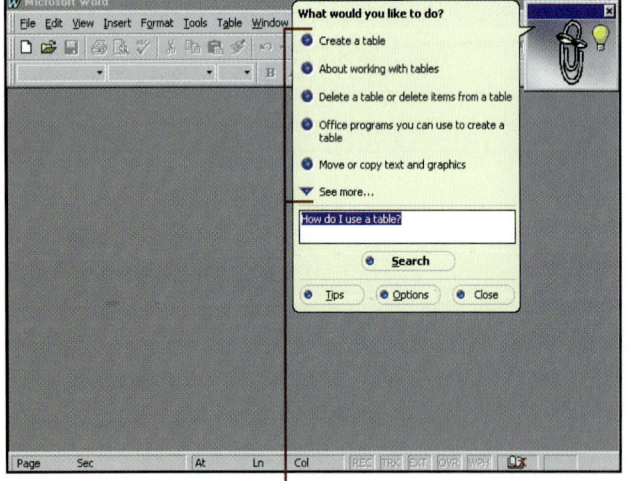

List of related topics

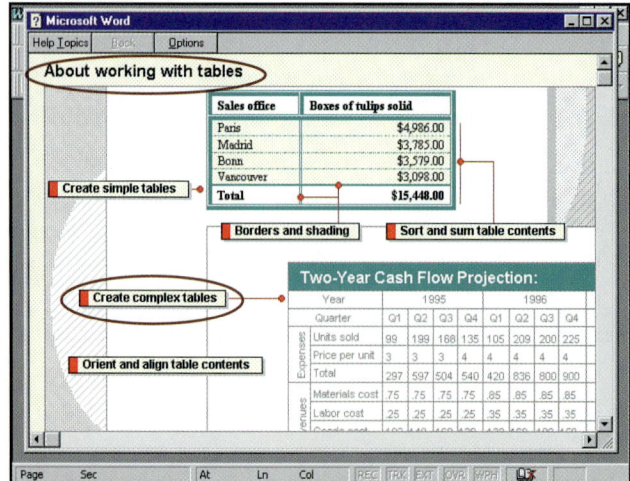

3. Click the suggested topic, **About working with tables**.

182 Learn Word 97, Second Edition

More information about tables is displayed.

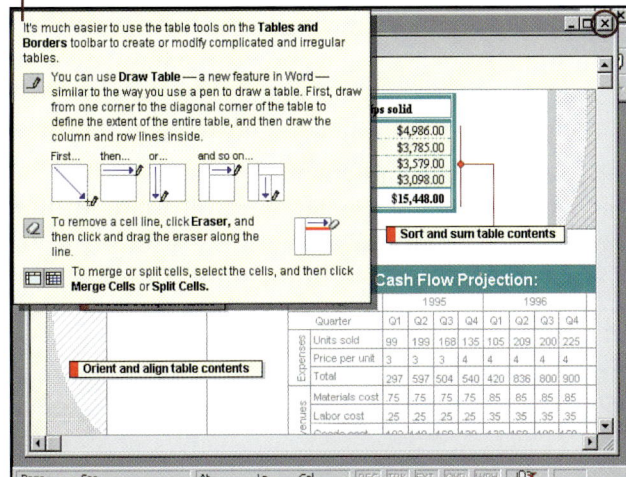

4 Click the section labeled **Create complex tables**. Further information about this issue is displayed.

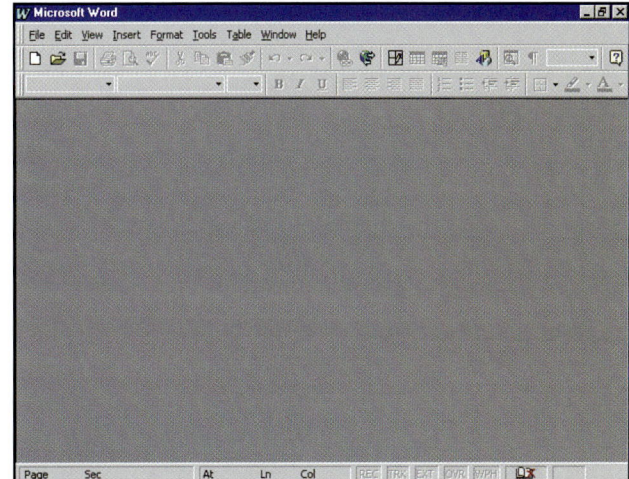

5 Read this help screen to learn more about creating complex tables. Click outside the display window to close it. Close the help window by clicking the **Close Window** button at the top right of the window. Close Office Assistant by clicking the **Close Window** button.

Lesson 8: References to Other Documents and Getting Help

Task 6

Using the Help Menu

Why would I do this?

You can also search the electronic manuals in more traditional ways. You can use the table of contents or the index. If you do not know the right term, it is hard to form the right question for the Office Assistant or to use the index. Sometimes, you do not know that a topic exists and are just searching for new and interesting skills that you might be able to use. The table of contents is a good place to start finding this type of help. In this task, you search for assistance by using the Contents help.

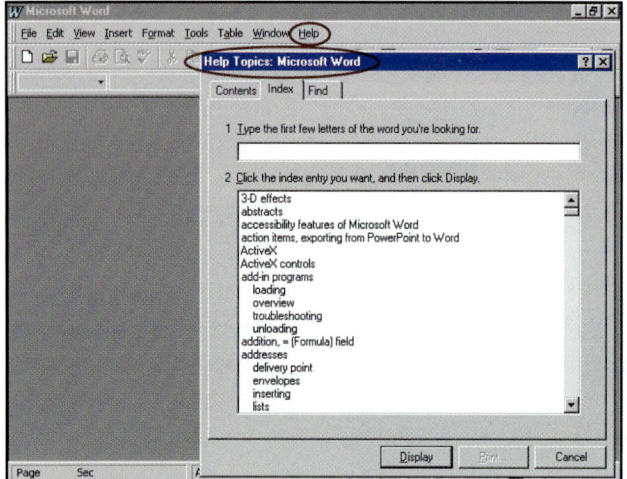

1 Select **Help, Contents and Index**. The **Help Topics** dialog box is displayed.

2 Click the **Contents** tab to display a table of contents for the online help manuals.

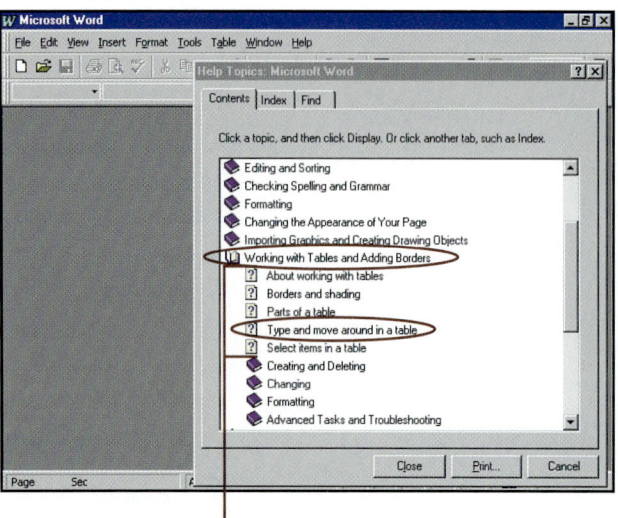

3 Double-click the topic **Working with Tables and Adding Borders**. A list of subtopics is displayed.

A list of subtopics is displayed.

184 Learn Word 97, Second Edition

4 Double-click **Type and move around in a table**. A list of key combinations that help you move quickly among the cells in a table is displayed.

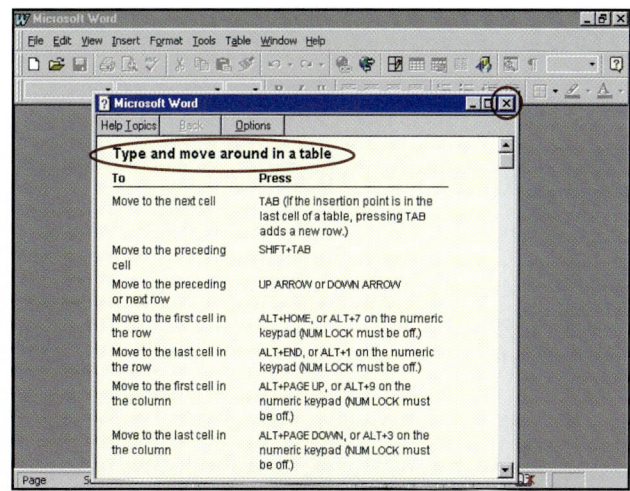

5 Click the **Close Window** button to close the Help window. Leave Word open for use in the next task.

Lesson 8: References to Other Documents and Getting Help   185

Task 7

Getting Help on the Internet

Why would I do this?

Sometimes, the program does not behave as you think it should and the help manual included with the program does not answer your questions. Another place you can go to get help is Microsoft's online support on the Internet, where you can search their knowledge base. If that does not help, you can go to the *newsgroups* section and post your question. Other users and experts from around the world see your question and post their suggestions or share their experiences. In this task, you go to Microsoft's support Web page and use several types of help.

1. Choose **Help**, **Microsoft on the Web**, **Online Support**. If your computer is connected to the Internet, the **Support Online** page opens.

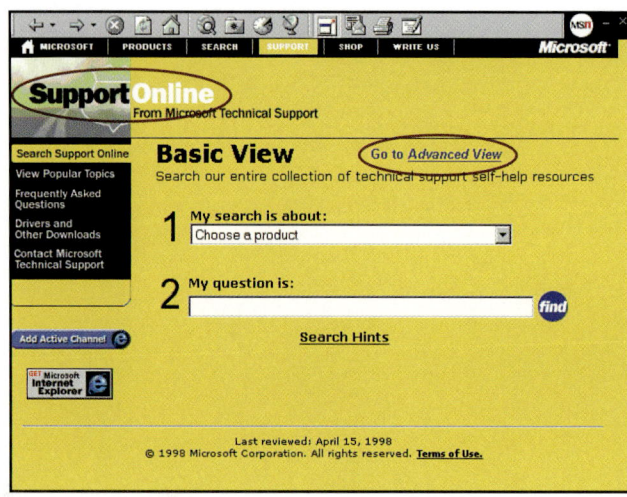

In Depth: Pages change rapidly on the Internet, and it is likely that Microsoft's technical help page will change several times during the useful life of this book. If the pages you see are not the same as those shown in the book, you should still be able to find the topics that are discussed. The browser that you use may also differ from the one illustrated here (Internet Explorer 4.0, using the Full Screen option).

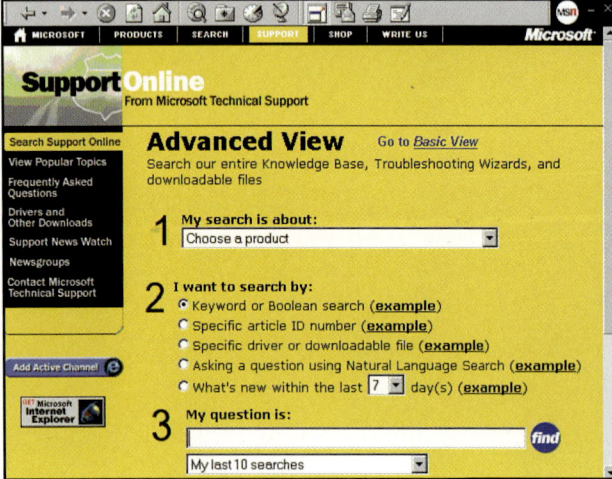

2. Click **Go to Advanced View**.

   The Advanced view offers several choices for searching the database of articles and helpful resources.

186 Learn Word 97, Second Edition

3 Click the list arrow next to the **My search is about** box and select **Word for Windows**. Click the button in front of the **Asking a question using Natural Language Search** option to select it. Type <u>**Can I use tabs within the cells of a table?**</u> in the **My question is** box.

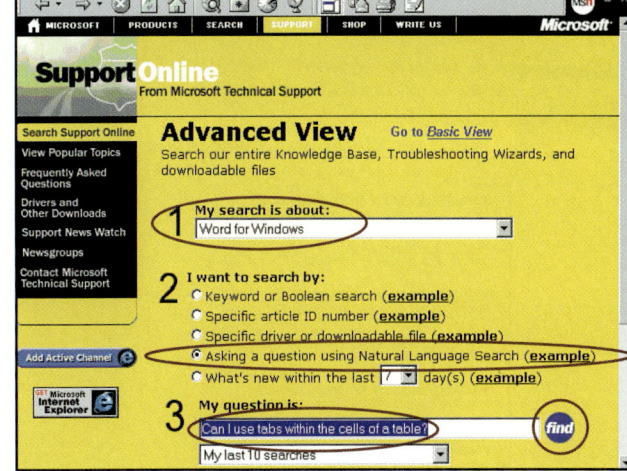

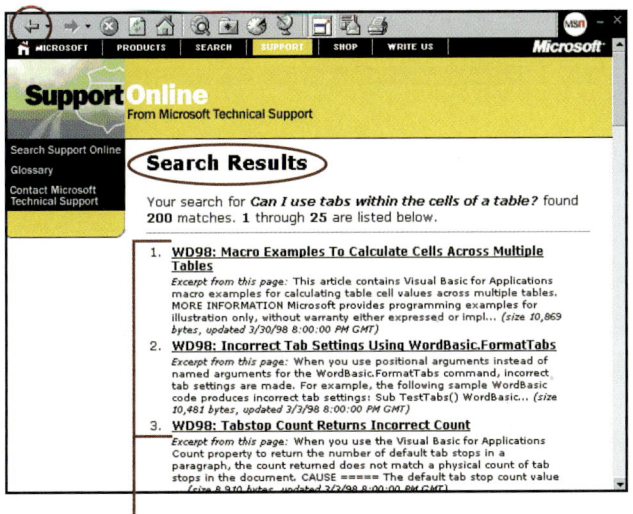

Click on one or more of these options and explore.

4 Click the **find** button next to the question. Explore the different topics that are available from this window.

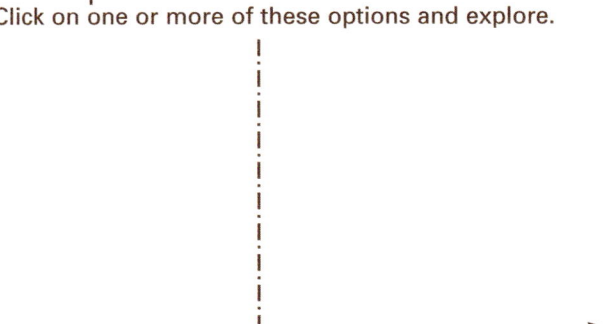

5 Click the **Back** button repeatedly until you return to the opening page, **Support Online, Advanced View**.

Lesson 8: References to Other Documents and Getting Help 187

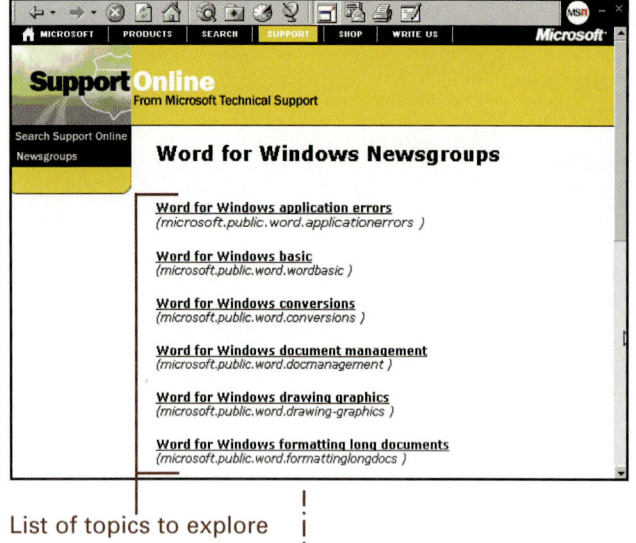

List of topics to explore

6 Click **Newsgroups** and then click on the appropriate selections to get to the newsgroups related to Word. (The options used change often. At the time of this writing, they were **Microsoft Office Family of Products** and **Word for Windows**.)

In Depth: Newsgroups provide you with the ability to read and ask questions about Word. The advice given here is from other users and is not guaranteed to be accurate, but it is often a good place to go if you cannot find the answer anywhere else.

7 Click on one of the discussion topics, such as **Word for Windows document management**, to display a list of messages. Your newsgroup reader opens (the reader shown is Microsoft Outlook Express).

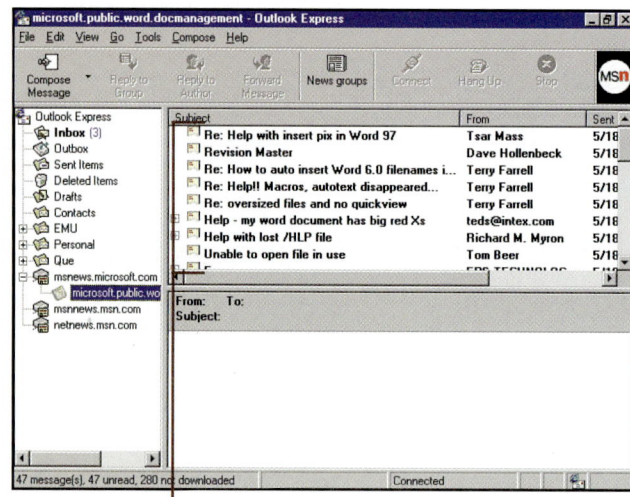

List of messages available for viewing

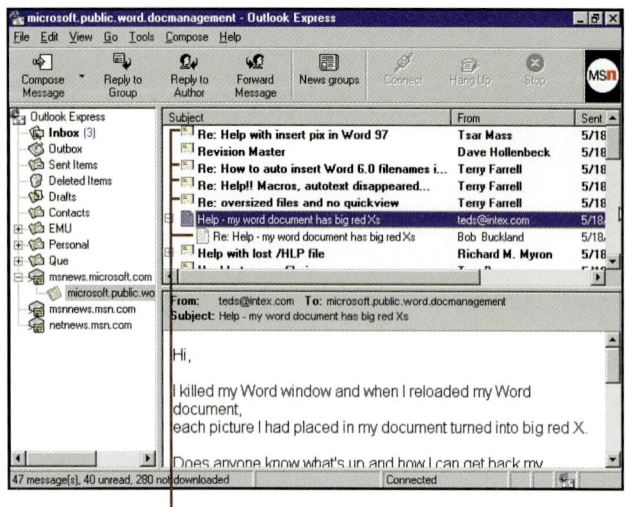

Examples of responses

8 Click on the + sign next to one of the messages. The responses to the message are listed. The title of a response begins with **Re:**.

188 Learn Word 97, Second Edition

9 Click on a response to open it.

The response is shown. Many newsgroup readers are also set up to display the original message as well. It is usually set off by > or < symbols.

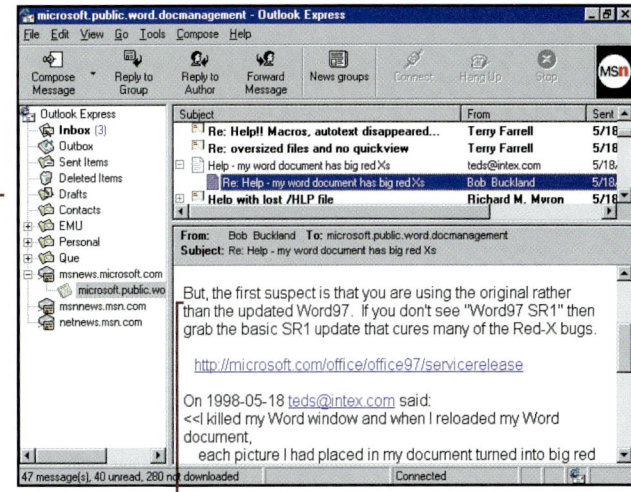

Response, original message

10 Close your newsgroup reader, but keep your Internet browser open. Use the taskbar to switch back to Word if necessary.

Lesson 8: References to Other Documents and Getting Help

Task 8

Finding Reference Books and Self-help Textbooks

Why would I do this?

Computer software is constantly changing, and you will need to upgrade your skills or add new skills. You may not have time to take a class, or you may feel that you do not need to know as much as an entire class would cover. You may have an occasional need for a very specific tool in Word that is not covered in a class. In these situations, it is valuable to have additional resources available. If you found this book easy to use on your own, you may want to use one of the other books in the **Learn** series to teach yourself Excel, PowerPoint, Access, Windows 95, Windows 98, or the Internet.

Another type of book you may consider is a reference book. Reference books are not designed to be read from cover to cover; instead, they are used to find detailed instructions on how to perform specific tasks. Most of the large publishing houses have Web sites where you can look at descriptions of their books and place orders for them. In this lesson, you take a look at Que Education and Training's Web site as an example. You also see how to use the Web toolbar in Word with your browser.

1 Click the **Web Toolbar** button.

In Depth: Word 97 has a Web toolbar that can be opened and closed by clicking the Web Toolbar button. This toolbar looks like the toolbar you see on a Web page. You can use this bar to enter a *URL* address and then press ⏎Enter to activate a search on the Web.

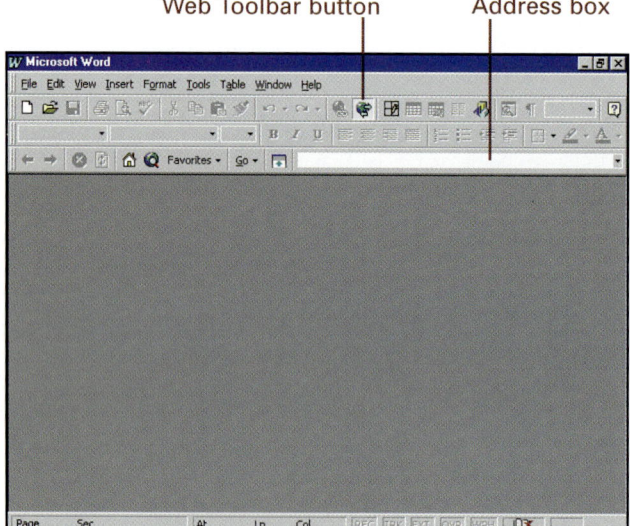

Web Toolbar button   Address box

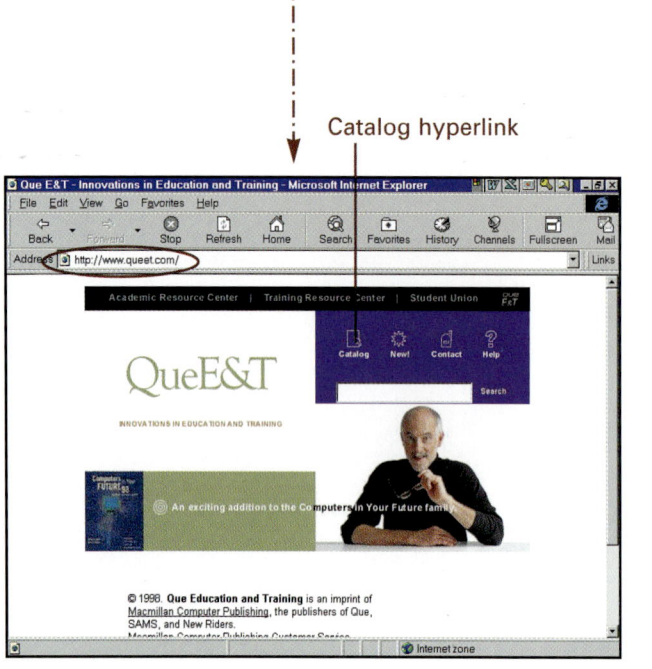

Catalog hyperlink

2 Click the Address box. Type **http://www.queet.com** in the **Address** box and press ⏎Enter. The program automatically launches your registered browser if it is not already running and then opens Que Education and Training's home page. Click the **Catalog** hyperlink to see a list of Que Education and Training's books.

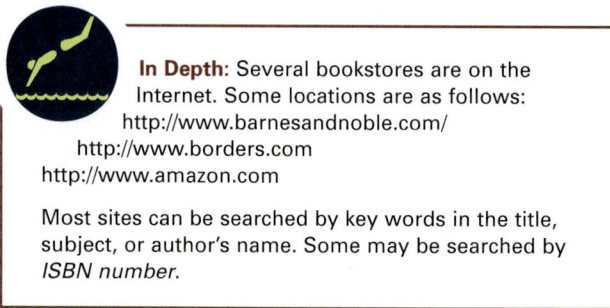

In Depth: Several bookstores are on the Internet. Some locations are as follows:
http://www.barnesandnoble.com/
http://www.borders.com
http://www.amazon.com

Most sites can be searched by key words in the title, subject, or author's name. Some may be searched by *ISBN number*.

3 Click the **Learn** hyperlink.

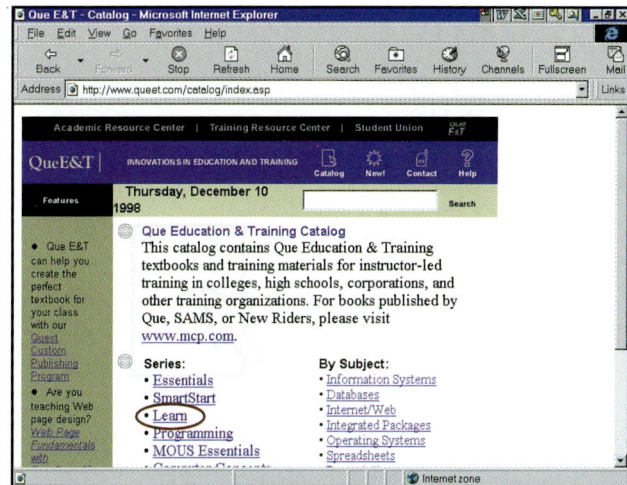

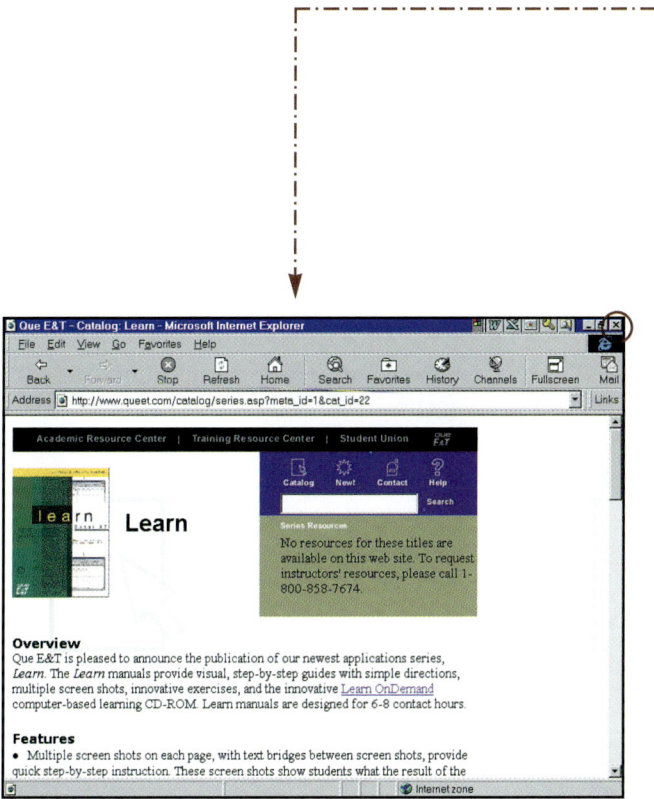

4 This page displays information about the other books in this series. It also has hyperlinks to other book series by Que Education and Training that take different approaches in terms of the depth and illustration of the lessons.

5 Close the browser. Close Word unless you plan to continue with the following exercises.

Lesson 8: References to Other Documents and Getting Help   191

Student Exercises

True-False
Circle either T or F.

T F **1.** It is possible to have two Word documents open at the same time.

T F **2.** If you select text in one document and copy it to the Clipboard, you can use the View option on the menu to switch to a view of another document and paste the text in the second document.

T F **3.** The name of a bookmark can have more than eight characters and can include spaces and punctuation marks.

T F **4.** It is possible to hyperlink from one Word 97 document to a specific bookmark in another Word 97 document.

T F **5.** Hyperlinks may be used to connect to other documents on your computer, but they do not work if the document is on another computer.

T F **6.** To use the Office Assistant, you type in single words for it to look up. It does not work with normal sentences.

T F **7.** When Word 97 is installed on a computer, a help file can also be installed that can be searched like a manual. It has an index and a table of contents.

T F **8.** To use the Microsoft on the Web help option, you must have an Internet connection.

T F **9.** Newsgroups are official postings from Microsoft employees that describe recently discovered bugs in the software and how to fix them. Postings have been reviewed for accuracy by Microsoft.

T F **10.** If you want to find out what other books are available to continue your studies, most major publishers have home pages on the Internet where you can find out how to order them.

Identifying Parts of the Word Screen

Refer to the figure and identify the numbered parts of the screen. Write the letter of the correct label in the space next to the number.

1. _____
2. _____
3. _____
4. _____
5. _____
6. _____
7. _____
8. _____

A. Web toolbar

B. Text that is hyperlinked

C. Insert hyperlink

D. Back

E. Emphasis and alignment of hyperlinked text

F. Display or Hide Web toolbar

G. Close

H. Forward

I. Name and folder of file that is currently in use

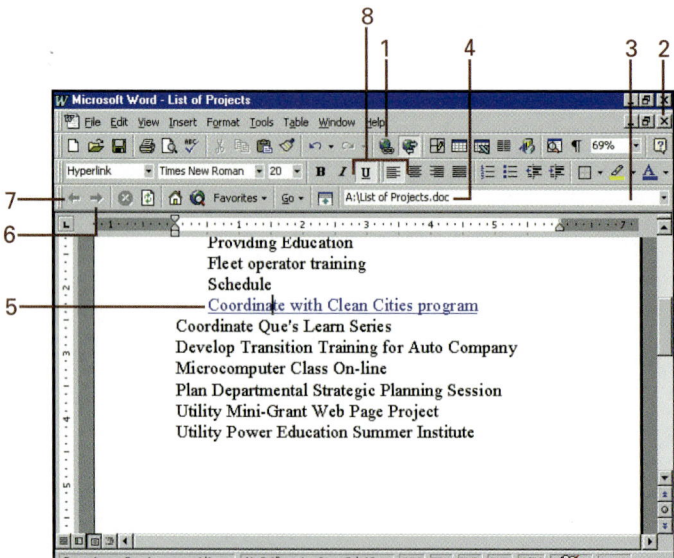

Matching Exercises

Match the following statements to the word or phrase from the list on the right. Write the letter of the matching word or phrase in the space provided next to the number.

1. ____ Method used to copy text from one document to another
2. ____ May not include a space between words in its name
3. ____ Abbreviation for the location of a page on the Internet
4. ____ A reference point in a document
5. ____ A connection between a document and another document or Web page
6. ____ Animated figure that appears when you choose Help, Microsoft Word Help
7. ____ Method used to ask for help after selecting Help, Microsoft Word Help
8. ____ Type of help available on the Internet that enables you to read messages and responses from other Word users
9. ____ Examples of publishers' addresses on the Internet, where more books on this subject can be found
10. ____ Method of identifying hyperlinked text

A. Office Assistant
B. Newsgroups
C. URL
D. Bookmark
E. Underlined text in blue
F. Name of a bookmark
G. Type in a question in sentence form
H. Hyperlink
I. Select text, copy, switch documents, and paste
J. www.queet.com, www.computing.mcgraw-hill.com

Application Exercises

Exercise 1—Copy Text from One Document and Paste It into Another

When you are finished with this exercise, you will have copied the description of a Web page that is designed as part of this lesson.

1. Launch Word. Open **Less0805** from the sutdent files. Save the file as **AFV Proposal**.
2. Open **Less0806** and save the file as **Web**.
3. Select all of the text in the **Web** document and copy it.
4. Select **Window** and switch to the **AFV Proposal** document.
5. Scroll to page 6 and place the insertion point on the line below the last line on that page.

6. Click the **Paste** button to paste the text in this page.

7. Choose **Window** from the menu to switch back to the **Web** document. Close the **Web** document.

8. Save your work and leave **AFV Proposal** open for use in the next exercise.

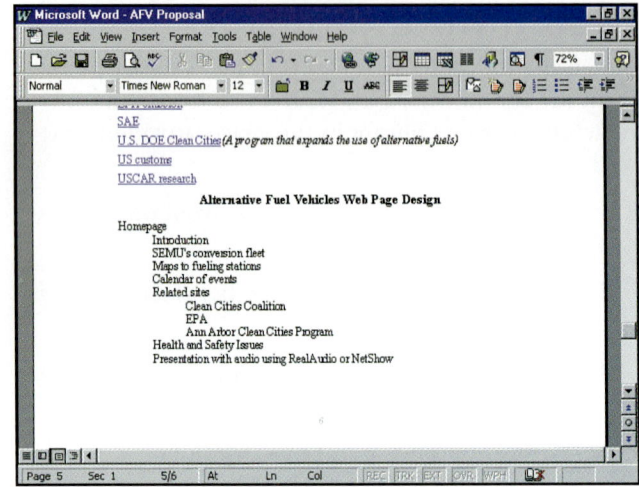

Exercise 2—Insert Bookmarks in a Document

In this exercise, you add bookmarks to several spots in the text to make it easier to find them and to link to them from other documents. Use the **AFV Proposal** document that was opened in the previous exercise.

1. Scroll to page 6 and place the insertion point to the right of the heading **Providing education on health and safety issues relating to compressed natural gas vehicles**.

2. Choose **Insert**, **Bookmark** from the menu.

3. Type **Education** and click **Add**.

4. Save the document and leave it open for use in the next exercise.

Exercise 3—Create a Hyperlink Between Two Documents

In this exercise, you link a reference document named **Timeline** to a corresponding description in the proposal.

1. Open **Less0807** from the student files. Save the copy as **Timeline**.

2. Select the text **Completion of educational materials**.

3. Click the **Insert Hyperlink** button on the Standard toolbar to open the **Insert Hyperlink** dialog box.

4. Click the **Browse** button next to the **Link to file or URL** box and find the location of the **AFV Proposal** document. Select it; its location is automatically entered in the box.

5. Click the **Browse** button next to the **Named location in file** box and choose the **Education** bookmark. Click **OK** to finish.

6. Click in the hyperlinked text to test it. It should bring up the **AFV Proposal** document and go to the bookmarked location.

7. Save your work and leave the document open for use in the next exercise.

Exercise 4—Add a Hyperlink to a Web Page

In this exercise, you create a hyperlink from selected text in the **Timeline** document to the Environmental Protection Agency's (EPA) Web site.

1. Scroll to page 6. Select the text, **EPA**, which is listed as one of the related sites in the Web page design. (It is part of the text that you pasted into this document in exercise 1.)

2. Click the **Insert Hyperlink** button.

3. Type **http://www.epa.gov** in the **Link to file or URL** box. Click **OK**.

4. Click on the linked text to test it. The EPA's Web site should come up if your computer has an Internet connection and a registered browser.

5. Close all the documents that are open, but leave Word open.

Exercise 5—Get Help from Microsoft Online Support

1. Choose **Help**, **Microsoft Word Help**.

2. Type **How do I see where the bookmarks are?** and click **Search**.

3. Click the **Show bookmarks in a document** option.

4. Click the **Options** button and select **Print Topic**.

5. Close the help window and the Office Assistant window.

6. Close Word.

Glossary

AutoComplete A tool that looks at the first four letters of a word and displays the AutoText entry (if one exists) for quick completion of the word or phrase.

AutoCorrect A tool that automatically identifies and corrects common spelling and typographical errors.

AutoFit A tool in the Table menu that changes the width of the columns to custom fit the data that has been entered.

AutoFormat A tool in the Table menu that enables you to choose from many different table styles.

AutoText A tool that lets you enter commonly used text with a few keystrokes.

Back arrow An arrow used in a browser to move to a page that was downloaded prior to the current page.

Borders The sides of the cells in a table.

Browser A program such as Netscape or Internet Explorer that helps you connect to the Internet and view Web pages.

CD-ROM (compact disc–read-only memory) An optical storage device used to store data permanently.

Cell The intersection of an individual row and column in a table.

Center To align the text in a paragraph so that the center of each line of text is halfway between the margins.

Clip art A graphics image provided by Microsoft or another company that can be inserted into a document.

Clipboard A temporary storage area where data is placed when it has been cut or copied. The Clipboard can only hold one set of data at a time, and it is overwritten when the next group of data is cut or copied.

Copy Command used to duplicate text from one part of a document and place it in a second location.

Cut To remove text from the document and store it in the Clipboard.

Cut and paste Method used to move text from one location to another using the Cut and Paste commands.

Default A setting in the program that is used unless it is changed by a specific action. Depending on the type of default, you can change it by going to the appropriate dialog box, selecting a new setting, and then specifying it as the default.

Drag and drop A method used to move text from one location to another by first selecting the text, dragging it with the mouse to the new location, and releasing the mouse button to drop the text in the new location.

Floppy disk A magnetic storage device used to store data that can be written to as well as read.

Footer The area at the bottom of a document that is reserved for dates, page numbers, text, or graphics. The footer is displayed on each page unless you specify otherwise.

Format Painter A tool that enables you to reformat paragraphs with the click of a button.

Forward arrow An arrow used in a browser to move to a page that was downloaded subsequent to the current page.

Handle A small square on the edge or corner of a picture or clip art image that is used to resize the image.

Hanging indent A format that extends the first line of a paragraph to the left of the rest of the paragraph.

Header The area at the top of a document that is reserved for dates, page numbers, text, or graphics. The header is displayed on each page unless you specify otherwise.

Hyperlink A link that connects a word or a label in one location to a file in another location. A hyperlink can be used to go directly to information in another file.

I beam pointer The symbol that shows the location or position of the mouse on your screen.

Insertion point A blinking vertical line that indicates where text will be inserted in the document.

International Standard Book Number (ISBN) An identification number used by book publishers.

Internet A worldwide communications network of computer connections that allows people to have access to thousands of online resources.

Justify To align the right and left edges of text in a document so that both of the vertical edges are straight.

Leaders A series of characters, such as dashes or periods, that provide a visual connection between widely separated text on the same line. Leaders are commonly used in tables of contents, in which the page number is at the far right of the page.

Left Justify To align the left edge of the text.

Local area network (LAN) A system that uses telephone lines or cables to join two or more personal computers, enabling them to communicate with each other.

Margins The empty spaces between the left, right, top, and bottom edges of the paper and the beginning of the text in your document.

Newsgroups Discussions between individuals at an Internet site.

Office Assistant An animated feature of Word that guides the user to additional information and help.

Page break An artificial break that is placed in a document in order to move the text following the break to a new page.

Paste To place the contents of the Clipboard at the insertion point.

Print Preview A utility that displays the layout of the document as it will appear when printed.

Read-only memory (ROM) A storage medium used to store programs, files, and other computer reference material that cannot be changed.

Right Justify To align the right edge of the text.

ScreenTip A box providing additional information that pops up when you point at a button or hyperlink.

Scrollbar The bars located on the right and bottom of the screen that allow you to move the document up and down or side to side on the screen.

Table A list of information set up in a column-and-row format.

Uniform Resource Locator (URL) An address on the Internet.

Web A system of computers and files, formally known as the World Wide Web (WWW), on which users may view and interact with a variety of information.

Web toolbar A toolbar that has a browser.

Word wrap A feature that moves text from one line to the next in a paragraph so that the text fits within the document's margins.

WordArt A Word subprogram that enables you to create artistic images with text.

Index

Symbols

- (dash), 82
< (greater than), 189
> (less than), 189
- (minus sign), xvii, 89
+ (plus sign), vii, xvii, 89, 188-189

A

addresses, email, Macmillan Technical Support, xxiii
Align Right button, 109-110, 115
aligning
    page numbers, 78
    text, 46-47
        in tables, 109-110
All command (Edit menu), 170
All Folders window (Windows Explorer), vii
Amazon Web site, 190
application, closing, 15, 38, 118
arrows, Back or Forward, 179
AutoComplete, 137-139
AutoCorrect, 124, 136
    command (Tools menu) or dialog box, 134-135, 137
AutoFit, 114-116, 124
AutoFormat, 114-116
AutoText, 137-139

B

Back arrow, 179
Backspace key, 8-9
Barnes and Noble Web site, 190
Bold button, 43-45, 106-108
Bookmark
    command (Insert menu), 172, 174
    dialog box, 172-174, 177

bookmarks, 172-175
books, reference, 190-191
bookstores on Internet, 190
Border button, 111-113
borders, 149-151
Borders and Shading
    command (Format menu), 111-113
        Borders tab, 149
    dialog box
        Borders tab, 111
        Preview area, 150
        Shading tab, 112-113
Borders tab (Borders and Shading dialog box), 111, 149
Borders Web site, 190
Break command (Insert menu) or dialog box, 87, 92
Browse button, 177
browsers, *see* Web browsers
bulleted lists, 50-53
Bullets button, 52, 63
buttons
    Align Right, 109-110, 115
    AutoFit, 116
    Bold, 43-45, 106-108
    Border, 111-113
    Browse, 177
    Bullets, 52, 63
    Center, 46-47, 85, 118, 150
    Change, 127-128
    Close Application, ix, x, 15, 38, 118
    Close Window, ix, 15, 94, 144, 171, 183, 185
    Concept, xviii-xix, xxi
    Cut, 32-33
    Demo, xix, xxi
    Find Next, 140-141
    Find Now, xv
    First Page, 88
    Font, 44
    Font Size, 44

Format Painter, 56, 58
Ignore All, 11
Increase Indent, 52
Insert, 157
Insert Column, 105
Insert Date, 83
Insert Hyperlink, 176, 180
Insert Rows, 105
Insert Table, 101
Insert WordArt, 161
Install, xii-xiii
Italic, 85, 108
Justify, 47
Learn On-Demand, xxiii
More/Less, 142
Multiple Pages, 90
Next, xii-xiii
Normal View, 3, 86, 91
Office Assistant, 182
Open, 23-24
Paste, 33, 171
Print, 14, 38, 132, 163
Print Preview, 88
Redo, 35
Replace, 143
Replace All, 143
Save, 13-15, 25, 27, 38, 151
Search, 182
Shadow, 150
Show/Hide, 32-33
Size, 44
Spelling, 127
Switch Between Header and Footer, 80, 85
Teacher, xvi, xix-xx
Undo, 34-35
Uninstall, xv
view, 3
Web Toolbar, 190

C

CD-ROM (compact disc-read only memory)
    drive letters, 23
    files, installing, xii-xiv
Cell Height and Width
    command (Table menu), 116-118
    dialog box
        Column tab, 116
        Row tab, 117-118

cells, 100, 110-113
Center button, 46-47, 85, 118, 150
centered alignment, 46
Change button, 127-128
changes in documents, tracking, 130-133
characters, hidden, 32
clip art, 148
    inserting, 152-153
    resizing and moving, 154-155
Clip Art tab (Microsoft Clip Gallery), 152
Clipboard, 32-33
Close Application button, x, 15, 118
Close command (File menu), Word 97, x
Close Window button, 15, 94, 144, 171, 183, 185
closing documents, 14-15
colors, text, 180
Column tab (Cell Height and Width dialog box), 116
columns, 100
    adding, 105
    AutoFit, 114-116
    selecting, 109
commands
    Edit menu
        All, 170
        Find, 140
        Go To, 174
        Replace, 142
        Select All, 48
    File menu
        Open, 43-44, 75, 101
        Page Setup, 75, 89
        Print, 38, 67, 93
        Print Preview, 88
        Save As, 25
    Format menu
        Borders and Shading, 111-113
        Borders and Shading, Borders tab (Format menu), 149
        Font, 45
        Paragraph, 48-49, 53-54, 58, 60-61, 84, 151
        Picture, 158, 160
        Tabs, 63
    Help menu
        Contents and Index, 184
        Microsoft on the Web, 186
        Microsoft Word Help, 182

Insert menu
    Bookmark, 172, 174
    Break, 87, 92
    Date and Time, 82-83
    Page Numbers, 78
    Picture, 152, 156
Learn On-Demand menu, Exit, xxiii
Select Table, Select Table, 115
Table menu
    Cell Height and Width, 116-118
    Insert Columns, 105
    Insert Rows, 105
    Insert Table, 102
    Select Table, 110, 118
    Table, AutoFormat, 114
Tools menu
    AutoCorrect, 134-135, 137
    Options, 5
    Options (Spelling & Grammar tab), 125
    Options, Edit tab, 36
    Track Changes, 130, 132-133
View menu
    Header and Footer, 80
    Ruler, 64, 75, 155
Window menu, Resume, 171
Windows Explorer
    Copy (Edit menu), viii
    Find (Tools menu), viii
    Open (File menu), viii
    Paste (Edit menu), viii
    Rename (File menu), viii
Word 97
    Close (File menu), x
    Customize (Tools menu), ix
    What's This? (Help menu), ix
components, Word 97 window, ix
Concept
    button, xviii-xix, xxi
    mode (Learn On-Demand), xviii
concept of *Learn Word 97, Second Edition*, x
Concurrent mode (Learn On-Demand), xviii-xix
Contents and Index command (Help menu), 184
Contents
    tab (Help Topics dialog box), 184
    window (Windows Explorer), vii
Copy
    button, 33
    command (Edit menu), Windows Explorer, viii
copying files, viii
Ctrl+B keyboard shortcut (bold typeface), 45

Ctrl+End keyboard shortcut (to end of document), 6
Ctrl+Home keyboard shortcut (to beginning of document), 6
Ctrl+I keyboard shortcut (italic typeface), 45
Ctrl+U keyboard shortcut (underline typeface), 45
Customize command (Tools menu), Word 97, ix
Cut button, 32-33
cutting text, 32-33

D

dash (-), 82
data files (student), uninstalling, xv
Date and Time command (Insert menu) or dialog box, 82-83
dates in headers and footers, 82-83
decimal tabs, 65
Delete key, 8-10, 28-29
deleting text, 28-29
Demo
    button, xix, xxi
    mode (Learn On-Demand), xxi-xxii
dialog boxes
    AutoCorrect, 134-135, 137
    Bookmark, 172-174, 177
    Borders and Shading
        Borders tab, 111
        Preview area, 150
        Shading tab, 112-113
    Break, 87, 92
    Cell Height and Width
        Column tab, 116
        Row tab, 117-118
    Date and Time, 82-83
    Edit WordArt Text, 162
    Find and Replace, 140-144, 175
        Go To tab, 174
    Font, 45
    Format Picture
        Position tab, 159
        Wrapping tab, 158-160
    Grammar, 126
    Help Topics, Contents tab, 184
    Highlight Changes, 130
        tracking changes in color, 131
    Insert Hyperlink, 176, 180
    Insert Picture, 156
    Interactive Training—Lesson Selection, xviii, xx
        Search tab, xxi-xxii

On-Demand Uninstallation, xv
Open, 23-24
Options, Spelling & Grammar tab (Options dialog box), 5
Page Numbers, 78
Page Setup, 75
    Layout tab, 89
    Margins tab (Page Setup dialog box), 76
Paragraph, 49, 58-61
    Indent and Spacing tab, 48, 54-55
Perform Uninstall, xv
Print, 38, 67, 93
Save As, 13-14
Spelling and Grammar, 127
Table AutoFormat, 114
Tabs, 63-64
Topic, xviii
Welcome, xii-xiii
dictionaries, 10-11
digital photographs, 156-157
directories, Select Destination Directory, xiii
disk drives, moving to, vii
documents
    active, 170
    AutoComplete, 137-139
    AutoCorrect, 134-136
    AutoText, 137-139
    bookmarks, 172-175
    bulleted lists, 50-53
    changes, tracking, 130-133
    characters, hidden, 32
    clip art images
        inserting, 152-153
        resizing and moving, 154-155
    closing, 14-15
    dictionaries, 10-11
    digital photographs, 156-157
    errors, correcting, 8-10
    fonts, 43-45
    footers, 74, 80-83
    grammar, correcting errors, 10, 12
    hanging indents, creating, 58-59
    headers, 74, 80-83
    headers and footers
        formatting, 84-85
        turning off, 89
    images, wrapping text around, 158-160
    insertion point, 8
        changing locations, 7
        moving, ix, 26

leaders, 62, 64-65
line spacing, changing, 48-50
linking, 176-179
margins, 74
    setting, 75-77
moving around in, 6-8
moving information, 169-171
Normal view, ix
Office Assistant, opening and closing, 5
opening, viii, 3, 23-24
page breaks, 74
    inserting, 86-87
Page Layout view, ix, 79
page numbers
    aligning, 78
    inserting, 78-79
page ranges, printing, 92-94
paragraphs
    adding spaces after, 60-62
    adding spaces between, ix
    Format Painter, 56-58
    indenting first lines, 54-55
Print Preview, 88, 91
    turning off headers and footers, 89-90
printing, 14, 38
rulers
    displaying, 64, 75
    viewing, 155
saving, 13-15
    on floppy disks or with a different name, 23-25
scrollbars, 6-8
spaces, inserting, 26
spelling, correcting errors, 10-11
tables
    adding columns, 105
    adding rows, 104-106
    aligning text, 109-110
    AutoFit, 114-116
    AutoFormat, 114-116
    centering, 116-118
    entering information, 102-104
    formatting borders, 110-113
    formatting text, 106-108
    inserting, 101-102
    moving around in, 104
    shading, 110-113
tabs, 62-66

text
- adding words, ix
- changing formatting, 45
- correcting grammar or spelling errors, 10-11
- cutting and pasting, 32-33
- deleting, 8-10
- entering, 3-6
- finding, 140-141
- finding and replacing, 142-144
- grammar checking, 5
- hyperlinked, editing, 178-179
- inserting, 26-27
- jagged lines below, 5
- manipulating, ix
- printing selected, 66-67
- redoing, 34-35
- selecting, 47-48
- selecting and deleting, 28-29
- selecting and replacing, 30-31
- spell checking, 5
- undoing, 34-35
- word wrap, 5
- wrapping around images, 158-160

titles, WordArt, 161-163
viewing with Web toolbar, 179
word wrap, 5
WordArt, 161-163
words, italicizing, 85

dot leaders, 65
dragging and dropping text, 36-37
drives
- drive letters, 23
- hard
  - installing files from CD-ROM, xii-xiv
  - uninstalling files from CD-ROM, xiv-xv
- moving to disk drives, vii

E

Edit menu commands
- All, 170
- Find, 140
- Go To, 174
- Replace, 142
- Select All, 48
- Windows Explorer
  - Copy, viii
  - Paste, viii

Edit tab (Tools menu commands, Options), 36
Edit WordArt Text dialog box, 162

editing text (hyperlinked), 178-179
email addresses, Macmillan Technical Support, xxiii
End key, 6
Enter key, ix
errors, correcting, 8-9
- grammar or spelling, 10, 12

exercises for students, vi
Exit command (Learn On-Demand menu), xxiii
exiting
- Learn On-Demand, xxiii
- Word 97, x

F

F1 key (Office Assistant), 182
figures in lessons, v-vi
File menu commands
- Open, 43-44, 75, 101
- Page Setup, 75, 89
- Print, 38, 67, 93
- Print Preview, 88
- Save As, 25
- Windows Explorer
  - Open, viii
  - Rename, viii
- Word 97, Close, x

files
- CD-ROM, installing, xii-xiv
- copying, viii
- finding, viii
- managing with Windows Explorer, vi-viii
- opening, vii-viii
- Readme.txt, xiii
- renaming, viii
- student data, uninstalling, xv
- Uninst.exe, xv

Find and Replace
- dialog box, 140-144, 175
  - Go To tab, 174
- tool, 142-144

Find command
- Edit menu, 140
- Tools menu, Windows Explorer, viii

Find Next button, 140-141
Find Now button, xv
finding
- files, viii
- text, 140-144
- Web sites, 181

First Page button, 88

floppy disks, documents, saving, 23-25
folders, All Folders and Contents windows
    (Windows Explorer), vii
Font
    button, 44
    command (Format menu) or dialog box, 45
Font Size button, 44
fonts
    changing, 43-45
    points, 44
footers, 74
    dates, 82-83
    formatting, 84-85
    text, 80-81
    turning off, 89
Format drop-down menu, 142
Format menu commands
    Borders and Shading, 111-113
        Borders tab, 149
    Font, 45
    Paragaraph, 58, 60-61
    Paragraph, 48-49, 53-54, 84, 151
    Picture, 158, 160
    Tab, 63
Format Painter, 56-58
    button, 56, 58
Format Picture dialog box
    Position tab, 159
    Wrapping tab, 158-160
formatting
    borders, 110-113
    headers and footers, 84-85
    text
        changing, 45
        in tables, 106-108
Forward arrow, 179

G

Go To Advanced view, 186
Go To
    command (Edit menu), 174
    tab (Find and Replace dialog box), 174
grammar
    checking, 5, 125, 127-129
        wavy green lines, 126
    errors, correcting, 10, 12
Grammar dialog box or shortcut menu, 126
graphics, borders, adding, 149
greater than symbol (<), 189

H

handles on clip art, 154-155
hanging indents, creating, 58-59
hard drive, files
    installing from CD-ROM, xii-xiv
    uninstalling from CD-ROM, xiv-xv
Header and Footer command (View menu), 80
headers, 74
    dates, 82-83
    formatting, 84-85
    text, 80-81
    turning off, 89
help
    Help menu, 184-185
    Internet
        bookstores, 190
        Microsoft Support Online, 186-189
    Learn On-Demand, technical support, xxiii
    newsgroups, + (plus sign), 188-189
    Office Assistant, 182-183
    reference books, finding, 190-191
    self help, 190-191
    topics, searching, xxi-xxii
    Web sites, searching, 190
Help menu, commands, 185
    Contents and Index, 184
    Microsoft on the Web, 186
    Microsoft Word Help, 182
    Word 97, What's This?, ix
Help Topics dialog box, Contents tab, 184
hidden characters, viewing, 32
Highlight Changes dialog box, 130
    tracking changes in color, 131
Home key, 6
horizontal scrollbar, 7
hotspots, xix
hyperlinks
    documents, linking, 176-179
    text
        color of, 180
        editing, 178-179
    Web pages, 180-181

I

Ignore All button, 11
images, text, wrapping around, 158-160
In Depth (lesson element), vi
Increase Indent button, 52

Indents and Spacing tab (Paragraph dialog box), 48, 54-55
indenting
- hanging indents, creating, 58-59
- lines, 54-55
- tab indents, 54-55

information, moving between documents, 169-171
Insert button, 157
Insert Columns, button or command (Table menu), 105
Insert Date button, 83
Insert Hyperlink button or dialog box, 176, 180
Insert menu commands
- Bookmark, 172, 174
- Break, 87, 92
- Date and Time, 82-83
- Page Numbers, 78
- Picture, 152, 156

Insert Picture dialog box, 156
Insert Rows
- button, 105
- command (Table menu), 105

Insert Table
- button, 101
- command (Table menu), 102

Insert WordArt button, 161
inserting
- spaces, 26
- text, 26-27

insertion point, 3
- documents, moving around in, 7-8
- moving, ix, 26
- placing with mouse, 9
- text, deleting, 8-10
- word wrap, 5

Install button, xii-xiii
installing
- files
  - from CD-ROM, xii-xiv
  - uninstalling from CD-ROM, xiv-xv
- Learn On-Demand, uninstalling, xiv-xv

interactive training, Learn On-Demand, xvi-xvii
Interactive Training—Lesson Selection dialog box, xviii, xx
- Search tab, xxi-xxii

Internet
- bookstores, 190
- help
  - finding reference books, 190-191
  - Microsoft Support Online, 186-189
- reference books, finding, 190-191
- *see also* Web browsers; Web pages; Web sites

Italic button, 85, 108

J-K

justified alignment, 46
Justify button, 47
keyboards
- insertion point, moving, ix, 26
- keys
  - Backspace, 8-9
  - Delete, 8-10, 28-29
  - End, 6
  - Enter, ix
  - F1 (Office Assistant), 182
  - Home, 6
  - PgDn, 6
  - PgUp, 6
- shortcuts
  - Ctrl+B (bold typeface), 45
  - Ctrl+End (to end of document), 6
  - Ctrl+Home (to beginning of document), 6
  - Ctrl+I (italic typeface), 45
  - Ctrl+U (underline typeface), 45

L

launching
- Learn On-Demand, xv-xvi
- Windows Explorer, vi-vii
- Word 97, x

Layout tab (Page Setup dialog box), 89
leaders, 62, 64-65
Learn On-Demand
- button, xxiii
- Concept mode, xviii
- Concurrent mode, xviii-xix
- Demo mode, xxi-xxii
- exiting, xxiii
- interactive training, xvi-xvii
- menu, commands, Exit, xxiii
- starting, xv-xvi
- system requirements, xi
- Teacher mode, xix-xxi
- technical support, xxiii
- toolbar, xvi
- uninstalling, xiv-xv

Learn Word 97, Second Edition, structure, v-vi
left justified alignment, 46
less than symbol (>), 189

lessons
- figures, v-vi
- In Depth, vi
- Pothole, vi
- QuickTip, vi
- visual cues, v

lines
- indenting, 54-55
- spacing, changing, 48-50

linking
- documents, 176-179
- Web pages, 180-181

lists, bulleted, creating, 50-53

M

Macmillan Technical Support, email address, xxiii
managing files with Windows Explorer, vi-viii
margins, 74
- setting, 75-77

Margins tab, 76

menus
- Format, 142
- Help, 184-185
- Special, 142
- Width drop-down, 150

Microsoft
- Clip Gallery, Clip Art tab, 152
- help
  - newsgroups, + (plus sign), 188-189
  - Support Online, 186-189
- on the Web command (Help menu), 186
- Word Help command (Help menu), 182

minus sign (-), xvii, 89
More/Less button, 142

mouse
- pointer, 3
  - placing insertion point, 9
- pointer shapes
  - arrow, 108
  - black down arrow, 108, 110
  - diagonal two-sided arrow, 154
  - downward pointing arrow, 109
  - I beam, 3, 7
  - left-pointing arrow, 107
  - magnifying glass with minus sign (-), 89
  - magnifying glass with plus sign (+), 89
  - small hand, 178-179, 181
  - white arrow, 7
- text
  - dragging and dropping, 36-37
  - selecting, 29

moving
- clip art, 154-155
- to disk drives, vii
- insertion point, ix, 26

Multiple Pages button, 90

N

names
- of bookmarks, choosing, 173
- of files, renaming, viii

newsgroups
- + (plus sign), 188-189
- help with Word 97, 188-189
- messages, < (greater than symbol) or > (less than symbol), 189
- readers, 188

Next button, xii-xiii
Normal view, ix, 91
Normal View button, 3, 86, 91
numbers of pages, inserting, 78-79

O

Office Assistant, 183
- button, 182
- opening and closing, 5

On-Demand Uninstallation dialog box, xv

Open
- button, 23-24
- command (File menu), 43-44, 75, 101
  - Windows Explorer, viii
- dialog box, 23-24

opening
- documents, viii, 23-24
- files, vii-viii

Options
- command (Tools menu), 5
  - Edit tab, 36
  - Spelling & Grammar tab, 125
- dialog box, Spelling & Grammar tab, 5

P

page breaks, 74, 86-87
Page Layout view, ix, 79, 91
Page Numbers command (Insert menu) or dialog box, 78

Page Setup
    command (File menu), 75, 89
    dialog box, 75
        Layout tab, 89
        Margins tab, 76
pages
    numbers
        aligning, 78
        inserting, 78-79
    ranges, printing, 92-94
Paragraph
    command (Format menu), 48-49, 53-54, 58, 60-61, 84, 151
    dialog box, 49, 58-61
        Indents and Spacing tab, 48, 54-55
paragraphs
    adding spaces after, ix, 60-62
    borders, adding, 149-151
    first lines, indenting, 54-55
    Format Painter, 56-58
    hanging indents, creating, 58-59
    line spacing, changing, 48-50
    text, aligning, 46-47
Paste
    button, 33, 171
    command (Edit menu), Windows Explorer, viii
pasting text, 32-33
Perform Uninstall dialog box, xv
PgDn key, 6
PgUp key, 6
photographs
    digital, 156-157
    text, wrapping around, 158-160
Picture command
    Format menu, 158, 160
    Insert menu, 152, 156
plus sign (+), vii, xvii, 89, 188-189
points, fonts, 44
Position tab (Format Picture dialog box), 159
Pothole (lesson element), vi
Preview area (Borders and Shading dialog box), 150
Print
    button, 14, 38, 132, 163
    command (File menu) or dialog box, 38, 67, 93
Print Preview, 89-91
    button or command (File menu), 88
printing
    documents, 14, 38
        Print Preview, 88-91
        page ranges, 92-94

Print Preview, 88-91
    turning off headers and footers, 89-90
text (selected), 66-67

Q-R

Que Education and Training Web site, 190-191
QuickTip (lesson element), vi
RAM (Random Access Memory), 13
readers, newsgroups, 188
Readme.txt file, xiii
Ready to Install screen, xiii
Redo button, 35
redoing text, 34-35
reference books, finding, 190-191
Rename command (File menu)
    Windows Explorer, viii
renaming files, viii
Replace All button, 143
Replace
    button, 143
    command (Edit menu), 142
replacing text, 30-31, 142-144
resizing clip art, 154-155
Resume command (Window menu), 171
Row tab (Cell Height and Width dialog box), 117-118
rows, 100
    adding, 104-106
    selecting, 107
Ruler command (View menu), 64, 75, 155
rulers
    displaying, 64, 75
    viewing, 155

S

Save As
    command (File menu), 25
    dialog box, 13-14, 25
Save button, 13-15, 25, 27, 38, 151
saving documents, 13-15
    on floppy disks or with a different name, 23-25
screens
    Ready to Install, xiii
    rulers, displaying, 64, 75
    Select Components, xiii
    Word 97, identifying parts, ix
ScreenTips, ix, 139
    Undo Paste, 34, 64

scrollbars, 6
    vertical, 8
    vertical and horizontal, 7
Search
    button, 182
    tab (Interactive Training—Lesson Selection dialog box), xxi-xxii
searching
    topics, xxi-xxii
    Web sites, 190
Select All command (Edit menu), 48
Select Components screen, xiii
Select Destination Directory, xiii
Select Table command (Table menu), 110, 115, 118
selecting
    columns, 109
    rows, 107
    text, 28-31, 47-48
self help, 190-191
shading cells, 110-113
Shading tab (Borders and Shading dialog box), 112-113
Shadow button, 150
shortcut menus, Grammar or Spelling, checking, 125-126
shortcuts, keyboard
    Ctrl+B (bold typeface), 45
    Ctrl+End (to end of document), 6
    Ctrl+Home (to beginning of document), 6
    Ctrl+I (italic typeface), 45
    Ctrl+U (underline typeface), 45
Show/Hide button, 32-33
sites, Web
    Amazon, 190
    Barnes and Noble, 190
    Borders bookstore, 190
    finding, 181
    Que Education and Training, 190-191
    searching, 190
Size button, 44
spaces
    adding after paragraphs, 60-62
    inserting, 26
special drop-down menu, 142
spelling
    checking, 5, 127-129
        wavy red lines, 125-126
    dictionaries, 10-11
    errors, correcting, 10-11
Spelling & Grammar tab, 5
    Tools menu, 125

Spelling and Grammar
    Checker, 127-129
    dialog box, 127
Spelling
    button, 127
    shortcut menu, 125
starting, *see* launching
status bar, view buttons, 3
students
    data files, uninstalling, xv
    exercises, vi
Switch Between Header and Footer button, 80, 85
system requirements, Learn On-Demand, xi

T

tab indents, 54-55
Table AutoFormat command (Table menu) or dialog box, 114
Table menu commands
    Cell Height and Width, 116-118
    Insert Columns, 105
    Insert Rows, 105
    Insert Table, 102
    Select Table, 110, 115, 118
    Table AutoFormat, 114
tables
    AutoFit, 114-116
    AutoFormat, 114-116
    borders, formatting, 110-113
    cells, 100
        shading, 110-113
    centering, 116-118
    columns
        adding, 105
        selecting, 109
    information, entering, 102-104
    inserting, 101-102
    moving around in, 104
    Office Assistant, 182-183
    rows
        adding, 104-106
        selecting, 107
    text
        aligning, 109-110
        formatting, 106-108
tabs, 62-63, 66
    Border (Borders and Shading dialog box), 111
    Borders (Format menu), 149
    Clip Art (Microsoft Clip Gallery), 152

Index 207

Column (Cell Height and Width dialog box), 116
Contents (Help Topics dialog box), 184
decimal, 65
Edit (Tools menu commands, Options), 36
Go To (Find and Replace dialog box), 174
Indents and Spacing (Paragraph dialog box), 48, 54-55
Layout (Page Setup dialog box), 89
leaders, 64-65
Margin (Page Setup dialog box), 76
Position (Format Picture dialog box), 159
Row (Cell Height and Width dialog box), 117-118
Search (Interactive Training—Lesson Selection dialog box), xxi-xxii
Shading (Borders and Shading dialog box), 112-113
Spelling & Grammar (Options dialog box), 5
Spelling & Grammar (Tools menu), 125
Wrapping (Format Picture dialog box), 158-160

Tabs
 command (Format menu), 63
 dialog box, 63-64

Teacher
 button, xvi, xix-xx
 mode (Learn On-Demand), xix-xxi

technical support, Learn On-Demand, xxiii

text
 aligning, 46-47
 aligning in tables, 109-110
 borders, adding, 149-151
 centering, 46
 cutting and pasting, 32-33
 deleting, 8-10
 dragging and dropping, 36-37
 entering, 3-6
 finding, 140-141
 finding and replacing, 142-144
 fonts, changing, 43-45
 formatting, changing, 45
 grammar, checking, 5
 in headers and footers, entering, 80-81
 hyperlinked
  color of, 180
  editing, 178-179
 images, wrapping around, 158-160
 inserting, 26-27
 jagged lines below, 5
 justified, 46
 line spacing, changing, 48-50

 manipulating, ix
 redoing, 34-35
 selecting, 47-48
  deleting, 28-29
  printing, 66
  replacing, 30-31
 spelling
  checking, 5
  correcting errors, 10
 in tables, formatting, 106-108
 typing, insertion point, ix
 undoing, 34-35
 word wrap, 5
 words, adding, ix

titles, WordArt, 161-163

toolbars
 Learn On-Demand, xvi
 Web, 190
  displaying, 178
  viewing documents, 179
 WordArt, 161

Toolbars command (View menu), 161

tools
 AutoComplete, 137-139
 AutoCorrect, 124, 134-136
 AutoFit, 114-116, 124
 AutoFormat, 114-116
 AutoText, 137-139
 Find and Replace, 142-144
 finding text, 140-141
 shortcut menus, checking spelling and grammar, 125-126
 Spelling and Grammar Checker, 127-129
 tracking changes in documents, 130-133

Tools menu commands
 AutoCorrect, 134-135, 137
 Options, 5
  Edit tab, 36
  Spelling & Grammar tab, 125
 Track Changes, 130, 132-133
 Windows Explorer, Find, viii
 Word 97, Customize, ix

Topic dialog box, xviii
topics, searching, xxi-xxii
Track Changes command (Tools menu), 130, 132-133
tracking changes in documents, 130-133
training, interactive, Learn On-Demand, xvi-xvii
typing, insertion point, ix
typographical errors, correcting, 8-10

U

Undo button, 34-35
undoing text, 34-35
Uninst.exe file, xv
Uninstall button, xv
uninstalling
    files
        from CD-ROM, xiv-xv
        student data, xv
    Learn On-Demand, xiv-xv
utilities, *see* tools

V

vertical scrollbar, 7
View
    buttons, 3
    menu commands
        Header and Footer, 80
        Ruler, 64, 75, 155
        Toolbars, 161
views
    Go To Advanced, 186
    Normal, ix, 91
    Page Layout, ix, 79, 91
visual cues of lessons, v

W-Z

wavy green lines, 126
wavy red lines, 126
    displaying, 125
Web browsers, Web toolbar, 190
    see also Internet; Web pages; Web sites
Web pages, linking, 180-181
    see also Internet; Web browsers; Web sites
Web sites
    Amazon, 190
    Barnes and Noble, 190
    Borders bookstore, 190
    finding, 181
    Que Education and Training, 190-191
    searching, 190
    see also Internet; Web browsers; Web pages
Web toolbar
    button, 190
    displaying, 178
    documents, viewing, 179
Welcome dialog box, xii-xiii

What's This? command (Help menu), Word 97, ix
Width drop-down menu, 150
Window menu commands, Resume, 171
windows
    All Folders (Windows Explorer), vii
    Contents (Windows Explorer), vii
    Word 97, components, ix
Windows Explorer
    All Folders window, vii
    commands
        Copy (Edit menu), viii
        Find (Tools menu), viii
        Open (File menu), viii
        Paste (Edit menu), viii
        Rename (File menu), viii
    Contents window, vii
    files, managing, vi-viii
    launching, vi-vii
Word 97
    commands
        Close (File menu), x
        Customize (Tools menu), ix
        What's This? (Help menu), ix
    exiting, x
    launching, x
    screens, identifying parts, ix
    window, components, ix
WordArt, 162-163
    Gallery or toolbar, 161
words
    adding to text, ix
    italicizing, 85
    wavy green lines, 126
    wavy red lines, 125-126
    wrapping, 5
Wrapping tab (Format Picture dialog box), 158-160

By opening this package, you are agreeing to be bound by the following agreement:

Some of the software included with this product may be copyrighted, in which case all rights are reserved by the respective copyright holder. You are licensed to use software copyrighted by the Publisher and its licensors on a single computer. You may copy and/or modify the software as needed to facilitate your use of it on a single computer. Making copies of the software for any other purpose is a violation of the United States copyright laws.

This software is sold as is without warranty of any kind, either expressed or implied, including but not limited to the implied warranties of merchantability and fitness for a particular purpose. Neither the Publisher nor its dealers or distributors assume any liability for any alleged or actual damages arising from the use of this program. (Some states do not allow for the exclusion of implied warranties, so the exclusion may not apply to you.)